DISCOURSES ON THE STATE AND GRANDEURS OF JESUS

EARLY MODERN CATHOLIC SOURCES

Volume 8

EDITORIAL BOARD

Ulrich L. Lehner
University of Notre Dame
Series Editor

Trent Pomplun
University of Notre Dame
Series Editor

Paul Richard Blum
Loyola University Maryland

Susannah Monta
University of Notre Dame

Jorge Cañizares-Esguerra
University of Texas at Austin

Felipe Pereda
Harvard University

Wim DeCock
KU Leuven

Jean-Louis Quantin
École Pratique des Hautes Études
(PSL)—Sorbonne

Simon Ditchfield
University of York

Erin Rowe
Johns Hopkins University

Carlos Eire
Yale University

Jacob Schmutz
Université Catholique de Louvain

Marco Forlivesi
D'Annunzio University of
Chieti-Pescara

Jean-Luc Solère
Boston College

PIERRE DE BÉRULLE

DISCOURSES ON THE STATE AND GRANDEURS OF JESUS

THE INEFFABLE UNION OF THE
DEITY WITH HUMANITY

Translated by LISA RICHMOND

THE CATHOLIC UNIVERSITY
OF AMERICA PRESS
Washington, D.C.

English translation, introduction, and notes copyright © 2023
Lisa Richmond
All rights reserved

Cataloging-in-Publication Data is available
from the Library of Congress

ISBN: 978-0-8132-3765-7
eISBN: 978-0-8132-3766-4

CONTENTS

Acknowledgments	vii
Abbreviations	ix
Introduction	1
Detailed Table of Contents	33
Preface	37
Discourse 1. On the Excellence and Singularity of the Sacred Mystery of the Incarnation	45
Discourse 2. On the Excellence of the Mystery of the Incarnation, in the Form of an Elevation	56
Discourse 3. On the Oneness of God in This Mystery	94
Discourse 4. On the Oneness of God in This Mystery	115
Discourse 5. On the Communication of God in This Mystery	141
Discourse 6. On the Communication of God in This Mystery	162
Discourse 7. On the Communication of God in This Mystery	182
Discourse 8. On the Communication of God in This Mystery	209

Discourse 9. On the Love and Communication of
God in This Mystery   246

Discourse 10. On the Three Births of Jesus   266

Bibliography   349
Index   357

ACKNOWLEDGMENTS

This work is dedicated to Charlène Cruxent, Marie-Ève Ménard, Joy Palacios, Christian Roy, Fr. Erik Varden, and Jonathan Mills, who have blessed me with their encouragement, and to all those who work in libraries and archives around the world, preserving old books and making them available in their original forms and in digital copies.

ABBREVIATIONS

ANF   *Ante-Nicene Fathers*. Edited by A. Cleveland Coxe, Alexander Roberts, and James Donaldson. 10 vols. Peabody, Mass.: Hendrickson, 2004.

CWS   *Classics of Western Spirituality*. 130 vols. New York: Paulist, 1978–.

FC   *Fathers of the Church*. Edited by Thomas P. Halton, Ludwig Schopp, Roy J. Deferrari, Bernard M. Peebles, and Hermigild Dressler. 127 vols. Washington, D.C.: The Catholic University of America Press, 1947–2013.

LCL   *Loeb Classical Library*. 550 vols. Cambridge, Mass.: Harvard University Press, 1911–.

NPNF   *Nicene and Post-Nicene Fathers*, Second Series. Edited by Philip Schaff and Henry Wace. 14 vols. Peabody, Mass.: Hendrickson, 2004.

OC   *Œuvres complètes de Pierre de Bérulle*. Edited by Michel Dupuy. 15 vols. Paris: Cerf, 1995–1996.

WSA   *Works of Saint Augustine*. Edited by John E. Rotelle, Boniface Ramsay, David G. Hunter, and Allan Fitzgerald. 44 vols. Brooklyn, N.Y.: New City, 1990–.

DISCOURSES ON THE STATE AND GRANDEURS OF JESUS

Introduction

The Son of God sent him before his face, […] like a new St. John, to point to Jesus Christ, to make him known to the world; and not only his mysteries, his actions, words, miracles, and sufferings, but also his Person, states, and adorable grandeurs; to cause him to be revered, served, adored, and loved; to form in us the living image of his life. This, if I may use these terms, was his apostolate and his mission.[1]

Pierre de Bérulle (1575–1629) is one of the foremost personalities of early modern Catholicism. Considered the founder of the "French school" of spirituality, he has had an enormous continuing influence, although today his name is almost unknown. This volume provides the first complete English translation of his most extensive published work, first printed in Paris in 1623 and titled *Discourses on the State and Grandeurs of Jesus, by the Ineffable Union of the Deity with Humanity, and the Submission and Servitude that Is Due Him and His Most Holy Mother in Response to This Wondrous State*. Composed in Bérulle's maturity, these discourses express his theology of the Man-God, whose self-emptying has enabled us to become "capable" of God.

Bérulle's Life and Occasion for Writing

Bérulle entered the world on February 4, 1575, at the Château de Cérilly near Troyes in the French province of Champagne, in a family belong-

---

1. François Bourgoing, "Préface aux prêtres de la Congrégation de l'Oratoire de Jésus-Christ, notre Seigneur," in *Œuvres de l'éminentissime et reverendissime Pierre Cardinal de Bérulle*, ed. François Bourgoing (Paris, 1644), xx https://gallica.bnf.fr/ark:/12148/bpt6k6568438c. Unless otherwise noted, translations of French and Latin texts are provided by the present translator.

ing to the nobility of the gown (*noblesse de robe*, a rank based on hereditary administrative positions). His father, Claude de Bérulle, died seven years after Pierre's birth. His mother was Louise Séguier, a member of the prominent family of this name. Louise was a pious woman, and under her influence and that of his Séguier uncles, Bérulle grew as a devout and serious young man. In about 1591 he began his studies at the College of Clermont, and a few years later he enrolled at the Sorbonne. His uncles decided that he would become a jurist as his father had been, and he embarked on the study of law.

In 1593 Bérulle began to associate with a group of Parisians who were seeking to infuse French Catholic life with the spirit of Tridentine reform. The group included Barbe Acarie, a figure of central importance to this movement and a relation of Bérulle's; Benoît de Canfeld, author of the influential spiritual guide *The Rule of Perfection*; Richard Beaucousin, a highly regarded spiritual director; and Pierre Coton, the king's confessor. In 1594, Bérulle's uncles acceded to his desire to abandon study of the law and enter instead into theological study. Bérulle became a priest in 1599. He made a retreat with the Jesuits in 1602 to further discern his vocation; the resulting conviction was that he should remain a secular priest.

One project of Barbe Acarie and her circle was to bring some of Teresa of Ávila's reformed Carmelites to establish communities in France. Bérulle travelled to Spain for this purpose, and by dint of much negotiation with the religious authorities, the first community of Carmelite women was established in France in 1604. By the time of Bérulle's death in 1629, there were forty Carmelite convents in the kingdom. Clement VIII's bull authorizing the French Carmelite foundation placed these religious under the charge of three non-Carmelite priests: Pierre de Bérulle, Jacques Gallemant, and André Duval. Teresa, however, had specifically indicated in her *Constitutions* that Carmelite sisters were to be under the jurisdiction of Carmelite brothers. The Acarie circle's reasons for urging the pope to place the French Carmelites under the authority of Bérulle and his colleagues were that no Carmelite brothers were established in France at that time and that such an arrangement would be politically prudent in light of the tense political relations between France and Spain. Further, such an arrangement had precedent; Clement VIII's bull was modelled on a rule already in place for a Carmelite foundation in Rome. But the irregularity of the situation provoked controversy. For those who opposed the arrangement, "The question was raised whether Pierre de Bérulle's jurisdiction over the Carmelites was legitimate, and whether the transmission of the order's 'charism' depended more or less exclusively on their being governed by the discalced order of men."[2]

In 1611, Bérulle founded the French Oratory, a congregation of priests with a particular focus on Marian devotion, prayer, and the renewal of the priesthood. This community was modeled on the Roman Oratory of Philip Neri. Bérulle introduced to his Oratorian colleagues a "vow of servitude" that he had composed, perhaps inspired by a similar vow to the Blessed Virgin Mary that he had encountered in Spain. He also encouraged some of the Carmelites to profess it, and in 1615 he took the step of introducing it to the Carmelites at Chalon "in the form of an ordinance." He did not consult Gallemant and Duval before doing so (an act of unilateralism that he may have regretted), and a serious ambiguity was introduced from the start by his referring to the vow as "particular" yet "essential and original to the order."[3]

Was Bérulle intending this as a fourth Carmelite vow, another and more momentous departure from Teresa's *Constitutions*? Bérulle's critics were suspicious, and for many years Bérulle was not particularly concerned with explaining himself. Denys de la Mère de Dieu, the head of the Carmelite men's congregation that had been established in Paris in 1610, pressed the issue. When a Carmelite of the convent in Bordeaux gave Denys a copy of the vow she had found in a sister's cell after the latter's death, Denys seized upon it to attack not only Bérulle's right to impose this vow but now also Bérulle's doctrinal orthodoxy, since a transcription error in the copy appeared to open Bérulle to a charge of monophysitism. Whether Denys knew that the copy had

---

2. Stéphane-Marie Morgain, *Pierre de Bérulle et les Carmélites de France: La querelle du gouvernement 1583–1629* (Paris: Cerf, 1995), 18. Morgain's book provides an in-depth study of the controversy.

3. Rémi Lescot, "Introduction historique et théologique," in Pierre de Bérulle, *Discours de l'état et des grandeurs de Jésus*, ed. Joseph Beaude, Blandine Delahaye, Michel Join-Lambert, and Rémi Lescot, *OC*, 7:xxix.

been imperfectly transcribed is unknown, but he sent the document to Louvain and Douai and succeeded in obtaining its condemnation by these faculties of theology. He wrote letters to Rome, charging Bérulle with heresy and other failings and issued pamphlets to stir up opposition in Paris. The title of one pamphlet neatly conveys the charges of innovation and unilateralism: "Observations on a Certain Fourth Vow, Added to the Three Solemn Vows by Master de Bérulle, Who Is Currently Proposing It to the Carmelite Nuns in the Kingdom of France and Introducing It into Convents on His Own Personal Authority."[4]

Bérulle waited many years before responding publicly. This response was his *Discourses*, a sweeping expression of his doctrine of the Incarnation and its relation to his vow of servitude. The discourses demonstrated his deep knowledge of Scripture and of the Church Fathers and were buttressed by several dozen approbations of his orthodoxy supplied by such prominent churchmen and theologians as the Cardinal Richelieu (who later turned against him politically), Joseph Tremblay (the Gray Eminence), Jean-Pierre Camus, Sébastien Zamet, Cornelius Jansen (not yet under theological suspicion), and Jean Duvergier de Hauranne (the Abbé de Saint-Cyran).

The discourses were printed along with a "Narrative of What Has Occurred Concerning a Piece of Devotional Writing Composed in Honor of Jesus Christ Our Lord and of the Mystery of the Incarnation," followed by the text of the vow to Jesus and the vow to Mary and an additional set of approbations specifically for the vows. By describing the vow as "essential and original [*essentiel et primitif*] to the order," he explained, he meant that it transcended the Carmelite order: it was founded not in this or that religion (way of devotion) but in "the religion of Jesus," in the primitive Church, in what came before all religious orders and was foundational to them all. In fact, "this vow and this elevation to Jesus is only a recognition and ratification" of our baptismal vows, he said; and to support this point he cited a passage from the Catechism of the Council of Trent:

The pastor will have the Christian people understand that it is right and appropriate for us to consecrate and render ourselves subjects, even slaves, to

---

4. Morgain, *Pierre de Bérulle et les Carmélites de France*, 360.

our Redeemer and Lord, forever; and in fact, when we received the baptism we did so profess, for we declared that we renounced Satan and the world and dedicated ourselves completely to Jesus Christ.[5]

The vow was not necessary, Bérulle explained, but it could be useful. What was essential was to cleave to Jesus Christ and accept his power over oneself, not only by constraint and necessity (for even the damned must do this much) but "by the choice and movement of our will, [...] as the captives of his love as well as of his power."[6]

While continuing as Superior and Visitor of the French Oratorians and Carmelites, Bérulle was also active in public life. In his earlier years he was engaged in disputations with French Protestants, and he served as the Jesuits' informal liaison in France during their expulsion from the kingdom from 1594 to 1603. In later years, Bérulle represented the king and court on several diplomatic missions. In 1619 he participated in negotiating the Treaty of Angoulême, which reconciled Marie de Medici and her son Louis XIII. He negotiated the marriage between Henrietta Maria, daughter of Henri IV, and Charles I of England in 1624. In the following year, he was instrumental in concluding the Treaty of Monçon between France and Spain. He was made a cardinal by Urban VIII in 1627. René Descartes's early biographer Adrien Baillet also records that Bérulle was instrumental in encouraging Descartes at a pivotal moment in 1628 to pursue his new philosophy.[7] Bérulle died on October 2, 1629, of an apparent heart attack while celebrating the Mass, at the moment that he was "proffering these words of oblation of servitude, *Hanc igitur oblationem servitutis nostrae*," thus "confirming his vow by his death."[8]

Bérulle's disciple François Bourgoing collected and published Bérulle's works in 1644, but attention to his writings did not long survive his death.[9] There are several reasons that we might posit for its

---

5. Bérulle, "Narré," *OC*, 8:39–41, 44. The citation given was to pt. 1, art. 3 of the Catechism. The quoted passage in fact comes at the end of art. 2.

6. Bérulle, "Narré," 43.

7. Adrien Baillet, *La Vie de monsieur Descartes* (Paris, 1691), pt. 1, bk. 2, chap. 14, vol. 1, pp. 160–66, https://gallica.bnf.fr/ark:/12148/bpt6k75559n.

8. "This oblation therefore of our service." Bourgoing, "Préface," v.

9. "Much evidence suggests that Bérulle had been forgotten by the 1640s, and

fading. One is that Bérulle, although learned, did not dedicate himself particularly to authorship but to establishing institutions and exerting influence through personal relationships. Bourgoing has recorded that Bérulle believed that "our Lord asked of him works rather than words, and that he did not send him to speak, but to act."[10] Other than the discourses, the writings of his mature years consist primarily of meditations on the lives of Jesus, the Blessed Virgin Mary, and Mary Magdalene, as well as talks or sermons he delivered to the Carmelites or Oratorians that were taken down by listeners and later printed. Perhaps also his literary style associated his writings with the past, for it would soon be discarded by other authors in favor of the new elegance of modern French.

His ongoing influence, however, was substantial, as successive generations of priests and religious diffused and adapted his teachings. The following are only the most prominent of his many followers: Charles de Condren (1588–1641) succeeded Bérulle as head of the Oratory, continued to found seminaries, and was deeply involved in domestic missions. Jean-Jacques Olier (1608–57) likewise continued Bérulle's emphasis upon priestly formation, founding the Compagnie de Saint-Sulpice (Sulpicians) and supporting missions domestically and in New France (Canada). Olier's *Treatise on Holy Orders* was used for centuries as a primary text for priestly formation. Jean Eudes (1601–80) founded the Congrégation de Jésus et de Marie. In the following century we find Jean-Baptiste de La Salle (1651–1719) and Louis-Marie Grignion de Montfort (1673–1716), among others, deeply influenced by Bérulle. The present-day theologian Yves Krumenacker has estimated that "in 1789, more than two-thirds of French seminaries were in the hands of inheritors of Bérullism,"[11] and many religious congregations that began or re-

---

inventories made after death indicate that his works were rarely found in libraries, even those belonging to members of the Oratory." Yves Krumenacker, "Entre histoire et mémoire: L'École française de spiritualité," *Théophilyon* 4, no. 1 (1999): 48. Yet Bérulle's writings did not enter complete oblivion, as they were reprinted several times in the following centuries. The most recent edition is that of Cerf, 1995–.

10. Bourgoing, "Préface," iii.

11. Yves Krumenacker, "École française de spiritualité," in Alain Tallon et al., *Histoire du christianisme en France* (Paris: Armand Colin, 2014), chap. 16, p. 273. See also Krumenacker, "Entre histoire et mémoire," 58.

emerged after the Revolution likewise found themselves in conformity with it. In the early twentieth century, the historian Henri Bremond revived interest in the person of Bérulle by the emphasis he placed on the cardinal in his landmark *Literary History of Religious Thought in France*, a multivolume work published between 1916 and 1936.[12]

Bremond is typically cited as the creator of the epithet *French school*. Krumenacker has demonstrated, however, that the term likely came into existence as far back as the mid-nineteenth century (being first applied narrowly to the Sulpicians) and that in 1913 the Sulpician Georges Letourneau "broadened its meaning to include the whole group of spiritual writers from the seventeenth to the nineteenth century that were read in Sulpician, Oratorian, Eudist, and Lazarist seminaries."[13] Bremond modified the term's meaning once again by extending it back to Bérulle and the Oratory. The precise nature and scope of the school has been contested among scholars since Bremond's day. We will not focus on the term but on what the discourses reveal of Bérulle's personal synthesis of theological and spiritual influences and emphases.

The Discourses

Within Bérulle's lifetime, the discourses were first printed in 1623, reprinted in that same year, and then a third time in 1629. The 1629 printing has been used as the source for this translation, given that it is the last one printed before Bérulle's death and therefore the last that can reasonably be supposed to have benefited from his review.

This is a work of mystical theology and doxology, not an expression of Bérulle's own mystical experience. Bourgoing remarked that the work could have been titled *Panegyric on the Incarnation, or, the Faith by This Mystery Explained*.[14] In expounding the theology underlying his vow of servitude, Bérulle ranges over a vast territory, often circling around his themes, sometimes spiraling closer in and other times further out, sometimes returning to and amplifying earlier points, and

---

12. Henri Bremond, *Histoire littéraire du sentiment religieux en France depuis la fin des guerres de religion jusqu'à nos jours*, 11 vols. (Paris: Bloud et Gay, 1916-36).

13. Krumenacker, "L'École française de spiritualité," 263-64.

14. Bourgoing, "Préface," xiv.

sometimes repeating points in a manner that may strike the reader as redundant. Because it is the longest of his works, and it was written near the end of his life, we may be tempted to seek in this text the definitive expression of his thought. Instead, we must bear in mind that these discourses were written in response to a particular situation, and while they presumably include everything that Bérulle considered necessary to accomplish his purpose, they may not include all that is important to his thought as a whole.[15]

Even if we knew nothing about the circumstances of its composition, within the work itself Bérulle provides several indications that it should not be interpreted as an entire statement of his doctrine. We have his remark in a brief note to the reader (not included in this volume) that the need to await receipt of some of the approbations "delayed the printing and gave me time to add several other discourses."[16] This remark suggests that he may not have viewed the discourses as one definitive set, either before or after making the addition. We also have Bérulle's word in his preface that he had conceived of a vast body of work, of which these discourses would form only the first part. He would compose additional discourses "if God will give us the leisure and grace to set them forth" (p. 43 in this volume). The ones being offered to the public in 1623 treated only of "the oneness of God" and of "the communication of God in this mystery"; future discourses, he said, would treat of God's fullness, life, love, holiness, sovereignty, and conduct. Bérulle did publish a short work in 1629 bearing the title *Part Two of the Discourses on the State and Grandeurs of Jesus, in Which Begins, The Life of Jesus*. Yet this text does not seem to fit clearly into the schema that Bérulle had outlined in his preface of 1623.

Sources and Influences

Bérulle draws on many sources: the Bible, certainly, and the Church Fathers, both Eastern and Western, as well as later theologians. The reader

---

15. For an introduction to Bérulle's thought as a whole, see M. Vetö, *Pierre de Bérulle: Les thèmes majeurs de sa pensée* (Paris: L'Harmattan, 2016).

16. Bérulle, "Au lecteur," *OC*, 7:33. Presumably this is discourse 10, which is in three parts.

will also note Renaissance humanist themes such as the man-as-microcosm motif, and references to classical authors and to contemporary science.¹⁷ Of the various streams that make up Bérulle's intellectual and spiritual inheritance, there are two in particular that we will mention here. The first is the Neoplatonism of Pseudo-Dionysius, and the second is the "Abstract school" of mysticism that we may contrast with Teresa of Ávila's emphasis on the person of Christ.

Neoplatonism is a name applied retrospectively to the dominant school of thought in the closing centuries of the ancient era (c. 250–650). The thinkers of this period, among whom Plotinus (205–70) is the most significant, sought to synthesize, clarify, and extend the inheritance that they had received from antiquity. Bérulle would have appropriated this thought through Augustine of Hippo and the Cappadocian Fathers (Basil of Caesarea, Gregory of Nyssa, and Gregory Nazianzen) and more directly through Marsilio Ficino's Latin translations of Plato, Plotinus, and Pseudo-Dionysius that were produced in the fifteenth century. Of these, Pseudo-Dionysius is the writer who most influentially conveyed this school to the thinkers of Bérulle's time.

The esteem in which Pseudo-Dionysius was held for more than a thousand years of Christian thought can hardly be exaggerated. This author appropriated the identity of the Dionysius who is mentioned in Acts 17 as an Athenian member of the judicial court, the Areopagus, and was converted by St. Paul. We do not know whether the author meant to deceive his readers by this appropriation or only to adopt the mantle of another person with symbolical or representational intent, following a common rhetorical practice of his time. Regardless of what Pseudo-Dionysius intended, the effect was that his writings were accorded a very high status, since the person that he claimed to be or to represent was among the earliest adherents of the Christian faith after the first disciples themselves. By the time of Erasmus (1466?–1536), many scholars had come to believe that this author had not lived in the first century but at several centuries' remove, and the writings of Pseudo-Dionysius were beginning to decline from their peak of authority. (It is

---

17. Erik Varden offers a perceptive study of Bérulle's use of humanist thought. See Erik Varden, *Redeeming Freedom: The Principle of Servitude in Bérulle* (Rome: Editions Sankt Ottilien, 2011), chap. 1.

now believed that this author lived and wrote in the late fifth or early sixth century.)

Just as Pseudo-Dionysius had expressed his Christian teaching in the terms and concepts of Neoplatonism while also transforming the earlier Neoplatonic material, Bérulle absorbed and transformed the Dionysian inheritance. To recognize how suffused the discourses are with terminology, concepts, and emphases drawn from this beautiful and fertile school of thought, let us briefly summarize it as it existed in late antiquity.

God, or the One, is beyond being (as the source of all being) and transcends qualification. Nothing can rightly be said concerning God. God is the cause and origin of all. From the One first comes Intellect, understood as the outer effect of the One's inner activity. Neoplatonists spoke of Intellect as the second *hypostasis* (substantial being, distinct reality—only later in Christian doctrine did this word come to mean *person*). Intellect's inner activity produces, in turn, a turning-back to the One, as Intellect seeks to understand itself in the contemplation of its origin. Intellect's inner activity overflows into the third hypostasis: that of Soul. From Soul comes what we call nature, or the physical world. Looking back at Intellect, which is its cause, Soul's outer activity produces the cosmos. Neoplatonic philosophers thus posited the activity of all things as that of abiding in the One, emanating from the One, and returning to the One, as an ontological hierarchy of relations and affinities, and not as activities in space or time. All things come into being from the One, and all things are continuously sustained in their being by the One, just as rays of light come into being and are sustained in their being by the sun.

Bérulle's discourses make repeated reference to the sun as a preeminent image of God, to flowing and outpouring, and to procession to multiplicity and return to oneness. The writings of Pseudo-Dionysius also deeply influenced Bérulle in "the exemplarism that forms the basis of Bérulle's entire theology,"[18] and his teaching of ontological hierarchy

---

18. Paul Cochois, "Bérulle et le pseudo-Denys," *Revue de l'histoire des religions* 159, no. 2 (1961): 175. Vincent Vasey, however, remarks, "That he was inspired by the exemplarism of Plato is another way of saying that Bérulle's thought is imprinted by Patristic thought, Greek Fathers of course, and in particular St. Augustine." Vincent R.

particularly influenced Bérulle's conception of the priesthood and servitude. Bérulle's teaching concerning the priestly state was particularly pertinent given that the priesthood was a primary locus of Tridentine reform. Bérulle's purpose in establishing the French Oratory was to assist in this renewal effort. The priestly calling was a vocation to participate in the eternal priesthood of Jesus Christ, who is both perfect sacrificer and perfect sacrifice, and to mediate between the divine and the human. This mediation was grounded in the authority and task handed down in ordination and was exercised in holiness of life in conformity to the model provided in Jesus Christ. Following Bérulle, Jean-Jacques Olier, for example, stated that the priest "must be regarded as a living Jesus Christ."[19] Thus the priesthood is grounded as much in the Incarnation as it is in the Eucharist. "The adoration of the Word and the dignity of the priesthood are inseparable for Bérulle. Christ is priest by reason of the hypostatic union."[20]

The other current of thought that requires special mention is known today as the Northern, Rheno-Flemish, or Abstract school of spirituality. Some of the primary figures associated with this movement are Eckhart von Hochheim (Meister Eckhart, c. 1260–1328); Jan van Ruusbroec (or Ruysbroeck, 1293–1381), author of *The Spiritual Espousals* (1340s, printed in French in 1606 in a translation by Bérulle's associate Richard Beaucousin); Hendrik Herp (or Harphius, 1410–77), author of *The Mirror of Perfection* (1440s, printed in French translation in 1617); and the unknown author of *The Pearl of the Gospel* (1530s,

---

Vasey, "Mary in the Doctrine of Bérulle on the Mysteries of Christ," *Marian Studies* 36 (1986): 68.

19. Jean-Jacques Olier, *Traité des saints ordres* (Paris, 1676), 378, https://numelyo.bm-lyon.fr/f_view/BML:BML_00GOO0100137001101213879. Drawing on comments by Jacques Maritain, Clare McGrath-Merkle argues that Bérulle improperly "expanded Trent's notion of the priest as the representative of Christ in the offering of the sacrifice of the Mass into the notion that the priest not only acts in the person of Christ at the Mass but, in fact, assumes the person of Christ at all times" and that a direct line of influence can be traced from Bérulle's teaching to today's "crisis of the priesthood." Clare McGrath-Merkle, *Bérulle's Spiritual Theology of Priesthood: A Study in Speculative Mysticism and Applied Metaphysics* (Munster: Aschendorff, 2018), 353–54.

20. Stéphane-Marie Morgain, "La prêtrise selon Pierre de Bérulle," *Revue d'histoire de l'Église de France* 83 (2007): 145.

printed in French in 1602 in a translation by Beaucousin). Another of Bérulle's associates, Benoît de Canfeld (or Canfield, 1562–1610), was an influential author whose *Rule of Perfection* (1609) is also representative. This school emphasized self-abasement and renunciation of self-love, with a view toward complete dependence on God and conformity to his will. It was abstract (in the sense of removed or drawn away) in that it taught that mystical union with God follows the extinction or overcoming of all sensory and conceptual awareness and all activity of willing. Canfeld's *Rule* describes three movements of the will of God (exterior, interior, and essential) occurring through what he taught as the three states of Christian life: active, contemplative, and super-essential. Of God's essential will, Canfeld writes:

> This essential will, then, is purely spirit and life, totally abstract, pure in itself, and stripped bare of all forms and images of created things, corporal or spiritual, temporal or eternal. It is not apprehended by sense, the judgment of man, nor by human reason. It is beyond all capacity and above all understanding of men, because it is nothing other than God himself. It is not something separated from God, nor yet something joined or united with God, but it is God himself and his essence.[21]

Thus, for the Abstract school, union with God "naturally assumes the bypassing of all that is created, even the humanity of Christ."[22] Bérulle's short work *On Inner Abnegation*, written when he was eighteen, is an expression of Abstract spirituality, discussing primarily the beginning stages of this path. It was written under the guidance of Richard Beaucousin, his then spiritual director, and expresses a stepwise method of lists and rules for spiritual advancement. While it speaks of God in almost every sentence, it speaks of Jesus only a few times and only in passing.

Bérulle's later, mature thought, influenced in part by the writings of Teresa of Ávila (1515–82), represents a crucial departure from the Abstract school. In contrast to these Abstract authors, Teresa taught that meditation on Christ in his human nature was of immense spiritual

---

21. Benoît de Canfeld, *Renaissance Dialectic and Renaissance Piety: Benet of Canfield's Rule of Perfection. A Translation and Study*, trans. Kent Emery (Binghamton, N.Y.: Medieval & Renaissance Texts & Studies, 1987), rule 3.1, p. 176.

22. Louis Cognet, *De la dévotion moderne à la spiritualité française* (Paris: Fayard, 1958), 14.

value even for those souls most advanced in the mystical way. "In some books written on prayer," Teresa wrote, we are taught that the unitive way requires that we leave behind all thought of corporeal things, even the corporeal being of Christ, so that the soul might "approach contemplation of the Divinity."[23] But she had come to believe that such teaching was an error and a hindrance. God may work in the soul in such a way that union with him occurs with the cessation of all thought of corporeal images, she affirmed, but this is not to say that the soul should actively desist in such contemplation. After following this path for some time, Teresa had come to view herself as "a dreadful traitor": "Is it possible, my Lord, that it entered my mind for even an hour that You would be an impediment to my greater good?" she asked.[24] "God desires that if we are going to please Him and receive His great favors, we must do so through the most sacred humanity of Christ, in whom He takes His delight."[25]

The Message of the Discourses

The title of the work conveys its fundamental theme: this is a meditation on the state (*état*) and grandeurs (*grandeurs*) of Jesus. The meaning of *grandeur* is relatively straightforward: *grandeur* is greatness, in size or in quality. *État*, however, requires some elaboration. This noun (earlier spelled *estat*) descends from the Latin *status*, denoting the fact

---

23. Teresa of Ávila, *Book of Her Life*, in *Collected Works of St. Teresa of Avila*, trans. Kieran Kavanaugh and Otilio Rodriguez (Washington, D.C.: Institute of Carmelite Studies, 1980), 1:191.

24. Teresa, *Book of Her Life* 22.4, in *Collected Works*, 1:192.

25. Teresa, *Book of Her Life* 22.7., in *Collected Works*, 1:194. See also her *Interior Castle* 6.7:

One should not withdraw through one's own efforts from all our good and help which is the most sacred humanity of our Lord Jesus Christ. [...] For if they lose the guide, who is the good Jesus, they will not hit upon the right road. [...] The Lord Himself says that He is the way; the Lord says also that He is the light and that no one can go to the Father but through Him, and "anyone who sees me sees my Father." They will say that another meaning is given to these words. I don't know about those other meanings; I have got along very well with this one that my soul always feels to be true.

In *Collected Works*, 2:339–40.

or condition of being in a standing position, or a particular way of standing, from the Latin verb *sto, stare*, to stand. By extension, the word denotes the disposition or condition, that is, the state, of a person or thing that persists through some length of time. Littré's dictionary, for example, defines *état* as "a way of being that is fixed and enduring," and quotes Fontenelle: "By the word 'happiness' we mean a state or situation such as one would wish it to endure without change; happiness differs in this way from pleasure, which is only an agreeable but short and transitory feeling, and cannot be a state."[26] The states of Jesus are his active and abiding dispositions or ways of being, and because he is eternal, they too continue eternally. As Bérulle explained,

> We must consider the perpetuity of these mysteries [of Jesus] in a certain way. For they are over in certain respects, and they remain and are present and continue forever in another way. They are over as to their execution, but they are present as to their power; and their power never ends, nor will the love in which they were accomplished ever end. The spirit, then, the state, power, and merit of the mystery is present always. The Spirit of God by which this mystery was worked, the inner state of the outer mystery, the efficacy and power that makes this mystery living and working in us, this powerful state and disposition; the merit by which he obtained us for his Father and merited heaven, life, and himself; even the actual savor, the active disposition by which Jesus worked this mystery, is always living, actual, and present to Jesus. […] This means that we should treat the things and mysteries of Jesus not as over and passed, but as living and present and even eternal, from which we also must gather a present and eternal fruit.[27]

Thus, as concerns ourselves, Bérulle writes, "We have two ways of serving him: one by actions alone and the other by state. We should choose this way that is abiding, secure, and permanent" (p. 155 in this volume). The vow that Bérulle was proposing was a vow to enter and remain in the state of servitude. In the words of François Bourgoing, "The state of servitude is a special manner of belonging, which does not consist so much in willing, desiring, and avowing this servitude as in a permanent

---

26. Émile Littré, ed. *Dictionnaire de la langue française* (Paris: Hachette, 1872), s.v. "état."

27. Bérulle, *Œuvres de piété, OC*, 4:312–13. Bérulle was not the originator of *state* in this sense; the idea is also found in Abstract writers such as Ruusbroec and the author of *The Pearl of the Gospel*.

quality and disposition, which our Lord impresses and sets in the heart so as to make it entirely his own." He went on: "It is not a preparatory oblation, but one that is complete and entire. It is not done proximately and for a time, but for always, as being perpetual and irrevocable."[28]

The state of Jesus that Bérulle describes and honors in this text, and to which the vow of servitude looks as its exemplar, is Jesus' state of self-emptying, in the mystery of the Incarnation. The Incarnation is for Bérulle the focus of the Christian faith. Bérulle makes this assertion immediately, in the first several paragraphs of his first discourse. The divine Word has come into the world to establish a state of grace and the divine assembly of the Church. He teaches "the science of salvation" (45), by teaching us who he is. His death on the cross is one part of who he is, but the Crucifixion is not Bérulle's primary focus either for the Word's identity or for his saving work. Instead, the Incarnation is "the cause of [our] salvation" (46). In it, God is "working the salvation of the world" (46). "For the divine life is founded in the miracle of miracles," Bérulle writes, "that is, in the mystery of the Incarnation [...] in relation to which all other miracles are only intimations or consequences of this first miracle or preparations for it" (71).

Bérulle takes as his primary biblical warrant for this assertion the Gospel of John. References to Scripture are present throughout Bérulle's writing, but John is the biblical book that Bérulle draws on most. This is not surprising, since from the earliest days of the Church, John's Gospel was considered the most spiritual and theological of the four Gospels and the one that most clearly elucidated the Church's understanding of the Trinity and the Incarnation. Eusebius, for example, described John's purpose in writing his Gospel as follows: "But, last of all, John, perceiving that the external facts had been made plain in the Gospel [of Mark], being urged by his friends, and inspired by the Spirit, composed a spiritual Gospel."[29]

Christians who are taught that Christ's death is what saves from sin and gives humankind entry to eternal life may be startled to realize that this is not the primary message of John's Gospel. Instead, "This is life

---

28. Bourgoing, "Préface," x–xii.
29. Eusebius of Caesarea, *Church History* 6.14.7, trans. Arthur Cushman McGiffert, *NPNF* 1 (Buffalo, N.Y.: Christian Literature Publishing, 1890), 261.

eternal, that they might know you, the only true God, and Jesus Christ, whom you have sent" (Jn 17:3). While not denying the essential salvific power of the Cross, the primary locus of the salvation message in John lies in the Incarnation, and because of the Incarnation also in the Trinity. Bérulle is a faithful disciple of John on this point as on many others. Indeed, John begins his prologue unequivocally with these themes. The primary narrative tension throughout this Gospel is, Is Jesus the Son of God? And will those who encounter him decide for or against his identity? Furthermore, sin in the Gospel of John is understood primarily as the rejection of Jesus' testimony concerning his identity and relationship to the Father. The modern commentator Gail O'Day writes, "In the Fourth Gospel, 'sin' is not a moral category about behavior, but is a theological category about one's response to the revelation of God in Jesus."[30] Sin is spiritual blindness, the unwillingness to see the Light of the World, the One whom Bérulle calls the Sun and the Dayspring. Further, O'Day remarks,

> the Fourth Gospel insists on placing the incarnation as the starting point for any conversation about atonement and reconciliation and not isolating Jesus' death on the cross as the sole moment of reconciliation. Jesus' glorification, the events of his "hour," complete what began in the incarnation (cf. 12:28), but the incarnation itself is the locus of reconciliation.[31]

Irenaeus was the first of the Church Fathers to make substantial use of John's Gospel, arguing in his *Against the Heresies* (c. 180) that in Christ humankind is "summed up" and restored to the image and likeness of God. Bérulle appropriates Irenaeus's thought at numerous points in the discourses. Not only does humanity regain what was lost in Adam through the infinite condescension of the Man-God, but humanity gains more: men become "sons of God," participants by adoption in God's divine being, which is a gift that Adam did not originally

---

30. Gail R. O'Day, *John*, in *New Interpreter's Bible Commentary* (Nashville: Abingdon, 2015), 8:555.

31. O'Day, *John*, 8:608. She also emphasizes here that the fourth Gospel stresses the relationship of God the Father and God the Son, and, by participation, mankind's relationship with the Godhead—themes of capital importance in Bérulle's discourses as well. "The Fourth Gospel [...] suggests a way of understanding reconciliation that takes *relationship* as a serious theological category."

receive. The Incarnation is itself soteriological. Bérulle quotes Gregory Nazianzen: God "enters into a new and second union with us, a union much more excellent than the first, [...] for in the earlier one he gives us his likeness, but in this one he deigns even to take on our nature, which is a kind of interchange and union much higher and more divine" (128). Several centuries after Irenaeus, Augustine of Hippo composed his commentary on John, as did Cyril of Alexandria. Bérulle's discourses draw on both of these works. Further, Augustine's *On the Trinity*, and Hilary of Poitiers's work of the same title, use the Gospel of John as a primary source. As the footnotes to the text will demonstrate, Bérulle draws heavily on Hilary's work in particular.

We are accustomed to describing the Incarnation as God becoming man. It is this, Bérulle affirms, but it is also man becoming God. Thus, Bérulle refers to the Man-God as well as to the God-Man, sometimes even in the same sentence. As the Man-God, the Incarnation is "the supreme deifying of human nature, which remains human within the very state of this divine union and yet receives, into a being created and finite and like our own, uncreated and infinite grace" (62). Similarly, Bérulle speaks of "humanity made divine" and "deity made human." Bérulle goes to great lengths to explain the doctrine of hypostatic union because it is the basis of his vow of servitude. He describes the hypostatic union through various images in his long second discourse. It occurs by "the divesting that Jesus' humanity has of its own and ordinary subsistence, so that it might be clothed in a subsistence that is other and extraordinary to this nature" (77). Alternatively, he proposes an agricultural metaphor: "The eternal Father, as the gospel's divine cultivator" engrafts the Word on human nature as on a plant (77). Then again, we might think in terms of politico-legal analogies: "This humanity is separated from its own subsistence and personhood and is endowed with that of the eternal Word," a "rich, royal, and precious investiture" (84). Or we might think of the Incarnation as a sun that is no longer only reflected in a mirror but becomes one with the mirror (214). In each case, we must have recourse to metaphor and analogy; we have no way of understanding such mystery directly. Bérulle quotes Augustine: "God the Word took man to himself in an ineffable way" (135).

The nub of the Incarnation is that there is "oneness of subsistence," that is, one person, who is both human and divine, and "by this means, it introduces into the mysteries of God and the intimate and secret subsistence of his Word a new oneness that was not there before" (111). Within the Godhead there is because of the Incarnation a new kind of oneness, worthy of greatest praise and adoration, which now "unites the world with God, God with man, and created being with uncreated Being" (112). And crucially, this oneness is eternal: since the event of the hypostatic union, "the humanity has never been and will never be for one single moment without this same subsistence always actuating and suffusing it, always as though informing and sustaining it" (125). The Real Presence in the Mass is temporary, but the hypostatic union endures forever. "God will dwell in this humanity eternally, in such a way that man will be God for as long as God is God, and the Son of man will be Son of God for all eternity. For such is the supreme Majesty's good pleasure, to give himself to man by an indissoluble and eternal union" (161).

The motive power of the hypostatic union is divine love. Moreover, "in this mystery God is love and nothing but love" (237). Love is discussed in the discourses in relation to each person of the Holy Trinity. In discourse 4, Bérulle treats of the Holy Spirit, "who in the Godhead is love" (115), whose infertility within the Godhead is expressed in a fertility powerfully exercised beyond the Godhead in the Creation and then supremely in the overshadowing of Mary. Also in discourse 4 Bérulle treats briefly of the love of the Father and the Son, "a striving and outpouring" of self-giving, an "ecstasy of eternal and uncreated love" (126) from which the God-Man results. God will be man forever, "in the extraordinary power and adorable might of his [the Father's] love and charity toward the man born of Mary, to whom he says in a wholly particular sense, *In charitate perpetua dilexi te* [I have loved you with an everlasting love]" (126). This love holds immense power, for it is able to empty, hold captive, indeed to crucify a God. Discourse 9 provides us with Bérulle's most extended discussion of the love of God. In this discourse Bérulle distinguishes two expressions of love in the Godhead. The first is the "natural and necessary" love among the divine persons. The second is the "free and voluntary" love that produces the Incarnation. The second is what provokes the astonishment of Bérulle, via an imagined astonishment of Jesus:

Can it be? Can God, who is sufficient and fulfilled in himself, God who fills himself and all things by the fullness of his being, love something outside himself? [...] This is a point most worthy of astonishment: that love, so great a love, of the world might be in the Godhead. This is a secret that philosophy has not fathomed; it has indeed spoken of God's greatness, as first cause, but little or not at all of his love toward the things that exist outside of his being and that are other to his essence. (248, 252)

By this love, "men are exalted and made gods, according to the word of God himself: *Ego dixi, dii estis* [I have said, you are gods]. And in loving man, God is humbled and made man, in such a way that we have, by this love's strange and wondrous power, a God-Man on the earth and men gods in heaven" (253).

Perhaps another reason that Bérulle does not view the Crucifixion as the primary locus of salvation is that he appears to be oriented, in some passages, to Duns Scotus's understanding of the motive of the Incarnation. In this view, God would have become incarnate even if the Fall had not occurred, because the Incarnation's supreme purpose was to enable man to become "as gods" and to enable God to be adored by a God. Our humanity in Christ has been lifted up to heaven, and Christ is the first fruit of humanity-made-divine, the firstborn among many brothers (Rom 8:29). The Incarnation makes possible "a kind of created deity" (66). This Humanity who is Jesus is therefore the father of the age to come (Is 9:6), through whom we become sons of God by adoption, as he is Son of God by nature.

This is Bérulle's celebrated "Copernican revolution," namely, that "earth is a new heaven" (46), and that earth henceforth rules over heaven. The order of the hierarchies is changed; here we find an important innovation from the thought of Pseudo-Dionysius. Jesus is a new world, for "the mystery of the Incarnation is a complete reprise of the work of creation."[32] And in the terms of Scotus's second motif, the Incarnation enables God to be worshipped as he deserves. "From all eternity, there was indeed a God who was infinitely adorable, but there was not yet an infinite adorer. [...] You are now, O Jesus, this adorer, this man, this servant who is infinite in power, in position, and in dignity to fully satisfy this duty and render this divine homage" (88).

---

32. Cochois, "Bérulle et le pseudo-Denys," 182.

All of creation has been produced by God, the One, the source and principle of all, out of nothing. All of creation is continually sustained in its being by God, as rays of light depend on the sun. Man was made out of nothing, and man remains nothing apart from God's sustaining power and love. Man by his creaturely condition is complete dependency and complete poverty. We may call this the first kind of nothing, or the creaturely nothingness, which is the first kind of servitude. There is a second kind of nothing: the nothingness of our efforts apart from grace. We depend utterly upon God in the state of grace and of glory as much as we do by our nothingness in the state of nature. This is our second kind of servitude, as sons of Adam, participant in his sin. Then, supremely, there is the third kind of nothing: the self-emptying to nothingness of the Man-God, which is the state of the hypostatic union:

> But in addition to these two bonds, it pleased you to have a third, [...] a bond of love, and of a love that is precious and singular; a holy and sacred bond that binds your person to our nature; a bond that makes a new being, a new state, and a new order; a bond that makes a new man and a new Adam. A new man, I say; not merely a righteous man or a holy man, not an angelic man or a divine man, but a Man-God. (68–69).

The Son in his self-emptying opens the way and gives us the model for the third kind of servitude, that of the adopted son of God, an election of the will that comes by grace. Bérulle stresses that the self-emptying of the Son is twofold, in that the Son did not only take on a human nature but he took on a particular sort of human life, a life of hardship and opprobrium, beginning as a helpless infant. As St. Paul writes in Philippians 2:7–8, the God-Man "emptied himself" in the Incarnation and then "humbled himself" further in the life that he lived in Jesus.[33] Union with God is a participation in this self-emptying, this new being, new state, and new order: "Cause me to live and subsist in you as you live and subsist in one divine person" (69). Union with God is a participation in the Man-God. As Vincent Vasey observes, "What is

33. For a fuller discussion of this point, see Peter T. O'Brien, *The Epistle to the Philippians: A Commentary on the Greek Text* (Grand Rapids, Mich.: Eerdmans, 1991), 227–30, and Paul Holloway, *Philippians: A Commentary* (Minneapolis: Fortress, 2017), 120–21.

the idea and model of the mystical experience but the hypostatic union itself?"[34] In the hypostatic union, Bérulle says, "the life and actions of this human nature are not its own—not that they do not proceed from it as from their principle, but they do not belong to it as property" (78). The hypostatic union is a supreme state of servitude and relationship. The Son of God, who has complete independence of the Father in the property of his own person—a point that Bérulle stresses repeatedly[35]— is for this reason the perfect Servant because he is able to give himself perfectly and voluntarily to the Father. He is also the perfect Servant because he does not give up only his liberty, as an only-human servant might, but he gives up his human person entirely.

The Christian perfection that is the vision of these discourses is therefore not the annihilation of self-will in order to become a passive conduit of the divine will, as the Abstract spiritual writers would have it. Instead, it is an entire giving of the self into a complete relation of dependency upon the Father. This involves the will, certainly, but the heart of the transformation is participation in the Man-God's permanent state of *kenosis*, which is supremely described in Philippians 2. "You are the true life, you are the model of our life," Bérulle exclaims:

> O divine interchange! O adorable communication! O wondrous counsel of uncreated wisdom that separates Jesus' humanity from his human person so that it might give him the divine person! O separation! O divesting that is both the preparation for the new life of the Man-God and the model of the new life of man justified according to the Spirit! For just as the eternal Son of God in his human nature has no human person, that is, has no human *me* substantially and personally, so also the son of God by adoption, led by his grace, ought not to have any *me* morally and spiritually. (84)

"Just as ... so also." The reader will soon observe that there is no sentence structure more characteristic of Bérulle's text than this. Bérullism's conception of self-emptying is utterly relational and analogical. The words most central to Bérulle's discourses are all ones of relational import: cleaving (*adhérence*), belonging (*appartenance*), dependency or sub-

---

34. Vasey, "Mary in the Doctrine of Bérulle on the Mysteries of Christ," 75.

35. As, for example, at the end of discourse 6. That Jesus is at all times in complete control of what happens to him is also a theme of John's Gospel and another indication of the close relationship that Bérulle's theology has with this Gospel.

mission (*dépendance*), poverty or want (*indigence*), capacity (*capacité*), homage (*hommage*), bond (*liaison, lien*), regard (*regard*), and relation or relationship (*relation, rapport*). Consider the contrast in meaning and emphasis between Bérullian self-emptying and that taught by the Abstract school. Here for example are Herp's words at the very end of his *Mirror of Perfection*, which sum up his teaching:

> Thus I have shown, as best as I can, the entrance to the superessential contemplative life. [...] The impetuousness of this love is so great that when we are utterly engulfed by it we are being put outside of ourselves into God [...]. Thus our spirit becomes drawn into the spirit of God, and there it is being melted. Thus it flows into the immeasurable abyss, in which it is constantly being renewed and blissfully born, so that the Father can say to the spirit, "You are my son; this day have I begotten you" (Ps 2:7).[36]

Instead, Bérulle's theology of divine union, as expressed in these discourses, is that it is an inner disposition, abiding, secure, and permanent, of the faithful soul's participation in what Bérulle calls the state of the Man-God. In Bourgoing's words, it is "a permanent quality and disposition, [...] a complete and entire giving."[37] The vow of servitude is the vow to realize the inner disposition of the Man-God's *kenosis*. It is a self-giving that divine grace brings to completion. The most arresting and beautiful simile that Bérulle uses to describe this state is the burning bush of Exodus 3, in which Moses encounters the divine presence: "a bush that burns and is not consumed, always a bush and always burning, always a bush in the thorns of our humanity, and always burning in the flame of the Godhead" (62). Like the burning bush, when we have attained union with God we will be "not consumed but set ablaze in a fire of love and charity" (59). As the editors of the Cerf edition of Bérulle's works point out, Bérulle "turns away from any 'abstract' self-emptying and situates servitude in relation to the 'divesting of the human person' that occurs in the Incarnation of the Word. The nothingness to be recovered is not the losing of oneself in the Absolute but the absolute capacity to correspond to the will of the Creator,

---

36. Hendrik Herp, *Mirror of Perfection* 4.65, in *Late Medieval Mysticism of the Low Countries*, trans. Rik van Nieuwenhove, Robert Faesen, and Helen Rolfson, CWS, 164.
37. Bourgoing, "Préface," 10–11.

which the creature had *before the Creation*."³⁸ Jean Ruusbroec or *The Pearl of the Gospel* may have been sources for Bérulle's concept of *état*, but according to these writers, we are to model ourselves on Jesus in all his states.³⁹ Although Bérulle would agree with that, his own message hinges specifically on the state of Jesus' *kenosis*. The title of his work, we should recall, is *The State*, in the singular. "He is not always being born, nor always suffering, but he is always Jesus, always himself," Bourgoing writes, "always a God emptied in our nature."⁴⁰

Augustine began his *Confessions* by asking, "Is there some place in me where my God may enter, the true God, the God who created the heavens and the earth? Is it possible, Lord, that there might be in me something that is capable of containing you?" The mystery of the Incarnation is that the infinite greatness and capacity of the deity has indeed been encompassed, or comprehended, in our humanity, and that from his fullness we have all received grace upon grace (Jn 1:16). Humankind is, by adoption, "capable of God." What a precious gift, Bérulle says, to be in want of God, the necessary precondition for becoming capable of God. "O, what dignity, to be capable and in want of one's God!"⁴¹ This is in part why Bérulle so deeply venerates the Virgin Mary: "Never was a creature so in want and hungering for God as the Holy Virgin. Never did a creature have such complete hunger and thirst for God."⁴²

Union with God effects completion of a circle: We come from God and are nothing in ourselves. We depend every moment on God as the one and only source of being. The purpose of our lives, our fulfillment as created beings, is to return to God, but this time as a new (or original) sort of nothingness. Just as the Son of God emptied himself in an ineffable and supreme downward movement, so also may we ascend to the Godhead with him, highly exalted. In the words of Cyril of Alexandria, in the Incarnation "we were all in Christ [that] the whole of

---

38. Rémi Lescot, "Introduction historique et théologique," 7:xxvii–xxviii. See also Jean-Michel Le Lannou, "Le 'sacrifice du moi' selon Bérulle," *Revue des Sciences Religieuses* 78, no. 2 (2004): 205–30.

39. See, for example, Ruusbroec, *Spiritual Espousals* 1.2, in *Spiritual Espousals and Other Works*, trans. James A. Wiseman, CWS, 48.

40. Bourgoing, "Préface," xix.

41. Bérulle, *Œuvres de piété*, 4:22.

42. Bérulle, *Œuvres de piété*, 4:383.

humanity might be raised up to his status, so that the verse, 'I said, you are gods and all of you sons of the Most High' might through applying to one of us come to apply to us all."[43]

The Translation

An obituary for the noted translator Gregory Rabassa describes the work of literary translation as "chronic, Talmudic agonizing."[44] I have thought of this phrase many times in preparing this translation. Bérulle wrote his text in French instead of Latin, a rather surprising choice in his era for a work intended for a learned readership. In my search for the most suitable English words, I have made extensive use of French and French-English dictionaries produced in the early modern era and in the centuries following, and of the surpassingly useful *Oxford English Dictionary*, which contains all English words and their meanings, whether obsolete, archaic, or presently in use.

Translation is a replacement for the original, one step removed from the thing in itself, a partially satisfying substitute for those who cannot encounter the work directly. There have been arguments about the nature of translation, and how best to realize it, for as long as there have been translators and critics. I view translation as an effort of analogy, of likeness. The task of the translator is to strive to be faithful to the archetype and work from a deep relationship of appreciation and respect toward it, ideally of love toward it. My understanding of what it means to translate faithfully has been influenced by Robert Alter's translation of the Hebrew Bible. Alter gives priority to the careful choice of words that are truly English yet able to convey the foreign quality of the source, he uses one English word for one Hebrew word as much as possible, and he places great importance on conveying the Hebrew rhythm and other literary qualities of the text.[45]

---

43. Cyril of Alexandria, *Commentary on John* 1.9, quoted in Joel C. Elowsky, ed., *John 1–10. Ancient Christian Commentary on Scripture. New Testament 4a* (Downers Grove, Ill.: Intervarsity, 2006), 45.

44. Margalit Fox, "Gregory Rabassa, A Premier Translator of Spanish and Portuguese Fiction, Dies at 94." *New York Times*, June 15, 2016.

45. Robert Alter, *The Hebrew Bible: A Translation with Commentary*, 3 vols. (New

This translation seeks to respect the tenor of the seventeenth-century text by using English words and expressions that do not strike the ear as jarringly modern, that is, appropriate only or primarily to the twenty-first century. Any translator from French to English must also take care to not raise the register of the text, that is, make it more formal-sounding, an unfortunate result that can easily occur when one translates a French word by its most direct equivalent in English. The most direct translation of the French word *filiation*, for example, is the English word "filiation," but the English word stock also offers the alternative of "sonship." For reasons that ultimately go back to the Norman Conquest of 1066 and the social conditions that arose from it, Norman French–derived words (*filiation, terrestrial, ascend, impotent*) convey a more formal or official sense, while Anglo-Saxon–derived words (*sonship, earthly, go up, powerless*) bear a less formal and more personal or affective sense: what the philologist Henry Bradley has called a "greater richness of emotional suggestion."[46]

I have considered it vitally important to preserve Bérulle's rhythm to the extent possible with English syntax. The discourses' grand rolling power is an outstanding feature of this text that will strike the reader immediately. Although I have sometimes divided Bérulle's long paragraphs into more than one paragraph, I have seldom separated his "periods" into shorter sentences, and I have tried to place rhythmic stress on the same words and constructions that Bérulle stresses. The discourses abound in rhetorical features, many of which contribute to its rhythmic quality: parallelism, chiasmus (the same content or structure, but in reversed order), isocolon (the sequence of sentences or phrases of equal rhythm, length, or grammatical structure), and antithesis (opposition or contrast of ideas). This translation attempts to represent each of these faithfully.[47] Bérulle makes repeated use of several syntactic constructions that may be viewed as literary expressions of his

---

York: Norton, 2019); and Alter, *The Art of Bible Translation* (Princeton: Princeton University Press, 2019).

46. Henry Bradley, *The Making of English* (New York: Macmillan, 1924), 106–7.

47. For an in-depth discussion of rhetorical features in the discourses, see Anne Ferrari, *Figures de la contemplation: La "rhétorique divine" de Pierre de Bérulle* (Paris: Cerf, 1997).

theology of exemplarism. The first of these is the "*comme* ..., *aussi* ..." analogy. Each instance of this construction is translated consistently as "just as ..., so also ..." The lower or subordinate item follows the higher or superordinate item as its model and exemplar. In this way it participates in the higher reality and finds its cause and fulfillment there. Through both his words and his rhetorical style, Bérulle is teaching us that our true life consists in participating in the life of the Son of God.

A second example of Bérulle's theological exemplarism that is enacted in his prose style is his frequent use of triplet constructions, or what we might call verbal trinities. The translation tries to keep these trinities in place. Bérulle frequently describes something by using three adjectives or gives a verb three direct objects. We need look no further than his first sentence in discourse 1 to find the Word described as "the splendor, power, and glory of the eternal Father," and his Incarnation as establishing "a holy academy, a state of grace, a divine assembly" (45). (Note also that this first sentence names the three persons of the Holy Trinity.) Bérulle is not drawing only on the classical rhetorical models but more importantly on the view that all creation is a participation in the reality of the Godhead—the ultimate model.

The third and most important literary expression of Bérulle's theology of exemplarism arises from the discourses' very genre. Despite the title, this is a work not of discourse alone but of discourse and elevation (*élévation*), even "discourse in the form of an elevation."[48] We typically think of discourse as a reasoned exposition on a factual or theoretical subject, set forth in an argument or linear progression (from the Latin *discursus*, "running"). The genre is associated in our minds with such concepts as length, rationality, formality, and sequence. Elevation at its most literal and prosaic, by contrast, denotes not horizontal but vertical movement. By extension, elevation is "an uprising of the mind to God,"[49] "a prayer of desire,"[50] "movement toward God with all one's

---

48. Elevation and its relationship to discourse have been the object of several detailed studies by Christian Belin. See Christian Belin, "Le 'discours en forme d'élévation' selon Bérulle," *Littératures classiques* 39 (2000): 253–64; and Belin, *La conversation intérieure: La méditation en France au XVIIe siècle* (Paris: Honoré Champion, 2002), chap. 10.

49. John of Damascus, *Exposition of the Orthodox Faith* 3.24, trans. S. D. F. Salmond, *NPNF* 9, p. 70.

50. Bérulle, *Collationes*, quoted in Cochois, "Bérulle et le pseudo-Denys," 188.

being, in prayer, starting from the contemplation of a mystery of the faith,"⁵¹ "a lively and affective movement of the soul toward God,"⁵² "the lifting up of the soul (in adoration); a devout exaltation of feeling."⁵³ In one of his sermons, Bérulle defines adoration as follows:

> The creature's primary duty and most frequent exercise is to adore its God. To carry out this duty, we must understand these two terms, "adore" and "God," and know what God is and what it is to adore. To adore is to have a very high idea of the thing we are adoring and a will that gives itself over in submission and humility to the excellence and dignity that we believe or know it to have. This very great respect in the mind, and this consent of the will that gives itself completely to this supreme dignity that it conceives of, is what produces adoration. For it requires not only thought but also the affection that submits the adoring person to the thing adored by the exercise and coming together of the two faculties of the soul, the understanding and the will, both used and applied concerning the subject that we want to or ought to adore.⁵⁴

Adoration is thus an activity that begins in thought and involves the will in response to what thought represents to it. To the extent that what we think of today as feelings are concerned, the feelings aroused are those of esteem and consent—this type of "affection" is the motor of the soul's submission, that is, it converts the thought into an active application of the will. For Bérulle, then, affection is closer to will than to emotion or feeling; it is "the state of the mind as regards some specific object; disposition towards something; inclination."⁵⁵ Christian Belin notes that for Bérulle, "it is always a matter of rising up [...] by one's thoughts, and not against them or as an adjunct to them."⁵⁶

The lifting of the heart in adoration necessarily recalls for us the physical elevation of the species in the Mass, which is the supreme moment of invitation to worship. Just as in the Mass the Real Presence is offered to God on the altar, so also spiritual elevation can become

---

51. Cochois, *Bérulle et l'École française* (Paris: Seuil, 1963), 186.
52. *Dictionnaire de l'Académie françoise*, 1st ed. (1694), s.v. "élévation," https://www.dictionnaire-academie.fr/.
53. *Oxford English Dictionary* (Oxford: Oxford University Press), s.v. "elevation," last modified March 2023, https://www.oed.com.
54. Bérulle, *Œuvres de piété*, 4:4.
55. *Oxford English Dictionary*, s.v. "affection," last modified March 2023.
56. Belin, "Le 'discours en forme d'élévation' selon Bérulle," 254.

a complete giving of the self, a complete oblation. This is the sense in which elevation may become vow, as for example in Bérulle's "Vows or Elevations to God on the Mystery of the Incarnation."[57] Teresa in her several written works alternates between discourse and apostrophe, in which she speaks directly to God. Centuries earlier, Augustine did the same in his *Confessions*. But Bérullian elevation is more than apostrophe. As Paul Cochois notes, "Berullian elevations, although they owe much to those of St. Augustine, are not merely theological meditation that changes to prayer of wonder":

> All of these expressions are characterized, in fact, by a double movement. First the giving of self, oblation proper: "I give myself to you," "I make a vow of servitude to God"; then the desire for mystical possession, in which the Virgin, Christ, or God himself can alone initiate: "Use me according to your power and good pleasure. Work in me."[58]

The Eucharist in turn represents the lifting up of the Man-God upon the cross, the ultimate act of self-giving or oblation. The Crucifixion is simultaneously an expression of humility and of glorification, described in the Philippians 2 passage that asserts each of these movements in dialectical tension. In her commentary on the Gospel of John, Gail O'Day notes a "distinctly Johannine idiom for Jesus' death, resurrection, and ascension: 'lifted up' [*hypsoō*], which means both 'lift up' and 'exalt.'"[59]

> The Fourth Evangelist asks the reader to hold two meanings together. [...] As the serpent was lifted up in the wilderness, so the Son of Man must be lifted up on the cross. The double meaning of *hypsoō* implies, however, that the physical act of lifting up is also a moment of exaltation. [...] The cross as humiliation is actually exaltation.[60]

I suggest that for Bérulle *élévation* therefore encloses within its meaning both an upward and a downward movement. To engage in elevation is to abase oneself in adoration toward God and, by divine grace, to be

---

57. Bérulle, "Vœux ou élévations à Dieu sur le mystère de l'Incarnation," *OC*, 8:59.
58. Cochois, "Bérulle et le pseudo-Denys," 188.
59. O'Day, *John*, 539. John contains three instances of Christ's foretelling that he will be "lifted up": 3:14, 8:28, and 12:32.
60. O'Day, *John*, 471. Consider in a similar manner the theme of the Son of Man's ascent and descent in John's Gospel at 1:51 and 3:13.

exalted to the status of son of God by participation in his state of servitude. As Belin says, it is "an interior dynamic of the heart's affection, a constant spiritual exercise of complete and permanent cleaving to the Mystery of the incarnate Word."[61] The literary genre of elevation is the ultimate expression, on the literary plane, of Bérulle's doctrine of exemplarism, encapsulating Bérulle's entire theology of divine union. On the spiritual plane, elevation is a relationship in which both man and God play a part. As guests invited to the marriage feast, "we must remain in our humble place until we hear the words, 'Friend, come further up.'"[62]

61. Belin, "Le 'discours en forme d'élévation' selon Bérulle," 261.
62. Bérulle, *Collationes*, quoted in Cochois, "Bérulle et le pseudo-Denys," 189, referencing Lk 14:10.

Discourses
on the State and
Grandeurs of
Jesus

Detailed Table of Contents

Preface — 37

Discourse 1. On the Excellence and Singularity of the Sacred Mystery of the Incarnation — 45

Incarnation, epitome of the faith and of God—God is adored and adores in greatness and humility—Earth is a new heaven—The praise of silence—The author's reason for composing this work—Supreme Oneness, the Man-God and God-Man.

Discourse 2. On the Excellence of the Mystery of the Incarnation, in the Form of an Elevation — 56

The true Sun—The Copernican revolution—Elevation to the Trinity and to the Holy Humanity—Participation—Bonds of creation, of grace and love, and of servitude—Three lives of Jesus—Economy of the Incarnation—Naked capacity and pure void—Jesus the infinite Adorer—Servant and lord.

Discourse 3. On the Oneness of God in This Mystery — 94

God is one in existence, in work, and in rest—Platonists and pagans—Muslims and Jews—Only Son—The Eucharist extends oneness—Jesus' life begins and ends in oneness—Oneness of essence, of love, and of subsistence.

Discourse 4. On the Oneness of God in This Mystery — 115

Holy Spirit, divine worker of oneness—Infertile in the Godhead, fertile beyond the Godhead—His two capacities of love and of oneness—Incarnation produces a oneness of God and man beyond that of "two in one flesh" or of Christ and his Church—Eucharist is a second, temporal union—Incarnation is an eternal union—Death and hell did not separate this union—The incomprehensible God causes himself to be comprehended—The first union with man was of likeness; the second is of nature—A new order—Earth is now above heaven—A new exercise of Providence—A wondrous circle.

Discourse 5. On the Communication of God in This Mystery — 141

Word as Image of the Father—His birth in time reflects his procession from the Father—His divine and human natures reflect his production with the Father of the Holy Spirit—That he is first-born among many brothers reflects his first procession in the Godhead—He is the Dayspring, the rising Sun—He is shoot, flower, and fruit—He is able to send the Holy Spirit—He is able to dedicate all things to the Father and dedicate himself as first fruits—He restores in us the image and likeness of God—He is father of the age to come, making his natural sonship a living source of adoptive sonship—We must model our life on his, as pure relation to God—God is made man in order to make men gods.

Discourse 6. On the Communication of God in This Mystery — 162

Trinity, Incarnation, and Eucharist correspond to Father, Son, and Spirit—We are drawn to heaven by a chain of love—God communicates himself and dwells in Creation by nature and by grace—All creation depends on him constantly, as light depends on the sun—Demons and sinners can separate themselves from God by free will but not by natural will or by essence—Created being is only participated being—Jesus' dependency is human and natural; his independence is divine and personal—This makes him able to effect our salvation, to satisfy the Father "from what is his own"—The author's critics do not understand these truths.

Discourse 7. On the Communication of God in This Mystery 182

God ceaselessly communicates himself according to each created thing's nature and condition—God communicates himself in the Trinity, Incarnation, and Eucharist—Each communication extends to another—The Word, father of the age to come, makes us gods by participation, living images of the divine Being, and sons by adoption—Purpose of the Son's coming is to cause us to return to God—Jacob's ladder—In Jesus Christ all the fullness of God dwells bodily—Jesus Christ dwells fully in his humanity—Mediator between God and men.

Discourse 8. On the Communication of God in This Mystery 209

The sun is the image of Jesus—He represents himself in us—Christian faith as an art of painting—The Sun came down from heaven—Not reflected in a mirror but becoming one with the mirror—Human nature belongs singularly to the Word—The divine splendor communicated to his humanity—A love that crucifies—The author asks for blessing on his community.

Discourse 9. On the Love and Communication of God in This Mystery 246

The love in the Trinity is natural and necessary; the love in the Incarnation is free and voluntary—Jesus' astonishment that God so loved the world—Knowledge draws its object up to itself; love draws the lover down to the object—We possess God on earth by love, and in heaven by knowledge—Jacob's ladder—The new Adam is made for the old Adam—Jesus enters all the states of human life—Jesus is a new world.

Discourse 10. On the Three Births of Jesus 266

Preface. His birth in his Father's bosom in the life eternal—His birth in the Virgin's womb in his life temporal—His birth in the grave in the life immortal—Today I have begotten you.

On the First Birth of Jesus. Eternal Dayspring—The Father performs the offices of both father and mother—The Church is the mother of the faithful—A God begetting and a God begotten—Sonship equal to the fatherhood—He is begotten of the living God; we are begotten of the God dying on the cross—Generation and procession—God surpasses our knowledge.

On the Second Birth of Jesus. Mary's integrity—The Creation proceeds from God as God; the Incarnation proceeds from God as Father—He holds his humanity by human sonship as he holds the deity by divine sonship—Man as epitome—Divine motherhood of the Virgin—Her powerful *Fiat*—The flow of life and love between Jesus and Mary—The Father's authority and that of the Mother.

On the Third Birth of Jesus. Jesus the phoenix—Defers his glorification and ascension out of love—Three lives, three dwelling places—In Jesus dwells all the fullness of the deity bodily—The example of Mary Magdalene—Let us find our life in obedience, our freedom in servitude, and our glory in submission to him, our Sovereign Lord.

Preface

God in his inestimable goodness willed to redeem the world that he had created by his infinite power. He begins the gospel on earth with a heavenly conference between the Virgin and the Angel, who announces to her that the only Son of God wills to be conceived in her and to be born into the world by her, so that he might be the Redeemer of the universe.

It seems to me that this angel from heaven is Jesus' forerunner to the Virgin just as this earthly angel that was foretold in Malachi is Jesus' forerunner to Judea.[1] To be precise, these angelic words convey the gospel of the eternal Father to the Most Holy Virgin just as the apostolic words truly convey the gospel of Jesus to sinners.

This gospel of God the Father is singularly high and wondrous, for it is the principle of the gospel of Jesus, just as the Father who ordains it is the principle of Jesus' person; and it is ordained in order to make known

---

1. Mal 3[:1] (original marginal note). The 1629 edition contains marginal notes, identified in the present edition with the phrase "original marginal note." Any material following this phrase in the footnote is provided by the present translator.

Whenever Bérulle quotes the Bible or another source in Latin (either in the body of the text or in an original marginal note), the Latin has been retained. If he does not also provide a (French) translation, I have given an English translation in a footnote. If he does provide a (French) translation, or if he quotes only in French, I have translated Bérulle's words into English.

Bérulle presumably owned copies of the Vulgate, the Septuagint, and other translations of the Bible; many passages would also be deeply familiar from liturgical use. It seems evident that Bérulle sometimes quotes Scripture and other sources from memory, and he does not always use the same words each time. References to a book title or to a biblical chapter and verse seem also to have been given from memory in some cases. I have supplied corrections where I was able to identify them.

to the world the Son of God, Son of man, and a Virgin Mother of God, formerly qualities unknown and secrets hidden from heaven and earth.² The gospel of Jesus is singularly sweet and favorable, for it is a principle of grace on the earth, it pardons sinners' transgressions, and makes in the world a countless number of adoptive children of God. This gospel of the eternal Father is announced in order to communicate the divine Word to the Virgin, and by her to communicate it to men and angels, and to spread on earth the uncreated and substantial grace, that is, the person of the only Son of God, who is the grace of the Father. This grace descends on the Virgin as a heavenly dew, causing her to be fertile with the salvation of the universe and beget a Man-God on the earth. The gospel of Jesus is made known in order to communicate the holy word of God to men, instruct them in the secrets of heaven, and spread on earth the grace of God, which makes men holy and lifts them up to heaven. This gospel of the Father opens heaven to the Virgin and opens to her even the Father's bosom, which had been closed from all eternity, so that she might receive from this fatherly bosom into her virginal womb the only Son of God, who wills to be the son of the Virgin Mary in the fullness of time just as he is the Son of God the Father within eternity.³ The gospel of Jesus opens heaven to sinners, pours on them its heavenly influences,⁴

---

2. The French noun *principe* is translated as "principle." In Neoplatonic thought, the principle (Greek: *archē*) from which all else comes is variously called the First, the One, or the Good. In some places in Bérulle's text, "fountainhead" might be a better choice than "principle," given how much this latter word in English is associated with impersonal notions of proposition, rule, and law. Near synonyms are *commencement* (translated as "beginning"), *cause* ("cause"), *origine* ("origin") and *source* ("source"), which denotes an origin in general or the origin of a watercourse specifically, that is, a spring. The phrase *source vive* is translated as "living source" or "wellspring," that is, a spring from which water flows.

3. The French noun *sein* is translated as "bosom," "breast," or "womb." It denotes the breast itself, the lap, womb, mind, or heart, or the innermost part, and is closely associated with the notions of affection, shelter, intimacy, and secrecy. Its possible French senses permit Bérulle to use the word in relation to God the Father and to the Virgin Mary, that is, to the bosom of God and to the bosom and womb of Mary. Thus, many passages in these discourses contain a fullness of interpretation that cannot be expressed in English.

4. Ultimately from the Latin *fluo* (to flow, stream), *influence* in both French and English formerly denoted a fluid that was believed to stream forth from the stars and affect what occurred on earth.

and makes them children of God and citizens of heaven, if they will be faithful to Jesus, keeping his laws and living under his rule.

This gospel of the eternal Father is borne by an angel who announces it to the Virgin, an angel who is among the greatest angels and princes of heaven. The gospel of Jesus is borne by sinners, whom he makes angels of his word in order to announce it throughout the earth.[5] The first gospel occurs softly, in Nazareth, in a cabinet, in private, in silence, in stillness, and, as Scripture says, *dum medium silentium tenerent omnia*.[6] The second gospel is made known in the universe, at noonday, in the sight of the peoples, with a burst of words and miracles. The first takes place between just two people: the one living in heaven, the other living on earth. The second takes place among all mortals, of all times, all ages, and all lands, to the end of the world. The first takes place between an angel and a virgin, but a virgin more heavenly and angelic than this angel, a virgin hidden and unknown to the world and to every mortal man, as she is called in Isaiah;[7] but a virgin who in heaven is more known and illustrious than any other person in heaven or on earth. The second takes place among men—some holy, others sinners, some apostles and others called, some sent and others invited—and seeks to establish the kingdom of God among men, the kingdom of heaven on earth.[8]

This heavenly conference between the angel and the Virgin is for great things, the greatest that will ever be accomplished in the course of the ages and even in eternity. This gospel of the eternal Father to the Virgin contains in epitome the doctrine of salvation and conveys to the children of men the seed of all the fruits of the gospel of the Son of God.[9] It is the base and foundation of Jesus' state and rule. The

---

5. The literal meaning of *angel* (from the Greek *angelos*) is "messenger."

6. Wis 18[:14] (original marginal note). *Cum enim quietum silentium contineret omnia*, "When a peaceful stillness held all things." Bérulle follows an alternate liturgical wording.

7. Jerome wrote that the Hebrew word *almah* used at Is 7:14 means both "virgin" and "hidden." See Jerome, *Against Jovinianus* 1.32, trans. W. H. Fremantle, G. Lewis, and W. G. Martley, *NPNF* 6 (Buffalo N.Y.: Christian Literature Publishing, 1893), 370.

8. The literal meaning of *apostle* (from the Greek *apostolos*) is "one who is sent."

9. The French noun *abrégé* is translated as "epitome" or "recapitulation." It denotes a representation in miniature (not an abridgement).

Church must show the world what takes place in Nazareth, what occurs in this secret, what takes place in the blessed moment that conveys the salvation of the ages and accomplishes the most high mystery of the Incarnation in the world's midst.

The first point of this angelic colloquy, this divine embassy, this gospel of the eternal Father, concerns the Virgin. The angel addresses himself to her and greets her, as full of grace, as honored with the presence of the Lord, as blessed among women. The praise is limited to this sex not because she lacks excellence and advantage over all men and even over the angels, but as a noteworthy sign and illustrious mark of the dignity that he has just announced to her, of the position that she will enter, which applies only to women. This is the position of mother, but of Mother in regard to God, which exalts her and gives her power and authority over all that is created.[10] It is an excellent privilege and an incomparable position that is reserved to this sex and to the most holy Virgin Mary, truly blessed among women on this occasion and thereafter established in grace, glory, and power over all men and angels.

But this angel, after having worthily spoken to the Virgin in this way and having taught us the grandeurs of this wonderful person, her fullness of grace, her divine motherhood, and the Lord's presence in her, which is the foundation of this fullness and the principle and endpoint of this blessed motherhood, he goes on to the second point in this heavenly embassy and announces to her the grandeurs of the one who will be her son.[11] And the first words of this great angel upon so great a subject are these: *Hic erit magnus, et filius altissimi vocabitur,*

---

10. The French verb *regard* is translated as "regard" (in some instances: "look upon," "concern"), and the noun *regard* is translated as "regard" (in some instances: "look"). The meaning is often close to the French nouns *relation* and *rapport*, both of which are translated as "relation(ship)." To regard something is to have relation to it; to attend, esteem, or have care or concern for it.

11. The French noun *grandeur* is translated as "greatness," but in the plural form as "grandeurs," since "greatnesses" seems awkward in English. The French noun *terme* is translated as "endpoint" (in a few instances: "extent," "limit"), denoting the extent, outer limit, or boundary of something, the point at which it concludes or ceases. It is translated thus in order to distinguish it from the French noun *fin*, translated as "end," which denotes the opposite of beginning, the accomplishment, or goal or purpose toward which something is directed.

etc. Et regnabit in domo Iacob in aeternum, et regni eius non erit finis.[12] He impresses Jesus' grandeurs, his divine sonship, his supreme power, and eternal kingdom on the Virgin's mind by his illumination at the same time that he explains them to her by his words. Great words, sweet words to the one who is to conceive him, bear him, and love him as her son; and words great and sweet also to the one who serves Jesus, loves Jesus, awaits the coming of Jesus, and as the apostle says, *iis qui diligunt adventum eius.*[13] Thus this heavenly embassy and these angelic and evangelical words speak of nothing but grandeurs, the grandeurs of Jesus and of Mary: incomparable grandeurs, grandeurs henceforth eternal! Grandeurs that are the most high, divine, and accomplished possible after the uncreated grandeurs of the divine persons!

These grandeurs of the only Son of God and of the one that it pleased him to choose for his most holy Mother will be the subject of these discourses that we have proposed to write, just as they are the venerable subject of the angel's words and of this heavenly embassy. Following the example of this angel of light, we will speak of the grandeurs of Jesus and of the Virgin Mary, but we will begin with the grandeurs of the one who is the origin of the grandeurs of his most holy Mother. For Jesus is the foundation and new principle of all grandeurs outside of God, and Jesus is in particular the root and basis of his holy Mother's grandeurs. He is the root of Jesse more than Jesse is his root, and he refers to himself thus in Scripture: *Radix Iesse.*[14] He is the root of Mary more than Mary is his root, and he bears his Mother in the state of grace more than his Mother bears him in the state of nature. The Virgin does not subsist in the order of God's council except by the submission and relation that she has to her only Son, and to the will that he had to be her son and to cause her to be his Mother.[15]

---

12. Lk 1[:32] (original marginal note). "He will be great, and will be called the Son of the Most High, etc. And he will reign in the house of Jacob forever, and of his reign there will be no end."

13. 2 Tm 4[:8] (original marginal note). "Those who love his coming."

14. "Root of Jesse." Is 11:1, 10; Rom 15:12.

15. The French noun *conseil* is translated as "counsel" when referring to advice or judgment, and as "council" when referring to the place or body where or by whom the advice or judgment is made. Bérulle later makes a distinction between *conseil* and *cabinet*. As the editors of the Cerf edition of Bérulle's works remark, "The author uses

For the grandeurs of Jesus may be considered in himself, in his relation to God his Father, and in his relations to us. And we will find in all these points that the angel has reason to say, "He will be great." Great, I say, absolutely, without modification and without restriction, as being great in everything—great in himself, in his divine relations, and in his states and offices, etc. He is great in himself: for he is great in his person, in the deity of his first nature, and in the subsistence communicated to his second nature.[16] He is great in his relations to the divine persons: for he is Son of the one and Principle of the other. He is great in regard to us in his states, qualities, offices, and privileges, for he is Head, and we are his body and members; he is Spouse, and we are his heart and delight; he is Father, and we are his children; he is Shepherd, and we are his flock; he is Teacher, and we are his disciples; he is Redeemer, and we are his captives; he is King, and we are his subjects; he is the sacrificial Priest, and we are his hosts—living hosts that he sacrifices to his Father's glory. In sum, he is everything, he is our everything; he is the life, the light, and the salvation of the world. Thus, heaven and earth concur in confessing this supreme greatness: heaven, by placing its crowns at his feet and crying, *Dignus est Agnus accipere virtutem et divinitatem*;[17] and

---

with precision the two technical terms *conseil* and *cabinet*, corresponding to the royal jurisdiction of the times. [...] The king, in his cabinet, deliberated with chosen counsellors on particular questions, perhaps secret; in his council, with members of the law (particularly ministers of State), he would take official decisions." Join-Lambert and Lescot, notes to Bérulle, *Discours*, OC, 7:86n2, 7:190n3. The French noun *dépendance* is translated as "dependence," "dependency," "submission," or "subordination." It means to be subject or subordinate to something else, to take one's support or follow necessarily from something else, to require a relation with something else in order to be complete. It is the condition opposite of independence. *Dépendance* is the objective condition of all that exists outside of God, not a subjective account of the creaturely experience. The French verb *dépendre* has likewise been translated as "depend" or "submit." "Depend" has been used in passages where the notion of contingency seems most salient, and "submit" where the notion of will seems most salient, but the alternate translation may be equally apt in a given instance.

16. The French noun *divinité* is translated as "deity," "divinity," or "Godhead," depending on the particular nuance suggested in each instance. The French noun *subsistance* is translated as "subsistence." The three Persons of the Trinity share one substance (essence) as God, yet each has his own subsistence (person, hypostasis).

17. Rv 5[:12] (original marginal note). "Worthy is the Lamb to receive power and riches."

earth, by rendering homage to him as to its God,[18] its Sovereign, and its Savior, according to this prophecy: *Et adorabunt eum omnes reges terrae, omnes gentes servient ei.*[19]

Each of these grandeurs indeed deserves its own discourse, and perhaps many discourses. We offer now to the public the first part of these discourses: that which concerns the grandeurs of Jesus in himself and in his mystery of the Incarnation, in distinction to his other grandeurs and his other states and mysteries that dedicate him to us. Indeed, we are setting forth just one part of this first part. For we have treated only of *The Oneness of God*,[20] and of *The Communication of God in This Mystery*, intending to avoid taxing the reader's mind by providing many discourses under one heading, and scattering here and there some seed of the other discourses that are to follow: *On the Fullness of God, On the Life of God, On the Love of God, On the Holiness of God, On the Sovereignty of God, On the Conduct of God in This Holy Mystery*, etc., if God will give us the leisure and grace to set them forth.

The grandeurs of Jesus and of the Virgin Mary are the object that delights heaven, delights it without end. This is the daily bread at the table of the blessed, the ordinary and delightful dishes at their heavenly banquet. Blessed are they who are sustained and nourished by these dishes in this life. All that we can say and think on earth are but little crumbs that fall from heaven, that we must collect from the table of our masters: *Micae quae cadunt de mensa dominorum.*[21]

---

18. Although "homage" (French: *hommage*) is used today in the general sense of respect or acknowledgment, its older meaning, still current in Bérulle's day, involved the notions of relationship and service. In feudal custom, a lord would endow a vassal with a fief, and the vassal would pledge fealty (make an oath of loyalty), becoming the lord's "man" (whence the word "homage," from the Latin *homo*, man).

19. Ps 71 [72:11] (original marginal note). "And all the kings of the earth will adore him, all peoples will serve him."

20. The French noun *unité* is translated as "oneness" (in a few instances: "unity") and in the plural as "unities," since "onenesses" seems awkward in English. *Unité* is the state of being one in origin. It is translated thus in order to communicate more clearly Bérulle's Pseudo-Dionysian vocabulary and to distinguish this word from the French noun *union*, which is translated as "union" and denotes the coming together of two or more things that earlier were separate. Bérulle makes a distinction between *unité* and *union* at several points in the text.

21. "Crumbs that fall from the masters' table." Mt 15:27.

Following the example of the humble Canaanite woman, we ask for them, we hope for them, and we await them from you, O Jesus my Lord! From you, who have so much love for us, who have so many rights and powers over us, who deign to make us yours on so many bases and singularly yours by the singular mystery of the Incarnation. You, who want on earth to quicken us by your death, wash us by your blood, uphold us by your spirit, raise us by your grace, instruct us by your word, and nourish us by yourself. You, who are the true and living bread, the heavenly bread, the bread come down from heaven, and as bread you desire to nourish us on earth with the substance of your body and in heaven with the communication of your divine essence.

Discourse 1

On the Excellence and Singularity of the Sacred Mystery of the Incarnation

When the divine Word who is the splendor, power, and glory of the eternal Father was sent into the world, he wanted to establish in it a holy academy, a state of grace, a divine assembly to be led and nourished by his Spirit. This he wanted so that he might speak to earth the language of heaven, teach men the science of salvation, and raise them to a high and sublime knowledge of God, by making known to them the greatness of his essence, the plurality of his persons, the depth of his counsels, and the singularity of his works. Concerning these, human reason cannot instruct them.

One of the first and primary points that we are taught in this school of wisdom and salvation that has been established and revealed to the world is the sacred mystery of the Incarnation. This mystery is so exalted that it exceeds the reach of all thoughts of men and of angels. It is so excellent that it contains and comprehends in itself both God and the world. And it is so profound that it is hidden from all eternity in the most secret thought of the Ancient of Days[1] and in the very bosom of the eternal Father, in so high and ineffable a manner that the great apostle rightly calls it in several places, *The mystery hidden from all*

---

1. Cf. Pseudo-Dionysius, *Divine Names* 10.2: "They call him Ancient of Days because he is the eternity and time of everything; and because he precedes days and eternity and time." In *Complete Works*, trans. Colm Luibheid, *CWS*, 120.

eternity in God, who created all things.[2] Yet this mystery that is so high and excellent, so deep and hidden, is fulfilled on earth in the fullness of time, to be set forth in the sight of earth and heaven, so open is it to all. It is fulfilled on earth to be the object of the peoples' faith, the anchor of their hope, the cause of their salvation, and the fulfilment of God's glory in the universe. For it is by this mystery that heaven is opened, earth is sanctified, and God is adored, with a new adoration, an ineffable adoration, an adoration formerly unknown to earth and even to heaven: for heaven had many adoring spirits and an adored God, but it did not yet have an adoring God. It is by this mystery that God is on earth humbling his greatness, and covered with our frailties, clothed in our mortality, is himself among us, as one of us, working the salvation of the world. This mystery is that earth is a heaven, a new heaven, where God dwells in a manner higher and more august, holier and more divine, than he formerly dwelt in the highest heaven. It is in faith, love, and homage to this sacred mystery that God himself, not his angels and servants,[3] is establishing a religion on the earth that will never be changed or removed from the earth.[4] He has reserved it for the latter days just as this mystery also bears the ultimate marks of his eternal power, love, and wisdom. It is in this mystery that the Church must be blessedly and divinely occupied and the piety of souls increased, delighted in astonishment and wonder as they contemplate this object. In it may be ineffably discovered and perceived the majesty of the divine essence, the distinction of his persons, the depth of his counsels, and the eminence, excellence, and singularity that God wanted this matchless[5] work to have—that is, all that is great, all that is holy,

---

2. Eph 3:9; Col 1:26 (original marginal note).

3. Bérulle is perhaps alluding to Is 63:9, which, when translated from the Septuagint, reads, "Not an intercessor, nor an angel, but the Lord himself." The Church Fathers considered Is 63:9 to be a key verse confirming the identity (same being) of God the Father and God the Son. See Jaroslav Pelikan, *The Christian Tradition: A History of the Development of Doctrine*, vol. 1, *The Emergence of the Catholic Tradition, 100–600* (Chicago: University of Chicago Press, 1971), 177.

4. Bérulle often uses "religion" (French: *religion*) with the sense of religious devotion.

5. The French adjective *unique* is translated as "matchless" (in some instances: "one," "only," "sole"). It does not mean unique in the sense of what is special or creative. ("The Only Begotten Son" is in French the *Fils unique*.)

all that is wondrous, and as an epitome and summary of all that the oracles of the faith reveal and instruct us about God and his works. This divine mystery is as the center of created and uncreated Being. It is the matchless subject in which God willed, willed forever, to comprehend and reduce to miniature the world and himself, that is, both his own infinity and the scope of the universe.

There are certain peoples who are well known in profane antiquity and famous in sacred literature, who were honored with the guardianship and tutelage of God's people and of the only Son of God himself in the state of his nonage and childhood.[6] Their writings and teachings were full of enigmatic and hieroglyphic figures. Their custom was to represent religion by a certain tongueless animal, to demonstrate that God, whose goodness, greatness, and majesty surpass all eloquence, should not be adored in tongue and words but in thought and understanding.[7] Let us set aside the thoughts of these profane ones and seek out the judgments of holy and divine souls. The one who was so devoutly consecrated to God's praises and who provides the Synagogue and the Church with sacred words for praising God at all times and throughout the world (I mean the sacred king, prophet, and poet of the Hebrews) divinely hymns, *Tibi silentium laus, Deus in Sion* ("To you silence is praise, O great God in Zion"). This is how St. Jerome says that the Hebrew language renders this verse that is, in the standard version, *Te decet hymnus Deus in Sion*,[8] to teach us that the hymn and praise that is properly fitting to God's greatness is a praise not of words but of deep silence.

What is fitting to God and religion may be rightly applied to this most high, great, and sacred mystery of the Incarnation. For in its state and scope it encompasses God himself, it establishes within the universe an everlasting and universal religion, it is the consummation of

---

6. The Egyptians (original marginal note). See Mt 2:13–15, quoting Hos 11:1. Cf. Ex 4:22.

7. The crocodile. See Herodotus, *History* 2.68–69, trans. David Grene (Chicago: University of Chicago Press, 1987), 160–61; Aristotle, *Parts of Animals* 5.33 (690b), trans. A. L. Peck and E. S. Forster, *LCL* 323, p. 393; and Plutarch, *Moralia* 5, trans. Frank Cole Babbitt, *LCL* 306, pp. 173–75.

8. Ps 65:1. "A song of praise befits you, God in Zion."

God's purposes and counsels upon the children of men, and it renders, not on earth only but in heaven itself, a wonderful worship and honor and an eternal and singular homage to the Godhead. The greatness, therefore, and the sublimity of this most high mystery should be adored in sacred silence and not profaned by our thoughts and words. We should imitate the temperance and reserve of the angels, who cover and veil themselves at the sight of so divine an object and who dwell in astonishment and wonder as they behold his glory. For it is about the Son of God, the Son of God made man, that the greatest prophets recount this famous vision of the angelic spirits and one of the greatest apostles explains it in the holy Gospel.[9] We, therefore, following their example and moved by a subject so excellent that it can render eloquence itself mute, should have recourse to the eloquence of works and services, praising, loving, and adoring Jesus Christ our Lord with all our power and beseeching him that all our life may be to him forever a devout and constant thanksgiving and an everlasting tribute and homage of servitude.

I would prefer to remain silent like this, and such was my intention until now. But a just defense causes me to break my silence, so that I might justify a work of piety against certain persons whom Christian temperance and charity do not permit me to name so as not to affect a holy vow through the fault of some individuals. They condemn what they do not understand, as though they wished to imitate those who, as St. Jude says, *blaspheme what they know nothing about.*[10] They speak from reasons that are not from theology and from interests that do not regard the crucifix. They lose their composure from inclinations that do not come from the new man and are unsuited to the school of the Cross. They publicly say and do what no law can justify, no reason can defend, no pretext can excuse, and no skill can cover up except by a clever silence. I have no desire to respond to these assaults and proceedings; they are worthier of correction than discussion, of scorn than words, and of forgetting than remembering in the memory of men. I will not attend to their attacks, defamatory pamphlets, and slanders

---

9. Is 6[:2]; Jn 12[:28–29, 40–41] (original marginal note).
10. *Quae ignorant, blasphemant* (original marginal note). Jude 1:10.

that are being spread with as little charity as truth and will remain in "silence, which is the best response," in the words of an ancient author.[11] I do not wish to devote my time, mind, and pen to these kinds of writings and responses, which are of little use to the public, unbecoming to my profession, and unhelpful in the matter.

Therefore, instead of responding with counterarguments, after ten years of patience and silence and after three years of tempests and storms stirred up in France and Italy by persons born to this practice, after numerous slanders and six offensive and defamatory pamphlets that have been sedulously spread even abroad, I am setting forth this discourse. I am doing so not to speak of their persons, intentions, or conduct but to speak of Jesus, his supreme state, and his wondrous grandeurs. Of Jesus, who was in former times the stumbling block to the Jews, who foretold that he would be so even to Christians, to his people, his Israel, his children; and who is still a stumbling block, in this matter, to those who have sought to oppose the homage and servitude rendered to him. I make this discourse public, therefore, in order to maintain this pious intention in a pious way, in honor of him, and to arrest the course of assaults by reasoning and sweetness. It is this present necessity that compels me, O Jesus my Lord, only Son of God, only Son of Mary, as well as the advice of persons who honor your grandeurs and mysteries and want to belong to you forever by a particular homage. About them I must say to you with St. Augustine, *Hi sunt servi tui fratres mei, quos filios tuos esse voluisti dominos meos, quibus iussisti ut serviam, si volo tecum de te vivere.* ("These are your servants, and as such they are my brothers. You have wanted them to be your children, and as such they are my masters. And you have commanded me to serve them if I want to live with you and by you.")[12]

---

11. Euripides (original marginal note). See Euripides, frag. 977: "Silence is an answer in the eyes of the wise." In *Fragments*, trans. Christopher Collard and Martin Cropp, LCL 504, pp. 560–61. Cf. Plutarch, *Moralia* 7: "For while Euripides asserts that silence is an answer to the wise, we are much more likely to need it in dealing with the inconsiderate, for reasonable men are open to persuasion." Trans. P. H. de Lacy and B. Einarson, LCL 405, p. 69.

12. [Augustine,] *Confessions* 10.4 (original marginal note). See *Confessions*, trans. R. S. Pine-Coffin (Harmondsworth: Penguin, 1961), 210.

Pardon then, O Sovereign Lord of men and of angels, if by their command and on this occasion I break my silence and intention and dare to speak of you, you who are the adorable Wisdom, the ineffable Word, and the wondrous Splendor of the eternal Father, his divine Word by whom he speaks to himself and to his creatures. On a subject that concerns the Son of God and the peace of heaven and earth, of God and men, I must not mix in the words and cavils of these contentious persons. They have neither great meaning nor great foundation, and in my opinion the light of this discourse is enough to cast away these shadows and clouds. If need be, I will hold them in reserve for later, because this discourse speaks of the union of the eternal Word with our humanity, and it must convey only gentleness and softness, in keeping with the state and nature of this mystery in which the goodness and softness of God himself is apparent, as the apostle says.[13] It is not as though it would be very difficult for me to respond to them, and in few words. But just as ancient peoples would remove the gall from the sacrifices that were offered up for domestic peace and concord, so also in this discourse, which I offer to God and to the public in honor of the peace and union that he has established with us through the sacred mystery of the Incarnation, I likewise wish to remove gall and bitterness.[14]

O Lord, deign to receive this offering from a hand so unworthy and a mind so feeble to make known your grandeurs and praises. And as I begin this work, let me address you in the words of the most humble and learned, most holy and wise, and most modest and devout teacher that the earth has produced and that you have yet given to your Church. In his lofty, holy, and divine words, therefore, which he declares at the end of one of his works, I will say to you at the beginning of this one,

---

13. Ti 3:5 [3:4] (original marginal note).

14. "More important [than libations and gifts] was the sacrifice generally celebrated on the wedding-day [...]. [I]t appears to have been the custom to remove the gall of the victim, and not burn it with the rest of the inner parts, and this was supposed to indicate symbolically that all bitterness must be absent from marriage." Hugo Blümner, *Home Life of the Ancient Greeks*, trans. Alice Zimmern (New York: Funk & Wagnalls, 192–?), 137.

On the Excellence and Singularity of the Sacred Mystery 51

Domine Deus meus, una spes mea, exaudi me, ne fatigatus nolim te quaerere; quaeram faciem tuam semper ardenter. Tu da quaerendi vires, qui invenire te fecisti, et magis magisque inveniendi te, spem dedisti. Coram te est firmitas et infirmitas mea; illam serva, istam sana. Coram te est scientia, et ignorantia mea; ubi aperuisti, suscipe intrantem; ubi clausisti, aperi pulsanti. Meminerim tui, intelligam te, diligam te: auge in me ista donec me reformes in integrum. Multa dicimus et non pervenimus, et consummatio sermonum universa, tu es ipse. Cum pervenerimus ad te, cessabunt multa illa quae dicimus, et non pervenimus; et manebis unus omnia in omnibus, et sine fine dicemus unum, laudantes te in unum, et in te facti etiam nos in unum. Domine Deus, quaecumque dicam de tuo, agnoscant et tui: si qua de meo, et tu ignosce et tui. ("O my God, my Lord, my only hope, answer my prayer, lest, worn out by the troubles of this life, I fail to seek you. I want to seek your face and to seek it always ardently. You who have given me the grace to find you and the hope of finding you more and more, give me also the strength to seek you. Before your eyes my strength and frailty are present; preserve my strength, restore my frailty. Before your eyes my understanding and ignorance are present. Where you have opened the door to me, receive me as I enter in. Where it has pleased you to close it to me, deign to open to the one who knocks. May you be impressed on my memory, may I know you, may I love you. Increase these gifts in me until you establish me in my perfect form. We pour ourselves out in many words, yet without attaining the goal we long for, and it is you, O Lord, who are the culmination, the perfect fulfilment, of all our speech. When we have attained you, this multiplicity of thoughts and useless words will pass away, and you will remain in oneness, alone all in all. We will all speak the same thing unendingly, praising you in unanimity and oneness, just as we also will be gathered and restored in you in perfect oneness and unanimity. O Lord my God, may you and yours approve of what I say of you, for I have taken it from you. And if in these discourses there is something that is mine and not yours, may you and yours pardon it.")[15]

After an eternity of abiding, occupation, and working within himself, God willed to go out beyond, as it were, by a new manner of working. That is, after the internal emanations that occupy him blessedly and divinely in his essence and eternity and that constitute the divine persons of the Holy Trinity, he willed to work beyond himself and to make creatures capable of knowing, serving, and adoring him. He resolved to create the world that we see. And although he was able to

---

15. Augustine, *On the Trinity* 15.28 (original marginal note). See *On the Trinity*, trans. Edmund Hill, *WSA*, pt. 1, vol. 5, pp. 436–37.

draw forth many worlds out of the treasures of his power and wisdom, he willed to produce only one, to represent the oneness of his essence in the oneness of his work. And so, as this God contemplated himself and loved his oneness, he wanted to depict it still more vividly and consecrate it in greater holiness within this same world. And as he had made one world in honor of his oneness, he wanted to choose within this world one Subject and have one work to himself that would be matchless and singular, unlike any other, exceptional and surpassing all others. He wanted this work of his hands to have an excellence perfectly corresponding to the worker's excellence and a oneness perfectly corresponding to his oneness. This is the divine mystery of the Incarnation, the supreme work of the Godhead, the masterwork of his power, goodness, and wisdom, the work particular to God (thus his prophet calls it by this word: *Domine, opus tuum*), an incomprehensible work, and one that comprehends God himself.[16] It is a work and triumph of uncreated love, in which love triumphs blessedly over God himself. It is a matchless and singular work and mystery in the world, which the eternal wisdom has accomplished as the work of his works and the mystery of his mysteries, who blesses by his presence, fills by his greatness, governs by his power, and sanctifies by his influences both heaven and earth.

We see God's oneness as though impressed on this mystery's oneness and this work as though engraved on a precious diamond. We see that in this world in which there are many natures capable[17] of his greatness, God chooses only one, and that in passing over the angelic nature he chooses human nature to unite with himself. We see that in the expanse of humankind, in which there are many members, he chooses only one, and that among the children of men there is but one Son of man[18] who is the Son of God. We see that within God himself,

---

16. Hab 3[:2] (original marginal note). "Lord, your work."

17. The French adjective *capable* is translated as "capable," in the sense of able to receive, take in, contain, hold, be filled, have room for, or be susceptible of. The noun *capacité* is translated as "capacity."

18. Bérulle follows the interpretive tradition of understanding the biblical title *Son of Man* as referring to Christ's human nature, and more specifically to human nature that is born of a human mother. See, for example, Irenaeus: "This Son of God, our

in whom there is plurality of persons in oneness of essence, there is but one person who became incarnate, although the Father and the Holy Spirit have equal power to perform a similar communication of their divine subsistence. In this way, God's oneness is honored no longer only in the world's oneness, as it was formerly in the Creation, but it is honored in the very oneness of a divine and uncreated person, in this masterwork of the Incarnation.

Let us speak more simply and give greater clarity and breadth to this thought. Let us say that this is no longer the oneness of an earthly and elemental world, a material and sensible world, but the oneness of a new work and a new world. It is a world of grace, of glory, and of greatness, a world completely heavenly, glorious, and divine. It is a world that equals and encompasses God himself as part to it (if we may speak in this way), and that proclaims, praises, and adores God's oneness. For Jesus is a world, a great world, according to true theology and for many other reasons that philosophy has never possessed for calling man a little world, as will be said elsewhere. And in Jesus we adore the oneness of a divine person who, subsisting in two different natures, is divinely and ineffably employed in proclaiming, honoring, and serving the supreme oneness of the divine essence.

O Supreme Oneness, how lovable and wondrous you are in the Godhead and in the most divine of its works! How adorable you are, for God himself employs in your honor the oneness of his Word in two associated natures, and he employs it forever, just as you are eternal and everlasting! How blameworthy mortals are to consider and attend to you so little and violate you so freely in your works! For they do not consider that God is Oneness, he does all things for oneness, and he does all things by oneness itself. The oneness of his power, essence, and understanding is the principle of all that he works outside himself and in all his works. He seeks to draw all things to himself and to his holy oneness, by the oneness of his Spirit in grace and the oneness of his Word in the Incarnation. He employs this mystery, and in it one of the

---

Lord, was both the Word of the Father and the Son of Man. Since He had a human generation from Mary, who was of the human race and was herself a human being, He became the Son of Man." Irenaeus, *Against the Heresies* 3.19, trans. Dominic Unger, Ancient Christian Writers (New York: The Newman Press, 2012), 3:94.

divine persons, to honor the oneness of the divine essence. O oneness of essence, adorable in the Holy Trinity! O oneness of person, adorable and lovable in the Incarnation! Oneness of divine essence and of divine person in these two mysteries, singularly adorable and lovable, seeking to draw us to God and his oneness! Yet audacious persons, by feeble reasoning and strong passions, rupture so freely the unity of faithful persons by heresies and the unity of obedient hearts by rebellion!

But let us set these thoughts aside, so that we can return to our discourses and mysteries. Let us say that when God had established three different orders in the universe, the order of nature, of grace, and of glory, in each of which there are many members filling earth and heaven with an almost infinite variety of creatures and a wondrous diversity of things, he wanted to form a new order in which there would be just one member, sole and unparalleled. For if we contemplate the order of nature, how many stars are there in the sky, plants on the earth, birds in the air, fish in the sea, animals in the forests, millions of men, thousands of angels? And if we pass on to the order of grace, how many are the just? How many prophets and patriarchs? How many martyrs and confessors? How many virgins? How many souls who serve God, in innocence or in penitence? If we ascend to the state of glory, how many saints are there, and how many different ones? How many seraphim, cherubim, thrones, virtues, and dominations, how many powers and principalities, and the many other names unknown in this age and acknowledged in the other?[19] But in the order of the hypostatic union, which is the supreme order, the light of faith instructs us that there is just one single Member. And just as it teaches us that there is but one God, so also does it teach us that there is but one Man-God, and one God-Man. For just as there is but one only Son in the bosom of the Father, so also did God desire there to be but one Son of Man who would be Son of God. He wanted this Son of man, born of the Virgin Mary, to be matchless and singular, not in his human being but in his divine state, not in his nature but in his dignity. God wanted him alone to be encompassed in this ineffable order of personal union with the deity, as the sole Member

---

19. These terms of St. Paul are understood as names of angelic ranks. See Eph 1:21; Col 1:16.

of this wondrous order. By contrast, he wanted each of the orders of nature, of grace, and of glory to be shared and communicated to so many members that their number is infinite.

Jesus therefore enters alone into this ineffable order, and there is no man or angel who may accompany him there. Just as in the celestial orders and hierarchies each angel fulfills its kind with dignity and sufficiency without any other member present, so also the only Son of the Virgin, the Angel of Great Counsel,[20] occupies this great order all alone without any other ever being admitted. In him God desired to cease the course of his works, as in his masterwork. In him God willed to comprehend and complete his greatness, power, goodness, and ineffable communication of himself, for he could make nothing greater, holier, or more divine than Jesus and did not want to ever make anything equal.[21]

Jesus therefore is alone on earth, in heaven, in time, and in eternity. He alone, I say, possesses uncreated and infinite being among the many that possess grace and glory. Jesus alone has the divine essence as one of his essences and the divine person as his own person. Jesus alone is seated at the right hand of the Father, alone placed on the throne of the Godhead, alone worthy of being adored by all creatures. He alone is worthy of possessing our hearts and minds, our affections and thoughts, just as he alone possesses the divine essence and person in an ineffable manner, distinct and particular to himself, in the sacred mystery of the Incarnation.

---

20. This is how the Septuagint (*megalēs boulēs angelos*) translates the Hebrew *pele' yoets* at Is 9.6: "Messenger of Great Counsel." Cf. Pseudo-Dionysius, *Celestial Hierarchy* 4: "Because of his generous work for our salvation he himself entered the order of revealers and is called the 'angel of great counsel.'" In *Complete Works*, 159.

21. Cf. Leo, Sermon 22: "Though incomprehensible, he willed to be comprehended." In Leo the Great, *Sermons*, trans. Jane Patricia Freeland and Agnes Josephine Conway, FC 93, p. 81; and Leo to Flavian, Letter 28, in Leo the Great, *Letters and Sermons*, trans. Charles Lett Feltoe, *NPNF* 12 (Peabody, Mass.: Hendrickson, 2004), 40.

Discourse 2

On the Excellence of the Mystery of the Incarnation, in the Form of an Elevation

Those who contemplate a precious and excellent object find themselves pleasantly taken aback in astonishment and wonder when they first see it, even before they recognize in detail the particular features of the subject they are contemplating. This astonishment, which would seem to impress a feebleness on the soul, gives it strength and vigor, for it draws strength from its feebleness and rises to a greater understanding and a higher and more perfect knowledge. This is what happens to us at the first sight and thought of the excellence, preciousness, and singularity of Jesus Christ our Lord and of the sacred mystery of the Incarnation. For being deeply and keenly moved by the greatness of this excellent object introduced in the preceding discourse, we believe we must rise up to God and praise him in his matchless work, returning later to consider further Jesus' state and grandeurs and fathom the secrets and depth of this most high mystery.

As such we are like a person who has emerged from a cave and deep darkness, is set down on a high mountain, and sees the sun.[1] Never

---

1. References to God as sun or light can be found in many passages of the Greek Platonists, in Scripture, the Church Fathers, and later mystical writers. Plato's myth of the cave seems particularly evoked by Bérulle's passage here. See Plato, *Republic* 7 (514a–518d), trans. Paul Shorey, *LCL* 276, pp. 118–35. Consider also Ruusbroec, *Spiritual Espousals* 2: "We wish to compare this first coming [of Christ to the soul] to the powerful shining of the sun which, from the moment of its rising, gives light to the

having seen it before, he beholds it in the clearness of a lovely day as it rises in our hemisphere, adorning and embellishing the universe and quickening it with its rays and light. Moved by the aspect[2] of so beautiful an object, he would surely be overcome with delight at this sight and be compelled to honor God in this work of his, without pausing to measure this great star's size and dimensions according to the rules and principles of astronomy or trying to investigate and observe the properties of its light, the efficacy of its influence, the periods of its motions, and the other perfections of this great heavenly body. In the same way, we who emerge from the darkness of earthly things and begin to contemplate the true Sun of the world, the Sun of this sun that sheds its light on us, the Sun of righteousness who gives his light to every man coming into the world, are, as it were, overcome with astonishment and set aflame by love and wonder at the first radiance and sight of this splendor. We are constrained to interrupt our discourses, so that at the beginning of this work and from the first thought of so worthy a subject we might rise up to God upon the grandeurs of his only Son and the state of this most holy mystery. Let us rise then to the contemplation of God made man and approach this sanctuary in a spirit of humility and piety, seeking far more to enter by reverence and love into knowledge of him than by knowledge to enter into love of him—although we desire to receive both of these qualities and impressions from him as we guide our thoughts and affections toward an object and mystery of both love and knowledge.

The Egyptians worshipped the sun and called it inordinately the visible son of the invisible God. But Jesus is the true sun, who looks upon us with the rays of his light, blesses us with his aspect, and governs us with his motions. He is the sun whom we ought always look to

---

entire world and pervades it with its radiance and warmth. [...] A person who wishes to experience the radiance of the eternal sun, which is Christ himself, must have the power of sight and must make his abode in mountainous country." In *The Spiritual Espousals and Other Works*, 77–78.

2. "Aspect" (French: *aspect*) is the side that faces something. In the context of astronomy or astrology, it denotes the relative position of the heavenly bodies, or their position relative to the earth. These positions were believed to affect what happened on earth.

and adore. Jesus is truly the only Son of God, and neither the sun nor any other created thing in heaven or on earth can compare to him in this position. Jesus is the only Son and the visible Son of the invisible Father, as we will say elsewhere. Let us say here that he is the sun not of the Egyptians deceived in their fables but of Christians instructed in the school of truth and in the light of this sun, who is the sun of the supernatural world—a sun that desired to be depicted and represented by this sun that is only his intimation and representation. For the sun is the image of God, the father of nature, the universal principle of life. And Jesus is the true and living image of the eternal Father; he is his image in his divine person and in his sacred humanity as united with the deity. He is the author of the world and the father of human nature, by his power in producing it and his love in redeeming it. He is the source of grace and the principle of true life, on earth and in heaven, in time and eternity, in men and in angels, in grace and in glory. The sun was formed at the midpoint of the days devoted to the world's creation, and it was set among the creatures, some higher and others lower, to give light to them all. Jesus, the Splendor of the Father, causes himself to be seen in the world and comes into the world by grace, at the midpoint of time, as the old law comes to a close and the new law begins. By the light of his grace, he enlightens the fathers who came before him and those who came after, for according to the Scriptures they are both like stars shining by the brightness of this sun, among whom he rises and appears to the world.[3] And just as the light that was created and subsisted from the world's first day was united with the body of the sun on the fourth day, so that, in it and through it, the sun could be a body and principle of light on earth and in heaven, so also the eternal light, the light not created but uncreated, the light subsisting in the Godhead, is in the fourth millennium united and incorporated into Jesus' humanity in order to make, in him and through him, a body and principle of life, grace, glory, and light for all eternity.

One of the most famous astronomers of antiquity was so enamored by the primary object of his science, the sun, that he desired the power to view and contemplate it closely and to be burned and consumed as

---

3. Phil 2:15.

he beheld it.⁴ Jesus is the object of the science of salvation and the science of Christians. The teacher and apostle of the world proclaims openly that his science is to know Jesus.⁵ Will Christians therefore not be moved by love and desire to see and contemplate this primary object of their faith, their science, and their religion? Will they not have a stronger desire for the sun of their souls than this philosopher had for the sun of the earth, a sun that was common and set forth to the sight and use of both men and beasts? And will they not be ardent to approach closely this Sun of righteousness, to be not consumed but set ablaze in a fire of love and charity as they look upon him?

An excellent thinker of this age wished to assert that the sun rather than the earth is at the center of the world, that it does not move, and that the earth, in keeping with its round shape, moves in relation to the sun.⁶ By this contrary position, he saved all the appearances prompting our senses to believe that the sun is in constant motion around the earth. This new opinion has not been greatly followed in the science of the stars, but it is useful and should be followed in the science of salvation, for Jesus is the Sun who is unmoving in his greatness and who moves all things. Jesus is like his Father, and being seated at his right hand he is unmoving just like the Father and gives motion to all things. Jesus is the true center of the world, and the world should be in constant motion toward him. Jesus is the sun of our souls, from whom they receive all graces, lights, and influences. The earth of our hearts should be constantly moving toward him, so that it may receive in all

---

4. Eudoxus [of Cnidus] (original marginal note). See Plutarch, *Moralia* 14: "Eudoxus prayed to be consumed in flames like Phaëthon if he could but stand next to the sun and ascertain the shape, size, and composition of the planets." Trans. Benedict Einarson and Phillip H. de Lacy, LCL 428, pp. 65–69.

5. 1 Cor 2[:2] (original marginal note).

6. Nicholas Copernicus (original marginal note). Copernicus (1473–1543) outlined his theory in *On the Revolutions of the Heavenly Spheres*, printed in 1543. During Bérulle's own time, Johannes Kepler (1571–1630) and Galileo Galilei (1564–1642) published mathematical and empirical findings that supported the Copernican theory. Copernicus was not the first to posit a heliocentric cosmology, as he himself noted; Aristarchus of Samos advanced this thesis in the third century BC, and it also formed part of earlier Pythagorean thought. Kepler's work was placed on the Index in 1616 because it presented the heliocentric theory as a certainty.

its powers and parts the favorable aspects and beneficial influences of this great star. So let us train the inclinations and affections of our soul toward Jesus and rise up in the praises of God on the subject of his only Son and the mystery of his Incarnation, by the thoughts and words that follow.

Trinity holy, divine, and adorable in the oneness of your essence, the plurality of your persons, the equality of your grandeurs, the origin of your eternal emanations, and the ineffable joy that you have in yourself, which is the wellspring of heavenly bliss: I praise you and bless you, I adore and give thanks to you for this counsel that is most high and deep, most hidden and sacred, this counsel wholly divine and wholly wondrous that you have kept from all eternity to one day and forever unite human nature with your divine essence![7]

O eternal and all-powerful Father, out of your full power you produce, within yourself and not in another's womb, an only Son who is your equal. And you produce him always, without ever ceasing from this divine, singular, and ineffable production, which just like your own essence has no end and no beginning. I love and adore you as the eternal and all-powerful Father—always Father and always begetting your Son, the living, matchless, and eternal image of your grandeurs! I praise you and bless you for giving this same only Son to this humanity drawn from the Virgin and for giving him in infinite love as a gift so great, singular, and absolute that our nature receives into itself the person of your only Son for its own person and subsistence and, in him, your very essence!

O eternal Word, I revere you, I love and adore you, as the Son, the only Son of God, emanating always from the eternal Father, without subordination and without want,[8] having in yourself the fullness of

---

7. Leo, Sermon 1 *On the Nativity* (original marginal note). See Leo, Sermon 30: "The Birth of Our Lord and Savior, [...]. This great 'mystery,' planned 'from all eternity' for the salvation of the human race and reserved 'for the end of the ages.'" *Sermons*, 125. Leo repeats this theme in other Nativity sermons as well.

8. The French noun *indigence* is translated as "poverty" or "want." It denotes lack, pressing need, resourcelessness, destitution; a condition of emptiness, absence, and suffering that yearns to be filled or relieved. Bérulle stresses that our condition of poverty is a high blessing, for the greater our poverty, the greater our capacity for God. Michel Dupuy remarks that while for Pascal mankind's condition is wretchedness

uncreated being, as the life, wisdom, and power of the Father and (if I dare say so) another himself,⁹ and as a principle, with him and by him, of a divine person in the Holy Trinity! O Son of the Eternal One, eternal as he is and his equal! O God from God, proceeding from the Father alone, who is the wellspring of deity! O light from light, light in your essence and in your person, proceeding as the light and splendor of the Father. O life, wellspring of life; *Apud te est fons vitae*, as your prophet exclaims!¹⁰ You are in the Father's bosom as in your rest, and the Father is in you as in the one who has his life and essence and who is his Word and knowledge! You are one with the Father in oneness of essence and principle, and you are, in him and with him, the wellspring of life and love in the Godhead itself, the source of divine and uncreated life and eternal love, subsisting and personal, equal to you and another yourself! May you be blessed forever, for as the source of life in the Godhead you willed to be so in our humanity. As a principle of love in the Holy Trinity you willed to be, by a new mystery, a new principle of a heavenly love on earth and in heaven. As Son of God in eternity you willed to be the Son of man in the fullness of time. And despite the grandeurs of your eternal birth, you willed to humble yourself, take on a birth in time, and make yourself nothing, by uniting yourself in love to human nature, in the Virgin's womb!¹¹ Love that sets at nought, love that makes itself nothing, which I revere and adore, for it causes a human nature to exist and subsist in the greatness of a divine person, and it has its origin in an outpouring of uncreated and infinite love!¹²

O Holy Spirit, Spirit of the Father and of the Son, proceeding from them in oneness of origin and binding them together in oneness of love and spirit, an eternal Spirit and love that subsists personally in the

---

(*misère*), Bérulle's emphasis on *indigence* "conveys not only emptiness, absence, and suffering but also the desire, call, and instinct toward God." Michel Dupuy, "Bérulle et la grâce," *XVIIe siècle* 170 (January–March 1991): 47.

9. The French phrase is *un autre lui-même*.
10. Ps 35:10 [36:9] (original marginal note). "With you is the fountain of life."
11. The French verbs *anéantir* and *dépouiller* are translated as "destroy," "empty," "negate," or "set at nought," and *s'anéantir* and *se dépouiller* as "empty oneself" or "make oneself nothing." The noun *anéantissement* is translated as "self-emptying."
12. The French noun *excès* is translated as "abundance," "outpouring," or "overflow." It does not denote excess in the modern English sense.

deity and divinely brings the eternal emanations to completion: I adore you and give you thanks for this holy and wondrous working by which you accomplished the sacred mystery of the Incarnation! You are in eternity the divine endpoint of the divine emanations, and you are in the fullness of time the principle of a new state, the state of hypostatic union, which is the source and origin of all the holy works, all the emanations of grace, which heaven and earth revere! In the Holy Trinity you are the sacred bond between the divine persons, and in the Incarnation you bind a divine person to a human nature! In the former, you receive from the eternal Word, in his Father's bosom, his own essence in your emanation; and in the latter, you give to this same Word, in his Mother's womb, a new essence, by your working, by clothing him in our humanity! O Holy Spirit, you are the spirit of love, and you carry out on earth this work of love, this divine union, this incomparable covenant that joins earth to heaven, created being to uncreated Being, and God to man, by so close a bond that we have a God-man and a man-God forever! May you be forever blessed in this holy work that accomplishes the Incarnation of the Word and the supreme deifying of human nature, which remains human within the very state of this divine union and yet receives, into a being created and finite and like our own, uncreated and infinite grace. It is like a new and wondrous bush before the face of God for the people's salvation, like the bush of Horeb before the face of Moses: a bush that burns and is not consumed, always a bush and always burning, always a bush in the thorns of our humanity, and always burning in the flame of the Godhead.

O holy Humanity, chosen by the eternal Father from among all creation to alone enter into the state of sonship that is not by adoption but by nature, to be united forever with his Word and share in his deity in oneness of person, to be holy by the same holiness that makes him holy and makes him Holy of Holies, although in another way, and to be the cause of all holiness of heaven and earth: I praise you, I love and adore you, in the personal union that you have with the Godhead, in the new life that you have and that you possess in the source of life, in the intimate and secret communication of the divine perfections that belong to you in a singular way, without detriment to the conditions and limitations of your created being and as to a nature subsisting in the

Godhead! I praise you in the infinite dignity and in all the powers and offices that you receive in this position, in the relationship, belonging, and appropriation that you have with the Holy Trinity—with the Father in the sonship of the Word made human who proceeds from him, with the Son in the subsistence that you receive from him, and with the Holy Spirit in the working by which he produces you and unites you with the Word! And I praise you, finally, in the supreme state—wholly divine and wholly wondrous—that you have entered into by this hypostatic union, and in all that results from it and belongs to it, all the portions[13] due to this divine state according to the order of power, wisdom, and benevolence of the eternal Father toward a nature that is so close to him and that has a greater intimacy with him than does any other nature, after his own essence, for it is intimate and joined together with him through the subsistence of his Son!

In this state and subsistence, you are an abyss of marvels, a world of grandeurs, an abundance of eminences, excellences, and singularities. You are the center, circle, and circumference of all God's emanations beyond himself![14] You are God's masterwork and the work in which, emerging out of himself, he himself spends his greatness, power, and goodness and in which he encompasses himself so that he might become as part of his work, raise it above all the works of his hands, and dignify and deify it in himself! You are the throne of glory and great-

---

13. The French noun is *apanage*, originally referring to a means by which a feudal king would endow his male issue with a portion of his property. Later it came to denote any provision or appropriation, or that which necessarily follows upon something else, as for example given in Nicot's *Thresor*, s.v. *apanage*: "Infirmities are the *apanages* of human nature." The older meaning specific to a royal father and son is clearly relevant to Bérulle's usage.

14. Cf. Nicholas of Cusa, *On Learned Ignorance* 1.21:

A circle is a perfect figure of oneness and simplicity. [...] The infinite circle, which is eternal, [is] without beginning and end, indivisibly the most one and the most encompassing. Because this circle is maximum, its diameter is also maximum. And since there cannot be more than one maximum, this circle is most one to such an extent that the diameter is the circumference. Now, an infinite diameter has an infinite middle. But the middle is the center. Therefore, it is evident that the center, the diameter, and the circumference are the same thing.

Trans. Jasper Hopkins (Minneapolis: Banning, 1981), 75–76.

ness in which the fullness of the Godhead dwells matchlessly, divinely, and bodily, as the great apostle says, a worthy herald of this very great mystery's glory![15] In the Holy Trinity, the Son of God is joined with his Father in oneness of essence, and here he is joined with this humanity in oneness of person. The same Son of God, in the Godhead, is joined with his Father in oneness of principle to produce the third person of the Trinity; and here he is joined with this humanity in oneness of person to be a principle, with it and by it, of the whole order of grace and of all the holiness of earth and heaven. The being and order of nature are accorded to the Father by his Son. The being and order of grace and of glory are accorded to the Son by this humanity, and he works and accomplishes it by this humanity, for he has elected and chosen it to be an instrument joined with the Godhead.[16] The divine essence is a grace of substance, and you, O holy Humanity, as united with the Word, are another kind of substantial grace and personally subsist in divine and uncreated holiness! Just as accidents and properties flow from substance, have their being in it, and depend on it, so also the effects of grace have their root and subsistence in you, O humanity made divine! O deity made human! Thus, this Man-God, this incarnate Word, this only Son of the eternal Father in heaven and of Mary on earth is, in the order of grace, what substance is in relation to accidents and what the sun is in relation to light. He has an eminence, influence, and power—a supreme eminence, a universal influence, and a singular and absolute power—over the whole state of grace and over all the effects that proceed therefrom! And just as in eternity, by the essence that he receives from his Father, he is the principle of the Holy Spirit, the eternal and

---

15. Col 2[:9] (original marginal note).

16. Cf. Aquinas, *Summa Theologica* 3.62.5 "Whether There Be in the Sacraments a Power of Causing Grace":

A sacrament in causing grace works after the manner of an instrument. Now an instrument is twofold; the one, separate, as a stick, for instance; the other, united, as a hand. [...] Now the principal efficient cause of grace is God Himself, in comparison with Whom Christ's humanity is as a united instrument, whereas the sacrament is as a separate instrument. Consequently the saving power must needs be derived by the sacraments from Christ's Godhead through His humanity.

Trans. Fathers of the Dominican Province (Westminster, Md.: Christian Classics, 1981), 4:2353.

uncreated Spirit, so also in the course of time, by the essence that he receives from his Mother (that is, by the instrument of our humanity), he is a new source, a deep and powerful source, of all created holiness, all infused graces, all divine helps, and all holy workings of earth and heaven, of time and eternity.

O abundance! O abyss! We cannot count the stars in the sky, the leaves on the earth, or the grains of sand in the sea, although their value and number are limited. But who will be able to count the number and appraise the value and singularity of all the effects of grace? Of all its effects, I say, in heaven in all the saints, on earth in all the righteous, and even in the sinners who resist the grace offered to them? Who will be able devoutly to contemplate what is borne by the length of the ages to the end of the world, and the infinity of an eternity's duration? Of an eternity, I say, that has no other life than the life of grace, that is nothing but holiness in all its ways, and that is wholly filled and occupied with the effects of grace and glory? All these effects, whether of God toward men or of men toward God, regard you, O Jesus, and will forever regard you as their origin. They will forever be supported, sustained, and founded in you as in their substance. O substance! O origin of grace! How great a thing this says of Jesus in regard to grace!

The order of nature and this whole universe that we see, which is so diffuse and extensive in wonderful diversity, is divided between two different beings, one of which is substance and the other accident. These comprehend all the variety in this world. So also the order of grace has its substance and accidents. It has its substance in the incarnate Son of God and its accidents in his saints and servants. But it has this advantage: that the Man-God is the matchless and singular substance of the whole order of grace, whereas the order of nature is divided and diversified into many kinds of substance. Thus, the order of grace, being more excellent and closer to the Godhead, is also closer to the oneness that is so lauded in the Godhead. It has but one deified substance, just as there is but one divine essence and substance. This Jesus, whom we are considering as a precious, excellent, and matchless substance in the order of grace, does not only sustain it as substance sustains all accidents that concern it. He is also an original substance of the whole order and state of grace.

For grace, on earth and in heaven, flows and emanates continually from Jesus, just as accidents flow from their substance and light on earth and in heaven proceeds from the sun. And, to raise us to a worthier object and more divine model, this emanation of grace is a kind of created deity, about which God said, *Ego dixi, dii estis*,[17] and is an excellent imitation of this great, noble, and first emanation of the Son in the Godhead, who looks upon the Father as his Father and principle. In this way, we must confess and honor two different emanations in Jesus, one arising from the other: his emanation from his Father in his own person, and the emanation that grace has drawn from Jesus, in homage and imitation of that which he himself has from his Father. This second emanation reveals and manifests to us a wondrous and perpetual state of Jesus, a state drawn from the greatest secrets and founded in the highest mysteries of the Christian religion and that should serve as a rule and guide for our piety toward him. For just as in the Holy Trinity the divine persons have relationship and relation with their principle and origin, and they subsist only in its properties and relations and live blessedly in this mutual regard, relationship, and love, so also in the order of grace, which is a perfect imitation, a living portrait, and a formal participation in the Godhead, all created holiness has an excellent relationship with the Son of God and a singular regard toward the incarnate Word and the life in Jesus, as the one who is Life, who calls himself by this name and who is its principle and model. Spirits endowed with this created holiness, in adoring and regarding Jesus in this way, adore and imitate in the divine and uncreated holiness the Holy Spirit's eternal regard and relationship toward the Father and the Son, and that of the Son toward the Father as toward his origin. So that, just as uncreated holiness subsists in the mutual relationship of persons who proceed toward those from whom they proceed, so also created holiness might have its subsistence in this singular relation, regard, and relationship toward Jesus and toward his holy Humanity from which it comes. And in this way, we might contemplate Jesus, love Jesus, and live in Jesus, for he is life, and he wants to be our life from this moment and for eternity.

---

17. "I have said, you are gods." Ps 82:6; Jn 10:34.

O Humanity divinely subsisting, divinely living, divinely working! You are worthy in this divine and infinite position of yours, and you are infinitely—infinitely times infinitely—worthy to govern all that is created and that can be created and, by a power of excellence, to have dominion over all that can be ruled. For even insensible nature is responsive to your commands, as we see in the tempests, winds, storms, and wrathful elements that obeyed you, *maiestate conditoris*,[18] to use the holy words of a great saint and teacher of the Church.[19] This worthily demonstrates the homage and submission that even insensible things have rendered to the Creator's powerful authority and august majesty, made visible and manifest in you, O sacred Humanity! You are worthy to gain and merit all that can be gained and merited, to sanctify all that can be sanctified, and to abolish and blot out all that is to be blotted out and pardoned, for you are holy by the very holiness of the divine essence. You are the center of created and uncreated being, for you have as the one a divine person and you have as the other a finite and limited nature. You are the new and singular object of God and men, for the eternal Father looks upon you as united with his Son, the Son as united with himself, and the Holy Spirit as united with the one who is his origin and the principle of his eternal emanation. And we all regard you as the spouse of our God, the ark of our covenant, the temple of our deity, and the source of our salvation.

In honor therefore of your grandeurs, powers, and favors, of your grandeurs in yourself, your powers over all, and your favors toward us; in honor also of all the divine objects that we have contemplated and all the mysteries that have a relation to you; in honor of the Holy

---

18. "By the majesty of the Maker."

19. Mt 8[:23–27]. Jerome [*Commentary on the Gospel of Matthew* 1]. *Ex hoc loco intelligimus quod omnes creaturae sentiant Creatorem. Quas enim increpavit et quibus imperavit sentiunt imperantem,* [*non errore haereticorum, qui omnia putant animantia, sed*] *maiestate conditoris, qua apud nos insensibilia, illi sensibilia sunt* (original marginal note). "From this passage we understand that all created things perceive the Creator. For those to whom the rebuke and the command are given perceive the one giving the command. This accords with the majesty of the Creator [but not with the error of the heretics, who think that all things have souls]. Things which are insensible to us are sensible to him." Jerome, *Commentary on Matthew*, trans. Thomas P. Scheck, FC 117, p. 103.

Trinity, the Father, Son, and Holy Spirit, ordaining and working the ineffable union of human nature with the eternal Word; and in honor of the Most Holy Virgin, in whom this divine union was accomplished and consummated: I address you and rise up to you, O Jesus my Lord! I speak to you the words of one of your apostles in his rapture, and I want to speak them to you with the same spirit and affection: *Dominus meus et Deus meus* ("My Lord and my God").[20] In this view and thought of your grandeurs, I offer and present myself to you in the state and the humble and blessed condition of servitude. I offer and make to you a firm, assured, and unalterable resolution of perpetual servitude, O Jesus Christ, my Lord and my God, my Life and my Savior! Of servitude, I say, to you, to your humanity made sacred and divine, and to your deity made human. For your humanity is made divine not only by the infusion and deification of grace but by a much nobler infusion and impression, that is, by the infusion and impression of the Word himself who communicates his own person to this humanity. And likewise, your deity is made human, which is to say, clothed in our humanity as in a new substance that comes and cleaves to it, by the sustenance and communication that it receives from the existence and subsistence belonging to the Godhead. O greatness! O goodness! O love! O ineffable bond of the Godhead with humanity! I bind my being to you, therefore, by the bond of perpetual servitude, in honor of the holy and sacred bonds that you want to have with us on earth and in heaven, in the life of grace and of glory. And I form this holy bond with all my power, beseeching you to give me more grace and power to bind myself to you with a greater, holier, and closer bond.

Our being is bound to you, O my God, by your greatness and by its poverty, that is, by its need of being sustained by you so that it does not fall back into the nothingness that your powerful hand drew it from. Our being is also bound to you by your goodness and by its helplessness, for it is not able to perform any work of salvation if it is not joined with you by grace. This is a bond that belongs only to the good and that separates them from those who are miserably separated from your self. But in addition to these two bonds it pleased you to have a third, wholly

---

20. Jn 20[:28] (original marginal note).

specific and corresponding to you alone: a bond of love, and of a love that is precious and singular; a holy and sacred bond that binds your person to our nature; a bond that makes a new being, a new state, and a new order; a bond that makes a new man and a new Adam. A new man, I say; that is, not merely a righteous man or a holy man, not an angelic man or a divine man, but a Man-God, who sustains, governs, and delights heaven and earth.

I adore your being, O my God, as the upholder of all being, in the bond that is first, necessary, and universal to all created being, common to those who are good and who are evil. I implore your goodness and mercy that I may be bound to you forever by the second bond, by the bonds of your love, the impression of your grace, and the infusion of your spirit. But I go further: I yearn for you, O my Lord Jesus, and I want to be part of you, have part in the new grace of your new mystery of the Incarnation! In honor of the wondrous union of your humanity with the very Godhead, I want to unite myself with you so that I might be in you, live in you, and fructify in you as the stalk does in its vine.[21]

O my Lord Jesus, cause me to live and subsist in you as you live and subsist in one divine person! Be my all, and let me be part of your mystical body, just as your humanity is part of a divine composition that subsists in two such different natures![22] Cause me to be bone of your bone, flesh of your flesh, spirit of your spirit, and to experience the effect of your holy prayer, on your final day and on the way to the cross, when, after you prayed for your apostles, you implore the eternal Father that we might be one with you as you are one with him:

> *Non pro eis autem rogo tantum, sed et pro eis qui credituri sunt per verbum eorum in me. Ut omnes unum sint, sicut tu Pater in me, et ego in te, ut et ipsi in nobis unum sint; ut credat mundus quia tu me misisti. Et ego claritatem, quam tu dedisti mihi, dedi eis: ut sint unum, sicut et nos unum sumus. Ego in eis et tu in me, ut sint consummati in unum.* ("For I do not pray only for them but also for those who believe in me by their words. So that all may be one, just as you are in me, O my Father, and I am in you, that they also may be one in us,

---

21. Jn 15:1–17. Cf. Bonaventure, *The Mystical Vine: Treatise on the Passion of the Lord*, trans. José de Vinck, in *Works of Bonaventure* (Patterson, N.J.: St. Anthony's Guild, 1960). Bérulle's text contains many echoes of this meditation of Bonaventure's.

22. The French noun *composé* is translated as "composition."

and that the world may believe that you have sent me. I have also given them the glory that you have given me, that they may be one, as we are one; I am in them and you in me, that they may be consummated as one.")[23]

O sacred words of the Word eternal! O efficacious prayer of the only Son of God! O words of adorable union of the Son with the Father! O prayer of desirable union of the Son with us and of us with him! O oneness! O union! I unite myself therefore with you in honor of the oneness that you have with the Father and the Holy Spirit. And I unite myself with you in honor of the ineffable union that you have with our nature in the mystery of the Incarnation. In truth, I find myself far distant and separated from you and from your sacred humanity, in the infinite dignity that it has by this divine and personal union. But your humanity also, in its pure and natural state, is separated from the Spirit of the Godhead that quickens it. As therefore this quickening Spirit and this eternal Word has come near to it, and in you, O Jesus, was united with it, was made flesh with it by an infinite condescension, deign to come near to me, unite yourself with me, incorporate yourself in me, so that I might be, might live, might work in you, be led and directed by you, and be possessed by you, just as the Spirit of your deity singularly sustains, directs, and possesses this soul and this humanity that is personally united with it.

In this divine state of Jesus, I revere and adore the life, self-emptying, and working of the deity in this humanity and the life, exaltation, and deification of this humanity in the deity! I marvel at the actions humanly divine and divinely human that proceed from this new and mutual life of the Man-God in his twofold essence—the one eternal and the other temporal, the one divine and the other human, and yet so intimately, so divinely, joined in holiness! O life! O source of life! O fullness of life! O Jesus, you are life! Just as in God all is life, so also all is life in Jesus, and we see that in him even death is life! For his death is life to us, and gives us life, and does not separate him from the true life, since death does not separate his soul or body from the deity that is true life.

When God, who is life, brought the world into being, he desired

---

23. Jn 17:20–23.

to create an intimation and image of himself as life, and he desired to form three lives that move on the earth, which he brought together and united in Adam and his descendants: vegetable life, animal life, and human life. But, if we take these three lives as being in all men, in the second Adam he established and ordained on earth three other kinds of life that are wholly new, holy, divine, and worthy of a new man and a new Adam: divine life, by the union of the divine essence and person with human nature; pilgrim life and meriting the salvation of the universe, by the union of the soul with the eternal Word and with a body both deified and passible; and glorious life, by the union of this soul with the glory of the divine essence and divine persons. Three unions and three lives that are completely heavenly, divine, incomprehensible, and miraculous. For the divine life is founded in the miracle of miracles, that is, in the mystery of the Incarnation, which surpasses the power and understanding of created nature. It is the masterwork of the Godhead and the marvel of marvels, in relation to which all other miracles are only intimations or consequences of this first miracle or preparations for it.

We therefore see that God does not strive only over nothingness,[24] as in the Creation, or over dust and ashes, as in the Resurrection, but—what surpasses all thoughts of men and of angels—he strives over himself, over his own person and greatness, so that he might abase himself to our meanness, exalt our lowliness, and by these two different movements join the Most High to dust and mire and make a Man-God on the earth. And just as, in this divine life, God wanted to join together two natures that were so far apart, so also, in the life of the Son of God living as passible and mortal among men, it pleased him to join two very different states and lives, of which one is the life of glory and the other of toil, one of bliss and the other of merit, one of joy and the other of suffering, one of greatness and the other of humility. Two lives bound together, in the state of the Son of God's life from his birth in the Virgin until his death, and bound inseparably. O most singular state!

---

24. The French noun *effort* is translated as "striving." It denotes a strenuous putting forth of power, laborious attempt, struggle, or exertion. The phrase *faire effort* is translated as "strive": to contend, struggle, fight against, or use one's forces to overcome or conquer resistance.

O life most worthy of consideration! O state that experiences the Son of God's striving over himself and his own life! A constant and ongoing striving for thirty-four years, without a single moment of interruption! A striving over the state not of nature or of grace but of glory! Of glory, I say, which seems rather an exalted state to have its rights and privileges violated! A state, striving, and miracle of the Son of God over himself, corresponding to him alone, particular and singular to him, for him alone among all the saints and not even for his Most Holy Mother! A striving that instructs and urges us to make a salutary striving over the state of our defective, wretched, and imperfect life, so that we might honor the one who for our salvation undertakes a striving, such a striving, over the powerful, blessed, and wondrous state of his glory!

Who will lead us into the contemplation of these three lives of Jesus, the one divine, the other pilgrim, the third glorious? Who will open to us their treasures and secrets, their grandeurs and mysteries? Who will enable us to see the effects of deity, some wrought and others suspended for a time, in this humanity? For the course of the Son of God's mortal and pilgrim life is divided into two kinds of states that are very different and, as it were, contrary to one another. One is a state of infusion and communication of many graces, effects, and singular, excellent, and divine qualities that the humanity receives from the deity hidden within it. The other is a state of suspension and separation from many other graces and effects that this same deity, according to its greatness and close bond with this humanity, was to work in it and through it and that are abundantly communicated to it in heaven but were nevertheless often held back and suspended until the time of his glorious and heavenly life, for our salvation's dispensation. For although Jesus Christ our Lord had the fullness of the deity so intimately joined with his human nature, he still wanted to experience on earth, in his humility, the separation from many kinds of graces and singular effects of his deity that were owed to his humanity upon entering into the state of hypostatic union and that are rendered abundantly to him in heaven. And what is wondrous: appearing in the eyes of men as a sinner, he wanted to experience this separation on earth, in the angels' sight, as a mark of likeness to the flesh of sin, as a means of expiating within himself the deprivation that sinners experience of so many graces that they would receive from God if they were not in his disfavor, and as a precious and particular subject that honors on earth, by a state of holy and divine deprivation, the state that sinners dishonor on earth and under the earth by a malign and wretched deprivation of God's grace and love.

These two states in the course of the Son of God's life are most worthy of singular consideration, and we have sufficient indications of each, scattered throughout the account of his life. For it is a noteworthy indication of this humble state of separation that the moment of the Transfiguration lasted so briefly, when it ought to last forever, and that it was not only a radiance of his soul's glory but a radiance and a testimony to the deity that is always living in this soul and body, according to St. John Damascene.[25] And yet we see that when his holy Humanity is emptied of this radiance and splendor, it returns directly to its previous state, the state that was common and ordinary to his humility but most extraordinary to his greatness and dignity. Similarly, an indication of this other state of abundance is the emanation of so many marvels recounted in Scripture, in which we see that for three years it pleased him to impress the marks of his greatness and power within the world, on the earth and the waters, on animate and inanimate things, on storms and tempests, on men and even on demons, on souls and bodies, on the living and the dead, and on all kinds of sick who were all healed. Some of his healings were wrought by his word alone, others by the laying on of his holy and powerful hands, still others by the touch of

---

25. John of Damascus, "Homily on the Transfiguration of Our Lord Jesus Christ": He transfigured himself before the disciples, he who was always in like manner glorified and radiant in the effulgence of the Godhead. For indeed having been begotten of the Father in a manner without beginning, he has acquired the natural spendor-without-beginning of the Godhead, not afterward to acquire being or further glory. [...] And if, therefore, that holy body was never without a participation in the divine glory but from the very beginning of the hypostatic union it was enriched with the perfect glory of the invisible Godhead so that there might be one and the same glory of the Word and of the flesh, nevertheless the glory existing in the visible body was obscure and reckoned as invisible by those who do not comprehend things unseen even by angels, by prisoners of the flesh. He was therefore transfigured, not by taking on that which he was not nor by changing into that which he was not, but by manifesting to his own disciples (when he opens their eyes) that which he was.

Trans. Harold L. Weatherby, *Greek Orthodox Theological Review* 32, no. 1 (1987): 15–16.

his sacred and deified flesh, some even by the simple touch of his robe. This was done not only to mark his power over animate and inanimate things but also to mark the power residing in this deified flesh, emanating from this precious flesh, which was much more effective than all the simples of the earth and divinely effective for the healing of all kinds of infirmities.[26] In one, it pleased the Son of God (so that we might enter into a knowledge of the holy and divine emanations that went out from him) to say these words, worthy of deep consideration: *Quis me tetigit? Novi enim virtutem exisse ex me.* ("Who touched me? For I know that a power has gone out of me.")[27] And he inspired one of his evangelists to say likewise on another subject, *Virtus de illo exibat, et sanabat omnes* ("A power went out of him, and he was healing them all").[28]

For this humanity, as the sacred abode of the Godhead that holds all things in eminence, is also the reservoir and treasury of all kinds of singular graces, powers, and properties from which an infinite number of miraculous, excellent, and divine effects can emanate in heaven and on earth, in men and in angels, and on all the subjects on which it will please him to work and employ his power. For just as the creatures are emanated from God, and God constantly produces that which comes out of this wellspring of all being, so also from the Man-God must constantly emanate a world of excellent effects of life, grace, glory, and splendor worthy of the Godhead and worthy of a humanity subsisting in the Godhead and living by the Godhead. The sun has just one or two emanations beyond itself that we know of, and it has them constantly, for we see how it continually emanates light and influence. Do we not want this Sun of the sun, this wellspring of grace and glory, this Man-God Jesus (who has all things in himself and holds all, either in existence or in eminence) to have a constant emanation of grace, light, life, holiness, and love, as well as all other kinds of divine and excellent qualities and workings? And to have this emanation with much more power, continuity, and activity than does this sun that we see, which is only his intimation and representation? Jesus, then, is a state of fullness,

---

26. A *simple* is an archaic term for a medicine made of one ingredient; a plant used for medicinal purpose.

27. Mk 5[:30]; Lk 8[:46] (original marginal note).

28. Lk 6[:19] (original marginal note).

infusion, and communication of graces and effects, emanating from the Godhead in humanity and flowing from the deified humanity into creatures as from a fullness of life and grace, in which men and angels participate, according to his beloved disciple's testimony.[29]

This infusion and abundance is owed to Jesus from the moment of the Incarnation, but it was at many points divinely suspended and arrested for a certain time by God's counsel. Thus, his mortal and pilgrim life is rightly distinguished by these two states: the one of deprivation and the other of fullness and infusion of many graces and effects, some of which were powerfully suspended and others divinely wrought and communicated to this humanity. This is well worthy of a separate discourse that we will reserve for another time. Both states, in this humanity that receives from them either communication or suspension, deserve an equal honor, which we ought not to omit in the present elevation. For to subjects that are eminently and divinely great and high, all is great, high, and equal. In this humanity, therefore, both the working and suspension of these divine effects should be equally precious and venerable to us, just as we see that, in the Godhead, to produce and not to produce them is equally divine and adorable in the persons of the Holy Trinity. For the sky is not adorned with as many stars nor the earth studded with as many flowers as this sacred humanity is embellished, sown, and differentiated with a countless number of divine and supernatural effects that the Godhead, testifying to its presence and subsistence, would either work or suspend in it continually. There is no time, place, or circumstance that is not made radiant by the working or suspension of some grace or wondrous effect that this humanity was to experience within itself or work outside of itself, as a mark of a splendor so vivid, a greatness so powerful, and a majesty so august, equally present, and permanent in all its different states. Let us conclude this point, then, by marveling at what we cannot express in so few words nor understand with so little knowledge, and let us say, in rising up to God: O what effects, either wrought or suspended in this sacred humanity! And O what effects of a deity so present, powerful,

---

29. *De plenitudine eius nos omnes accepimus.* Jn 1[:16] (original marginal note). "From his fullness we have all received."

and acting in a humanity that is made so worthy and capable of the divine workings! For it is made capable of them, not by grace alone but by an uncreated essence and person dwelling within it, united with it, personally living and subsisting in it.

Let us pass from earth to heaven and from his life of humility to his life of glory. Who will enable us to understand this high state of glory that the divine wisdom and goodness reserved for a soul wholly its own and for a humanity exalted to the highest point of honor and the closest and most intimate union to which God's power can carry a created nature, that is, to personal union with the Godhead? O precious, O singular, O incomprehensible state of Jesus' glory, which must be adored and cannot be fathomed, and which surpasses all the glory of both men and angels, surpasses it incomparably!

As I consider all that occurs in the soul, body, and heart of Jesus, in the states of his three different lives, who will enable me to know the particular features of the Son of God's life, inner and outer, on earth and in heaven? What life! What pleasures! What thoughts! What affections! What knowledge! What exaltations! What humilities! What elevations! What homage! What thanks! And what love of a soul drawn out of nothingness, covered in glory, exalted in a moment above all that can be created, and joined personally with God himself! O life! O power! O majesty, coming forth from a deity that is living and subsisting in this created nature! O splendor of light eternal! O king of glory! O sun of righteousness! Sun that causes the light of the heavens to fall into shadow and that darkened the sun itself on your final day on earth: *Illumina tenebras meas.*[30] Deign to look upon my darkness, and cause me to love you and know you! May I share deeply in your light! May I marvel and contemplate your grandeurs! May I fathom your mysteries! I address myself to you, O essential Wisdom! As I adore your being in the oneness of God and in the subsistence of the Word to which you are singularly appropriated, and as I adore your wonderful resourcefulness in carrying out and fulfilling your works, give me this grace, so that I may fathom the wondrous secret of this your masterwork and announce and explain the divine resourcefulness by which you have

---

30. Ps 17 [18:28] (original marginal note). "Give light to my darkness."

been able to join this Word with human nature, in the sacred mystery of the Incarnation.

There is a secret, then, in this new mystery, a motive in this great work—God's masterwork—and a singular means that the divine Wisdom found to join earth with heaven in this way, as a point and center, the invisible with the visible in one same subject, and to join created being with uncreated Being in one same person, and in a way that does not mix and confuse two beings and two natures that are so far apart and so joined together both. There is a secret, I say, a motive and means unknown to the heavenly intelligences, and a divine resourcefulness. It is the divesting that Jesus' humanity has of its own and ordinary subsistence, so that it might be clothed in a subsistence that is other and extraordinary to this nature. It is divided and separated from its own subsistence, which it had by right and which it is blessedly separated from at the moment of its production. Just as in grafting, the trunk that is to carry the graft is divided and affected—and the fruit of this graft that the gardener chooses is a fruit that is extraordinary to the tree being grafted—so also the eternal Father, as the gospel's divine cultivator, chose on earth an uncultivated plant (if we consider it in its origin and nature), which is the humanity bearing the likeness of the flesh of sin.[31] In it he separated the nature from the person that had belonged to it innately and that should naturally flow from its existing and actuated essence. He substituted the heavenly graft, the divine subsistence, the person belonging to his Son, in place of the human subsistence that was precluded. He did this in such a way that this plant, divided and, as it were, affected in this way in what is so intimate, particular, and innate to its being, bears different fruit that belong not to itself but to the graft that it receives. This nature, thus divested and reclothed, has henceforth a being that is different not in its essence but in its existence and subsistence. As a result, its life, movements, and actions no longer belong to it or for it as property but belong to the one who divinely sustains it. For there is this difference to note between the graft of the gardener and the divine graft of the eternal Father, the heavenly gardener: instead of the graft's being sustained by the uncultivated trunk on which it is grafted,

---

31. Is 5:1–7; Jn 15:1; Rom 8:3, 11:13–25.

here the Word—as a divine graft that is engrafted on human nature as on an uncultivated plant, in its likeness to sin—is the sustainer of this same nature. He who sustains the world with three fingers sustains this humanity in a more powerful and singular manner. He takes it to himself, sanctifies it, and deifies it in his person. Whence it follows that the life and actions of this human nature are not its own—not that they do not proceed from it as from their principle, but they do not belong to it as property, either in terms of logic or in terms of law and morality.

I regret enlarging on this subject and using words here that are more suited to academic theses and the schools than to sermons and discourses on the faith. But the reader will please pardon me, for necessity constrains me to do so in order to forestall, as a precaution, the objections that some people may raise. I would pray them to be willing to stay silent out of temperance or else desire to take the trouble to consider attentively and fathom the verities that the faith teaches us. Then we will all have one same sentiment, accompanied by charity, in the things of the faith, as the apostle commands us.[32] For they do not realize that by contesting this truth they touch the heart of Christianity, which has for its treasury and font the actions and sufferings of this humanity, not only as humanity but as the Word's humanity, that is, as the humanity that belongs in its nature and actions and qualities to a divine, uncreated, and infinite being, who takes up this human nature's essence, state, and merit into an uncreated existence and subsistence, a divine condition and dignity, and a price and value that are inestimable.[33] Let us say to them that the actions of this humanity cannot be judged as belonging to itself in logical terms. For they do not correspond to it alone, as would be necessary for something that belongs completely to one thing, following logicians' rules. For these actions also correspond to an underlying substance that is other to this

---

32. Rom 12:16. *Idipsum invicem sentientes.* Phil 2:2. *Idem sapiatis, eandem charitatem habentes, unanimes, idipsum sentientes, nihil per contentionem, neque per inanem gloriam* (original marginal note). "Be of one accord among yourselves." "Having the same understanding, the same love, of one mind, one sentiment, nothing by contention or vain glory."

33. Cf. Athanasian Creed: "Not by conversion of the Godhead into flesh; but by assumption of the manhood into God."

humanity, if we consider it only within the state and limits of nature.[34] Let us say to them that in terms of either common and natural right or even divine and supernatural right, this humanity's actions belong to the Word and not to itself. For as a person substituting for the right of human nature, and as a person divine and uncreated, the eternal Word takes this humanity to himself by an infinite power and love. He unites it with himself, makes it his own, rests and dwells in it as in his own nature, draws it beyond the limits of common and natural use, anoints and consecrates it with the unction of his deity, and takes right and authority over this humanity and its actions and everything that belongs to it. For all that is in Jesus Christ is founded in the hypostasis of his deity; and the eternal Word, as this human nature's divine underlying substance, is the possessor of all its actions and sufferings. He sustains, exalts, and deifies them in his own person when he sustains, exalts, and deifies the substance of this humanity. By this means, they cleave to the deity as by a common bond of hypostatic inherence. It is therefore evident that the Word has, in this way, lawful right and authority to use and determine his humanity's state, life, actions, and sufferings. It belongs to him and is truly, blessedly, and divinely his, by the wondrous power and singular possession that he deigned to take of this nature and of all that corresponds to this nature, divested of itself and worthily reclothed in him.

When a slave gives up or loses his liberty, he loses the right and authority that common birth gives him over his actions and the use of his own life, and this right is lawfully transferred from the person of the slave to the person of him who holds the slave in captivity. How much more is this sacred humanity itself discharged of this right and power to determine itself and its actions, and this right lawfully transferred from human nature to the divine person? For, seeing itself emptied of its natural subsistence so that it might be raised high in a subsistence as eminent as that of the eternal Word, not only does it willingly give up its liberty and freedom to him, as the happy slave of his power, greatness, and love, but it also gives him its natural right to subsist in

---

34. The French noun *suppôt* is translated as "underlying substance" in order to distinguish this word from the French *substance*, translated as "substance," and *subsistance*, translated as "subsistence."

itself, so that it might subsist in his divine person alone and be in his power and possession, not only in a moral, voluntary, and transitory way, like that of a slave in his master's hand and power, but also personally, perpetually, and naturally, as it were, if we may speak in this way. It is evident that to divest the human subsistence from the human nature is to separate it from something that is much more bound to and inseparable from the nature, much more particular and intrinsic, than freedom and liberty are in regard to the person who enters into servitude and slavery. For nature cannot be separated from its personal being except by the very author of nature, whereas this freedom and liberty are lost and separated from the free person by a thousand human events. Personal being enters into nature's jurisdiction and is its endpoint, completing it and in a sense belonging to the very substance of things. By contrast, freedom and liberty is only a simple accident and condition, which passes and disappears without the subject's involvement and enters only into the conditions of state, not those of person. This humanity, then, that is divested of what is as great and intimate to its essence as subsistence, and, according to the angelic teacher, divested of its existence, lies much more in the power and possession of the eternal Word who receives it and sustains it in its being than does the slave in the power and possession of his master.

And if, according to law,[35] a tree that is transplanted from one place to another and becomes rooted there, belongs to the owner of the second soil and no longer to that of the first—since it becomes in some way another tree by taking nourishment from new earth, although it has the same stock, substance, and vegetable soul, both in its kind and species and even in its individual nature, and as such continues to bear the same fruits and leaves—how much more will we say the same about this human nature, a heavenly plant, that in its species is an upturned tree, as Plato says, and that in this individual is even more accurately

---

35. L. 26. "But if §1. On acquiring ownership of things" (original marginal note). See Justinian, *Digest* 41.1: *Qua ratione autem plantae quae terra coalescent solo cedunt, eadem ratione frumenta quoque, quae sata sunt, solo cedere intellegunter* ("By the same reasoning that cuttings implanted in land become part of it, so seeds and corn sown in land become part of it"). Trans. Alan Watson (Philadelphia: University of Pennsylvania Press, 1985), 4:490.

an upturned tree in a much higher and more exalted sense, unknown to this great philosopher and known only to Christians?[36] How much more, I say, should we say that this humanity, drawn out of the infertile soil of the being that is common and ordinary to its specific nature, and blessedly transplanted into the soil belonging to the divine and personal being, to subsist and live forever in this new being of the divine Word, lies no longer in the power and possession of nature, which is the soil and state it is separated from, but lies in the power and possession of divine and uncreated grace, the new soil into which it is transferred by personal union with the one who is essential and subsistent grace? He bears absolutely the name of grace, both in the ancient writers and in the Scriptures itself. He is truly the substantial and hypostatic grace of whom St. Paul, according to all of the old Latin commentators and some of the Greek ones, says, *The grace of God has tasted death for everyone:*[37] that is, the Son of God, who is the author, essence, and source of grace.

In order for something profane to be offered to God, either consecrated by some religious ceremony and act or dedicated by men's will during the celebration of the divine service, it is withdrawn from the right of the individuals who lawfully possessed it. Their right, although real and lawful, remains thereafter suppressed, in the judgment of even the most uncivilized nations that have ever existed in the world. How much more therefore ought we to grant the same to this humanity that the Son of God gives and offers to the eternal Father as the sample, foretaste, and first fruits of our stock and nature, and that he chose from all

---

36. Cf. Plato, *Timaeus* 90a–b:

We declare that God has given to each of us, as his daemon, that kind of soul which is housed in the top of our body and which raises us—seeing that we are not an earthly but a heavenly plant—up from earth towards our kindred in the heaven. And herein we speak most truly; for it is by suspending our head and root from that region whence the substance of our soul first came that the Divine Power keeps upright our whole body.

Trans. R. G. Bury, *LCL* 234, pp. 245–46. Cf. Ruusbroec, *Spiritual Espousals* 1.4: "The tree of faith grows downward from above, since its roots are in the Godhead." *The Spiritual Espousals and Other Works*, 70. Cf. Hermes Trismegistus, *Asclepius*, in *Hermetica*, trans. Brian P. Copenhaver (New York: Cambridge University Press, 1992), 70.

37. Heb 2[:9] (original marginal note).

eternity to be consecrated even by the divine essence and employed by God's will for so great a service and so holy a work as the expiation of the world, the redemption of humankind, and the satisfaction of God's justice? This is a work and service that could belong only to a nature made holy, sacred, and exalted to the throne of the Godhead. Certainly this nature, neither in itself nor in its actions, should be considered according to the common and ordinary condition of the other natures of its kind. It must be considered according to its new condition and dignity, by which it enters blessedly and sublimely into uncreated nature and by which it singularly belongs, by so many rights and bases, to the eternal Word and, through him, to the Godhead.

Let us leave aside these persons, then, who take pleasure in remaining ignorant or in obscuring God's verities with their debates. Let us rise above in a humble and pacific spirit, the two principal qualities that our Savior ascribes to himself, he who is the subject of our discourses.[38] Let us contemplate plainly things that are so worthy and true, since they contain truth himself in his own person. And let us consider this: the eternal Word who communicates subsistence to this nature is the Son of God, is equal to God, and is God himself. This human nature is by essence in a state of servitude, and in regard to the Godhead it remains unalterable and perpetual in this state by its own nature and condition. As the Father contemplates his Son reclothed in this nature, he calls him by his prophet, on this occasion, his Servant: *Servus meus es tu, o Israel, quia in te gloriabor.*[39] When the Son of God comes to espouse this same nature, he loses nothing of the earlier right that he had over it as God, and by this union he takes a new right over it as spouse. By this, it belongs much more to him than to itself. The oneness and the intimacy of this union surpass all others and attain even to oneness of person between two such different natures. This gives the divine person a new authority over human nature. The excellence, sublimity, and deity of this person give him yet incomparably more right than is fitting for human persons to have over their own natures. The holy and sacred state that this nature enters into by very unction of the deity assigns and

---

38. Mt 11:29.

39. Is 49[:3] (original marginal note). "You are my servant, O Israel, in whom I will glory."

appropriates it completely to the deity, as we will come to see more clearly and amply in the discourse on the holiness of God in this mystery.

All of these rights that are so high, great, and lawful, are, if one can add something to them by use of the will, so humbly, truly, and blessedly accepted by this humanity. It desires to be emptied of the right that it would have over its actions and itself so that it may relinquish itself wholly, by its own resignation, into the power of the eternal Word. For it constantly accepts all of God's desires upon it, and particularly the divesting of its human subsistence, a divesting that the divine power and wisdom ordained in God's secret council, in order to accomplish something so high, great, and incomprehensible upon this humanity, and through this humanity upon us—that is, in order to make a Man-God on earth, give a savior to the world, and establish an eternal mystery, a mystery of mysteries, the work of God's works, binding the divine person to human nature.

For it is evident that in this mystery, the person that is substituted and divinely communicated to this nature is the foundation, sustenance, and fulfilment of this human and natural being, influencing all of the actions belonging to this nature in the way that corresponds to underlying substances and even more to a person who is divine and uncreated. Thus, it has a right over this nature and its actions that must be considered not only moral but also natural; not only natural but also supernatural, holy, and sacred; and not only supernatural, holy, and sacred but exceedingly supernatural, most holy, most sacred, and most divine. For it is founded in the holy authority, the sacred authority, the divine and absolute authority that this divine and uncreated person has over this nature, that is, over a nature that the eternal Word appropriates by a means that is so high, great, and divine that it is ineffable and adorable by men and by angels. For he establishes this humanity in a condition so eminent and exalted that, being united with the Word, it enters into dominion over all things, as much in heaven as on earth, and even receives communication of the person of the Word's independence from the other divine persons, as will be said in the sixth discourse. All the more then can we say that it is in so sublime a state that it is no longer subject to the laws that are common to nature, since in a sense even in its subsistence, deification, and the independence that it receives from the eternal Word it is not subject to the other divine persons, as we will demonstrate elsewhere. For it belongs so matchlessly and singularly to the eternal Word. If it belongs to him so particularly, even in regard to the divine persons, how much more will it belong to the Word in regard to itself and its actions?

Let us conclude then and note that by the ordinance of God, this humanity is separated from its own subsistence and personhood and is endowed with that of the eternal Word. This humanity accepts most willingly this loss and separation and transfers to the eternal Word most freely itself, its own actions, and all that originates from it. From the first moment of its creation, this humanity lost its subsistence, and also from this first moment it accepted most willingly the counsel of God who desired to separate it from its subsistence. By this loss and separation, it also loses the right and ownership that it would have to act and subsist in itself, and these actions cannot, in terms of right, be adjudged as belonging to it, for it is no longer the possessor of its state and actions. This whole right is lawfully transferred to the eternal Word, who enters into possession of the human nature's state, actions, and sufferings to use them according to his divine will. Just as, in return, this nature enters blessedly into right of the state, grandeurs, and goods of the divine sonship, by an ineffable interchange and communication.[40] O happy transfer! O honorable divesting! O rich, royal, and precious investiture! O divine interchange! O adorable communication! O wondrous counsel of uncreated wisdom that separates Jesus' humanity from his human person so that it might give him the divine person! O separation! O divesting that is both the preparation for the new life of the Man-God and the model of the new life of man justified according to the Spirit! For just as the eternal Son of God in his human nature has no human person, that is, has no human *me* substantially and personally, so also the son of God by adoption, led by his grace, ought not to have any *me* morally and spiritually.[41]

---

40. The French noun *commerce* is translated as "interchange." It denotes relations, converse, congress, intercourse, reciprocal exchange of thoughts and feelings, ongoing familiarity, or relationship.

41. The French noun translated here as "me" is *moi*. In general use, the *moi* denotes the human person or self; in moral contexts more specifically it denotes self-attachment,

I therefore honor this divesting that Jesus' humanity has of its own subsistence. And then, in honor of this divesting and as far as your greatness and my condition brings it to your homage and glory, I renounce all power, authority, and liberty that I have to dispose of myself, my being, and all of its conditions, circumstances, and belongings. I release them entirely into the hands of Jesus, his divine soul, and his humanity anointed and made sacred by the deity itself. I release them in honor of this humanity, for the fulfilment of all his desires and powers upon me. I go further: I want there to be no more me in myself, and I want to be able to say with St. Paul, *Vivo ego, iam non ego, vivit vero in me Christus* ("I live, and not I, but Jesus Christ lives in me").[42] Following the profound reasoning of St. Augustine, I want the spirit of Jesus to be the spirit of my spirit and the life of my life. Just as the Son of God, by right of subsistence, possesses the human nature that he has united with his person, so also I want Jesus by right of special and particular power to deign to enter into possession of my spirit, my state, and my life. I want to be nothing but a naked capacity and pure void within myself, filled with him and not with myself, forever.

This intention I make to you, O Jesus my Lord, and to your humanity made divine, a humanity truly yours in its deification and truly mine in its humiliation, griefs, and sufferings. To you and to it I make a complete, absolute, and irrevocable oblation and gift of all that I am through you in the being and order of nature and of grace, of all that depends therefrom, of all the natural actions, indifferent actions (if there may possibly be any), and good and virtuous actions that I will ever perform; and this as far as I have some power by nature and grace to determine them. I devote the totality of this my power to make myself yours, to dedicate all to you, and to dedicate all that I can thus dedicate to the homage and honor of your sacred humanity, which I take and regard henceforth as the object to which, after God, I make the relation of my soul and my life, inner and outer, and of everything that is mine, without exception.

---

self-love, or ego in the condemnatory sense. In Bérullian terms, we could say that the *moi* is the illusion of self-sufficiency or independence, the desire to be one's own, and thus the condition opposite complete relation to God.

42. Gal 2:20.

Now, in this divesting that we have just considered, Jesus enters into a life divinely human and humanly divine by the intimate union of his two natures subsisting in the oneness of his person. And the only Son of God, the eternal Word, the splendor, power, and glory of the Father, takes on the form of a servant. He takes it on in two ways: one, by taking on our human nature in the mystery of the Incarnation and humbling within it the infinite and supreme being of his deity even to the nothingness of our humanity; and the other, by humbling this same humanity in the state and mystery of a life of labor and pilgrimage on earth. I say that he humbles this humanity of his, thus united and exalted to the throne and state of a divine person, even to a state and form of humble life serving his creatures and, in the end, even to the opprobrium and the cruel and servile agony of the Cross. These are great mysteries, holding and taking captive your greatness and sovereignty, O Jesus, in a state of humility and servitude, by the sacred bonds of obedience to the eternal Father and by love toward human nature! Great mysteries, demanding by a right most powerful and just that I devote the nothing that I am to serving and adoring you in this new and humble state!

In honor then of this twofold state and form of servanthood to which I see your divine Incarnation, your life of labor, and your humble cross reduce your supreme greatness, I offer and present myself to you, I dedicate and consecrate to you my life of nature and of grace. I want to serve you not only by my vows and actions but also by a state and condition that dedicates me to you and gives me a singular relationship to you, so that just as you always are mine, I may always be yours and there may be in me a permanent quality that renders you a perpetual honor and homage. And as I see that through your twofold self-humbling that was done for the love of men you are doubly the slave of our love, I also want to be the slave of your greatness, your self-humbling, and your love. I want my life and actions of nature and of grace to belong to you as the life and actions of a slave, yours forever. I dedicate myself completely to you, O Jesus, and to your sacred humanity, by the most humble and subject condition that I know: the condition and relation of servitude. I confess this as what your humanity is owed, as much for the greatness of the state to which it is exalted by hypostatic union as for the willing outpouring and humility to which it gave and emptied itself for my salvation and my glory, in his life, his cross, and his death. To this intention, end, and homage, I place and establish now and forever my soul, my state, and my life in a state of submission and in a relationship of dependency and servitude in regard to you and to your humanity that is both deified and humiliated in this way.

Great and wondrous Jesus, I have contemplated and adored you in your grandeurs! May I contemplate and adore you also in the state of your humility and servitude! For you are both Son and servant, without the state of your own natural sonship affecting or being affected by this state and office of servitude. Just as the divine nature does not, in you, alter and affect human nature in its own essence, but on the contrary, by preserving it, enhances and raises it even to an infinite state and dignity, so also your eternal birth and greatness enhance and make all the more wondrous and adorable the state of humility and servitude to which it pleased you and the eternal Father to reduce and empty yourself for our salvation. In the house of the eternal Father, you are, O good Jesus, both Son and servant, always Son and always servant, and also only Son and only servant. You are the only Son, specifically and by nature, among all the children of God, and you are the only servant, chosen and singular, among all the servants of God! You are this chosen servant of whom the eternal Father speaks by his prophet: *Ecce servus meus, suscipiam eum, electus meus complacuit sibi, in illo anima mea.*[43] You are this chosen servant in whom alone the Father delights and, through him, takes delight in us. You are this chosen servant who alone serves God with a kind of service that belongs only to you, serving him to take away sins from the earth, to satisfy his justice, and to reconcile him perfectly with human nature. This surpasses the power of every creature that will be separated from uncreated grace. You are also this chosen servant who alone serves God as he is worthy of being served, that is, with an infinite service, and you alone adore him with an infinite adoration, as he is infinitely worthy of being served and adored. For, before you, this supreme Majesty could not be served and adored by men or by angels with this kind of service in which he is loved and adored according to

---

43. Is 42[:1]; Mt 12[:18] (original marginal note). "Behold my servant, I will uphold him, my chosen one, in him my soul is pleased."

the infinity of his greatness, the deity of his essence, and the majesty of his persons. From all eternity, there was indeed a God who was infinitely adorable, but there was not yet an infinite adorer. There was indeed a God worthy of being infinitely loved and served, but there was no infinite man or servant, fit to render an infinite service and love. You are now, O Jesus, this adorer, this man, this servant who is infinite in power, in position, and in dignity to fully satisfy this duty and render this divine homage. You are this man who loves, adores, and serves the supreme majesty as he is worthy of being loved, served, and honored. And just as there is a God worthy of being adored, served, and loved, so also there is in you, O my Lord Jesus, a God adoring, loving, and serving him for all eternity, in the nature that was united with your person in the fullness of time. O greatness of Jesus, even in his state of humility and servitude, to be alone worthy of rendering a perfect homage to the deity! O greatness of the mystery of the Incarnation, to establish an infinite state and dignity within created being! O divine use of this divine mystery and this humble state of servitude, since by means of it we have henceforth a God who is served and adored without any kind of defect in this adoration, and a God who adores without affecting his deity! We have his supreme majesty so worthily, perfectly, and divinely served and adored, by a subject who is divine and infinite in his person and by a service that is so high and exalted that every creature adores him in it.

Thus, all is divine, all is infinite, and all is adorable in the object, the state, and the use of this most high and divine mystery. Thus, O Jesus, you are humble, great, and wondrous! Thus, you are both vassal and lord! Thus, you are the only Son and servant of the Most High! Thus, you are God, and you are man! And these different natures, these many states and conditions, are and subsist in one single person, whom I adore, whom I love, whom I want to confess and serve in all his grandeurs, offices, and desires. By your grace and power, in your honor and in honor of the love and service that you render to the eternal Father and that you deign to render even to men, may men know you, may they love you, may they serve you. May they contemplate your grandeurs, give and consecrate their lives to your life, and fathom the marvels and secrets of your life. You are Life, O Jesus, and your life is twofold, just as you have a twofold nature, for each of these natures is living, is blessedly and divinely living. Your life is doubly hidden, that is, it is hidden in its own greatness and sublimity and in its wondrous lowliness and humility. Life hidden in deity, life hidden in humanity, and life hidden in the humility of a suffering and pilgrim life on earth. I say, life hidden in the deity, for this life is hidden in the bosom of the Father. There it is and dwells in inaccessible light, and the greatness of its light serves as its shadow and veil, as darkness and obscurity, in regard to all created nature, which cannot see this life except by the light of glory. By this light alone we see the Godhead that lives and subsists in itself and subsists and lives in this humanity also.

This truth is so clear and evident that only common sense (assuming faith), and the simple apprehension and understanding of terms, are needed to understand it. And yet some people of this age err in such a way that, for fear of identifying them more clearly, I hesitate to reply or recall them. But their strong emotion compels me to at least tell them that what distances me from these fights and counterarguments is the feebleness of the reasons that they cite, and my own inclination. I would not find it difficult to convince them of what I do not wish to name in order to treat them with more respect than they themselves render to the prelates in this matter, who have designed to authorize it publicly by their writings.[44] Their condition requires and disposes them to be children of light; may they not become the friends of shadows and darkness and end up, against their own purpose, as partisans of the Prince of darkness in his principal qualities, one of which is contained in his name and the other noted in St. John, who calls him the "accuser of our brothers"[45] and of those who seek to bear the impression, mark, and imprint of Jesus. They are not established as judges in the Church of God, to regulate the words that must be used in discussing the faith, and the defamatory pamphlets that they are publishing hardly testify to the temperance and ability of their authors, whoever they may be. If they do not understand these propositions concerning the theology of the incarnate Word, they should not examine, judge, or condemn them, for that surpasses either their understanding or their authority.

44. The publication of the discourses included endorsements by noted prelates. See Introduction.

45. Rv 12[:20] (original marginal note).

It is no vice not to understand them, but it is blind and self-forgetful to presume to understand and undertake to judge them without capacity, obligation, and authority.

But let us leave these persons and their disputes; let us pray for them and return into the light of this discussion and subject. Let us adore Jesus in his hidden life, in his own greatness, and in his own light. This is the life of the Godhead in itself and in the bosom of the Father. It is the life of the deity in his humanity. It is the subsistence of the humanity in the deity, which surely no one can see unless he sees God. And it is the life of his soul in its glory, the life hidden from the men and apostles who lived and conversed with Jesus, the life known to the angels and to them alone, in the light not of their grace but of their glory. This twofold life, the glorious life and divine life of Jesus, is yet hidden in the humility of his mortal and pilgrim life on earth. O Jesus, you live in glory and in deity, and this glory and deity is hidden in the humanity, infancy, and flight into Egypt, and in the opprobrium of the Cross. You are God, and you are seen in the nature and appearance of man, as your apostle says.[46] You are glorious, and you suffer! You are life, and you die! You are king, the king of glory, and you flee away! You are Son, the only Son of God, and you live for thirty years as the son of a carpenter, as a carpenter and commoner! O human life of Jesus! Humble life, powerless life, suffering life, dying life, life dead on a cross and in a grave! But life high in its humiliation, life powerful in its powerlessness, life glorious within its cross, life subsisting in death and the grave! Life, even then adored by the glorious angels and the suffering demons, even when hidden by this life in the cross, in death, and in the grave! By this life buried in the earth, by the power of this new King of heaven and the kingdom of heaven proclaimed on earth, and even when buried in the earth! O what secrets, what grandeurs, what marvels! O what things hidden from our minds, from our understanding! From our minds that experience and receive more shadows than light and are more fit on earth to adore by reverence than to fathom by presumption the essence or counsels of God in his works, and in his greatest work, which is Jesus! Let us therefore rise up to him on the points proposed and say to him

---

46. Phil 2[:7] (original marginal note).

as we adore him: O life hidden in humanity! O life hidden in sublimity! O humble life! O great life! O human life! O divine life! O uncreated life! O incarnate life! O suffering life! O glorious life! O subject life! O ruling life! O Jesus, living, powerful, and ruling in heaven and on earth, according to this holy word from your sacred mouth as you entered into the state of your glory and your kingdom: *Data est mihi omnis potestas in caelo et in terra* ("All power is given to me in heaven and on earth")![47] May I confess you, O Lord my God, may I marvel at you, may I adore you. May I accept all your powers over me, embrace all your desires, and dedicate and consecrate to you what is already yours on so many bases and that I want to be yours also on the new basis of my free choice and will and by the present oblation that I make and renew to you. I dedicate and consecrate my life, all the moments of my life, to you in honor of the states and moments of your life! With this present intention, I want each moment of my life and each of its actions to belong to you, O Jesus my Lord, and to your sacred humanity, with as much right and power as though I offered them to you each individually.

O Jesus, O only Son of God, O life! True life and the author of life:[48] may you be blessed forever, in your deity and in your humanity and in your subsistence that forever binds this humanity to your divine essence and makes this humanity holy with the greatest holiness that can be communicated to any creature. That is, it makes it holy by the same holiness that the Father gives his Son and that the Son and Father give the Holy Spirit, which is the holiness of the divine essence! For this essence that is communicated by divine generation and procession in the mystery of the Trinity is the very same that is communicated in the birth of Jesus in the mystery of the Incarnation (although in a different way). It is communicated in order to sanctify this humanity with a holiness so high and new that it makes God man and man God, that it makes Jesus incapable of sin, the source of all holiness, worthy of redeeming the life of men, giving life to the angels, appeasing a God of wrath, satisfying him in strict justice, and honoring him with an infinite love, honor, and service that is worthy of his majesty, by the infinite

---

47. Mt 28[:18] (original marginal note).
48. Acts 3[:15] (original marginal note).

dignity of the person who renders this homage and service to him in his human nature. O deity! O holiness! O humanity! May I know, may I fathom, may I adore your grandeurs! You are, O holy Humanity, the sacred temple of Deity, the temple that is foremost in excellence and matchless in singularity! The temple in which the deity rests more blessedly, more worthily, more wondrously than it does even in the order and state of glory, which holds sway in heaven as the order of grace does on earth. This point is certain, and yet it has served as a pitfall to our critics. But I appeal to them, either better instructed or better disposed, for there is nothing but extreme carelessness or extreme passion that can oppose this truth that is so clear and accepted by those who fathom the great mysteries of the faith under the veil of simple words. For the divine and eternal Word rests in this humanity as in his own nature and as in a nature that he appropriates, matchlessly and singularly, by the communication of his subsistence and not only by the infusion of some grace or accidental light. Jesus Christ applies this word "temple" to Jesus Christ himself, calling his body the temple that the Jews would destroy and that he would rebuild in three days.[49]

O holy Humanity, you are the only one among all creatures whom the eternal Father chooses to exist and subsist in his Word, and whom he calls out of them all so that you might enter by this means into the state of his sonship that is not adoptive but natural and particular, and to experience and receive the intimate and secret communications of the divine perfections (insofar as your created being permits) as a result of this state, subsistence, and divine sonship that is so freely communicated to you. This means a world of excellences, precious things, and singularities, all of which, either known or unknown, revealed or unrevealed, proclaimed on earth or reserved for the light of heaven, I revere and honor as I ought and as you desire me to, O Jesus my Lord! I give and abandon myself to the supreme sovereignty that cannot be communicated to the state of created things, which your humanity possesses by this state of divine sonship. I deliver myself over to the excellent, absolute, and particular power that this wondrous and adorable state gives him over every created thing. I dedicate and consecrate myself

---

49. Jn 2[:19–21] (original marginal note).

wholly to you and to it. I want it to have a special power over my soul and state, over my life and actions, as over that which belongs to it by a new and particular right, by virtue of the free choice that I now make to submit to his sonship and sovereignty forever.

And since your power infinitely surpasses ours, I implore you, O holy and deified soul of Jesus, to yourself deign to take the power over me that I cannot give you and to make me your subject and slave in the way that I know not and that you know. Since (whether I will or not) I am the slave of the cost of your blood, I want also to be the slave of your grandeurs, self-humbling, and love. I want to be yours and to serve you according to your particular counsels upon me, not only by my actions but also by the state and condition of my being and my inner and outer life. I implore you to hold and treat me on earth no longer as one of your hired hands, as the prodigal son wished, but as one of your slaves, as your Church teaches, and as one who abandons himself to all your desires, delivers himself over to all your powers, and offers himself to experience the effects pleasing to you of your greatness and sovereignty over what belongs to you.

And as it pleased you to give yourself to us and make yourself ours through the holy Virgin, permit me also to give myself to you through her. I implore her therefore, as Mother of my God, to deign to will to be Mother of my soul; as Mother of Jesus, to offer me to Jesus and to hold and consider me herself henceforth as a slave of her Son; and as such, to have him give me a share in his ways and eternal mercies.

Discourse 3

On the Oneness of God in This Mystery

Those whom the grace and light of faith raise to the contemplation of divine things consider and adore the majesty of God, as existing, as working, or as governing and triumphing within himself and his works. They confess him, in all these ways and qualities, to be sovereignly, divinely, and wondrously One. For, if we consider him as existing, he has this in a distinctive and singular way. The first point and foundation of the greatness of his being is that his existence is his very essence.[1] For he is one; he is the principle of all oneness; he is even Oneness itself in his nature and essence. Thus, he has oneness in his existence. The proofs of this are so common in Scripture that it would have to be copied out completely in order to state them all, and the signs of it are so universally impressed on nature that all its effects would need to be produced in order to demonstrate this truth by as many testimonies. For this oneness is in so many kinds and is so strongly portrayed in all things that to fail to acknowledge or understand it is to fail to acknowledge or understand one's own self. It shines forth in all God's works like so many mirrors that reflect and represent it to us. It is engraved so deeply on all natural things that nothing has ever been able to remove its lines and marks. This mute voice of nature makes itself heard in the recognition of this truth, to those who know how to listen well. Even if the thickest darkness of error clouded the best minds, universal nature

---

1. Cf. Aquinas, *Summa Theologica* 1.3.4, vol. 1, p. 17: "Whether Essence and Existence Are the Same in God": "His essence is his existence."

has spoken so clearly and so in keeping with the oneness of its God and maker, in the voice of its first and most excellent philosophers, that all have concurred in confessing and making it known to the world. To argue from texts and reasoning is therefore superfluous, and it should be enough for us to assume this truth, adore this oneness, and listen with a humble spirit to this oracle of God speaking of himself to his people, through his servant Moses: *Audi Israel: Dominus Deus tuus Deus unus est* ("Hear, Israel: the Lord your God is One").[2] But what we should attentively consider is the wondrous excellence and power of this oneness within God himself. For as his essence has an ineffable fertility in his oneness (which in God necessarily results in the plurality of persons, persons who are divine, infinite, and uncreated), this fertility does not divide the oneness. Instead, the perfection of this oneness is the reason for this fertility. The oneness remains unalterable in this plurality, and the oneness is all the more wondrous, ineffable, and adorable therein.

If we contemplate God not only as existing in himself but as working, both in himself and beyond himself by two kinds of workings that proceed from him, in each of them he works as one and in oneness, notwithstanding the plurality of his persons. For it is by the oneness of his essence, power, and understanding that the world is produced. This is why the world bears the image of God's oneness, as the mark of its maker and the ensign and arms of its Lord. And for this same reason it owes homage to God, not only because his being is the divine, first, and sovereign being but also because of his supreme oneness, from which the world originates. For God, not only as God but as oneness, is the principle of this universe. Similarly, the internal workings and divine emanations are fulfilled in oneness, which is all the more wondrous given that they proceed from persons to whom plurality belongs as oneness belongs to the essence. Yet in these divine persons, as working and as producing, we find a wondrous oneness. For God is one not only as God but also as Father, and he is the sole principle of his beloved Son. And the Father and the Son together produce the Holy Spirit, producing him not in difference or plurality but in oneness of origin, coming together as one single principle toward this adorable and wondrous work.

---

2. Dt 6:4; Mk 12:29.

If we contemplate God not in his existence or working but in his rest, we again find and adore him in oneness. For the doctrine of the faith and the public and solemn prayers of the Church teach us daily that God lives and reigns in the oneness of the Holy Spirit. In him he has his life and rest, his glory and love, and in him the perfect oneness, fertility, and communion of the divine persons are blessedly accomplished and brought to completion.

As God therefore lives, works, and reigns in oneness, that is, lives in oneness of essence, works in oneness of principle, and reigns in oneness of love, it is not a wonder that he conforms his works to oneness and that the greater and loftier the things are that he has to perform, the more he works them according to his oneness. And when he has a supreme work and mystery to perform—the work and mystery of the Incarnation—he works it in an excellent manner, a wholly new, singular, and unparalleled manner, in oneness. This mystery is to be his masterwork, the work that he wants to establish as a triumph over his creatures (as we will demonstrate elsewhere), and the work by which he wants to triumph over himself, that is, over his divine perfections. For he himself leads as in triumph his greatness in humility, his power in powerlessness, his wisdom in infancy, his love and justice and mercy in the cross. He is therefore in this work as in a triumph, in which he triumphs not over others but over himself and causes his creatures to be ashamed if they do not give him the power of triumphing over them through this work, since by it he triumphs over himself.[3]

Therefore, as he has a work to perform that is so much his own, so great and divine, he works it according to his dignity. He accomplishes it in a manner corresponding and proportionate to the excellence of his principle, the oneness of his incarnate person, and the oneness of his eternal essence. What is more, as he professes in this work to taking

---

3. A triumph is a Roman military and religious procession, in which great victories of Roman generals were marked and celebrated. Included in the procession were the most redoubtable members of the conquered side, led in chains as slaves and on their way to death, to further magnify the glory of the one who had conquered them. The image described in this passage is therefore of a victorious God who has conquered not an external enemy but himself, who has defeated his divine perfections by their antitheses. In this procession, humility leads in triumph the greatness that it has conquered, powerlessness leads power, etc. Cf. 2 Cor 2:14.

no thought of himself and his greatness so that he might abase himself to our wretchedness, he does not set aside his holy oneness. This is worthy of deep and particular consideration. As he covers his glory so that he might enter into this work and ennoble and exalt it by his own self-humbling, he desires to make his oneness more illustrious and lauded, more remarkable and glorious than ever. He wants it to triumph in the triumph over his works, that is, in this august and sacred mystery of the Incarnation. For he impresses on this work a new kind and manner of oneness that is singular to it, wholly distinct and specific to it, that does not correspond to any of his works nor ever will. He wants this great mystery to be a living image, a perfect model, and a divine subject of the divine oneness, because it contains the oneness of an uncreated person in two different natures and is matchless and peerless among God's works. We seem to have here an evident conflict, a formal opposition, between the two supreme perfections of the divine essence, that is, between his goodness and his oneness. For his oneness wants this work to be matchless, and his goodness would like to extend and communicate it to many subjects. God is a wellspring of constant emanations beyond himself, and it is fitting and natural for goodness to extend and be communicated without end and limit (just as light extends to the point of infinity if it encounters no opposition and resistance). Who therefore will not think that this high and sublime communication of the deity, which renders so much glory to God and so much honor to the world, and which is in itself so lovable, wondrous, adorable, and desirable, should not be extended to many subjects, just like the communication of nature, of grace, and of glory? But it is appropriate in this mystery of peace, in this mystery that establishes peace between heaven and earth, God and men, to find peace within the very throne of God and among his divine perfections. Therefore we say that as God's oneness and goodness are the two perfections of the deity that are most acknowledged and lauded, God wanted to take both of them into consideration in this masterwork. He wanted to honor his goodness by performing in it the greatest, richest, and most intimate and abundant communication of himself that his divine power could accomplish beyond himself. And he wanted to honor his oneness by resolving to never again do anything in the world that is like this singular mystery. For he did not want to separate his supreme oneness from its right and power to take this great work to itself, and he wanted to enhance this great work, his supreme work, with this kind of oneness that makes it dear and precious, excellent, matchless, and incomparably praiseworthy.

Oneness is the first property that philosophers ascribe to created being. It is the first perfection that Christians confess and adore in uncreated Being. It is what Scripture demonstrates to the faithful most frequently. And the Platonists, who are the highest among the pagans in the knowledge of things sublime, men truly divine among the naturalists, and theologians among the philosophers, speak of nothing so divinely as they do of oneness.[4] In their teaching's elements and secrets, they teach their followers that the divine essence and fertility lies in oneness. Indeed, they even dare to say, in a manner of speaking that is full of their mysteries, that God has oneness and not being, since oneness, according to their high understanding, is something prior and superior to being. The demons, who have lost the love of God but not the knowledge of him (which is deeply impressed on their nature) and who are sworn enemies of the divine grandeurs and perfections, render in their particular malice a striking testimony to this truth. For, in their battles against God on earth, the first and greatest was against his oneness. This battle was waged furiously for four thousand years in the world's first, strongest, longest, and most widespread heresy: that of polytheism. This heresy was insinuated from the time of the earthly paradise, having its foundation in man's first sin and in the devil's first word (*Eritis sicut dii*),[5] and thereafter spread throughout the earth. This heresy that is so powerful and old was not overcome except by the new, powerful, and adorable oneness of this precious mystery, for a Man-God was needed to eradicate it from the earth, whereas the other heresies were destroyed by his prophets and servants. And we see that ever since this Man-God lived, walked, and spoke on the earth, the earth has not been able to persevere in this error, for the oneness of its Creator has been acknowledged in all lands and by the majority of the earth's inhabitants, despite being deprived of the light of faith and

---

4. Naturalists are materialist philosophers, such as the Stoics and Epicureans.
5. "You will be as gods." Gn 3:5.

profoundly buried in the darkness of heathenism. This universal recognition of the oneness of one God, in the universe formerly occupied with paganism and the worship of an infinite number of false gods, is the first grace that has come forth from this mystery, which bears and contains in itself the true light, the uncreated light that gives the world the light and knowledge of the true God. It is the first truth that the incarnate Word impressed on the earth, impressed so deeply by this divine imprint of the eternal Father's substance that nothing can remove it. It is the first ray of his light, spread through all the universe, and it is so strongly spread by the birth of the true Sun that the darkness of error and sin has never since been able to obscure this truth. Nor will it ever obscure it while the world endures, as it did in earlier times under the law of nature and the written law. It is the first effect that is visible and made known to the world of the omnipotence of his oneness, that is, of the oneness of his person, subsisting in the plurality of different natures and honoring by a new mystery the oneness of his eternal essence. And finally, this light and knowledge of God's oneness is a grace so abundant and broad and a favor so powerful and universal that it is communicated not only to the faithful dispersed throughout the world but has extended even to those who are enemies of the name Christian, as though by a back-flowing tide of the grace of the Incarnation on the earth. For since the coming of the Son of God, the greatest adherents of paganism have been ashamed of their error and have affected to acknowledge the oneness of one supreme God within the diversity of their gods. Those who over time cut themselves off from Christianity did not, however, give up a belief in the oneness of one God, as though by a secret reserve of power that the only Son of God wanted to perform in honor of his oneness even within these faithless souls, when he gave them up and abandoned them to their errors and impieties, as is evident in all the peoples who are followers of Mohammed.

It is by a prevenience of this same grace, power, and favor that the Jews, formerly so inclined to idolatry, were unable to fall back into it as soon as the blessed time of Jesus' coming approached and he began to shine over our horizon in his dawn. This is something all the more remarkable in this people because they were inclined to idolatry from the cradle and from the birth of the law and synagogue, as is shown by the adoration of the Golden Calf, and persevered in it in every age and time thereafter, as is shown in the prophets. The divine oracles and severe chastisements of God's justice were not able to turn them from it. And yet, toward the last age of the world, after their return from Babylon, as the time of the Messiah approached, they did not return to idolatry. It was as though they sensed the blessed coming of the true light that was on the point of spreading its rays in the universe. Judah has never again been in these errors and darkness since the Son of God honored it with his birth and descent and since, like a sun, he enlightened this province with his presence.

This oneness, then, that is so intimate in God, so fitting to the creation, so deeply impressed on the world, so opposed by the demons, so well defended by the faithful, and so securely established, acknowledged, and honored by the efficacy of this divine mystery, was to be indicated in it, just as it is indicated by it. This is why God wanted to impress this oneness, this first and most lauded perfection, on the first and greatest of his works, that is, on the work of the Incarnation, making it matchless and unparalleled on earth and in heaven. Just as the order of the necessary and ineffable communications of the deity within itself, by the divine and personal emanations, is brought to completion and, as it were, arrested in the Holy Spirit who is the third person of the Trinity (without being able to pass into other divine and immanent processions), so also God willed to arrest, in his Son and in his united nature, the course and progress of the free and voluntary communications of his deity beyond himself. Thus, there will never be any other person than his eternal Word who communicates his subsistence to created nature, and this same Word will never give this grace except to human nature. Among the singular natures of our kind, there will only ever be this Humanity, drawn from the immaculate substance and body of the Most Holy Virgin, that will enjoy this supreme favor. This greatly exalts Jesus' grandeurs, and it increases our homage toward his divine person and his human nature. For we must carefully and devoutly consider that it is the Word alone, the only Son of God, who was made man for man's sake, and that this eternal Word desires to communicate his person and greatness only to this Humanity alone in kind and number. This Humanity alone, therefore, among all creation is the sole object of God's grandeurs and favors in the highest and most ineffable communication that can be made to a created essence. In Jesus, God blessedly arrests the course of his power, wisdom, and goodness, for he is not able to devote them to a worthier work. In the Creation, the hand of God working in the ordering of the universe arrested itself in man, and when he had formed him on the sixth day he entered on the seventh into his rest, for he had arrived at the highest point and his masterwork in nature. Similarly, God working within the supreme order of his graces and favors—that is, in the ineffable order of the hypostatic union—arrests his power, wisdom, and goodness in the new man, in our Immanuel, in his incarnate Son, as in a work and subject that is infinite, infinitely times infinite. In itself and in its dignity over the nature of God's other works, which never equal the divine perfections that produce them, this work equals these perfections that produce it in the world and that make up the divine mystery of the Incarnation. After he wondrously accomplishes this masterwork of supreme grace and favor, just as we can say devoutly that in eternity he takes his rest in the Holy Spirit, so also we may say that in the fullness of time he takes his rest in Jesus. He takes his delight in him, he is well pleased, and he calls us all to fix our minds and hearts in him and fits us to take our rest and pleasure in this divine object. For in Jesus he himself arrests the course of his works, the progress of his divine perfections, and the culmination of his graces, and establishes forever his glory, rest, and pleasure.

We recall from the preceding discourse that this work is a work and a mystery of oneness, which begins in a sacred council, an adorable and wondrous council, a secret council of oneness. It unites the Father in his thoughts, counsels, and works; it unites the Son in his state, grandeurs, and mysteries; and it unites men in their homage, sentiments, and affections toward him. For the eternal Father does not have to divide his attentions, purposes, and activities. He is not like the father of a family who has many children in his household, among whom he apportions his attention, care, and love, his states, honors, and goods. The Father has but one Son in his deity. He has but one Son to regard on earth and in heaven. He has but one beloved Son, in whom he is well pleased. He has but one mediator to give to his Church. He has but one prophet and one messiah to send to his Israel, his people. Thus he says, in the singular, *I will raise up a prophet for them.*[6] He says, in the singular, *This is my beloved Son. Listen to him.*[7] And Jesus Christ says of himself to his disciples, *One alone is your master.*[8] His beloved disciple says of him, *The only Son, who is in the bosom of the Father.*[9] His foremost apostle says of him, *He is the Lord of all.*[10] And the peoples say of him, *This is truly the Savior of the world.*[11] He is always sole and always matchless, matchless in his person and offices, matchless on earth and in heaven, matchless in the bosom of the Father and in his Church. Jesus alone is the beloved Son of the Father; Jesus alone is the messiah, prophet, and king of Israel; Jesus alone is the master, sovereign, and savior of the world. And the humanity of Jesus alone is the instrument joined with the Godhead, to perform his works on earth and in heaven. Jesus shares only in God himself, who communicates to him his own essence and glory, for he does not share with any angel or man the grandeurs, purposes, and activities of his Father. All is in him, for him, and by him, as reaching toward him, belonging to him, and subsisting in him, so that all may be united in him, and through him in his Father. For as Jesus is therefore the subject—the sole subject—of God's grandeurs and favors, and as he is present, alone and matchless, in the first and most eminent order of the Godhead's works, we do not have to divide our thoughts, sentiments, and homage. He must have them all, and he must have them alone in this position, just as he alone possesses in this great order this infinite and uncreated Being. He must have them, I say, alone and in this high degree that belongs to him alone, according to the supreme greatness that the most high mystery of the Incarnation confers on him. This is why the eternal Father willed to make in his Son and in his sacred humanity the final and highest production of his graces, and why he did not give him any assistant or associate in this great and supreme dignity that he gave him: so that he might unite us

---

6. Dt 18[:18] (original marginal note).
7. Mt 17[:5] (original marginal note).
8. Mt 23[:8–10] (original marginal note).
9. Jn 5 [sc. 1:18] (original marginal note). Jn 5 is nonetheless a relevant passage.
10. Acts 10[:36] (original marginal note).
11. Jn 4[:42] (original marginal note).

all to him and not divide our hearts and minds among objects that were equally lovable and honorable.

This is the deep counsel of the wisdom of God, worthy of being adored in its origin, revered in its subject, and marveled at in its conduct, for it is a counsel of God upon his only Son. It is a counsel of God upon a new state that he gives his Son and upon a state that he desires to give him beyond himself: a matchless state, unchanging and eternal and that will endure into the future for as long as God himself. This counsel of God upon his own Son is founded in a great secret that corresponds to the property of his eternal generation and has an excellent relationship with the oneness and singularity of his divine, personal, and uncreated Being. For just as in the Godhead his sonship is matchless, so also God willed, by an unchanging decree, that it be and remain forever communicated only to one nature alone among created things. As a result, when God wants his Incarnate Word to be present in many places in his new nature, he employs his power to create a new masterwork and a new mystery, in which he multiplies the presence and not the essence of this his nature. We see this in the most holy mystery of the Eucharist, in which the Son of God performs a miracle, a perpetual miracle, upon himself, that is, upon his body, blood, and soul. He employs his power to preserve the oneness of this precious blood and this living and animate body (living not only by the human spirit but also by the Spirit of the Godhead) and to maintain the oneness of this soul that subsists in the divine person, by multiplying their presence without multiplying their essence. A remarkable miracle! For it is performed so many times and in so many places. A perpetual miracle! For it will endure to the end of the world. A miracle of Jesus Christ and of Jesus Christ upon himself! For he is its author, and he exercises his power upon it—not upon dust, as in the resurrection of Lazarus, nor upon some parts of the body that are defective in nature, as in the healing of the sick, lame, and blind—but upon a body and a spirit, upon the most worthy and most holy body in heaven and on earth and upon the most exalted and sublime soul among the heavenly spirits, that is, upon the living and glorious body and the holy and divine soul of the Son of God. A miracle that is the greatest of Jesus' miracles!

For this reason he wanted it also to be the final work and miracle that he would perform in the free state of his mortal life and on his last day. For after this work there is only anguish, only captivity, only suffering, and only a continuous pilgrimage to the cross and to death. It is a worthy thought, and worthily honoring to the divine oneness, that the Son of God's greatest and final miracle in his free and pilgrim life is a miracle of oneness, a miracle wrought to preserve the oneness of Jesus within the wondrous effusion of the love of Jesus, who wanted to communicate himself in heaven and on earth to many souls and in many places. It was wrought to preserve by this means within the Church, which is one, the oneness of her God and Savior, who is one in his temporal nature just as he is one in his eternal nature. That is, it was wrought to preserve the oneness of his body, blood, and soul by multiplying their presence without multiplying their essence! It is also a thought worthy of the oneness of the Son of God, who, being one with his Father, devotes his greatest and final miracle to preserving the oneness of his human nature within this mystery and uniting us all to him in oneness by a mystery of oneness, which gives St. Paul reason to say, *We, who are many, are one bread and one body, all of us who are partakers of one bread.*[12] It is a mystery of oneness serving as a sacrifice to adore the oneness of God! It is a mystery of oneness serving as a miracle to preserve the oneness of his only Son in the Incarnation! It is a mystery of oneness serving as a sacrament to impress the oneness of spirit and grace on his children by adoption and to unite them among themselves and with him! This caused St. Paul to speak these holy and great words and this antithesis worthy of deep consideration: *That one same heavenly bread causes the many who partake of it to be one same body.* These words and antithesis are worthy of the profundity of this great mystery, the one supplement to the Incarnation, devoutly expressed by this great apostle and worthily serving the oneness of God incarnate.

It is appropriate to remark on the original reason for this perpetual miracle of the most holy Eucharist, which makes the Son of God's glorious body present to us in heaven and on earth and in many places on earth, and which multiplies this sacred body's presence but not its

---

12. 1 Cor 10[:17] (original marginal note).

essence. It is so as not to multiply the masterwork of the Incarnation and the Godhead's union of person with another singular nature. It is so as not to do in the world another work that is like it. It is so as not to establish many bodies and souls subsisting in the deity. And it is so as to preserve the oneness of the soul and body of the Son of God in the multiplicity of his presences. Heresy, proud and ignorant of God's mysteries, does not understand this, nor is it worthy of understanding the secret and mystery of oneness, since it is led and animated by the spirit of division. The faithful, however, who are humble and enlightened by the light of faith, know how to acknowledge and adore God's counsel in this miracle and mystery of the Eucharist, by which one body and one spirit, the body and spirit of Jesus, remaining one and singular in his being, is present in many places, so that without affecting his oneness he can be and can work in many places the many effects of his presence, grace, and glory. This point is so firm and unalterable in the secret counsel of the eternal Father that the state of hypostatic union is unparalleled and is never repeated. The divine work of the Incarnation is matchless and singular in the world. His power and goodness are arrested in this divine subject and are never employed again in producing a comparable work. So much did he resolve never to give the essence and person of his Son to any other particular nature in the way that it pleased him to give it to Jesus. So much does he desire us all to have forever, in Jesus and in Jesus alone, the source and origin of the oneness of spirit and grace that it pleased him to call us to in his Son. Just as the Son is eternally and divinely one with his Father by his first birth and one with us temporally and humanly by his second birth, so also does he reach out toward oneness and exhort us there by his word, lead us there by his example, draw us there by his power, and obtain it for us by his prayers, saying to the eternal Father, *O holy Father, may those whom you have given me be one, as we are one.*[13]

It is in this miraculous work of the Eucharist and in this thought of the divine unities that the only Son of God desired to conclude and complete his life. It is in this work and in this thought that he wanted to speak to God his Father in the most exalted, important, and solemn

---

13. Jn 17[:11] (original marginal note).

of his prayers, which he made to the eternal Father in the cenacle in Jerusalem, completing the greatest of his works, the most supreme of his mysteries, on his last day in his apostles' midst, and going to the cross to offer himself there as a sacrifice.

It is also in this thought that he desired to begin his new life on earth, his life divinely human and humanly divine. For he begins his life and his elevation to God at the same time. He begins to live on earth and to acknowledge God in heaven at one same moment and in one same place, that is, in the secret cabinet, the sacred oratory, the divine temple of the Virgin's heart and womb. When Jesus is newly conceived in this intimate and august place made holy and sacred by the working of the Holy Spirit, by the presence of the Word, and by the power of the Most High, he enters directly into his first occupation, in which his most secret communion, highest elevation, and the deepest and most powerful application of his spirit lies in the sight, homage, and love of the divine unities. Here we find two things blessedly joined together, both of them worthy of very great veneration: one is the first point in God's fulfilment of this work of his, and the other is the first contemplation of Jesus' soul, at the same moment, of this same work of the Incarnation that is a work of new and wondrous oneness.

We should therefore deeply venerate his divine soul, which beheld God in his essence, his persons, and his glory from the first moment of his creation. The apostle compels us to do so, if we know well how to consider it, when he describes the Son of God to us as beginning his entry into the world by a solemn profession that he makes to his Father, in which he adores him, acknowledges the new state that he receives from him in the Incarnation, and makes an oblation of himself as a slave (as we will say elsewhere), offering him his body as a host for the sins of the world and the deliverance of men, who were slaves of the prince of the world. For, if we bring together the apostle's word that reports to us this memorable oblation of the Son to his Father, with the teaching of the faith that Jesus' soul was thenceforth in the enjoyment of glory, it is evident that this great act of the Son of God's first profession and oblation assumes, by the object of the adoration of latria[14] and by the object

---

14. Adoration, worship.

of the oblation of the sacrifice that he made to his Father, that this holy soul beheld God in his essence and oneness, and that in beholding his essence he beheld the wondrous unities that are in the divine persons, if we consider them as produced and as producing. It should not be very difficult to persuade anyone of this if he considers that the greatness and the end of Jesus' divine and supreme state, in the mystery of the Incarnation, has its basis and foundation, its particular relation and relationship, and is wondrously comprehended, in the divine unities.

To better understand this truth, we must take up this discussion at a higher point and say that there are three holy, divine, and adorable unities that the excellence of our mysteries enables us to know, that the sublimity of the faith offers us, and that the Son of God contemplated, loved, and adored on earth: the oneness of essence, the oneness of love, and the oneness of subsistence. The oneness of essence in the Godhead that we adore, the oneness of love in the Trinity that we marvel at, and the oneness of subsistence in the Incarnation that we profess. The oneness of essence that the Son of God receives from his Father, the oneness of love that he produces with his Father, and the oneness of subsistence that he communicates to our humanity by his Father's will. According to St. Paul, the first activity of Jesus' soul undoubtedly lay in adoring his God and in beholding and contemplating God's oneness. It is his first duty and exercise. It is his first duty to adore him, and it is his first exercise to behold him, that is, to behold his essence and glory. Since this man who is called Jesus was God by this mystery and saw by the light of glory (which no one denies him) that he was God, there is no doubt that his first duty and work in this blessed view and life was to adore, in his human nature, the supreme oneness of the divine essence. Following the order of the eternal origins and emanations, in which he is the only Son of God and the second after the Father, he began directly to marvel and adore his Father's power to beget him and his own birth, subsistence, and matchless and eternal sonship in the bosom of his Father. And since Jesus' first work, in his deity, is the production of the Holy Spirit whose principle he is with the Father, then, following this order of the divine processions, he also beheld and adored at that moment this divine emanation, this eternal Spirit, this personal love whose source and origin he is in the Godhead and who is the bond, uncreated and ineffable, that unites the Father with the Son and the Son with the Father by an eternal oneness and by the oneness of spirit and ineffable love. Seeing these two natures, the one human and the other divine, being joined in oneness of subsistence, one divine and uncreated subsistence, he beholds, loves, and adores at the same moment this new oneness that makes him the new man—that is, makes him Man-God—by a new kind of oneness in which his being, state, and greatness consist. Just as (according to the relation of St. John)[15] our bliss lies first in the divine essence and then in beholding Jesus Christ our Lord and the ineffable oneness that unites two such different natures in him, so also the second object of the bliss of Jesus' soul lies in beholding himself, as subsisting within uncreated Being, and in beholding this same oneness that in uniting these two natures constitutes this divine composition, makes God man, establishes the new mystery of the Incarnation, and gives to the world a new object: an object thenceforth eternal, an object of greatness and love, of life and bliss. He who covers his grandeurs with his humility and who calls himself so often in Scripture the Son of Man for this reason, does not fail to acknowledge them. He does not ignore them or forget them. For at the first moment, he recognized and saw that being Son of Man he was Son of God. For just as in his deity he is Son of God by eternal generation, and in the humanity in which he is Son of Man he is Son of God by temporal communication of the divine essence to human nature, so also the Son of Man who is the Son of God is always beholding and always contemplating this excellent state, and always dedicating himself and this new oneness that makes him the new man to the homage of the supreme and uncreated Being's divine and adorable unities.

O new oneness! O holy oneness! O oneness of subsistence, how dear, how lovable, how honorable you are in Jesus, because his being and greatness consist solely in you, that is, in this oneness of personal subsistence! O soul of Jesus, when, drawn out of nothingness and united with God and beholding his glory, you saw this new mystery of the Incarnation, and when in beholding it you saw how he establishes a holy and incomprehensible oneness, a new but real, divine, and ador-

---

15. 1 Jn 1:1–4.

able oneness between two things so far apart, and you saw how your divine stability and subsistence lies in this oneness: what application, what love, what homage did you then render to this divine being that is your being, to this divine oneness that establishes this new, supreme, divine mystery of the Incarnation? Just as you, O Jesus, are the one alone who received and the first of all mortals who beheld this oneness of subsistence in your two natures, so also are you the first, even before the Virgin who conceived you and the angels who announced you, to have acknowledged and honored this divine and new oneness in the fullness of its marvels! You are the first who applied yourself to this holy oneness and who prayed to extend its grace, power, and effects so that our souls might be reunited with God, as St. John says.[16] You are the first who gave immortal thanks to the eternal Father for having established in you and in this oneness the center and origin of the oneness of grace and spirit that was to be communicated to angels and men and that must reign on earth and in heaven forever! In this way, then, O Jesus my Lord, you began your life and in this way you ended it, blessedly and divinely, in the Virgin's womb and in the cenacle in Jerusalem: in the thought, love, and adoration of the divine unities. In this way you continued on the earth, in Bethlehem, Jerusalem, Nazareth, Egypt, Judea, and in all the places that you honored and sanctified by your holy presence. In this interior exercise, part of the spiritual and contemplative life took place that you wanted to practice in order to work our salvation, provide an example to your children, and serve and honor the majesty of God on earth. Now that you are in heaven and established in the Father's glory, you are still in the thought and beholding of this same object, and your triumphant, heavenly, and immortal life has this same occupation that you had during the course of your humble, suffering, and pilgrim life. For you are the true life, you are the model of our life, you are this model that is shown to us on the mountain and to Moses and by which we are commanded to work. May our inner life therefore be occupied in contemplating, adoring, and imitating your inner life. May our spiritual life regard and imitate the exercises and occupations of your divine soul and sacred life. And imitating your

---

16. Jn 17.

example, let us all contemplate and adore, after you and through you, this divine object. Let us see that by these wondrous unities we have two holy, divine, and adorable trinities in our mysteries. We have a trinity of subsistence in oneness of essence in the first, highest, and most august mystery of the faith, in the person of the Father, Son, and Holy Spirit. And we have a trinity of essence in oneness of subsistence, in the sacred mystery of the Incarnation, in the essence of the soul, body, and deity of Jesus. One of these two trinities exists from all eternity; the other exists for all eternity. One is solely divine and uncreated, in its persons and essence; the other is both divine and human, divine in the person and human in two of its essences. One is adored and never adoring; the other is humbly adored and divinely adoring the most high, ineffable, and incomprehensible mystery of the Trinity, which is the wellspring of the Incarnation, its perfect model, and its final cause. In it this first Trinity, this eternal Trinity, this Trinity of persons is sublimely and solely, sovereignly and divinely acknowledged, served, and adored on earth and in heaven by this other, second trinity: a new trinity, a trinity of essences, which makes up the new man and is comprehended in this new mystery of the Incarnation.

As we see, these two trinities are founded in two divine and different unities: one in oneness of essence and the other in oneness of subsistence. The oneness of essence is the first before all, for it is eternal and unoriginate and is the origin of the unities that are in created and uncreated being. Indeed, it is the origin of the plurality of persons whom we adore in the Most Holy Trinity, for this plurality of persons comes from its fertility, and in its oneness they subsist. This plurality of persons, which is divine and adorable as one same essence, concludes in the oneness that is so often and clearly set forth in the public and solemn service of the Church, marking and celebrating so humbly and repeatedly the oneness of the Holy Spirit, *In unitate Spiritus sancti*: this is what the Church says in all the prayers that she offers to her God. O oneness of Spirit and personal love, uniting the divine persons to each other! For just as they are divinely united, or, rather, just as they are one in the origin of the emanations, that is, in the oneness of essence, they are also divinely united at the endpoint of the emanations, that is, in the oneness of spirit and love. O oneness of essence and oneness of love, encompassing in this way the most high mystery of the Holy Trinity and comprehending in these two unities the infinite extent of God's fertility! For the oneness of essence is the origin of God's fertility and communication within himself, and the oneness of love is the origin of God's fertility and communication beyond himself. God extends and communicates beyond himself by goodness and love, which are the singular properties of the Holy Spirit. O unities of love and essence, comprehending the incomprehensible, that is, the divine nature and persons! For the oneness of essence begins (if we may use this term) as principle-without-principle and the oneness of love closes and concludes as end-without-end the wondrous circle of the eternal emanations. The ineffable processions are as a divine movement within the sovereign, eternal, and unchanging being, beginning in oneness of essence and concluding and resting in oneness of love.

The other trinity, comprehended in the divine mystery of the Incarnation, is founded in the oneness of subsistence, a subsistence that is not absolute but relative, not essential but personal, fitting to the divine Word and applied to our humanity.[17] This oneness of subsistence is the foundation of this most high mystery of the Incarnation, of all the grandeurs that accompany it, and of all the effects that proceed from it, toward God or creatures, on earth or in heaven, in time or eternity. From it, there is a wondrous and incomprehensible result in the infinite diversity of things, things entirely holy, great, precious, and divine. This precious and excellent diversity constitutes, as it were, a new supernatural world within the natural one, a new world of grandeurs and marvels, wholly dependent on this matchless and divine subsistence. For just as the grandeurs and perfections of the divine persons come from the oneness of essence that is common to these persons, so also the grandeurs and perfections of Jesus come from this subsistence. It is therefore this oneness of subsistence that establishes this mystery of the Incarnation, and it is also this mystery that establishes in return this oneness of subsistence in two natures. By this means, it introduces into the mysteries of God and the intimate and secret subsistence of his Word a new oneness that was not there before. By contrast, these

---

17. The French adjective *relatif* is translated as "relative": related, having relation, or standing in some relation to another. Bérulle means objective relation, not our modern-day notion of "relativism."

two unities (the one of essence and the other of love) are as old as God himself and are eternal as he is. For men indeed used to adore on earth the oneness of the divine essence, and the angels indeed used to behold in heaven the oneness of love binding together the persons of the Holy Trinity, which is a kind of oneness unknown on earth before this new mystery of love and oneness and was confessed in heaven by those who, beholding the Godhead, beheld therein the oneness of its spirit and personal love. But (O secret of this divine mystery, noted in three different places by St. Paul!)[18] men by the state of the Judaic law and institution did not believe, and angels (according to the principal Fathers of the Greek Church, and many of the Latin ones) did not yet see and adore, this new oneness of subsistence. And what is more, according to the universal opinion of all theology, they did not know it in all its marvels and in all the circumstances that establish this matchless mystery's substance in the world. Rather, they believed, beheld, and adored the trinity of subsistence and not the oneness of subsistence to which heaven and earth now render a common homage, agreeing and concurring in one same spirit and adoration. And just as heaven and earth adore the oneness of divine subsistence that is in Jesus, so also are we all longing for the oneness of grace and glory to which he raises us by the mystery of his Incarnation. O oneness, powerful in its effects! O oneness, adorable in its deity! O oneness, new in its application! O oneness, wondrous in its activity and bond! For in this mystery, it unites the world with God, God with man, and created being with uncreated Being. Instead of there being oneness of essence among the uncreated persons, divine and equal to each other and, as such, worthy of this oneness of essence, this new and powerful oneness is between natures so far apart and unequal that one is divine and the other human, one uncreated and the other created, one eternal and the other temporal, one most powerful and the other most powerless. Yet they are united: united by a sacred, divine, and eternal bond in oneness of subsistence. This is a kind of oneness that, in this work, adores and regards the oneness of essence that is among the divine persons and the oneness of love that is between the eternal Father and Son. On earth and in heaven, it continually works

---

18. 1 Cor 3 [sc. 2:8–11]; Eph 3[:5–9]; Col 1[:26] (original marginal note).

the oneness of spirit, grace, and glory in which all creation must be established and completed.

Thus, God is living eternally in the oneness of his essence. Thus, God is working powerfully in oneness of principle. Thus, God is ruling blessedly in the oneness of his love. And thus, God is newly establishing his Son and his grandeurs in the oneness of the divine subsistence and is founding his state and kingdom in the oneness of this subsistence. O divine unities! O oneness of essence, oneness of principle, oneness of love, and oneness of subsistence! How wondrous you are, how lovable, how adorable, both in yourself and in your emanations and works! How much ought we to seek you in yourself, pursue you in your purposes, respect you in your counsels, cause you to shine in your works, and attend to you carefully in all that your spirit and grace cause us to undertake in your honor! How much ought we to cleave to the secret and powerful leading of your wisdom that brings all things back to oneness, just as all things come forth from oneness! For, according to St. Dionysius, "all things came out of Oneness by nature," and they pursue this oneness by a secret impulse of nature.[19] They return there by grace; they are swallowed up in it by glory. But above all created things, this humanity that we adore in Jesus returns and is swallowed up into another kind of wholly divine oneness, by a way that is also wholly divine and incomprehensible. The spirit of love establishes it in the new mystery of the Incarnation, in the new oneness of a divine person, and in the supreme state that bears in itself this oneness and dignity that is uncreated and infinite. By this mystery, Jesus is forever the center, principle, and root of the oneness of spirit, grace, and love to which he calls us, leads us, and strengthens us by the divine state of subsistence, by the course of his life, the merit of his death, and the efficacy of his prayers, for he desires and requests it earnestly. He wanted to pray three solemn and noteworthy prayers on the final day of his life, on the day of his griefs and sufferings, and as the Scripture says, *in diebus carnis suae*:[20] one in the cenacle in Jerusalem, according to St. John; the other in the Garden of Olives, according to St. Luke; and the third on the

---

19. See Pseudo-Dionysius, *Divine Names* 1, pp. 50–51.
20. Heb 5[:7] (original marginal note). "In the days of his flesh."

cross, according to St. Paul.²¹ Of these, he uses the first to obtain for us the grace of being wholly consumed in the supreme oneness that is in him and that he has eternally with his Father, according to these holy words recounted by the most intimate of his servants, most faithful of his apostles, greatest of his evangelists, and most loving and beloved of his disciples: *O my Father, may all those who believe in me be one, as we are one; and as you are in me, O my Father, and I am in you, may they be also one in us, so that the world may know that you have sent me. I have given them the glory that you gave me* (that is, I have given them my deity in my humanity), *so that they may be one, as we are one. I am in them and you are in me, so that they may be consummated as one and that the world may know that it is you who sent me and who loves them as you have loved me.*²²

---

21. Jn 17[:1ff]; Lk 22[:42]; Heb 5[:7] (original marginal note).
22. Jn 17:21–23.

Discourse 4

On the Oneness of God in This Mystery

The ineffable work and divine economy of the Incarnation of the eternal Word is a precious and sacred mystery of love and oneness, divinely accomplished in the fullness of time as the highest point and deepest secret of God's love and oneness beyond himself. Just as, according to the great author who is called the Areopagite, love is a heavenly power that divinely unifies what is furthest apart,[1] so also the Holy Spirit, who in the Godhead is love, is the one who unites uncreated being with created being and performs this great work according to the angel's annunciation to the Virgin, who said to her, *The Holy Spirit will come upon you.*[2] This Spirit of God, who is God himself, works in this work as the spirit of love and oneness. In keeping with his personal property, he seeks to work on earth, for earth and heaven, for men and angels, for time and eternity, a work that is precious and singular and a sacred mystery of love and oneness. So let us contemplate this divine worker, both in himself and in this work of his.

The Holy Spirit in the Holy Trinity is produced and not producing, but in his production he receives the oneness of essence that is common to the Father and the Son. He is produced by these divine persons who are distinct from one another, but by a wondrous secret he is produced by them in oneness of principle. And as we note these two holy and adorable unities in his production, the oneness of essence and the

---

1. Pseudo-Dionysius, *Divine Names* 4, pp. 79–84.
2. Lk 1:35.

oneness of principle, he himself is also produced within the Trinity as the oneness of spirit and love. So as we contemplate this Holy Spirit, the divine worker of this divine work, all that we seem to see in him is love and oneness.

These two points have a natural and perfect relation to one other, for love naturally reaches out toward oneness, and it is clear that a supreme and divine love must be Oneness itself. But what is quite strange as we contemplate the Holy Spirit is that although he is love in the Godhead, he is infertile in this Godhead (if so low a word may be used in speaking of what is so high and great), whereas love and fertility are naturally joined together. This is one of the most secret and unfathomable points in this profound mystery of the Most Holy Trinity, in which each point is an abyss in which the human mind is lost and swallowed up when it tries to investigate rather than to revere what surpasses the measure of its understanding. In humility of mind, then, and adoring the marvels of our faith and the secrets of the Godhead under the guidance and light of faith, let us pass from depth to depth and from one secret and marvel to another. In a spirit of love and reverence, let us say that by a secret just as strange and marvelous, this infertility of the Holy Spirit is as divine and adorable as the fertility that produces him. It proceeds from the power and fertility of his production and divinely expends and arrests the divine fertility in his person. This infertility is founded in the greatness, dignity, and property of his very person, who is blessedly produced as the divine endpoint and rest of the divine emanations within the Trinity. It is an infertility that, just as it comes forth from the fertility of God, so also it concludes in the fertility of God, that is, in the fertility of a divine person working beyond himself. For instead of its being particular to the eternal Word to be origin and also to be originate, it is particular to the Holy Spirit to be infertile and also fertile: infertile in himself and fertile beyond himself. And it is the property of his person to be in himself the endpoint that divinely brings to a close and blessedly arrests the divine fertility within the Most Holy Trinity. But he is the endpoint who receives, contains, and arrests in himself the fullness of this fertile nature, so that by receiving, preserving, and arresting this fertility he might spread it powerfully and divinely beyond himself. This is why, in God's works, just as power is ascribed to the Father and wisdom to the Son, so also fertility is attributed to the Holy Spirit. As soon as God begins to speak in the Scriptures and to work beyond himself, this fertility of the Holy Spirit is employed and lauded. For it is said in the opening of Genesis that at the beginning of the world's creation, at God's first work and before the world's first day, the Holy Spirit was moving and resting on the waters, *Incubabat aquis*[3] (according to the Septuagint), as though to impress his fertility on them and cause thereafter so many highly excellent creatures to emerge, which fill heaven and earth and make up this universe. God revealed this to his servant Moses so that we might understand that everything produced in the universe and differentiated thereafter in the six days of Genesis owes its relation and origin to the fertility of the Holy Spirit.

Yet the creation of this visible and sensible world is not enough to worthily bring the Holy Spirit's fertility to a close. It must be devoted toward a more exalted being and the formation of a more excellent world. It must have a greater object for its power and a worthier and more exalted end for its working. And because he is infertile in the Godhead by the condition that is particular to the mystery of the Trinity, he must, by a new mystery, be fertile in another ineffable manner. He must give new being to one of the persons subsisting in the fullness of the Most Holy Trinity, so that just as the fertility of God, in God himself, concludes in a divine person, so also the fertility of the Holy Spirit, beyond himself, may be directed to producing an already existing God (O strange marvel!), henceforth existing in a new nature. We see this in the world's regeneration, in which the architect of heaven and earth, the eternal Word, is clothed in human nature and comes to take up this new being so that he might give a new being to the world. The same Holy Spirit who began to work in the sensible world and in the order of nature, according to Genesis, begins to work within the invisible world and in the order of grace, according to the testimony of St. Luke. He forms the head of this order of grace and is the new principle of supernatural being, making a new heaven and a new earth and constituting a new world, to speak in the language of God himself in

---

3. Gn 1:2. "He brooded over the waters."

his holy Scriptures.[4] In his own person and in his two natures divinely united, he is himself an incomparable world. We see therefore that the Holy Spirit does not employ his fertility within himself but employs it beyond himself. He does not employ it in the archetypal world but employs it in the world that we may call "intelligible." He does not employ it within eternity but employs it in the fullness of time. For he impresses his divine fertility on the blessed womb of the Most Holy Virgin. He produces a God-Man and gives the eternal Word a new birth in human nature. Producing nothing within himself, he produces this divine mystery of the Incarnation blessedly beyond himself, as his supreme work, in which he represents his living portrait, making it his perfect image and applying the most excellent brushstrokes and the most vivid and deepest colors of his likeness.[5]

Let us summarize in a few words what we have set forth. Just as he is personally love and oneness in the Holy Trinity, he performs this work as a work and mystery of love and oneness. Just as he is love produced, not love producing, in the Godhead in which he alone does not produce one like him, so also Jesus, who is the work of the Holy Spirit who formed him in the Most Holy Virgin's womb and produced him as the love of heaven and earth, is a love produced, and not producing one like him in the being, order, and state of the hypostatic union. Just as the Holy Spirit is the endpoint and rest of the love of the Father and of the Son, arresting the incomprehensible movement of the divine emanations within the Godhead and spreading God's fertility beyond himself in his works, so also Jesus is the divine endpoint and rest of God's love working beyond the Godhead, spreading beyond himself the fertility of his Spirit within creation, in the order of grace and of

---

4. Is 65:17, 66:22; 2 Cor 5:17; 2 Pt 3:13; Rv 21:1–5.

5. Cf. Athanasius, *On the Incarnation* 3.13–14:

You know what happens when a portrait that has been painted on a panel becomes obliterated through external stains. The artist does not throw away the panel, but the subject of the portrait has to come and sit for it again, and then the likeness is redrawn on the same material. Even so was it with the All-holy Son of God. He, the Image of the Father, came and dwelt in our midst, in order that He might renew mankind made after Himself.

Trans. P. Lawson (Crestwood, N.Y.: St. Vladimir's Seminary Press, 1993), 41–42.

glory. And thus, the sacred mystery of the Incarnation is a work, a state, and a mystery of love and oneness, a masterwork of the Holy Spirit in these two divine qualities, and a masterwork that adores the distinct unities that are in the eternal persons, producing and produced. It is a masterwork that looks upon the Spirit of love and oneness as its principle and that stands in relation to it as to its exemplar, which is itself divinely expressed and vividly represented in this divine mystery of love and oneness. This point is particularly noteworthy, for it contains an excellent exercise that we ought to make and marks an adorable relation that this work has to the Holy Spirit and the divine unities, well worthy of being considered in the singular state of this divine mystery of the Incarnation.

Now, there are various kinds of subjects that can be united and joined together and various kinds of unions and unities that can be conceived by the mind of man and created by the Spirit of God. In contributing to this work, the Holy Spirit brings together two things so far apart, unequal, and separated as are created and uncreated being. And as he is himself the holy oneness that divinely unites the persons of the Godhead with one another, so also does he himself, in this mystery, unite one of the adored persons of the Trinity with one of the created natures in the universe. Thus, he accomplishes this great mystery not in union only but in oneness, as wrought by the Spirit of oneness, and he accomplishes it not in oneness as such but in oneness of person. For he who performs it is, in his person, spirit, love, and oneness. And since he is God, he performs this sacred mystery of love and oneness in oneness of divine person. May you be blessed, O holy and adorable Spirit! May you be blessed forever, both in yourself and in the most holy, excellent, and divine of your works! May you be blessed for having made and represented in it a living image of yourself and a holy and wondrous expression of the divine oneness that we adore in your essence and in the property of your person! It is a twofold oneness that we marvel at and confess in you and daily implore in our most sacred mysteries and public prayers! For they all blessedly close with this "oneness of the Holy Spirit" who is the endpoint of the divine emanations and who, in the property that constitutes his person, is the bond uniting the divine persons and the sacred oneness of the Father and the Son in eternity. For the faith instructs us that the Father and Son are divinely bound together not only by the oneness of their essence but also by the divine and ineffable oneness of the Holy Spirit.

Here is the cause and origin of the state and oneness that lies in this divine mystery. Here is the perfect idea upon which this perfect work is drawn and the accomplished model on which it is formed by a spirit as excellent as is the eternal Spirit, proceeding from the power of the Father and the wisdom of the Son. It is a work worthy of so worthy an author and of such a Spirit. But let us go further and direct our thoughts to contemplating the work, just as we have contemplated the worker. Since by his grace and leading we have grasped this truth in its principle and have drawn out the wondrous oneness of this mystery from its wellspring and origin—that is, in the holy unities that regard the Holy Spirit—let us pursue it in the state, effects, and circumstances of this divine work. Let us see that in this august mystery there is but one person subsisting in two different natures above the laws of the world's Author, who gives each nature its own subsistence, intrinsic and incommunicable to any other. Let us see also that there is but one divine person who enters into the state of this mystery, among the three persons whom the faith adores. This seems to go against not only the laws of created nature but also God himself and the inseparability that we confess among the divine persons when they work something that exists beyond the infinite being of their common essence. Let us see also that this supreme favor and uncreated grace are granted only to human nature and, within humankind, only to this one sacred Humanity. In this way, let us see and observe that this mystery is wholly encompassed within oneness. The oneness is indicated in its origin and state and in the principal parts that compose it (if we may refer to them like this, for want of nobler terms). For, in order to state briefly what has been said fully, it is a principle of oneness that produces in eternity the Holy Spirit working this mystery. This Spirit who is at work is oneness in the property of his person, and the work that he performs is a work and mystery of oneness. The greatness and stability of this mystery lies wholly in the sacred oneness of the divine subsistence, which is matchlessly communicated to this created nature and gives the world the divine masterwork of the Incarnation.

O oneness that makes a new being, a being worthy of adoration by all that is created! O oneness that sets forth a new order in the universe, sets a new center in the world, and establishes a new principle in nature! O oneness that gives a new sovereign to the angel, a redeemer to man, and a head to the Church of the living God! O oneness that establishes in heaven a new King of glory, on earth a means of life and immortality, and in the world a Sun of righteousness who spreads his light and rays to the highest heaven and the lowest point of earth! O oneness that crowns God's works and that triumphs in the two mysteries that the faith adores, that is, the Trinity and the Incarnation, which are two singular mysteries that belong distinctively to the Godhead, one in itself and the other in the single nature that alone is joined with it. For we see oneness shining in the divine essence in the mystery of the Trinity and in the divine person in the mystery of the Incarnation, that is, in all that is of God, if we distinguish in God only his essence and his subsistences. Let us say again: O truly holy and blessedly adorable oneness! For it gives a new Holy of Holies to earth and heaven, and it makes a new adorer and a new subject, newly worthy of being adored and of adoring. O divinely powerful oneness! For it extends its might over God himself, making him temporal from eternal, mortal from immortal, visible from invisible, passible from impassible, powerless from all-powerful, and creature from creator, according to the nature that he took on.[6] To say in a word what is ineffable, it makes God man and the Man-God. O Godhead! O humanity! O oneness! O great marvel! That two natures so far apart and unequal, the one so high and the other so low, might be joined together! That they might be joined by so perfect a union and so powerful a striving that humanity might be in personal oneness with God, and that what does not occur even between creatures might by the power of this mystery be in God and man! For, among natural things, sometimes we do see a kind of mixing and joining together, serving as an intimation and representation to represent the state of this mystery, but this is completely different. The more powerful and perfect the crea-

---

6. Cf. Leo, Sermon 30: "We rejoice, therefore, in both [natures], since we are not saved except with both. We cannot in any way divide the visible from the invisible, the corporeal from the incorporeal, the passible from the impassible, the tangible from the intangible, the 'form of a servant' from the 'form of God.'" *Sermons*, 130.

tures (that is, the intelligent beings, angel and man), the more closely they approach God in the perfection of their being, the more capable they are of uniting together and forming some kind of intimation and image of the oneness among the divine persons. But sacred theology teaches us that there is no kind of nature, fully developed and complete in its kind, that can enter into union like this with another created nature and be joined to it by a personal bond. Yet, by the power of the mystery of the Incarnation, humanity enters into this kind of union and oneness with God himself. It has a bond, closeness, and intimacy with God that it does not and cannot have with any other created nature and person, not in its affections only, nor in its effects, but in the essence, depth, and center of its being. O goodness! O power! O love! God and man are joined in oneness of person, which is the highest, closest, and most intimate union to which the divine omnipotence can exalt created nature. And just as, in the Holy Trinity, oneness of essence is as the original root and source of all the grandeurs that correspond to the divine persons, so also, in this mystery, oneness of person is the source of all the grandeurs and ineffable communications that are made and that can be made to this humanity.

But this goes beyond our purpose. Let us return to our discussion and restrict ourselves to the point, center, and oneness of our mystery. Let us observe how this oneness, which is so fitting to God, so impressed on his creation, and so perfect and intimate in this mystery, is excellent also in the manner in which it subsists. This manner is invisible to us but most visible to God and his angels. For those who used to see Jesus on his earthly way, speaking with men and living among them, saw nothing of the secret and mystery that the eternal Wisdom had hidden in him. Only the angels, who beheld his glory, beheld the wondrous oneness that united his divine essence with human nature in the person of the Word. They saw that this oneness was not transitory but permanent, not of accident but of substance, not temporal but eternal, and not subject to being interrupted even for one moment in the use, office, and function that it exercised in regard to human nature. Thus, this soul and body were and would be eternally subsisting in the Godhead.

What the angels beheld in the clarity of their illumination we must grasp in the darkness of our faith and consider all the more, since this point greatly reveals this most high mystery's excellence and dignity. Let us observe, then, how the divine mystery of the Incarnation closely binds and unites God and man with a kind of union that gives not only an inherent right and title to the possession and use that must be mutual and reciprocal between the two natures, the one divine and the other human (as are the covenants and contracts that people make on earth to bind themselves together). But just as this union is more divine, so also is it more powerful, active, and close. This sacrament between God and man is greater and higher than the one between those who are called in Scripture *duo in carne una*, and even between Jesus Christ and his Church.[7] I say that this sacrament between God and man is greater, for the terms *mystery* and *sacrament* befit the Incarnation well, and this is the ordinary language of the Fathers, as those know who read them and who see that they often extend the use of this word even to the Godhead and to the secret of the eternal procession. I say therefore that this sacrament is greater and higher than all other means that one might think have the power to give us some kind of union with God. The Son of God is always present in his Church, according to his word, *I am with you until the consummation of the age*,[8] but this promise is effective insofar as it has to do specifically with the assistance promised to his Church for teaching the doctrine of salvation. It is not necessary that he be always and at each moment working in the Church as a general body, or in her councils. It is enough that he is always protecting her and covering her with the shadow of his wings and leading her in the needs that arise, ready to enlighten her in his truths when these become obscured through time or heresies.

Jesus Christ our Lord is always in the world through the holy sacrament of the Eucharist—which is a second union that he willed to enter into with our persons, after and in honor of the one that he deigned to enter into with our nature through the Incarnation—although he is not always applied to us and united with us in this divine sacrament. For the Eucharist, in which lies the Father's substantial grace, joins and unites us with God only during certain moments. Truly—O greatness!

---

7. Gn 2[:24] (original marginal note). "Two in one flesh."
8. Mt 28[:20] (original marginal note).

O power of our mysteries!—during these moments we are really and substantially united with him as one single substance. That is, the body and blood of Jesus Christ are in both God and us: in God by personal subsistence, in us by real and sacramental residence. But when the most holy communion has concluded and the species have been consumed, we no longer cleave to the body of the Son of God in substance, and this precious flesh, the sacred bond that joins us with the Godhead, is no longer in us. What remains to us of the union that we have with God by means of the Eucharist is that the Son of God, who has chosen our bodies to be like living sepulchers of his living and glorious body, sanctifies them by a real impression of his grace and power. For once he has taken possession of our members as his own, through his body, and has made us all members of his body, of his flesh and bone, by this divine touch he has power over us as over that which is his and whose right and ownership lie with him.

But in this union of God with man through the mystery of the Incarnation, all is very different and accompanied by circumstances and conditions that are much higher and more advantageous. For it is not a substance united with God and different from God, as in the Eucharist, that is the means of joining deity with humanity, but it is the very person of the Word, who is one and the same with[9] the Godhead and is the sacred bond uniting humanity with God. And it is not only in certain moments, as in the Eucharist, that this union is accomplished in actuality, but in the Incarnation the sacred oneness that takes place between these two subjects, divinely and personally united, never ceases, never decreases, never ends. Instead, it remains always in its act, function, and power and way of acting. It exists always in the fullness of this power, act, and function. It always accomplishes its divine power and always performs its wondrous office. And as the person of the Word is divine and infinite, it has a wholly extraordinary and ineffable application to human nature. Lacking its subsistence, human nature needs that of the eternal Word, which, so to speak, actuates and suffuses this humanity in its essence, powers, and all its parts. He does so according to the extent of his power and infinity, as far as the creature is capable

---

9. The French phrase is *une même chose avec*.

of it, to the highest and ultimate point of its exaltation. Just as the divine essence always subsists in the eternal Word, so also the humanity has never been and will never be for one single moment without this same subsistence always actuating and suffusing it, always as though informing and sustaining it. As a result, all of the places that have been honored with the presence of Jesus' humanity have also been honored with the fulfilment and consummation of this divine oneness. The one is inseparably united with the other, for it draws all its subsistence and even its existence from this divine being. This Humanity therefore, everywhere that it is, exists in actual oneness of person with God. The earth bore the Son of man in this divine state of real, actual, and personal oneness with the Godhead for thirty-four years, in Nazareth, Bethlehem, Jerusalem, Egypt, Galilee, and Judea, on earth and sea, in towns and deserts, and in all the places of his pilgrimage in the world.

Death and hell itself received this soul and body in this divine state, in their bosom and circumference, and were never able to dissolve this divine oneness. The parts of human nature were separated at that time by the striving of the cross, but neither the soul nor the body could be separated from this oneness, for the divine person still accompanied the body to the tomb and the soul to limbo. Jesus' body was indeed separated from his soul by the power of death and of love suffering for the sins of men, but, by the eternal Word's more powerful love toward the Son of man, this body of the Son of man was not separated from God.[10] But—O marvel! O prodigy of the oneness of God in this mystery of the Incarnation, a oneness that is powerful and unalterable!—the nature of this flesh, separated from the soul and from life, was joined and mingled with the nature of eternity (to use the expression of a great bishop and ancient father of France),[11] and this body,

10. Cf. Gregory of Nyssa, *Against Eunomius* 2.13, trans. H. C. Ogle and H. A. Wilson, *NPNF* 5 (Peabody, Mass.: Hendrickson, 1994), 127; Hilary, *The Trinity* 10.57–60, trans. S. Mckenna, *FC* 25; Augustine, *Tractates on the Gospel of John* 47.9–13, in *Tractates on the Gospel of John, 28–54*, trans. John W. Rettig, *FC* 79; John of Damascus, *Exposition of the Orthodox Faith* 3.27, in *Writings*, trans. Frederic H. Chase, *FC* 37, p. 332.

11. Cf. Hilary, *The Trinity* 8.13, p. 285:

If the Word has indeed become flesh, and we indeed receive the Word as flesh in the Lord's food, how are we not to believe that He dwells in us by His nature, He who, when He was born as man, has assumed the nature of our flesh that is bound inseparable

dead and hanging on the cross and lifeless in the tomb, was even then consubsisting with the Godhead and as such worthy of being adored by men and angels.

Now that the Son of man is risen, heaven has received this sacred deposit of the love of God and men and, in this deposit, has received this divine oneness. Heaven holds it forever in its own glory, power, and greatness. This deposit will continue to subsist in this oneness unalterably and as long as God himself. For as long as he is God, he will be man. God is man not only by a lawful right and power that unites in actuality these two parts together from time to time; God is man by this oneness between these two natures that the divine subsistence makes always actual, complete, and consummated. God set the foundation of this oneness of his in the extraordinary power and adorable might of his love and charity toward the man born of Mary, to whom he says in a wholly particular sense, *In charitate perpetua dilexi te*.[12] For this charity is everlasting and never interrupted, that is, it is even everlasting in the striving and outpouring, in the ecstasy and oneness, of his love. It is a striving and outpouring in love for God to unite his own person to human nature and for the Son of God to give humanity this same essence that he received from his Father. And it is a wondrous ecstasy, in which God, emerging as though beyond himself, enters into created being and establishes there forever the rest, triumph, and oneness of his love. O striving! O outpouring! O ecstasy of eternal and uncreated love, and that wants to be just as eternal in the striving, outpouring, and ecstasy of his love! O supreme charity, divine and everlasting in its source and effect, or, rather, in its marvelous striving and ecstatic outpouring, which all other love, although excellent and divine, will never be able to approach! O strong and invincible charity, which nothing can alter! Nor will anything henceforth be able to separate this holy Humanity from this everlasting, sublime, and divine state of personal oneness with God!

By this oneness that is so penetrating, powerful, and lasting, God is truly, really, and substantially man, and man is personally God. God

---

with Himself, and has mingled the nature of His flesh to His eternal nature in the mystery of the flesh that was to be communicated to us?

12. Jer 31[:3] (original marginal note). "I have loved you with an everlasting love."

and man constitute but one same person, subsisting in two such dissimilar natures, living in such different states, and placed in conditions so removed from one another. Yet these natures, states, and conditions that are so different and unequal are brought together so divinely and intimately, so inseparably and unconfusedly, according to the definitions of the holy councils, that the faith confesses and adores its God in two such different natures, and the human and angelic mind becomes lost in the oneness and difference of this most high mystery.[13] For the name, the greatness, power, dignity, and majesty of God, insofar as it is communicable to the creature, resides and rests in this Humanity. God joins it to himself, quickens it in himself, and makes it consubsistent with his deity. By this means, when it is adored, God is adored in it, and when it speaks and walks, God is speaking and walking, and its footsteps should be embraced and its words heeded as being the steps and words of a God. And similarly, when this Humanity works or suffers, God is acting and suffering in it. Its actions and passions are divine, and as such they have an infinite merit and are of an infinite price and value through the ineffable relation, interchange, and communication that lies between the deity and humanity in the subsistence of the divine person. Thus, the incomprehensible God causes himself to be comprehended in this humanity. The ineffable God makes himself heard in the voice of his incarnate Word. The invisible God makes himself seen in the flesh that he united with the nature of eternity. The God overwhelming in the radiance of his greatness makes himself felt in his gentleness, softness, and goodness, according to these words of the apostle: *The goodness and softness of God our Savior appeared in the world.*[14] The one who sustains the world by his power sustains our

---

13. Council of Chalcedon (451 AD):

This one and the same Jesus Christ, the only-begotten Son must be confessed to be in two natures, unconfusedly, immutably, indivisibly, inseparably, and that without the distinction of the natures being taken away by such union, but rather the peculiar property of each nature being preserved and being united in one Person and subsistence, not separated or divided into two persons, but one and the same Son and only-begotten, God the Word, our Lord Jesus Christ.

Henry R. Percival, ed. *The Seven Ecumenical Councils of the Undivided Church: Their Canons and Dogmatic Decrees*, NPNF 14, pp. 264–65.

14. Ti 3[:4] (original marginal note).

humanity by his substance, and he devotes and applies his own subsistence to this created nature so that he might support it in himself. He joins it together with himself in so powerful and perfect a way that from these two natures thus united results this divine composition, this wondrous subject, Jesus Christ our Lord, true God, true man. He is a subject so powerful that he governs, delights, and sustains heaven and earth, angels and men. He is a subject so wondrous that he has qualities, experiences states, and receives attributions that are so new, strange, and different that the great theologian of antiquity rightly cries out,

O new and unprecedented mixture! O wondrous temperament![15] He who is, is made. He who is uncreated, is created. He who cannot be comprehended in any place is encompassed and comprehended in our humanity. He who enriches all is made poor. For he undergoes the poverty of our flesh so that we might possess the riches of his deity. He who is fullness is spent (for he gives up his glory for a time), so that I might take part in his fullness. O goodness! O mystery! I received the image of God in creation and did not preserve it; and God took on my flesh to give life to my soul and immortality to my body. He enters into a new and second union with us, a union much more excellent than the first, for in the earlier one he gives us his likeness, but in this one he deigns even to take on our nature, which is a kind of interchange and union much higher and more divine.[16]

In these thoughts, what should we consider and marvel at more: the greatness of God humbled like this in the nothingness of the creature, or the lowliness of man thus exalted to God's equal and placed on the throne of the Godhead? O marvel! O greatness! That man, who is but dust and ashes in his origin, according to the word of the very one who formed him and who said to him as he did so, *Pulvis es, et in pulverem reverteris*.[17] That man, who is but impotence and frailty in his state and progress and is but a vapor, even a momentary vapor, *vapor ad modicum parens*, as the holy Scriptures say.[18] That man, who is but wretchedness in his birth, life, and death (that is, in all his states) and

---

15. A well-proportioned composition or mixture.
16. Gregory Nazianzen, *Oration 42* (original marginal note). See Gregory Nazianzen, Oration 45, "Second Oration on Easter," in *Select Orations and Letters*, trans. C. G. Browne and J. E. Swallow, *NPNF* 7, p. 426.
17. "You are dust, and to dust you will return." Gn 3:19.
18. "A vapor appearing for a moment." Jas 4:15.

of whom an Ancient said, *O necessitas abiecta nascendi, vivendi misera, dura moriendi.*[19] That this man, I say, might live and subsist in the Godhead? That this man might be God, and that this God-Man might pass through all these degrees, undergo all these states, and ennoble them, sanctify them, and deify them in himself?[20] Thus we have, according to the teachings of our faith, and that we adore in our mysteries, a God being born in the manger, a God living and journeying in Judea, a God dying on the cross, and a God dead in the grave. By so strange a means he is made the redemption of humankind, the divine justice receives payment for our debts with a price of infinite dignity, and our deliverance from the captivity of the devil, from sin, and from death is carried out by a secret power that is hidden in the humanity, the life, suffering, and death, of a God.

This is what this oneness entails, which is divine and adorable in itself, wondrous in what follows and results from it, and lovable in its effects. This is what we must pursue and set forth in this discourse. For, by this new oneness, just as there is in the world a new being, a new man and a new Adam, so also is there a new order in the world and a new state in the universe: a state previously unknown for four thousand years. Of the four orders that compose and differentiate heaven and earth—the order of nature, of grace, of glory, and the supreme order, which is that of the hypostatic union—this great and new order is farther from and higher above the first than the first order is from nothingness, from which the divine omnipotence directly drew it. For between nothingness and the being of nature there is nothing that intervenes, and between man and nothingness there is only a partition, which is only mire. Man is formed from the loam of the earth, and the earth is taken from nothingness. There is, then, only this bit of loam that serves as a common wall between nothingness and man, but there is an infinite distance between God and man, between created and uncreated being. Yet these two beings are bound and joined together as in a point and center, and these two such different natures are united in

---

19. Sidonius Apollinaris [Letter 8.11.4] (original marginal note). "O how abject the necessity of being born, how miserable that of living, how harsh that of dying." See Sidonius, *Letters*, trans. William B. Anderson, LCL 296, vol. 1, pp. 462–63.

20. Cf. Irenaeus, *Against the Heresies* 2.22, vol. 2, p. 74, and 3.18, vol. 3, p. 91.

one same person. Thus, the hypostatic order and union is established in the world. In the Creation, God made the order of nature, and at the same time he established on earth the order of grace and in heaven the order of glory. These are three different and wondrous orders, in which he desired man to have a share. But here is a new order in the world, a new state in the universe. Here is a state that is incomparably more exalted above the order of glory than heaven is above the earth, than this glory is above the order of grace, than grace is above the order of nature, and that nature is above nothingness. It is this oneness of divine subsistence that introduces into the world an order so excellent and a state so exalted, an order so eminent and a state so privileged, an order so powerful and a state so precious that it is matchless in its subject and so extensive in its power that it extends over everything and demonstrates the effects of its power upon each of the other orders. It regenerates the universe, it fulfills heaven, it sanctifies the earth, it ennobles nature, it exalts grace, it crowns glory, it fills the angels with rapture, it makes bodies spiritual and our spirits divine, and it deifies our humanity in the divine person. And in sum, all that comes forth from God by creation and all that returns into God by sanctification looks upon this order, this divine state, this supreme mystery, this Incarnation as its resource and principle, as the point in which all is brought to completion, and as the end to which all must be dedicated, because it pleased God himself to originate, be encompassed, and concluded there, and to dedicate himself to it.

Now, as this new order follows from this new being, so also from this new order comes a change and something new in the conduct of divine Providence. For since God became incarnate on the earth, it is no longer heaven that governs earth but earth that governs heaven, and the first mover is no longer in heaven but on earth. It is God incarnate who is now the first mover, and the first heaven that used to move all the others has changed order and position and is now only the second mover. Even the order, state, and situation of the world's principal parts are reversed by the reversal that God performed in regard to himself in this mystery. For heaven is no longer above earth but an earth is above all the heavens, that is, the earth of our humanity living in Jesus Christ. This blessed portion of earth, taken like this into heaven, exalted above all the heavens, and subsisting in the eternal Word, is a new heaven that is unmoving in itself and moves all things. It is a new center of the universe, to which every spiritual and embodied creature is drawn. It is both center and heaven: the heaven that contains all things in its greatness and eminence, and the center that gathers all things in its oneness and draws all things by its strength and power. It is the fixed center of the universe, and it is placed not at the world's middle but at the lowest point of the earth and in the highest heaven, by a strange change and reversal in the order of nature. This pays homage to the new state of the eternal Word and to the reversal (if we may use this word) that we adore in the Author of nature, for he takes on a new nature in which, taking no thought of himself and humbling his greatness, he establishes the new and sacred mystery of the Incarnation, changing, reversing, and making all things new within the order of nature and of grace. In fact, we see that this wondrous change that is made on the earth passes from earth to heaven and from heaven to the celestial hierarchies. For it is no longer the angel who governs men nor the first angel who governs the heavenly spirits. It is a man who governs all men and angels, and the order of the hierarchies is made new by this renewal of being, power, and life within human nature. Instead of the angels taking their orders and receiving their commissions and divine models from their heads, and their heads taking these from the one who is first among them, now they all, even the first of the angels, take these on earth from a man, from a human child, a child three years, three months, and three days old.[21] The angels even learn from the men who cleave to this Man-God and serve him, from poor fishermen, from unlettered and ordinary men, by this reason alone: that they are his followers and apostles. The angels, I say, spirits who are wholly intellectual and established in glory, learn humbly from these men on earth the secrets of the divine power and of the humble and mysterious economy of the Incarnation, which in heaven and in the light of glory they do not know in its breadth and in all its marvels. This gave the apostle cause, when he spoke of this mystery, to say that he had "the task of proclaiming the glory and incomprehensible riches of Jesus Christ and of making known the mys-

---

21. Such a statement must evidently be taken as an expression of rhetorical consistency rather than as a historical detail.

tery hidden from all time in God, so that the Wisdom of God might be manifested to the powers and principalities by the Church, etc." (*Mihi omnium sanctorum minimo data est gratia haec, in gentibus evangelizare investigabiles divitias Christi, et illuminare omnes, quae sit dispensatio sacramenti absconditi a saeculis in Deo: ut innotescat principatibus et potestatibus per ecclesiam multiformis sapientia Dei, etc.*)[22]

There is even a change in the conduct and exercise of divine providence, in that formerly it looked upon only what is outside of God and had regard only for his palace and outer court (if we may speak like this about things that are so great, worthy, and exalted above our words and understanding). The principal part of this providence, which is predestination, was concerned with the angel and man only, that is, with intellectual nature capable of knowing and serving him. But since God in his sacred council ordained this order of orders and this state of hypostatic union, his providence enters into a much worthier concern, a much higher power, and a much greater and more honorable occupation than before. For God himself, as man, wills to enter into the jurisdiction of this providence. And just as he held council when he willed to create man and said, *Faciamus hominem*,[23] according to the text in Genesis, so also did he hold council to make man be God, which is a work much more excellent and which concludes and ends in God himself. By virtue of this great and secret council that God held concerning the fulfilment of this new mystery, his providence begins to be exercised upon so great a subject, it deliberates upon the Incarnation of the eternal Word, treats of the only Son of God's temporal birth, looks upon him as entering into this mystery, assists him in his new and mortal life, accompanies him in his journeys, establishes his house and family on earth, and ordains his states, his power, and his privileges.

Let us take this up from a higher point and rise up to humbly and steadfastly contemplate the Godhead in itself and in its sacred counsel upon its supreme work. From all eternity, the thought, regard, and love within God is in regard to himself, but his counsel is within him in regard to his creation only, and he deliberates only upon his servants. The greatness of his own essence, the blessed condition of his wholly

22. Eph 3:8–10.
23. "Let us make man." Gn 1:26.

spiritual and intelligent being, and the divine state of his supreme and unchanging life give him understanding and love of himself, but they do not necessarily give him any exercise and function beyond himself. He is sufficient to himself and has no need to act or do anything beyond in order to be occupied. By this thought, regard, and love that he has toward himself, as toward his matchless object that alone is worthy of himself, he is sufficiently, fully, and divinely self-occupied within himself. He delights blessedly in the greatness and bliss of his being. He produces in his bosom the persons who are originate in the Trinity, and they have no need to leave it, because this dwelling place that suffices to their birth and production suffices also to their eternal bliss. God therefore is eternally living and blessed in the one thought, one love, and blessed occupation that the greatness, fullness, and fertility of his own essence necessarily give him. He produces beyond himself only what pleases him and when it pleases him. His council treats only of his works, and his providence ordains and concerns only his creatures. But by the state of this new mystery, the council of God has a newer and worthier object. For he does not treat only of the kingdoms of earth or even those of heaven, as he did before, but now he deliberates upon this new oneness that he is establishing forever between the two natures: the one divine and the other human. He deliberates upon the person of his only Son, whom he wants to give to the world for its salvation, and he deliberates upon the ineffable communication that is to be between God and human nature. O greatness! O new dignity in the council of God! Never was this high, secret, and sacred council of the Godhead so exalted, honored, and occupied than when it arranged this divine mystery. Never was it so adorable and incomprehensible than when it established this supreme state. Do we not see how it is not a matter here of his producing a world out of nothing, but of his reducing, in a sense, the Author of the world to the state of nothingness? Of clothing his eternal Word, by whom all things are made, with our frailty and impotence? Of drawing the only Son of God from the bosom of his Father and abasing him to the point of human and created nature and to the nothingness of our mortality? Do we not see how it is not a matter here of God's exercising his power and righteousness upon dust and ashes, but upon a Man-God? And that it is not a matter here, as it was formerly in the earthly paradise, of condemning the sinner to death, but of delivering the only Son of God over to the power of darkness, to the opprobrium of the cross, and to the horror of death, following the words that the soldiers' presence drew from his sacred mouth: *This is your hour and the power of darkness.*[24] Do we not see how it is not a matter here of giving grace to the guilty, but of giving the grace of uncreated being to this Humanity? Supreme, divine, and infinite grace, the source of all grace!

Instead, then, of angels and men being called and ordained only to divine servitude and adoption as the culmination of their greatness and bliss, and instead of predestination until now never used for anything higher and more exalted, there is now a man called by God to something incomparably worthier and higher. There is a Son of man predestined to divine sonship. There is a Jesus, Son of man, *who is predestined Son of God in power*, in the words of his apostle.[25] This is the highest point from which the sacred council of predestination will ever ordain. Nothing can be proposed to it that is greater than this divine state of hypostatic union, just as there is no greater calling, no election more certain, and no charity more complete than that in which humanity is called and exalted to the throne of the Godhead, and Jesus Christ, son of Mary, in equality with God is established forever at his right hand and in his glory. But our words are too feeble to express things so great. Let us listen to the oracle of his age and the most excellent of teachers, in the most excellent of his polemical books, the teacher whom the Son of God chose for the defense of his grace that is his Incarnation's effect and end and the subject of the predestination of the elect. I mean St. Augustine, who, speaking of the predestination of the Holy of Holies and of all the saints in him, says these words:

Ipsum Dominum gloriae in quantum homo factus est Dei Filius, praedestinatum esse dicimus. Clamat Doctor Gentium in capite epistolarum suarum: Paulus servus Jesus-Christi, vocatus apostolus, segregatus in evangelium Dei (quod ante promiserat per prophetas suos in scripturis sanctis) de Filio suo, qui factus est ei ex semine David, secundum carnem: Qui praedestinatus est Filius Dei in virtute, secundum Spiritum sanctificationis, ex resurrectione mortuo-

---

24. Lk 22[:53] (original marginal note).
25. Rom 1[:4] (original marginal note).

rum. Praedestinatus est ergo Iesus, ut qui futurus erat secundum carnem filius David, esset tamen in virtute Filius Dei secundum Spiritum sanctificationis, quia natus est de Spiritu sancto et Virgine Maria. Ipsa est illa ineffabiliter facta hominis a Deo Verbo susceptio singularis, ut Filius Dei et Filius hominis simul; Filius hominis propter susceptum hominem, et Filius Dei propter suscipientem unigenitum Deum veraciter et proprie diceretur, ne non trinitas sed quaternitas crederetur. Praedestinata est ista naturae humanae tanta et tam celsa et summa subvectio, ut quo attolleretur altius, non haberet: sicut pro nobis ipsa Divinitas quousque se deponeret humilius, non habuit, quam suscepta natura hominis, cum infirmitate carnis usque ad mortem crucis. ("We say that the Lord of Glory, as man, is made Son of God, is predestined. The teacher of the Gentiles sets it forth clearly at the beginning of his epistles: 'Paul, a servant of Jesus Christ, called to be an apostle and chosen to proclaim the gospel of God (which he had formerly promised by his prophets in the holy Scriptures) concerning his Son, who was made his by the seed of David according to the flesh, who is predestined Son of God in power by the Spirit of sanctification, by the resurrection of the dead.'[26] Jesus therefore is predestined, so that he who was to be son of David according to the flesh would yet be Son of God in power by the Spirit of sanctification, being born of the Holy Spirit and the Virgin Mary. This is the singular susception[27] by which God the Word took man to himself in an ineffable way, so that he might truly and rightly be called Son of God and Son of man together: Son of man because of the man who is taken up by God the Word, and Son of God because of God the only Son, who takes and unites him with himself, lest one believe not in a Trinity but in a quaternity.[28] This exaltation of human nature is predestined to be so high, great, and supreme that there is nothing higher to which it may be exalted, just as the Godhead had nothing lower in which to humble itself for love of us than this human nature, taken on with the infirmities of the flesh to the point of death on the cross.")[29]

26. Rom 1:1–4.

27. The action of taking up, or taking upon oneself; reception, acceptance, or undertaking.

28. Cf. Augustine, *Tractates on the Gospel of John* 78.3:

Let us acknowledge the twofold substance of Christ, the divine, of course, by which he is equal with the Father, the human, than which the Father is greater. But both together are not two, but Christ is one—lest God be a quaternity, not a Trinity! For as man is one, rational soul and flesh, so Christ is one, God and man. And therefore Christ is God, rational soul, and flesh. We profess Christ in all these, Christ in them individually.

In *Tractates on the Gospel of John, 55–111*, trans. John W. Rettig, FC 90, p. 109.

29. [Augustine,] *On the Predestination of the Saints* 15 (original marginal note). See Augustine, *On the Predestination of the Saints*, in *Four Anti-Pelagian Writings*, trans. John A. Mourant and William J. Collinge, FC 86, pp. 254–55.

Now, in this change occasioned by the mystery of the Incarnation in the order and exercise of providence and in the counsel of God upon predestination, we learn a secret of God's counsel, we discover a property of his essence, and we observe a very noteworthy difference between his being and his state, between his cabinet and his council (if we may speak in this way about what is ineffable and express the divine grandeurs by a kind of analogy and proportion to human grandeurs). For God, in his cabinet, is occupied solely in himself and with himself. This cabinet is properly the bosom of the Father, filled solely with the being of God, in which there are only the divine persons, and in which God, blessedly occupied in the thought and love of himself, does not go out beyond his self. For he is the sole object of this occupation, and he dwells in himself by the property of his internal actions, which are vital and immanent. But when God enters into his council, he seems as though to go out beyond his self and his cabinet, by the state and condition of the things that he treats there, given that it belongs to God's council to deliberate upon and provide for only what is beyond God. God enters into his council in order to ordain the affairs of his state and kingdom and to treat of his creatures, even to treat with his creatures. Instead of his treating, in his cabinet, only with the divine persons, in his council he often enters into treaty and deliberation with his creatures themselves, as the holy writings testify to us.[30] In this way he seems as though he goes out beyond and enters a condition unequal to himself.

But in this new council that is held upon the sacred mystery of the Incarnation, we see both a blessed going-forth and a wondrous returning of God into himself, in honor of which we ought to dedicate and consecrate all of our soul's goings forth and returnings to God. For it seems that God goes as though outside of himself, in this subject, in a new manner, which leads the Son of God to qualify this mystery by the name of "going-forth."[31] For he goes out of his greatness to enter into our wretchedness. He goes out of his eternity to enter into a being that is measured by time and limited by the course of the sun. He goes out of his immortality to enter into our mortality. He takes no thought of

30. As, for example, at Gn 3:9–13, 4:6–15, 18:23–33.
31. Jn 16:28.

himself so that he might enter so far into the baseness of created being and unite himself so closely with his creation that God is man and man is God. And therefore, just as he goes in some manner outside of himself, so also does he return as though back into himself by this new counsel and this new mystery. For when he treats of a mystery that contains and encompasses God in himself, the result is that he treats, he ordains and deliberates, not upon the creatures but upon himself, since he is the supreme author and the wondrous subject of this sacred counsel and most high mystery. The eternal Word, going as though outside of himself so that he might enter into the performance of this work that he shares with the other divine persons and that is among those that the theologians call "works of God outside of his self," he returns as though into himself in a way that is distinct and particular to his person, by blessedly accomplishing this mystery and divinely completing it with his own subsistence.[32] By this means, he joins our humanity to his divine person and causes it to return into his Father. He returns there himself, in it and through it, in a new way, by the substantial state of his person and his divine sonship, which, as it is not only relative but all relation to his Father, causes God-Man to be in a perpetual state of relation to the Father: a divine, incomprehensible, and ineffable state, bringing supreme oneness, profound intimacy, and unchanging rest to the eternal Father.

Thus, by contemplating this work we see, follow, and adore eternal God, both as going forth outside of his self and as returning into his self by this new counsel and divine mystery. From this it follows that God, in the circumference of his works and in the movement of his counsels, is like a wondrous circle that is formed by ending at the same point where he started in beginning.[33] For God produces all things by his Word, the Word is the principle by which the world is created, and

---

32. Cf. *Catechism of the Council of Trent* 1.8: "Although the Son alone assumed human nature, yet all the Persons of the Trinity, the Father, the Son, and the Holy Ghost, were authors of this mystery. It is a principle of Christian faith, that whatever God does extrinsically, is common to the three Persons, and that one neither does more than, nor acts without another." In *Catechism of the Council of Trent Published by Command of Pope Pius the Fifth*, trans. Jeremiah Donovan (Baltimore: Lucas Brothers, [1829?]), 38.

33. Cf. Plotinus, *Ennead* 6.5.11, in *Ennead*, trans. A. H. Armstrong, LCL 445, vol. 6, p. 355; Pseudo-Dionysius, *Divine Names* 4.14–4.17, pp. 82–84.

the world is brought to completion in man's production, as the last of God's works.[34] By uniting human nature to his Word, God therefore unites and joins the last of his works to the principle of his works. What is more, since this human nature is the epitome of the universe and the subject in which, by the various degrees and conditions of its being, all creation is recapitulated, it is evident that when human nature is united with God, the universe itself, which came out of God, goes back to God, for in it the universe is reunited and joined with God in this divine mystery. God resolves in his counsels to create the world by his power and also to renew it by his love. The Word, who is the principle of this creation, is the wondrous endpoint to which this regeneration is blessedly accomplished and brought to completion by the ineffable union of his divine person to human nature. All of the new creatures of the new world are gathered in him, not only as their principle and origin but also as their rest and consummation. For if we raise our minds higher in the thought of the divine productions, we will see that not only does God work and produce outside of himself this great universe and excellent creatures, he also works and produces within himself the divine persons, and these productions are all the higher and more wondrous given that God infinitely exceeds all created things. God's first work is the production of his Word, and God's final work is the incorporation of this same Word in human nature. God's first work therefore joins with his last, in the person of the very Word, who is made flesh and brings the works and counsels of God to completion by completing this humanity in the divine mystery of the Incarnation. Thus, we have and adore a God producing within himself, producing there his Word who is his first production, and we have and adore the same God producing outside of himself, producing the man who is his last production and the final work of his hands, on the last of the six days employed in cre-

---

34. Gn 1; Jn 1 and 8; Col 1; Heb 1; Tertullian, *Against Praxeas*; Hilary [*The Trinity*, 3.4–10 and 8.48–50]; Augustine. Chaldean version of Jonathan [i.e., Chaldean (Aramaic) version of the Bible attributed to Jonathan Ben Uzziel (first century BC)]; *In Filio creavit Deus caelum et terram* [In the Son God created heaven and earth]; Thomas [*Summa Theologica*] 1.46.3 ["Whether the Creation of Things Was in the Beginning of Time"] (original marginal note). See Tertullian, *Against Praxeas*, trans. Peter Holmes, ANF 3, pp. 600–602; Hilary, *The Trinity*, 67–73 and 313–15; Aquinas, *Summa Theologica*, 1:244.

ating and forming the world. It is this God who gathers, reduces, and brings all things back to himself, by willing, ordaining, and causing human nature to be accomplished and brought to completion by the subsistence of his Word, and the creation to be joined with the Creator and man with God in oneness of person. In this incomparable work of our Creator and Re-Creator, all things return to the same point they set out from, that is, in God.

As we contemplate our mysteries, then, let us regard God as a wondrous sphere, not only in the sense that even pagan philosophy has acknowledged, but still more in a sense much higher and more exalted, which the light of faith teaches and reveals to us. For God is a sphere in his essence, understanding, and providence, who has his rest in his own center and has motion only within himself (if we may use this term in speaking of a perfectly unchanging being). Since this divine being who is all act, all spirit, and all intelligence has only his view of himself and of created things, the view and understanding that he has of himself is the emanation of his Son, and the view that he has of his creatures is the subject of his arranging and establishing of his providence. That is, the first view gives origin to his emanations, and the second gives occasion and matter to his counsels. In each of these we see that God is like a wondrous circle. For the divine emanations, as they proceed from God, are also brought to completion in God in the production of the Holy Spirit, who is God as are the Father and the Son who produce him. The counsels of God, as they go out from God, return to God in the deliberation that he takes of uniting a created essence with an uncreated person and of establishing in the world this wondrous oneness, which is the center and final point that arrests all his counsels and brings them to completion. For the Scriptures testify to us that he has done all things in his Son, by his Son, and for his Son.[35] God therefore is always himself, that is, God is always infinite and ineffable, always lovable and always adorable. God is always lovable and wondrous in himself, in his counsels, and in his works, and especially in his Work of works, in his Counsel of counsels, in his Mystery of mysteries. It puts an end to the division and disunion that sin set between God and man, it makes a new covenant

---

35. Col 1:15–20.

between God and us, much stronger and more advantageous than the first. It gives and produces in the world the Author of the world, and by an ineffable secret it makes God man and makes man be God in the adorable oneness of the person of the eternal Word with human nature. For this, may they be forever blessed—the eternal Father who ordains, the Holy Spirit who works, and the divine Word who accomplishes this most sacred, profound, and high mystery of the Incarnation.

Discourse 5

On the Communication of God in This Mystery

The more excellent things are, the more the understanding of them is worthy and desirable. It is better, says the great philosopher, to know a little about great things than to know much about lesser things.[1] Let us not be reluctant, therefore, to spend a little time going further into the secrets of our mysteries and knowing the greatness of this one that is God's masterwork, the secret of his secrets, the one that epitomizes and recapitulates all his mysteries—and which is an eternal mystery; in its faith the earth is occupied and in its sight heaven is blessed. For, in contemplating it, there are many great and high points that would all be indeed worthy of most particular consideration. The first that is encountered in the eyes of faith and the Church is the Word that is made flesh. The second is this flesh and humanity that is united with the Word. The third is this Word's subsistence, which is the bond of this oneness. The fourth is this Word's nature, which is the divine essence and which, in and through this person, is united with human nature. The fifth is that in this divine essence that has plurality of persons, the Word alone among the divine persons is the sacred, substantial, and personal bond uniting God with man. But it will be enough for us in this discourse to contemplate the divine Word, both in himself and in this work whose principal part he is—so to speak, for indeed he is as its

---

1. Cf. Aristotle, *Parts of Animals* 1.5 (644b), vol. 1, p. 3. Cf. Thomas Aquinas, *Summa Theologica* 1.1.5, "Whether Sacred Doctrine Is Nobler Than Other Sciences," vol. 1 p. 3.

whole. He is the deep and everlasting source of all its excellences and grandeurs, he is the firmament of all its powers and privileges, he is the influencing cause of its gifts, graces, and preeminences, and he is the wondrous bond of this divine mystery's supreme state.

The eternal Word is produced and producing in the Most Holy Trinity. This belongs to him alone. He has his source, life, and rest in the oneness of the eternal Father, who alone is this Word's Father and principle. He receives from him, in his generation, the oneness of his essence; he is the only Son of the eternal Father, as though spending all of his Father's power to beget. He produces with him the third person of the Trinity, not in difference but in oneness of principle (which is ineffable). In this production of his, he has his endpoint in the oneness of the Holy Spirit, in whom the unmoving movement of the divine emanations ceases and rests as in a center of love and oneness.[2] This oneness, proceeding from the Father and the Word, unites this Word again with the Father by a kind of oneness that is distinct from earlier kinds. For this oneness that is produced is the oneness of the Holy Spirit, implored in all our invocations and prayers: he who in the property of his person is the bond, the love, and the oneness of the Father and the Son.

By these truths, which are not subtle but secure and are all articles of the faith in the doctrine of the most high mystery of the Trinity, we see that the divine Word is wholly encompassed within the divine unities. We adore him in their midst, as on a throne where he has from all eternity his being and life, his rest and glory. We confess him as being most fittingly the principle and subject of the highest mystery of oneness that the divine goodness, power, and wisdom can perform.

To understand this better, let us consider that the eternal Word occupies the middle between the Father and the Holy Spirit in the order of the divine persons. Like the Holy Spirit he receives the oneness of the divine essence, and like the Father he produces the oneness of the Holy Spirit. These two unities are distinct in power and are both to

---

2. Cf. Gregory Nazianzen, Oration 29, "Third Theological Oration, On the Son": "There Unity, having from all eternity arrived by motion at Duality, found its rest in Trinity. This is what we mean by Father and Son and Holy Ghost." In *Select Orations and Letters*, 301.

be observed in the person of the Word. One is in his essence, and the other is in his person, whose principle he is. The one is original and inherent (for all unities have their relation to the oneness of the divine essence, as to the first), and the other proceeds and is originated. The one is neither produced nor producing, but the other is produced, and it constitutes within the Trinity a divine person, who is produced as uniting the other two persons together by a bond worthy of their being and greatness, by an eternal, divine, and personal bond.

It was said of an Ancient that he painted what was impossible to paint, and that he achieved his works so well that he gave life and motion to his brushstrokes and animated what is inanimate.[3] So much did they want to claim him as excellent in rising above art, nature, and oneself. What they ascribed to this famous painter with immoderate words is rightly and truly fitting to the only Son of God, on a much better basis and in a very different subject. For as the Son of God contemplated himself, he wanted by a will and power shared by the divine persons to depict himself in a living and natural way. As the best painter in the universe and the most excellent artist, he wanted to depict what seems impossible, by forming and representing in this mystery the first, most vivid, and express image of the eternal Father. For as the Word beheld himself rightly as the image that the Father formed of himself within himself, he wanted to depict and represent himself in a work of his hands. This is shared by the Father and the Holy Spirit, but I attribute it to the Word by a kind of ascription that is founded in the singularity of this mystery. As the Son is, in the Godhead, the living image and perfect idea of his Father, he desires in this work of his to be as the living and perfect image of himself. According to the preceding discussion, since there are two unities that are distinct in power and that regard him and have so particular a relationship to him—the oneness of essence that he receives, and the oneness of person that he eternally produces—he wants to honor these two unities of his in one work and one counsel of singular oneness. He desires, as it were, to paint and depict them vividly in this matchless work of his, and he desires that

---

3. The reference may be to Apelles. Cf. Pliny, *Natural History* 35, trans. H. Rackham, *LCL* 330. Clement of Alexandria at *Exhortation to the Greeks* 4 mentions Apelles as a master painter. See *Exhortation to the Greeks*, trans. G. W. Butterworth, *LCL* 92, p. 141.

this mystery of his, in its state and circumstances, might be like a kind of honorary tribute to them. So just as we see in the Eucharist that he is himself the representation and image of himself at Calvary, and that by his presence established in this religious sacrament and sacrifice on the Church's altar he continually honors the great sacrifice that he made of himself on the altar of the cross, so also, in this precious work (the first and supreme of his mysteries), he wants to be, as it were, the living image of himself in eternity. He wants to himself honor and represent his being and state in the Godhead in the new being and state that he deigns to take on in our humanity.

This is why, just as he proceeds in eternity and is the first who proceeds from the Father whom St. Dionysius calls the fount and source of Deity, so also does he want to be as though proceeding in the fullness of time.[4] He wants to take on and have here a new being, in honor of the uncreated being that he receives from his Father. He wants to produce a mystery in himself, in which he himself might honor and regard the mystery of his eternal procession. He wants to consecrate in honor of the first divine emanation the first, greatest, and most untellable of his works and mysteries. And just as he is distinct here in the property of the divine emanations—as it belongs to the emanation of the Word to be begotten of the Father, to proceed from him as Father and begetter, and to be constituted by birth and eternal sonship in the order of the divine persons—so also therefore does he will to be begotten in time. He wants to come into the world by birth, not by another way that would seem to be more appropriate to his greatness. He wants to be truly Son of man, as he is Son of God. He wants to receive from his Mother on earth a temporal essence and to preserve it to himself eternally, in honor of the eternal essence that he receives from his Father. And because this essence is one in the Trinity of the persons, he unites himself to one single essence in kind and number, so that he might honor within the order of created things, and imitate within the oneness of this nature deified in him, the oneness of essence that is in the Godhead. So that just as there is but one divine essence, so also there may be but one deified essence that honors by this new state and perfect relationship

---

4. Cf. Pseudo-Dionysius, *Divine Names* 2.7, p. 64.

the oneness of essence that subsists within the Most Holy Trinity. And if we contemplate the Word, not only as God but as God produced and begotten (that is, in the property of his person), we will acknowledge that he is properly, substantially, and personally living, and that by the power and quality of his procession he is produced as living, or rather as life, and as the life that is the source of life in regard to the person of the Holy Spirit who proceeds from him. For this Word proceeds from the living God as his living Son, as receiving from him his own life, and as producing with him the life and love of the Holy Spirit. The Word, then, according to his own understanding, is life, the principle of life, and he is the principle of the life of love. This is why he willed to live by a new life just as he lives by an eternal life. Uniting himself with our humanity, he wanted to constitute by himself, with it and in it, a mystery of life, love, and oneness and to be himself a new life in the universe just as he is life in the bosom of his Father. He wanted to be a new principle of the Spirit of grace and love within time, just as he is the principle that continually produces the Holy Spirit within eternity.

Let us take this thought further and see in this work how the Son of God wanted to reflect again upon himself—that is, upon his matchless and intimate work in eternity, which is the production of the Holy Spirit. For, seeing that this person produced is the bond of the divine persons, he wants his person producing to be the bond of both the divine and human being. This Holy Spirit, this person, who proceeds from him in the Holy Trinity, is the bond that so unites the two divine persons that they are perfectly united in the oneness of the Holy Spirit and yet persist in their personal distinction and plurality. Thus, he wanted his own person to be the sacred bond uniting the two natures in such a way that they persist in their natural distinction and properties and are perfectly united in oneness of person, without confusion and without any division, as the holy councils say. So just as in the first of our mysteries we have and adore one divine person uniting two persons together, so also in the second of our mysteries we have and adore one divine person uniting two natures together: one divine and the other human. It adores, imitates, and regards the oneness of the Holy Spirit, who is the third person in the order of the Holy Trinity and whose property it is to be the eternal bond of the two persons from whom he proceeds and whose personal love and sacred oneness he is. Let us conclude, then, and say that when we contemplate the divine Word, in his emanation or in his person or in his eternal production (that is, in all the points in which we may contemplate him within the Godhead), we see him singularly expressed and vividly represented by the state and the qualities of this divine mystery, which has a perfect relation with what is ineffable in eternity and is a portrait of God as he is.

With these thoughts taken at the source of life and the very being of the eternal Word, we contemplate him as on his throne and in his greatness, and we follow him in spirit as he comes down to our humanity. But we observe that the other divine persons remain in heaven and in glory; he alone humbles himself to earth, so that he alone may be clothed in human nature. This is not without foundation in the conditions corresponding to his person, for we have expressly pointed out not only that he proceeds in eternity, which he has in common with the Holy Spirit, but that he is the first who proceeds, which is distinct and particular to him. Since in this position he is the first to receive the deity that is to be communicated to the world, he also wants to be the first to come and give it to us. And we see that he is the first to come down from heaven in borrowed dress to give himself to the world. The Holy Spirit does not come down to earth to exercise a visible and manifest power until after this mystery and after the Son of God has consummated on earth all the ways in which he wanted to give himself to us by the many mysteries of his life and cross. As in a holocaust, it pleased him to be consumed in the outpouring of his love, to be reborn like a phoenix into a new life—a heavenly and immortal life, a life that prepares us for immortality.[5] As therefore the eternal Word is the first to receive this deity that is to be communicated to the world, he is the first to come and give it to the world. And just as he is the one alone who both receives and gives it in eternity, so also does he want to be the one

---

5. The earliest extant mention of the phoenix as a symbol of long life or immortality is found in Hesiod, *Precepts of Chiron*; see also Herodotus, *History* 2.73, p. 162. The phoenix as a type of Christ's Resurrection was first suggested by Clement of Rome, *Epistle to the Corinthians* 25–27, in *Epistles of St. Clement of Rome and St. Ignatius of Antioch*, trans. James A. Kleist (New York: Newman, 1946), 24–26, then by Tertullian, *On the Resurrection of the Flesh* 13, ANF 3, p. 554.

alone who gives it substantially, in giving himself personally to our humanity. Thus, this mystery is founded in the conditions corresponding to the eternal Word. Thus, by himself and not only by his Father's will, the Word is brought to give himself to the world in a way so precious and singular. Thus, he deigns to regard our frailty, to bear it up; our lowliness, to exalt it; and our humanity, to espouse it.

Just as he abases himself to us and our wretchedness, so also ought we to rise up to him and his grandeurs, so that we might know and adore them. Let us not be reluctant therefore to spend time considering the grandeurs of the only Son of God, since he seems to take no thought of them so that he might humble himself in our humanity. For his grandeurs—eternal grandeurs—are his by birth; let us consider then, in a spirit of honor and love toward him, this primacy of birth and origin that are fitting to the Word. For it says something great and incomprehensible to man, and it is adorable by every created spirit and fundamental to this mystery. It sets a distinction, a reality, a wondrous property in eternity and in the pure and simple being of God. It constitutes an eternal person in the Godhead. It conveys power that produces the third divine person, which makes fitting the serious and profound words of the great St. Hilary: *Divinitatis sacramentum, nativitatis natura consummat.*[6] This birth, forming the circle of the internal emanations, comprehends God's fertility and seals and encompasses the mystery of the Trinity in the efficacy of his production. For just as his procession is the first of the processions, so also is his production the last of the divine productions.

These things are worthy of deep consideration to the one who knows how to understand them, and they would indeed deserve a longer discussion. But let us pass beyond and approach our mystery more closely. Let us say that this birth of the eternal Word gives him the right to many uses, offices, and actions on earth and in heaven, in time and eternity. It regards this high mystery of the Incarnation as its representation and image and as a new state in which the Son of God is made *primogenitus in multis fratribus*, as St. Paul says.[7] This is a new

---

6. Hilary, *The Trinity* 7[.41] (original marginal note). "The nature of the birth completes the mystery of the Godhead." Hilary, *The Trinity*, 271.

7. "Firstborn among many brothers." Rom 8:29.

primogeniture, which imitates, adores, and regards his primacy of birth in the order of the divine emanations. It is an eternal primacy, honored in a hidden and first way in the state of nature and of law by the preeminences that are established in favor of those who are firstborn. For the Author of law and of nature aims only at great things within these base things; he thinks of spiritual things in a law that is gross and carnal. He thinks of divine and eternal things in what is human and temporal, and as he always dedicates his works and laws to himself, his purpose is to express and honor, by these rights and privileges of the children of men, the powers and grandeurs of his only Son. And it seems to me precisely according to the eternal Father's hidden intentions that these rights and benefits that are assigned to the eldest, on the human plane, are so many marks of honor and so many tributes that human birth renders to the divine birth. This is because the eternal Father, who contemplates and looks only upon his Son, or in his Son as in his Word and one mirror, looks upon and honors the birth of God in that of man and causes imperfect law and mute nature to acknowledge tacitly in the things of God what they are not worthy of knowing distinctly. And by the will of its author and legislator to fill up what its incapacity lacks, in this way the human birth renders honor and homage to the primacy of birth and origin that is fitting to his only Son within eternity.

So that all things work together for the honor of what is so high, this only Son, acknowledged and honored by nature and law in this way, also receives various names in holy Scripture that variously describe the greatness of this untellable birth and procession, according to the saying of Isaiah, *Generationem eius qui enarrabit?*[8] Thus, in the prophets he is called the Dayspring,[9] for he is a Sun as well as his Father is—and a Sun emanated from a Sun[10]—of whom he is called the Son

---

8. Is 53[:8] (original marginal note). "Who will explain his generation?"

9. Lk 1[:78–79] (original marginal note). The French noun *orient* is translated as "dawn," "dayspring," "east," or "rising sun." It denotes the rising sun, dawn, or daybreak; the quarter of the sky in which the sun rises; or the eastern part of the world. Thus, in this passage and in discourse 10, Bérulle remarks that "all that is dawn owes tribute and homage" to him who is the Dawn, as does the eastern orientation of our churches and the catechumens who "turn themselves toward the east as a sign of their homage and cleaving" to him.

10. Mal 4[:1–2]; Is 60[:1–3] (original marginal note).

of light even by those who had only a simple intimation and most obscure understanding of him, and also by those who, being his children, are called children of light in his Scriptures, to whom it pleased him to reveal and manifest himself.[11] But by this emanation, it is singular of him that although he is a Sun as his Father is, he is a rising Sun, which his Father is not. This sun that we see rising and setting daily is only his intimation and representation, whereas this Sun that shines in our darkness and rises in our hearts, according to St. John, is the true Dayspring whom we ought always look to and adore.[12] Toward him also, from the time that his birth was made known to the world, our temples are directed, which are the public and solemn places of our adoration. Thus, he is the Dayspring in the Godhead; he is the Dayspring in eternity. He is so much the Dayspring that he is without beginning, a Dayspring therefore eternal, but he desires also to be our Dayspring in the fullness of time. And thus, as a new Dayspring in our humanity, he comes to take his setting in our mortality.

Similarly, he is called Flower and Shoot, that is, the flower and shoot of the Godhead. This is the name that the Hebrew language gives him in Isaiah and that is preserved for him in the rich and blessed version of the Church.[13] This is the term that St. Dionysius calls him by in his *Divine Names*, which corresponds to him rightly and justly.[14] For the flower is the first ornament that the sun gives to nature when its course raises it over our hemisphere and brings it closer to us. The flower is what the tree, by its fertile power, first sprouts and produces in the amenity of spring, when the earth begins to be covered and laden with its offspring. The flower is the first of nature's productions and what the womb of the earth first germinates and unfolds by the heavens' gentle influences. So also the Word is the first emanation of God; he is the one whom the bosom of the Father first conceives and produces in eternity. He is the one who first proceeds from this sacred stock. That he is the firstborn of God even the Platonists say, for they learned this from our sacred writings, in which we read that he is the first fruit of the divine

---

11. Lk 16:8; Jn 12:36; Eph 5:8; 1 Thes 5:5.
12. 2 Pt 1:19; Rv 22:16.
13. Is 11[:1]; Is 4[:2] (original marginal note).
14. Pseudo-Dionysius, *Divine Names* 2.7, p. 64.

fertility.¹⁵ He therefore also wanted as first fruit—first fruit not of the earth but of the very Godhead—to be offered to the Godhead and to put himself in the state of being presented to God as the first fruit of all that is and ever will proceed from God. I call him flower, shoot, and fruit together, for what is scattered and divided in created things is brought together in God. The Word is fruit as to his procession's perfection and maturity. He is flower as to beauty, which rightly accords with his person and is ascribed to the Word not only by our teachers but even by the Platonists, our imitators, who perceived the intimations of our mysteries in their representations and saw something of their greatness in our prophets' figures of speech. And he is flower and shoot as to his power to produce a second person of the Godhead, because just as fruit comes from the flower and shoot, so also from the Son comes the Holy Spirit, who is the second person proceeding in eternity.

Now, from this comes a noteworthy distinction between the two persons who proceed, which is relevant to our discussion and causes us to come down precisely on our mystery's point and center, teaching us one of the principal reasons for which the Word, and not the Holy Spirit, enters into the work of the Incarnation to accomplish it by his hypostasis. Because the Word is the living source of the Holy Spirit who proceeds from him as well as from the Father, and who is called, from this point of view, the Spirit of the Son and the Spirit of truth, he dedicates to the Father both himself and this Spirit as being emanated from him. For it is his distinctive feature and his state in eternity to be an eternal and substantial relation of himself, and, as a result, of all that proceeds from him, toward the eternal Father as toward the principle and source of his being and of all original being. By contrast, the Holy Spirit, who is produced and not producing in the Godhead, does not

---

15. According to a teaching that began among Alexandrian Jews and was taken up by the early Church, Plato is said to have received his wisdom from Moses. This idea was revived by the Renaissance humanists. An associate of Bérulle, Pierre Coton, wrote that the Septuagint was in fact the second Greek translation of the Hebrew scriptures: "The first was that which Plato had, before the Macedonian monarchy, which Clement of Alexandria refers to." Coton, *Institution catholique* (Paris, 1610), 316–17, quoted in Dagens, *Bérulle et les origines de la restauration catholique (1575–1611)* (Bruges: Desclée de Brouwer, 1952), 25.

have the right to dedicate the Son to the Father nor give him to the world. If he had united himself with a created being, he would not have been able to employ and apply the work of the Word as something his own in this high and singular manner. For the Word is produced from the Father alone, he is sent by his Father alone, and he works by him alone, just as he receives from him alone his being and his life.

But since the only Son of God is the Holy Spirit's principle and source, he has power to dedicate him to the Father. He has power to give him to the world and to send him upon his apostles. He has power to apply him to the work of this mystery of his and to employ his work there as something whose origin is his own, which is the foundation of all that the Son works by the Holy Spirit insofar as he gives and communicates to him the power and deity by which he works. This removes all impropriety and imperfection in these lofty words and strong expressions that we have used in describing the relationship of the Holy Spirit to the Son in his holy workings, since what is only imperfect in created things is found, by a great marvel, to be without imperfection in divine and uncreated things. For it is marvelous that in the oneness and simplicity of God, there is plurality: plurality without division. It is marvelous that there is procession: procession without sequence. It is marvelous that this procession is without majority and superiority in the one and without minority and inferiority in the other.[16] And it is also marvelous that this sending, this application, this activity among the persons is without subordination; but it is founded in the greatness, singularity, and deity of their principle and origin. To encounter so many marvels is so worthy of God, so fitting to God, so natural to God that it is no longer marvelous that there be so many marvels together in the being of an infinite majesty—the being that is the principle of all being and the source and fullness of so many marvels.

Let us conceive of divine things therefore according to their divineness and not according to our baseness. Let us conceive of these uses, actions, and words without the imperfection of human reason. Rising up above ourselves, let us go from marvel to marvel and enter into wonder

---

16. *Majority* and *minority* are to be understood here in the sense of status according to age.

as we see that in the greatness of our mysteries and the sublimity of our faith we have and acknowledge two eternal and divine principles: not as the Manichean does, the one good and the other evil, the one in direct opposition to the other, but both good, both sources of divine goodness. The one first, the other second, but both equal, both divinely bound together, both regarding and loving each other mutually, and each in perfect sympathy with the other. The one subsisting in the Godhead only, and the other subsisting in the Godhead and humanity both. The one producing from all eternity, and the other producing for all eternity. The one is the eternal Father, the Principle-without-any-principle, alone producing and not produced, in whom we adore an authority (to speak according to the great teacher of France)[17] and a majesty that produces all that is produced beyond the Godhead and even within the Godhead. The other is the only Son of God, the father of the age to come, the true principle of life in the fullness of time through the sacred mystery of the Incarnation, and who is furthermore, in eternity, the principle of a divine person, but a principle that itself originates in another person, and who is, to speak according to the Council, "God from God, light from light."[18] He is God both producing and produced, which is incomprehensible, and in him we adore an infinite authority and dignity. He divinely dedicates to the eternal Father himself and everything without exception that proceeds from him, as his Holy Spirit, or proceeds and is dependent on him, as all that is created. Thus, it belongs to the Word in his eternity to be constantly dedicating to his Father the persons proceeding from his Father (that is, himself and the Holy Spirit) and to thus be worthily and divinely regarding, loving, and honoring, in the relation of himself and of all that proceeds from him, the most high and sublime majesty of the eternal Father, whom those who are nothing do not want to acknowledge, serve, and adore on earth.

As we contemplate the birth, greatness, and office of the eternal Word, we adore his being, his life, and his state in God his Father and his power that produces a divine and uncreated person within eternity.

17. Hilary, *The Trinity* 9 (original marginal note). Hilary discusses the Father's authority, and Christ's relationship with it, throughout this ninth book.
18. Nicene Creed, set forth at the First Council of Nicaea (325 AD). See Percival, *The Seven Ecumenical Councils of the Undivided Church*, 3.

We marvel at his birth and primacy in the order of the divine emanations, by which he dedicates to God the Father in eternity both himself and the Spirit who emanated from him. We acknowledge his right, by the condition of this birth of his, to place himself in a divine mystery, in which he may divinely, substantially, and personally dedicate to God's homage all that is created, just as in the Godhead he dedicates to God his Father all that proceeds and is uncreated. In this way, he is led and prompted by himself, that is, by his personal properties and perfections, to enter into a new state to his Father's glory and to accomplish this new mystery. For he is the first to emanate from God, and he desires to be in a state and condition by his human nature to be offered to him as first fruits, in recognition of all that universally proceeds from him. He is the one alone who has emanated from the Father alone, and he wants to be the one alone who constitutes by himself this new mystery. He wants to be the one alone who adores divinely and personally in his humanity the sole Principle-without-any-principle of all things, who is his eternal Father, the one whom St. Dionysius calls the origin and principle of all deity. He is the living image that the eternal Father produces in contemplating himself, and he wants to be, in a new manner, an image that lives and speaks of God's grandeurs and that by a divine power restores in us the image and likeness of the Godhead that was impressed on our nature and effaced by sin. He is the imprint of the Father's substance, and the Father gives and communicates his own substance to him by impression. He wants to be the seal and imprint impressing his own essence and subsistence on human nature.[19] In honor of his Father who impresses him on himself and who eternally gives him being, he desires to give us this being. He wants to apply and impress himself on created nature like a divine imprint. He is the uncreated Word by whom all things were formed, and he wants to be the incarnate Word by whom they may all be re-formed and raised to a greater dignity. He is the only Son of the Father, and he wants to create for him by his power, beget for him by his love, obtain for him by his merits, and give to him by his spirit many children who long for his glory. He wants to make his own natural sonship a living source of adoptive sonship. This makes him

---

19. Cf. Hilary, *The Trinity* 8.44, p. 310.

father and principle in the order of grace and of glory. It gives him glorious titles, rights, and privileges and gives us most glorious teachings. We must summarize these teachings before we go further, and from the Son of God's state in regard to his Father we must learn what our state toward him is meant to be. In the high and sublime life of the only Son toward the Father we must contemplate the life that we are to begin on earth and consummate in heaven, drawing the first brushstrokes and features of our perfection upon so accomplished a model, and forming ourselves in the life of the Spirit and in all virtue upon so divine a life and so precious and excellent an example.

For, just as the eternal Word proceeds in his divine being and has God for Father, so also do we proceed in our supernatural being (although in another way) and must acknowledge the Son of God as our father, from whom we all take our being and the life of grace. For this reason, he is given the name "father of the age to come" among the titles and qualities that were foretold in the oracle of his coming. Just as the Word and eternal Son of God always regards his Father because he is his Father, so also ought we to have a perpetual regard toward the Son, because he is our father. This regard of ours toward him should be one of supreme honor, most powerful love, and entire and absolute submission, desiring that our whole being might be eye and spirit so that we might be wholly devoted and occupied in this spiritual and divine regard toward the resource and new principle of our being. Just as the only Son of God has a constant relation toward his Father of all that he is, and his being and life consist in this relationship—even, to speak precisely, his life is nothing but a life that is substantially and personally relative of what he is, toward his sole principle—so also the use of our being and life should be totally devoted to the complete and absolute relation of all that we are, in the order of nature and of grace, by his eternal mercies. In the works of profane writers, fabled loves transformed people into other substances. How much more ought we to desire that the power of him who truly transforms things in their nature might be employed upon us, and that by virtue of his powerful love our being's substance might change its state and condition so that we might be blessedly converted in a pure relation toward him, in homage, love, and imitation of his personal substance, life, and subsistence that is wholly relative toward the eternal Father. Just as the Son of God so proceeds from the Father, regards the Father, and dedicates himself to the Father, that he is, notwithstanding this, most intimate in his Father and resides in him—*A matrice excessit, non recessit*, as the learned Tertullian says—so also should we be inseparably joined with the Son of God as the vine shoot is to the vine and as he himself is inseparably joined with his Father.[20] We should be and remain perpetually in him, just as he is and remains in his Father. We should always be living and working by him and for him, just as he lives and works by his Father, for he is both the principle and the end of our being and our life.

And finally, as the only Son of God beholds himself as unchangeable in his being, he wills to change his condition for his Father's glory and be made man so that he might live a kind of life in which he might suffer and work, which he cannot do in the Godhead. He even wills to preserve this new being always, to honor God his Father not only by his works and sufferings during the course of his pilgrim life on earth but also by a new and permanent state in heaven and eternity. Following his example, then, we should change our life and condition, and, to the glory of him who makes such a striving over his greatness, we should make a striving over ourselves, our activities, and our passions. We have two ways of serving him: one by actions alone and the other by state. We should choose this way that is abiding, secure, and permanent. We should embrace a manner of life that may of itself honor God's majesty and be the origin of many holy and virtuous actions, in honor of the state and life that the Son of God enters into by the sacred mystery of the Incarnation and in which he continues in the heavens eternally. All of these points and singular relationships are well worthy of exercising Christian thought and piety. They are like so many secure foundations, which establish the relationship that we should have and claim to have with the Son of God by the humble state of servitude that we vow to him, in honor of the relationship that he has with his

---

20. Tertullian, *Against Praxeas* (original marginal note). "He went forth from the bosom, he did not withdraw from it." The text, *A matrice non recessit, sed excessit* is found in Tertullian, *Apology* 21: "He did not withdraw from the bosom, but went forth." See *Apology*, trans. Sydney Thelwall, *ANF* 3, p. 34. Tertullian does write on a similar theme in *Against Praxeas* 8, p. 602.

Father by the wondrous state of his divine and eternal sonship. But it is enough to point this out here in passing; the practice and breadth of it is addressed elsewhere.

Let us continue the thread of this discussion in honor of the eternal Word, and let us observe that as we form ourselves like this in the practice of these divine relations, we honor the only Son of God by expressing his life and state within our own. By honoring him we honor his Father in him, who has given him to us through the outpouring and abundance of his love. It is a chain of love and honor, binding us to the Father and to the Son and causing us to imitate and adore the mutual love and honor that is between them. For the Son of God loves and honors his Father in looking upon him as his origin, and the Father loves and honors his Son in communicating to him his being and life and by impressing these on him. These two divine persons honor one another with an eternal honor, a mutual regard, and a mutual love. The life of the Father and the Son is therefore a life of honor, love, and contemplation, truly worthy of the greatness, dignity, and deity of these two eternal lovers. As these two divine persons contemplate, love, and honor each other in eternity in this mutual way, they also honor one another by a new way of honor in the new mystery of the Incarnation, which, to speak precisely, is a mystery, state, and exercise of mutual honor and love of the Father toward the Son, of the Son toward the Father, and of the Father again toward himself. For just as the eternal Father honors his Son in the Godhead in giving him divine being and life, so also does he honor him in our humanity, in various ways. He honors him by proclaiming him by the law and his prophets to be the sovereign, salvation, and light of the world. He honors him by employing the effects of his power and his greatest marvels so that he might be acknowledged as his only Son and as his equal in power, greatness, and majesty. He honors him by setting him forth as a visible god upon the earth and by manifesting his divine greatness under the veil of his mortality.[21] He honors him by appointing him within the ages as the principle of life, grace, and glory, just as he himself in eternity is the

---

21. Cf. Nicholas Copernicus, *On the Revolutions* 1.10: "[Hermes] the Thrice Greatest labels it [the sun] a visible god." Trans. Edward Rosen (Warsaw: Polish Scientific, 1978), 22.

principle of divine and uncreated life in the two persons proceeding from him. He honors him by emptying himself of all use and exercise of judging the world, in order to give this power to his Son, Son of God, Son of man, and to make him the universe's sole and sovereign judge. And finally, he honors him by filling his human nature with all the effects of deity and all the states of glory that can be communicated to him and that are properly owed to the man whose state is that of personal oneness with God himself. In this we must observe that in honoring his Son like this, the eternal Father honors himself, and that just as all proceeds from him, so also by a divine circle all returns to him, and the honor that he gives to his Son returns to himself. For in giving his Son the power, authority, and position of father toward us, and in making him our head and our second Adam, he gives to himself in a sense the new position of head of a subject as honorable as is Jesus Christ our Lord, who confesses and adores God as his Father and head—as his Father in his deity and as his head in his humanity, according to this divine oracle: *Caput Christi Deus*.[22]

We see clearly, then, as we follow so many divine relations and truths, that by an excellent means, a divine state, a new fatherhood, and an eternal mystery, God honors the divine and eternal being and name of Father that he has in regard to his only and eternal Son. It remains then to explain how, in the work of the Incarnation, the Son honors his Father. For it is evident that he honors him in honoring his own birth and eternal sonship, since it is in regard to it and it alone that he is father in eternity. He honors this birth by taking on a new birth and sonship in the world and by impressing his divine sonship on our humanity by his subsistence. He also honors his eternal Father by establishing himself in a state and singular mystery in which, being Son, he becomes the serf and slave of the Father, as is said elsewhere. In being made man, he wants to render tribute and homage to the eternal Father for all that is created, and honor for all that he has received from him in eternity. Still possessing the being of his deity, he offers God to God, since he offers himself who holds the rank of divine person in the Trinity. Being truly and perfectly God-Man and Man-God, he is

---

22. 1 Cor 11[:3] (original marginal note). "The head of Christ is God."

assuredly the most worthy subject that God's power may ever produce, and he prepares for him the greatest sacrifice, the most holy host, and the most wondrous holocaust that God's holiness will ever be able to receive.

Just as this mystery is most high in itself and in all that belongs to it, so also all is most singular, august, and divine in it, both in its causes and in its circumstances. The Holy Trinity as a whole is divinely and singularly occupied in establishing this work that is also distinctively his work. It treats of it in the highest and most secret of its councils, without admitting any other to this sacred council. As God, the eternal Father ordains it, and as Father he is the first principle of this divine work. For it is he who as Father, and as only Father, sends his Son alone to accomplish it. The only Son of God comes into the world, not through his gifts or through his effects as before, but in his own person and in a manner that is wholly new and unknown on earth and in heaven. In the time ordained by God, which the Scriptures call "the fullness of time"[23] (for reasons that will be explained another time), in the light of letters and in the flowering of the most powerful empire,[24] the Light and Power of the eternal Father willed to be seen and felt upon the earth. In the month, therefore, on the day, and at the moment chosen by divine wisdom, heaven opens and the eternal Word descends to the earth to accomplish this mystery himself. He comes into the world four thousand years after having created it, in order to be one of its inhabitants, to honor it by his coming, to sanctify it by his presence, to establish in it his power, to be the Center, Sun, and Savior of the world, and to cause the rays of his love, greatness, and mercy to shine in it forever. Each of the three persons of the Godhead makes this work his own by fitting and distinct operations. Thus, just as the Father sent his Son, so also, before descending to the earth to accomplish this great work that had not yet been and that will never have its peer, the Son sends the person of the Holy Spirit, as being his by origin. He does this to prepare, before his coming, this work that is his own work in so many respects and on such singular bases; so divine is this work in its

---

23. Gal 4:4.

24. Rome's military and cultural apogee occurred from the first century BC to the first century AD.

substance, principles, and circumstances. For the angel who announces it to the Virgin says specifically, *The Holy Spirit will come upon you*[25]— that is, if we follow this sacred word's specific meaning, not God simply in his deity that is common to the three persons, but this particular person who is emanated from the Word, this third person subsisting in the Godhead, this person who is called, in distinction to the others, the Holy Spirit. This Spirit of love and oneness, in his own person, contributes to this work that is also a work of divine love and oneness. By a special appropriation that is founded in his love and oneness, he arranges the matter that is to be actuated by the divine being, by drawing this body from the Virgin's substance, forming and arranging it, and rendering it capable of receiving not the power only but the person and subsistence of the Word. He wills to make him gloriously alive and consubsisting in his Godhead.

Here we are brought, by the perfections and conditions that are fitting to the Word, right into his work and mystery. By the properties and productions of the divine persons, we are brought to the production of this divine work. We have come to the blessed day, the remarkable day in our calendar, in which God, coming down from his greatness in his goodness and from his righteousness in his mercy, wills to unite himself with our humanity. Here we are at the moment, the precious moment in time and in eternity, the moment to which all our moments should be dedicated, the moment in which this great God, as though taking no thought of himself so that he might remember us, desires to be clothed in our mortality. Here we are at the point of the wondrous state in which God enters into our wretchedness and man enters into the grandeurs of God. For the Word is made flesh, God is made man, man becomes God, and God is made man in order to make men gods.[26] This is a great saying, expressing in few words mysteries that are most high, which thought cannot adequately adore nor tongue

---

25. Lk 1[:35] (original marginal note).

26. Ps 82:6; Jn 10:34. Cf. Athanasius, *On the Incarnation* 8.54, p. 93; Irenaeus, *Against the Heresies* 3.19, vol. 3, pp. 92–93; Clement of Alexandria, *Exhortation to the Greeks* 1, p. 23; Origen, *Contra Celsum* 3.28, trans. Henry Chadwick (Cambridge: Cambridge University Press, 1953), 146; Augustine, Sermon 166.4, in *Sermons 148–183*, trans. Edmund Hill, *WSA*, pt. 3, vol. 5, p. 209.

adequately express! What shall I say, readers, yet what shall I not say? I must say to you with one of the Church's oracles and in his words: *Suscepi tractanda divina homo, spiritalia carnalis, aeterna mortalis. Ubi aperitur, pascor vobiscum, ubi clauditur, pulso vobiscum.*[27] I knock therefore at the door of uncreated and incarnate Wisdom, and I ask him for his light and leading: *Ut loquar infirmus fortia, parvus magna, fragilis solida.*[28]

What is stronger than this mystery, which destroys sin, conquers the devil, overcomes God in his anger, and holds him captive willingly in love toward the one who offended against him? What is greater than this mystery, which draws man out of nothingness, resurrects him in glory, exalts him to heaven forever, and, in making men gods by grace—as he himself says, is brought to completion as though in its principal subject, in a Man-God, not by grace but by subsistence and in oneness of divine person?[29] What is more certain and sure than this mystery, since the sins that inundated the earth for four thousand years and rose up to heaven were not able to keep it from being accomplished? After it was accomplished, the horror of a deicide could not dissolve it—the horror, I say, of a deicide that covered the heavens with darkness, eclipsed the sun, disturbed the universe, and caused horror to insensible nature. For, despite this calamity and this merciless attempt that was made upon the life of a God, the state of this mystery remained subsisting and unalterable in the parts that were separated from the humanity, and it was made new in the reunion of the same parts and in the same humanity that was made new by the glorious resurrection. It was made new so that it might never again be altered or interrupted for a single moment. For at the point of the resurrection, the only Son of God gives this humanity a new life, a heavenly life, an immortal life.

---

27. Augustine, *Tractates on the Gospel of John* 18.5 [18.1] (original marginal note). "I have spoken to you of divine things, I who am but a man; of things wholly spiritual, I who am carnal; of eternal truths, I who am subject to death. If the truth is opened to me, it nourishes me along with you; if it remains closed, I knock along with you." See *Tractates on the Gospel of John, 11–27*, trans. J. W. Rettig, FC 79, p. 125.

28. Augustine, *Tractates on the Gospel of John* 48.10 [10.11] (original marginal note). "In my weakness, I set forth to you a strong doctrine; in my meanness, great teachings; in my fragility, firm truths." See *Tractates on the Gospel of John, 28–54*, p. 236.

29. Jn 10[:34]. *Ego dixi dii estis* (original marginal note). "I have said, you are gods."

He chooses it to be the companion of his glory, he sets it on his throne and at the right hand of his Father. He sets himself within it as on a throne, as on the most worthy throne, the most eminent and exalted there is, apart from the bosom and divine essence of the Father. God will dwell in this humanity eternally, in such a way that man will be God for as long as God is God, and the Son of man will be Son of God for all eternity. For such is the supreme Majesty's good pleasure, to give himself to man by an indissoluble and eternal union. And such must be man's good pleasure also, to give himself to God with such power and efficacy that no solvent in the world could be capable of dissolving and rupturing this union. We want this to be so, O Jesus my Lord, and we offer our vows and wishes to your infinite Majesty! Let us be yours, as you are ours! Let us be yours forever, as you are ours forever! Let us be your members and you be our head, as God himself is your head! Let us live in you and through you, as you live in your Father and through your Father! Let us be capable of you, filled with you, just as you are capable of God, filled with God in all fullness! Be our all, our sufficiency, our fullness, just as the fullness of the deity rests blessedly in you! And thus, living and established in you who are our life and our firmament, by your grace may we say forever, truly, in the spirit and words of your apostle, *Who will separate us from the love of Christ? etc.*[30]

30. Rom 8[:35] (original marginal note).

Discourse 6

On the Communication of God in This Mystery

There are three mysteries that serve as our faith's principal exercise and object, differentiating and separating it from the academies and religions that have been introduced and set forth in the world, and that testify that it is truly divine, singular, and excellent, above the light and capacity of nature. The first is the mystery of the Most Holy Trinity. By its power we were created and formed, in its belief we are now baptized and justified, and in its enjoyment we will one day be glorified. The second is the Incarnation, in which human nature, singularly exalted, is united with God its first principle and joined with him in a new, holy, and wondrous way, and, as is said elsewhere, in a way whose state was previously unknown to earth and heaven. By this new and supreme life and holiness that has been established on the earth, the rule of death is destroyed, sin is set at nought, and mortals are declared children of God, capable of eternal life, heirs of heaven, and coheirs of Jesus Christ, receiving from him his grace and glory as in exchange for our nature that he deigned to take on among us. The third is the Eucharist, in which God gives and renders to us this same nature that he deigned to take on from us, as a sacred deposit. Having received it from us and dignified it in himself, he gives it back to us in abundance. For in this nature, he gives us his grace, his Spirit, and his deity, and by his divine and sacred touch he impresses on our bodies (as the Fathers say) a power that prepares us for the glorious resurrection and heavenly life.

He communicates to the whole substance of man a new and supernatural right, a secret and wondrous power, a vital and seminal quality of rebirth and incorruption, of resurrection and immortality.

These three mysteries are excellent and divine, profound and inscrutable, and precious and distinctive to the Christian religion, which is preeminent in having in its state and practice a trinity of mysteries that subsist in the Church's faith and doctrine and adorn and enhance her belief—just as there is a trinity of infused and supernatural qualities that adorn, enhance, and complete the powers and faculties of the faithful soul, and a Trinity of divine and eternal persons that shine forth and subsist in the Godhead. This trinity of mysteries is a sacred number, which in this way renders the Church's public and solemn profession august and venerable. In the economy of our faith, it renders a supreme honor and homage to the Trinity of the divine persons, whom these mysteries regard and honor in a singular way. For just as the soul serves the most high, august, and sacred Trinity inwardly by the three infused gifts and practices of faith, hope, and charity, so also does the Church acknowledge and adore it outwardly by the trinity of mysteries that the Church makes known and announces to men for their salvation and to the glory of these three divine, wondrous, and adorable persons. One of these three great mysteries is distinctive and particular to each of them. For in the Trinity, the Father is considered as a fontal Deity (to speak with the one who is called the Apostle of France):[1] the one who subsists in himself, the one without principle and origin, and the one principle-without-principle of the two other divine persons, that is, of all that proceeds in the Godhead. In the Incarnation, the Word is adored as the one who subsists in humanity and the one who himself works the salvation of the world in and through this humanity. And in the Eucharist, the Holy Spirit is devoutly and solemnly invoked, so that by his power the common and everyday substance of the species that are offered on the altar may be changed and transformed into the excellent and precious substance of the body and blood of the only Son of God.

It is particular to these mysteries that just as the divine essence is and rests in each one of the divine persons, so also the deity itself is

---

1. Dionysius, *Divine Names* 2[.7] (original marginal note). See *Complete Works*, 64. (This author was often identified with Denis of Paris, patron saint of France.)

encompassed within each one of these mysteries: whether in oneness of essence as in the Trinity, in property of person as in the Incarnation, or in concomitance as in the Eucharist.[2] This makes them singularly august, exalted, and adorable. It is also their distinctive feature to regard Jesus Christ and men and to have an excellent and singular relationship to these two particular objects. For the Trinity looks upon Jesus Christ as Son, as only Son of God, which is his first and greatest quality. The Incarnation looks upon him as father, and even from his infancy the prophet calls him the father of the age to come.[3] The Eucharist looks upon him as spouse, since in it he is joined with each one of us, not only by his gifts and favors but still more by himself and in his own person, with his precious body and blood being the perfect bond of him with us and of us with him. Likewise, the Trinity looks upon man as its image and likeness and as its masterwork in the universe. The eternal Word, in the Incarnation, looks upon human nature as the object of his divine love, the subject of his eternal covenant, and the being that is to be divinely and eternally united with his eternal and divine essence. And Jesus Christ, in the Eucharist, looks upon man as his dwelling place and temple, the living temple of his body, living and shining forth in glory.

It is also precious and singular of these three mysteries that they relate to each other as well as to a certain center of excellence and perfection, and that they are linked together by a mutual relation and reciprocal bond. The Son of God speaks of this in several places, and particularly in St. John (chapter 17). After instituting the holy Eucharist and communicating the apostles, he divinely dedicates the oneness that he has with his Father in the most high mystery of the Trinity, and the oneness that joins him to us in the sacred mystery of the Incarnation, to the oneness that he wants us all to have with him through the Eucharist and with his Father through him. This sets the foundation and establishes in the world the oneness of grace and spirit that he desires for his apostles and his Church.

To better understand these sublime truths, we must consider how in the Holy Trinity the Father's deity resides in substance and essence

---

2. Concomitance is the coexistence of the body and blood of Christ in each of the Eucharistic elements.

3. Is 9[:6] (original marginal note).

in the person of the Son by means of the eternal generation, according to these sacred words of the Son of God: *Ego in Patre et Pater in me* ("I am in my Father, and my Father is in me").[4] Following this, the same deity of the Son of God resides substantially and personally in his humanity by means of the Incarnation. Thus, the one in whom the Father resides is resident in this sacred humanity that is united with the Son of God in oneness of person, just as the Son is united with his Father in oneness of essence. And thirdly, the living and glorious body of the Son of God resides substantially and bodily in our earthly and mortal bodies by means of the Eucharist, in which we receive the living Son of God. In him we live with a holy and divine life, just as he lives by his Father, according to what he himself says in St. John (chapter 6). And in this way, we already enter into an excellent communication with the Godhead; and in this world already, by certain degrees and grades, we are united in substance with God.

This is what the Son of God, on his final day and in his holy prayer, speaks of to his Father with these holy words: *I have given them the glory that you gave me, so that they may be one, as we are one. I am in them and you in me, so that they may be consummated in one.* And in the preceding verse: *I pray for them, so that they may be one, just as you are in me, O my Father, and I am in you, so that they also may be one in us.*[5] Sacred words and oracles of the eternal Word, worthy of being engraved on heaven and earth by the hand of angels and men! Words and oracles that express these three mysteries to us, and in this trinity of mysteries, like divine knots and links that are divinely tied and interlaced with one another, God the Father joins substantially the body and nature of mortal and earthly men to the supreme essence of his deity, in this life already, through the humanity of his Son! It is as though we had in these divine mysteries not the feigned and fabled power of a profane love that links gods and men together, bringing the false gods down to earth and feignedly exalting men to heaven in order to set them as shining stars in the firmament; but the true and holy power of an ineffable and incomprehensible love that links God and men together, produces a real and true humbling of the Son of God, who is God

---

4. Jn 10:38, 14:10–11.
5. Jn 17:21–22.

himself, and makes him man in order to make us gods. Through him, as by a strong and powerful chain, the eternal Father raises and draws us up to heaven, to the heaven of his deity.[6] It is a chain of love, for he speaks of it in this way himself.[7] It is a chain that draws us up and keeps us united with the Father by the Son, and with the Son by himself and by his sacred mysteries. It is a precious chain, exceeding all estimation and value; a sacred chain, blessedly and devoutly composed of the principal mysteries of the Christian religion; a divine and unalterable chain of oneness and charity, the charity of the Father and the Son toward men, of the Father's oneness with the Son in the Trinity, of the Son's oneness with human nature in the Incarnation, and of the oneness of the body of Jesus Christ with us in the Eucharist. It is a precious chain, sacred and divine, in which consist the greatest secret, the strongest tie, and the principal motive power of the true God's purposes, counsels, and works toward men. It is a chain made up of these three mysteries, like sacred and divine knots, like strong and wonderful links, by which the eternal Father draws us to himself and lifts us up forever to this heavenly kingdom, whose king is Trinity, whose law is charity, whose extent is eternity.

Pursuing these high and sublime thoughts and leaving for another time and discourse that which concerns the Eucharist, let us adore in our mysteries two divine, wondrous, and ineffable communications: that of the divine essence to the divine persons, which constitutes the most high mystery of the Trinity; and that of the divine person to human nature, which establishes the most humble, lovable, and divine mystery of the Incarnation. In the first communication, the divine essence that is perfectly one and perfectly communicable (which is a great secret among the secrets of the Godhead), is communicated in actuality to the divine persons. In the second, a divine person who is incommunicable in the Godhead is most intimately communicated to a created nature, in such a way that this person becomes just one subject, God and man. In this communication there is a most powerful application, most intimate union, and most perfect appropriation of the Word to this humanity and of this humanity to the Word. He makes it divine

---

6. Cf. Pseudo-Dionysius, *Divine Names* 3.1, p. 68.
7. This may refer to Jn 12:32.

and wondrous in person, exalts it above all that is created, places it in the supreme and singular order of the hypostatic union, and establishes it forever on the throne of the Godhead.

This deserves to be considered more attentively, explained more fully, and set forth more plainly. Let us consider, then, who he is who communicates himself in this way to human nature, what kind of communication and union he takes up with this nature, and what the result and portion is that belongs to this nature by virtue of this ineffable union and communication.

The more the one who deigns to enter into communication and union is powerful and exalted in his greatness and quality, and the more the one who receives it is of humble condition, the more this communication is worthy of being considered, valued, and honored. And if the communication that he makes is of something that is great in itself, dear and intimate to the one who communicates it, this communication will all the more powerfully move the heart with love and gratitude. If in addition it is abundant and lasting, it delights the mind in astonishment, wonder, and thankfulness. For the ineffable communication that is in this mystery will never end and will endure for eternity. It brings such an abundance of glory, greatness, and good that it encompasses within itself all that is excellent within created and uncreated being. It is the eternal Word who enters into communication with human nature. He is the second person of the Trinity, but equal to the first. He is the splendor and power of the eternal Father. He is the uncreated being who unites himself with created being, the King of glory with nothingness, God with man. In this union and communication, God does not communicate just his outward favor, his benevolence, his infused grace, and these precious gifts that follow and accompany it (that is, what proceeds from him and is inferior to him). Instead, he gives and communicates an uncreated being to this created being, a divine and eternal substance to a human and temporal substance, and his own person to our humanity.

We must take up this discussion at a higher point so that we might better understand the greatness of this mystery, the state of substantial and hypostatic grace that is communicated in it, and the singular gift that God makes of himself to this human nature (which the Son of God suggests and emphatically shows in these sacred words to the Samaritan woman: *Si scires donum Dei, et quis est qui loquitur tecum*),[8] and so that we might recognize what this august and sacred presence and this special dwelling place is that God has in this humanity. It is a presence and indwelling that is distinct and different from that which he has in heaven and on earth, in all his creatures, and even in the things that are most holy and sacred and more closely and finely joined with him by his grace and glory. God dwells properly in himself and needs no place for his dwelling; the place that is fitting to him and worthy of him is himself, where he dwells from all eternity before the creation of the world. It is fantasy to want God to dwell in imaginary places. His greatness deserves a better abode, and nothing is worthy of him except himself. He is himself a place for himself: *Ante omnia Deus erat solus, et ipse sibi, et mundus et locus, et omnia*, the learned Tertullian authoritatively states.[9] *Antequam faceret Deus caelum et terram, in se habitabat Deus, apud se habitabat, et apud se est Deus*, as the great St. Augustine blessedly and learnedly says.[10] Before going further in this discussion, let us make good use of this thought that is truly worthy of God and of the teachers who teach it to us, and as we contemplate the divine Majesty dwelling from all eternity within itself, let us withdraw our minds from base, worthless, and perishable things. Let us rise up above ourselves. Let us love and seek to be in God, in remembrance and honor of what he is eternally within himself. Let us adore him as the one who is the fullness of being and life, the one who is sufficient to himself and to all things, and the one who is infinite capacity, to whom it belongs to contain both himself and all things by his being's greatness and eminence, its extent and immensity. For when God willed to communicate himself beyond himself, after the intimate, eternal, ineffable communication that is among the divine persons, he created the world,

---

8. "If you knew the gift of God and who it is that is speaking to you." Jn 4:10.

9. [Tertullian,] *Against Praxeas* 5 (original marginal note). "Before all things, God alone existed, and he was for himself world, place, and totality." See *Against Praxeas*, 600.

10. In the words of Ps 122 [123:1]. *Qui habitat in caelo* (original marginal note). "Who dwells in heaven." "'Where was God living before he made heaven and earth?' […] God was dwelling in himself; he dwells with himself; with himself he is God." Augustine, *Commentary on Psalm 122*, in *Expositions of the Psalms* (*Enarrationes in Psalmos*) *121–150*, trans. Maria Boulding, WSA, pt. 3, vol. 2, p. 33.

and the world is in God as in the one who preserves and contains it. God is within the world and in all the parts of the world, just as the soul is in the body and in all the parts of the body. For this reason, the Ancients called him the World Soul.[11] He is in all things by presence, by essence, and by power, without any of the imperfections and disadvantages that the meanness of our understanding can grasp in the way that creatures are and exist. For those who bring together the elevated discourses of philosophy with the sublime contemplations of theology say blessedly and divinely that God is within the world without being encompassed in it, beyond the world without being excluded from it, above the world without being higher than it, below the world without being lower than it; that he dwells in things by containing them and not by being contained by them; that he gives being, existence, and capacity to the world and receives nothing from the world; that he is infinite, immeasurable, and incomprehensible; and that he is this intellectual sphere whose center is everywhere and circumference nowhere.[12]

As there are various ways in which God is and dwells in his creatures, we will reduce them to two general and primary ones, under which the other lesser and inferior ones can be subsumed. God dwells in the world by his nature and by his grace. Let us set aside for another time the discussion of grace, and let us say for now that he dwells in it by his nature, in such a way that he is present to the world and joined together with it by two unions that are distinct and different in their principle and origin. The union of the simple presence that God has in all parts of this universe is founded in the spiritual nature, fineness, and immensity of the divine being, by virtue of which he is more intimately within each thing than light is in the translucent bodies

---

11. Plato posited that since the cosmos was a living unity, by analogy to other organisms it must have soul. See his remarks at *Statesman* 269d–273b (trans. Harold M. Fowler, LCL 164, pp. 50–51), *Philebus* 30a (trans. Fowler, LCL 164, pp. 264–67), and most fully, *Timaeus* 34a–37c (trans. R. G. Bury, LCL 234, pp. 62–75). In Plotinus's later development of this doctrine, the World Soul is the third of the three hypostases and has an upper part, occupied with contemplation, and a lower part, occupied with the world's creation. See Plotinus, *Ennead* 4.3.4 and 5.2.1 (trans. A. H. Armstrong, LCL 443, 444, pp. 44–45, 58–61).

12. This description is attributed to Hermes Trismegistus and to Alan of Lille, and it was used subsequently by many authors.

that it suffuses and illuminates and than the spirit is in the body that it governs and sustains. This caused St. Paul to say, *In ipso vivimus, movemur et sumus.*[13] The union of presence and dependency together (which is between God and the creatures) proceeds from the greatness of his majesty and the infinity of his essence that fills heaven and earth, according to his holy word, and makes all things present to God and always dependent on him, in all the degrees of their being and in all their accidents and circumstances.[14] This dependency is founded in the eminence and sovereignty of the supreme and uncreated being and in the poverty and necessity of created being, which always needs to be joined with God necessarily as to its first cause and to receive his constant influence, for it depends on him much more absolutely than the ray does on the sun (if it is separated from the sun for one moment, it immediately loses its being and existence). For in this wondrous body of light and this star of the universe, the most express intimation and image of the deity that we have among visible and bodily things, it seems that God desired us to see with the eye how much all that is created depends always on uncreated being. Just as the sun is the first luminous star, a body and substance of light, and a wellspring of all the light that spreads in heaven, in the air, and on earth, and just as this light emanating from it has no stability in itself but constantly needs the presence of its sun, so also God is the first and supreme Existent, God is a substance of uncreated and infinite being, God is a wellspring of all created being. This created being cannot be separated from the supreme and uncreated Being, because it constantly and always needs to cleave to God and depend on God who is its origin. This is why God bears in his qualities this one that is primary and as though it were his motto: *He who is.*[15] It is his own Name, spoken by himself, his name so often expressed in his speech and particularly in his first and public patent that he gave to his servant Moses to assemble a people, raise up a state and commonwealth, and give a law in his name on the earth. It is this name and this quality that torments the demons and throws them

---

13. Acts 17[:28] (original marginal note). "In him we live and move and are."
14. Is 6:3.
15. Ex 3[:14] (original marginal note). A device or motto (French: *devise*) is a brief inscription that forms part of a heraldic livery.

into confusion, for they see and feel how necessarily, constantly, and sensibly they are without the presence and perpetual influence of their Creator that they can have no doubt of it. And yet they wanted, and want still, to be forever separated from it. This brings ruin and division upon them, not only in their kingdom but in themselves, in the motive power and reach of their own essence. This is worthy of much deeper consideration. For if their essence were not necessarily joined with God it would be nothing, and their will, which lies in their essence, is completely separated from God. But even though they separate themselves from him like this and cut themselves off by their depraved will from the influence of his love and goodness, they cannot cut themselves off from the continued influence of his greatness, power, and authority, or from their dependency. And what is highly remarkable is that this division in their kingdom and in their essence does not stop there: it passes into their very will, which is wretchedly divided and separated from itself by the condition of their first, natural, and necessary impulse that inclines them to the good. For God impressed this impulse on their angelic nature in its creation, and this impulse persists in hell just as their own nature does. Thus, their will, by this first impulse, cannot be separated from God, whom it knows most infallibly and senses most acutely to be the sovereign Good: the good that is necessary to every creature. And yet this same will, by free and voluntary action, separates itself from that good with all its power. And these unhappy spirits, dividing themselves from God in this way, divide first within themselves and from themselves and live forever wretched and damned, forever joined to and separated from God by their will, forever joined to God by their essence, forever joined to God by their natural will, and forever separated from God by their free and disordered will.

This is the wretched state of the sinner, who indeed can bring himself to ruin but cannot destroy his own essence, which necessarily lies in a state of want, cleaving, and dependency on its Creator and cannot be separated from him in any manner. For the first quality, the universal condition, the inseparable property of created things consists in this want, cleaving, and dependency. It can rightly be named a transcendent, primordial, and fundamental degree in every created being's order and state, essence and nature.[16] For created being is only participated being, unlike its first cause and not of the same kind, for the latter's being is infinite, existing by its own essence, and independent. This is so true that as there are in the Godhead two divine persons whose origin and principle lie necessarily in their subsistence, they have in this emanation itself a non-dependence. For it is so fitting and essential to the divine and uncreated Being to be independent, and so fitting and essential to every created being to be in want, cleaving, and dependent on its God, its principle and origin. It is only a simple being, limited and participated—which has nothing and can have nothing except in this general and universal condition of cleaving and dependency that bears a relationship to God its principle. This relationship is not of accident but of substance. It is not particular but universal and absolute, in all the degrees and states of its being. It is an essential, perpetual, and necessary relation toward God, to whom we all ought to correspond with all our power, in all states, objects, and circumstances.

In this view and thought, let us lift our eyes to heaven and our spirits to God. Let us rise up in his grandeurs and humble ourselves in our nothingness. Let us strive, with the help and prevenience of grace, to belong to God as much by our free will, insofar as our powerlessness can sustain it, as we are his by the condition of our nature. Let us cleave to God as much by the movements of his grace as we do by the poverty of our being. And losing ourselves like this in the abyss of his grandeurs and our nothingness, let us praise him for his blessed state, in which he is sufficient in himself and all else lies in want, whether on earth or in heaven, in nature and in grace, and even in glory. Let us marvel that Jesus alone, by the dignity of his person, is without want; Jesus alone is the fullness of sufficiency, both to himself and to all things. For he encompasses in himself the eternal Word who is his all, and, if one dare to say so, both his all and his part. He is in the divine state and wondrous order of the hypostatic union, in an ineffable way that is without dependency. For although the eternal Word emanated and is always emanating from the Father and looks upon him eternally as his origin and principle, he is, in this emanation from him and in this regard

---

16. A transcendent attribute or quality is one that applies to all beings without exception.

and relation toward him, without want and without dependency. And therefore, Jesus is sovereign in this position, so sovereign that even his being and state in our humanity in no way depends on any but himself, since he accomplishes and completes it.

This proposition will seem perhaps a bit daring and strange to some. But in addition to its being authorized, I beg them to defer judgment for a moment and let us lead them step by step by the truths of the faith and the precepts of theology. I am certain that they will see clearly that it in no way affects—on the contrary, that it honors—the action, work, and power of the Most Holy Trinity. For we must carefully consider that the eternal Word so proceeds from his Father that by the power and virtue of his origin he is God as God is, he is equal to God, and he is independent as God is. Therefore, he is also independent in his terminative application of this human nature, in his state, residence, and cleaving to this sacred humanity. He accomplishes his mystery of the Incarnation in a holy and divine manner, by the power that he has received from his Father in his origin and by his Father's will, but not in dependency upon his Father. For the eternal Father is indeed his father, but he is not his sovereign in the Godhead.

Let us contemplate then the eternal Word coming down from the highest heaven and from the bosom of his Father, by his Father's will but without dependency upon his Father.[17] He enters into this humanity as into a being that he desires to make specifically his own, by applying to it his subsistence that belongs only to him, that is his in the Godhead, that makes him distinct from the other divine persons, and that is fitting to his independence. He takes to himself completely this created being. He establishes his essence, presence, and power in it. He applies his person and subsistence to it. He sets his love and good pleasure within it. In it he does his will and works the salvation of the universe. And this humanity, not in its entity nor in its creation but in the matchless and singular belonging that it has to the Word who holds

---

17. Cf. Hilary, *The Trinity* 3.9, p. 71: "He fulfils the will of God the Father, as He declares: 'For I have come down from heaven not to do my own will, but the will of him who sent me,' not that He does not also will what He does, but He manifests His obedience in carrying out the will of His Father, while He Himself wills to fulfill the will of His Father."

it united with himself, and in the excellent and ineffable deification that it receives from him within, is not dependent on any other person than the eternal Word, who accomplishes this work and mystery by himself and by what belongs to him in the Godhead. He desires this human nature to be his without being the nature of the other divine persons, by communicating to it his personal deity, sonship, and property. For it is in this belonging that its state and grandeurs consist and that this supreme state of the hypostatic order and union subsist. It is by this wondrous entry of the Word into our humanity that this secret and sacred mixture (without any confusion) of God and man is made in the Man-God. It is by this divine ingredient that the remedy is prepared for our ills and the inexplicable composition of two natures (divine and human) in one underlying substance, from which results this divine composition, this wondrous Jesus Son of God, Son of man, God and man together. And this Jesus, who in his human and temporal nature depends on the Holy Trinity, has a manner of being in this most high and supreme state that is without dependency, since he encompasses in himself the eternal Word as his own person. By contrast, all angels, all men, and all saints together, however great and exalted they are or may be, for all eternity and in all their states of nature, of grace, or of glory, depend absolutely, necessarily, and perpetually on the divine Majesty.

This point is very high, particular, and remarkable in this mystery, and it consequently entails another doctrine regarding the actions of this humanity that the Word was pleased to join with himself. This humanity's actions, since they proceed from this created nature that still remains created in its nature and accidents, are dependent on the Most Holy Trinity. But since they are distinctive and belonging to the Word, since they subsist in him by the subsistence that he gives to the nature that produces them, and since they are truly his by the natural right that renders and assigns actions to the persons who act, in this sense and in this respect they belong to him as to the one who is the working nature's underlying substance, and they do not belong like this to the Holy Spirit or even to the Father. And if we may speak in this way about what is ineffable, they do not take their authority from any other dominion or sovereignty than his own, that is, from the greatness of the deity and the independence of his person. For because the eternal Word is Word and Son of God, he is sovereign in the Godhead and has no sovereign to rule over him. Thus, the Word, in his will to be and dwell, to act and work, in this nature of his that he has united with himself, is of the same will as the Father but is independent of the Father. As he possesses this humanity in a way and manner that is distinct and specific to him even in the Godhead (that is, as the only Son of God and by his subsistence), he has in his person a kind of right and ownership over this human nature and its actions that correspond to him alone and not to the Father. For although he is born of his Father and shares his Father's essence, the Father does not share with the person of his Son this right and ownership that the Son has over his actions and sufferings. The deification of this human nature, of its actions and sufferings, is properly the action—or, to say it better, the actuation—of the eternal Word who is distinctive to him and independent in his personal property. This is worthy of new and particular consideration and greatly increases the price of our redemption. It greatly exalts Jesus' actions and sufferings. It gives him a new right and a new means of satisfying the eternal Father, in strict justice (that is, *ex propriis*,[18] as the School puts it) by actions that are not only most pure, holy, and divine but also so fitting to the one who satisfies that as such they are not owed to the one who receives the satisfaction. That is, they are not owed to the person of the Father, who receives the actions and sufferings of Jesus Christ his Son as payment for our debts. He receives them not only as actions and sufferings but as deified actions and sufferings, and even as independent of him in a certain sense and way. For Jesus' nature, actions, and sufferings indeed depend on the eternal Father in their natural condition, but they are independent of him in their state and subsistence, in their personal property, in their deification, in the relationship that they have to an underlying substance that is both divine and independent, and in the belonging that they have to the Word who is divinely ascribed to this created nature and substituted for the natural right of the human person that is not there. The Word is forever the possessor of this human nature, its actions, and its sufferings, all of which therefore are the Word's and belong to him with a kind and sort of independence.

Let us summarize this discourse in a few words and observe that

---

18. "From what is his own."

this deity, independence, and sovereignty of Jesus, in his person, in his application to human nature, and in his right, power, and authority over it and over its actions, are founded in the greatness of his being, in the power of his origin, in the dignity of his eternal birth. And since he has this greatness by birth, he has it truly, rightly, and naturally. He has it in such a way that the Father's authority is not affected, for the Father is the one he receives it from. This independence that is divine, emanated from God, and possessed by Jesus, is most worthy of being considered by his people and marveled at and adored by all his subjects and children. It is an independence clearly set forth in this discourse, having its firm foundation in the Father's power to produce his Son as independent and in the Son's subsistence that is given to human nature and to its actions. These are two divine and unchanging foundations of the Church's faith in the two principal mysteries of her belief, that is, the Trinity and the Incarnation. Upon these, the state of the united nature, and the humanly divine and divinely human quality of its actions and sufferings, are established and supported. As they are human in their condition, they are raised up in the condition of this mystery and belong specifically to the person of the Word. They have an excellent relationship to him and a divine state in the property of his person, who has a right and authority over this nature and these actions as over something that is his: his by a right so lawful and natural, so powerful and divine, so natural and supernatural, that it cannot be worthily enough described nor humbly enough marveled at and adored. It is fundamental to our salvation, our redemption, and our greatness in eternity. Yet, a truth so high, important, and having so worthy a foundation is taken up and blamed in some new discourses that condemn and censure too carelessly this way of calling the Son of God's actions "humanly divine and divinely human." This way of speaking is founded in the state distinctive to this mystery, used by the Fathers of the early Church, and even borrowed by some modern authors in excellent works (if it were suitable to cite them here and interrupt the thread of this discourse that is directed toward something else).[19] This point is

---

19. The editors of the Cerf edition of Bérulle's works suggest that this is a reference to Francisco Suárez, *On the Incarnation of the Word*, a work that is not available in English translation.

not touched on except in passing, yet it deserves a much greater discussion and clarification and ought to be taken up in another place in order to satisfy the authors of defamatory pamphlets and "helpful opinions" that are in fact unsound and unhelpful.[20] These anonymous authors are ignorant censors of the piety and devotion that is being proposed toward Jesus Christ our Lord. This piety is founded in the earliest homage and sentiments of the Christian religion. It has its birth in baptism and in our rebirth in the Church. And it is authorized by the Church's voice and command in the catechism ordained by the holy and sacred council of Trent.

I would indeed wish that the time and patience of these new inquisitors permitted me to pursue the other points concerning Jesus' sovereignty over all things, and particularly over something so noble and divine, a subject so precious and excellent, as himself—that is, over his states, mysteries, and actions. But since it does not please them to give me this leisure, and their proceedings compel me to put this work forward, I will content myself in saying that by exalting Jesus' state and grandeurs in this way, and by describing his independence in the Godhead, we do no wrong to the Holy Trinity or to the eternal Father. For it is the same Trinity that, doing this work as the masterwork, produces the independence of Jesus. It is the eternal Father who, by himself and his Holy Spirit giving this humanity to his Son, causes Jesus Christ, God-Man, to be subsisting and living in this independence. In this way, when we adore Jesus' grandeurs, we adore in him the grandeurs of his Father who produces him in his eternity by the infinite power of his generation that is so divine and perfect that just as he originates from him, so also is he independent like him. As we adore within the Trinity an origin and emanation of the Son without dependency, which is incomprehensible, he also wanted us to notice and marvel at, in the Incarnation and humanity of his Son, something that is created and dependent, powerfully and divinely established within the being that is uncreated and independent.

It is the glory of God to do such a work. It is the glory of the Father

---

20. Denys de la Mère de Dieu's third pamphlet against Bérulle, published anonymously in 1622, was titled *Avis salutaire sur un certain quatrième vœu de religion* ("A helpful warning about a certain fourth vow of religion"). See Introduction.

to produce such a Son. It is the glory and the state of Jesus, God and Man together, to have in himself a human and natural dependency established within his divine and personal independence. And it is the glory and the life of men to know, to love, and to serve so high and divine an object. For he himself says to God his Father, *Haec est vita aeterna, ut cognoscant te solum Deum verum, et quem misisti Iesum Christum* ("This is eternal life, that they may know you, the only true God, and he whom you have sent, Jesus Christ").[21] These are holy words that we should hear with humility, consider carefully, and meditate upon deeply, for they are words of life—in their subject, because they speak of eternal life, and in their origin, because he who speaks them is Life itself, and life on the way to death. In these words, he worthily and clearly demonstrates his state and greatness, his mission and power to give life. And although he is going to death, and these words to his disciples and to his Father are only about the death and suffering that is near and imminent to him; although, I say, he is in this state and in these discourses, seems to appear only clothed simply in our humanity and mortality, lives as a man among men, and is saddened among his sad apostles: in their sight and presence, as though he were taking no thought of his mortal and suffering condition, he rises up, he joins and associates himself intimately with God as with the one who is his Father. He associates himself with him in the greatest quality, which is to be the object necessary to eternal life. And the Life speaking to Life before mortals—that is, the Son to the Father before his disciples—says authoritatively and blessedly these words, worthy of being engraved on our hearts by the point of his cross and sufferings: *Haec est vita aeterna, ut cognoscant te solum Deum verum, et quem misisti Iesum Christum.* With these words the Son binds himself to his Father, as pouring the true life into souls on his Father's behalf and with his Father, because he contains in himself the life and deity that is personally joined with the humanity, just as he himself is in essence One with God his Father. This humanity, in its states, actions, and circumstances, is a noteworthy and necessary part of our faith, jointly with the deity that it is united with in the object of the faith and in the working of our salvation just as it is

---

21. Jn 17:3.

united with him in one same subsistence. Although Jesus is established in two states that are very different from one other—the one divine and the other human, the one created and the other uncreated, the one dependent and the other independent—yet he is ours and acts in our salvation in both of his states. Christians must confess, serve, and love him in these two qualities, which the Creed of the faith tells us—that is, in his human, specific, and natural condition, and in his divine state, which is other to the earth, extraordinary and supernatural even in the supernatural order of grace. For Jesus is ours not only as man but also as God, which is wondrous. The prophet invokes him in this way, in this divine verse: *Benedicat nos Deus, Deus noster, benedicat nos Deus, et metuant eum omnes fines terrae*. We see here how, in honor of the three divine persons, the name of God is repeated three times. In honor of the second person of the Trinity, the second time that the name of God is repeated it is with the addition of a word that calls him *Our*. It calls him this alone among the other divine persons, *Deus noster*, as he alone is our Immanuel. This marks out the singular belongings and appropriations that make the Son of God specifically and solely ours by the mystery of his Incarnation. This moved this prophet to speak of God in this way and invoke his benediction in this form: *Benedicat nos Deus, Deus noster, benedicat nos Deus, et metuant eum omnes fines terrae* ("May God, our God, bless us; may God bless us, and may all the corners of the earth revere his Majesty").[22]

Just as the Son of God is ours, therefore, in a manner wholly distinct and specific to him, so also our humanity is his in a manner wholly distinct and specific to it. From this we should learn to be his completely and with all our power. For we must carefully consider that this humanity, drawn from the Most Holy Virgin, belongs to God in a way that is wholly different from all the other things in the world. God possesses it more blessedly, powerfully, and divinely than we could ever understand. The faith itself teaches us that it belongs to him in two ways, which both correspond to it alone and which in themselves are quite different. For instead of the divine nature's belonging to the Word by generation and not otherwise, and created things' belonging

---

22. Ps 66 [67:6–7] (original marginal note).

to him only by creation (in which all the other ways that they belong to the Creator are reduced and in which they are founded), this humanity belongs to the eternal Word by creation, as do all created things, and also by generation, which is the same basis by which deity belongs to him. For in eternity, the Word is God because he is Son of God, and he is Son of God because he is begotten of God. The same Word who is necessarily begotten within eternity desired to be begotten a second time, in the fullness of time, and by this second generation he wanted to impress on this humanity the adorable imprint of his divine and eternal sonship, which it receives and bears for an eternity. For he possesses this humanity not simply as God but as Son of God, and as such he impresses his own and personal subsistence on it. Thus, just as the Godhead belongs to the Word by generation, causing the divine sonship to subsist in the Godhead, so also this Humanity belongs to the Word by generation, causing the same sonship that we confess and adore as subsisting in the Godhead to subsist in the humanity. Therefore, just as the Word is Son of God in the Godhead in which he subsists by eternal generation, so also is he Son of God in the humanity in which he lives and subsists by temporal generation, by which the Father says to his Son, *Ego hodie genui te*, as we will demonstrate elsewhere.[23] This sacred humanity belongs to God, therefore, by both creation and generation. By high, divine, and ineffable generation, I say, that blessedly bears and divinely conveys the divine and eternal sonship from heaven to earth, from eternity to time, from the bosom of the Father to the Virgin's womb. It bears it in this glorious humanity, which by this means is transferred from the common and ordinary state in nature and in grace into the matchless, supreme, and extraordinary order of the hypostatic union. This is an order and a state of singularity, sublimity, deity, and independence, into which it enters by subsistence in the specific and independent person of the only Son of God. This is the precious and divine means by which this Jesus whom the eternal Father sends us, this Jesus whom the eternal Father gives us to be our father, savior, and sovereign, this Jesus in whom he placed our life, our eternal

---

23. "Today I have begotten you." Ps 2:7; Acts 13:33; Heb 1:5, 5:5. Cf. Augustine, *Confessions* 11 and particularly 11.13, p. 263.

life, this Jesus who is the object that the eternal Father offers us and the model that we should constantly regard, imitate, and adore—this Jesus, I say, is so great, so high, and so wondrous that in this new state and in this his mystery of the Incarnation, he is independent of the eternal Father. And yet this King of glory who is independent, even independent of the eternal Father, becomes for our sake humbly dependent on a Caiaphas, a Herod, and a Pilate; on some Jews, torturers, and idolaters; on suffering, on the cross, and on death itself. Let us imitate and adore therefore his humble submission. Let us submit to his laws, his love, and his power. Let us humbly depend on him who is divinely independent and whom the Father gives us—gives us forever—as independent. And as we render eternal homage and servitude to him, let us blessedly find life in his death, rest in his cross, salvation in his wounds, joy in his suffering, honor in his opprobrium, freedom in his captivity, and greatness in his humble and voluntary submission.

Discourse 7

On the Communication of God in This Mystery

One of the most noted philosophers of pagan antiquity and greatest masters of moral teaching contemplated the marvels of nature and the brevity of our human life and found it quite strange that man's days on earth are so brief for the contemplation of what lasts so long. He lamented, was dismayed, and cried out, *Homo ad immortalium cognitionem nimis mortalis* ("Man is too mortal for the understanding of things immortal").[1] And yet this great philosopher had as the object of his understanding only the roundness of the earth, the motion of the heavens, the splendor of the planets, and the beauty of this universe. What would have been the astonishment and raising of his mind, then, if he had been a Christian, and if, enlightened as we are by the light of faith, he had known a new world and new earth, a new heaven and new sun, and a Man-God who, by his course and by the regular, or rather, blessedly irregular, motions of his suffering life and his divine death, darkens the heavens, disturbs the elements, shakes the earth, fills hell with dread, delights men and angels, and, by ways full of such great marvels, establishes a new kingdom, an eternal kingdom, in the world? The object of Christians' contemplation is very different from that of naturalists, who study only in the book of the world and occupy themselves only with the profane sciences. These sciences seemed insipid to

---

1. Seneca, *On the Blessed Life* 32 (original marginal note). The text is found in Seneca's *On Leisure*, in *Moral Essays*, trans. John W. Basore, LCL 254, vol. 2, p. 193.

St. Augustine, because he found the incarnate Word nowhere in them. He saw Jesus Christ our sovereign Lord nowhere in them, and he read in them nothing of the outpouring of his love, the favors of his grace, and the power of his cross.[2] If this philosopher was right to complain that nature had given man so few years to contemplate the state of natural things, how much more rightly ought we to protest the brevity of our days for contemplating so great an object? Certainly, the life of man is too brief to contemplate so great a marvel. But God provides for this by his goodness, for he causes us to be reborn and live again by his grace, and he makes us immortal so that we may eternally contemplate this eternal object. We have nothing to lament but ourselves, that being immortal we profane our immortality by becoming attached to such mortal and perishable things, and that when this immortal object is revealed to us, we give it so little of our love and thoughts. We distract ourselves with so many things that are so mean, base, and profane, in light of a subject so high, great, and divine. Since the Son of God wants to think of us, treat with us, and humble himself to us; wants to come even within the limits of our being, make himself part of it, and be one of us; wants to be man as he is God, to live among men as he lives among the divine persons, and to attend to us, give and communicate himself to us and to our nature in a manner so high, singular, and ineffable: we should indeed, with a steady and ardent will, think of him, treat with him, and rise up to him. We should enter into the abyss of his graces and favors, desire to be like him, live only for him, and give ourselves to him in the outpouring of his grace and power. Our being, since it owes so much to his power and love, should belong wholly to Jesus. His name, greatness, and dignity should occupy our senses and fill our minds. His power and love should give life to our powers and suffuse the marrow of our soul. His Spirit should govern our spirit, sustain our life, and guide our actions. Our thoughts, words, and motions should incline wholly to him. Nothing should come forth from our mind that does not yearn for Jesus and long for his honor and glory. Nothing should enter into our mind that does not savor of the mind and fragrance of Jesus. Held captive by his love, we should see only

---

2. [Augustine,] *Confessions* 7.20–21 (original marginal note). See *Confessions*, 154–56, and 4.16, pp. 87–90.

Jesus, nothing should content us but Jesus, everything in him and by him should please us, and nothing without him and beyond him should satisfy us. We should confirm in ourselves these devout words of the devout St. Bernard: *Aridus est omnis animae cibus si non oleo isto infunditur, insipidus est si non isto sale conditur. Si scribas, non sapit mihi, nisi legero ibi Iesum: Si disputes, aut conferas, non sapit mihi, nisi sonverit ibi Iesus. Iesus mel in ore, in aure melos, in corde iubilus.*[3]

Jesus is therefore the subject of our discourse, and the object of our thoughts. We are glad to continue speaking of God performing this work, making a new Adam and forming a Man-God as the subject of his grandeurs and the culmination of his marvels. As we adore the goodness of God communicating himself thus to his creation, let us penetrate more and more into the ineffable communication of God in this mystery. Taking it up at a higher point and as though at its source, in order to lead and direct it gradually up to this work, let us see how the supreme Being, eternal and uncreated, intellectual light and inaccessible wisdom, the first and the principle of beings, the living God and the fount of life, equally lovable and adorable in his excellent and blessed nature, is in a ceaseless state of wondrous communication, according to the degree that each thing's nature and condition makes it capable of receiving. He communicates an intimation and trace of his existence to things lower and closer to nonbeing, such as simple bodies and elements. He communicates an intimation of his being and life to, for example, vegetable and sensitive things. As he goes higher in his work, he reveals and communicates himself more, by impressing no longer an intimation and trace but a more express image and a more perfect resemblance of himself and of his living and intelligent being, as is seen in the angels and in men.[4] And if they accept the leading of his good-

---

3. St. Bernard, *On the Song of Songs*, Sermon 15 (original marginal note).

All food of the soul is dry if this oil is not poured over it; it is insipid if its savor is not preserved with this salt. If you write, it has no savor for me unless I read Jesus therein. Whether you debate or discuss, it has no taste for me if the name of Jesus does not ring forth therein. Jesus is honey to the mouth, melody to the ear, and joy to the heart.

In *Works of Bernard of Clairvaux*, trans. Kilian Walsh (Kalamazoo, Mich.: Cistercian Publications, 1981), 2:110.

4. Cf. Pseudo-Dionysius, *Celestial Hierarchy* 4, p. 156; *Divine Names* 2.5, pp. 62–63,

ness, grace, and love, he also goes further and exalts them even to the sight and possession of his goods and grandeurs and to the enjoyment of his glory, giving them access, admission, and standing in his palace, his paradise, and his eternity.

But this infinite and wondrous being is in a much higher, more exalted, and more excellent state of self-communication, for we have and adore in the greatness of our mysteries three most secret and intimate communications, which are ineffable in themselves, incomprehensible to men and angels, and perfectly and directly divine. The first is the eternal communication of God the Father to his Son, in which he gives him his own essence. The second is the coeternal communication of the Father and the Son, giving their common essence to the Holy Spirit. And the third is the most lovable and adorable communication that the Word alone makes of himself and his person to the sacred humanity, drawn from the pure and immaculate substance of the Most Holy Virgin. In this way, just as we have a trinity of mysteries in the state of the faith (according to the preceding discourses) and we adore a Trinity of persons in the being of the Godhead (according to the teachings of our religion), so also we have and adore a trinity of communications in the divine being, which is the foundation of the present discourse. For the Ancients described God's infinite being to us as an intellectual sphere that comprehends everything and that cannot be comprehended. And just as its greatness is enclosed, encompassed, and completed in itself—that is, in the Trinity of the divine and eternal persons—so also the mystery, the circle, and the secret of the proper, direct, and ineffable communication of this being of God is comprehended, consummated, and fulfilled within himself in this trinity of communications. The first two are comprehended in the mystery of the Trinity, and the third is reserved for the sacred mystery of the Incarnation that completes, encompasses, and brings to a close the divine circle and the wondrous circumference of God communicating within himself and within this sacred humanity. There he blessedly and divinely arrests the point and greatness of the direct divine communications in one divine person, who receives into himself and his subsistence a created nature.

---

and 4.20, p. 86; Bonaventure, *The Journey of the Mind to God* 1.2, in *Works of Bonaventure*, 1:9–10.

These three communications are so precious, eminent, and singular that there is nothing similar on earth or in heaven that can serve us as an intimation and representation worthy of representing them. Their excellence and perfection are infinitely far from all other communications that nature and faith teach us of. They are such that we can believe and adore them on earth by grace, and behold and contemplate them in heaven by glory, but we cannot comprehend them either in earth or in heaven. For they comprehend the infinite, that is, they comprehend God himself, either in his nature or in his persons, and they are so powerful and sublime that they contain and involve in their efficacy an ineffable communication of the divine being. This is a communication so great, intimate, and perfect that it makes the persons who proceed coessential with their eternal principle, and it makes human nature, to which this communication is made, consubsistent with the Godhead.

In these two divine communications that are encompassed in the bosom of the eternal Father, one from the Father to the Son and the other from the Father and the Son to the Holy Spirit, we marvel how an essence that is wholly simple, indivisible, and unchangeable can be communicated to several hypostases. In the humility of faith, we adore the divine nature as being both perfectly one and perfectly communicable. This is one of the greatest secrets of the Godhead and one of the highest points that the faith teaches us. For the God of Christians is so very One that this oneness subsists in a plurality of persons, and thus in the divine being there is both oneness and plurality. This plurality is not a difference of persons, as though detached and separate from one another, as was the god of the Manicheans, one the principle of good and the other the principle of evil. Instead, these divine persons are bound together in love and communion. In the divine being we have perfect oneness, plurality, and communion: communion that is the foundation and model of every other communion, divine and human, natural and supernatural, as we will say elsewhere. This communication and communion of uncreated and eternal persons lies not only in love and mutual likeness, but—what is much more, and what surpasses the human and angelic mind (which cannot understand how, in God, the conditions of producing and produced occur)—this communication is founded in the origin and emanation of the persons from one other, which assumes oneness and fertility in the being of God. As a result, in the sublimity of our mysteries and in the greatness of the divine being whom we serve and adore, we have oneness and plurality by the distinction of persons, oneness and communion by the communication of persons, and oneness and fertility by the emanation of persons.

Now, this original and eternal communication of the Godhead, fertile within itself, is the cause and model of the temporal communication that God makes of himself, beyond himself, to our humanity in the mystery of the Incarnation. It is as an express imitation and an extension unto created being of the supreme and ineffable communication that is within the uncreated being among the three persons of the Most Holy Trinity. And if we wish to join mysteries to mysteries, yet without departing from the only Son of God as our sole subject in these discourses or from the divine communications that are the subject of the present one, let us say that the holy Eucharist is likewise an imitation of the mystery of the Incarnation and an application and extension of it even to each Christian and faithful person, just as the earlier mystery of the Incarnation is an imitation and extension of the supreme communication that is within the Holy Trinity by the communication of the eternal Word in our humanity. We have then in these three mysteries one same subject to contemplate and adore. We have one same Son of God divinely encompassed and comprehended in these mysteries of the Holy Trinity, the Incarnation, and the Eucharist: in the first in the oneness of his essence, in the second in the oneness of his person, and in the third in the oneness of his body. By these three unities, Jesus is living in three different and wondrous states, that is, in the bosom of the Father, in our humanity, and in his Eucharist. He is living, I say, in the bosom of the Father as Son of God, God from God, and principle of a divine person. He is living in our humanity as Man-God and in the world as the universal principle of life. He is living in the Eucharist as the Victim of God before the face of his Father and appeasing his wrath upon his altar, where he communicates the life of grace and the seed of glory to each one of us. Three states of Jesus, three very different states, three states worthy of honor, love, and most particular consideration, three states proceeding from these three unities, founded in these three mysteries, and honored by three remarkable and adorable communications in Jesus: the one that he receives from the eternal Father, the one that he makes to our humanity, and the one that he makes to his Church and to his faithful. That is, three distinct communications: of his essence in the Trinity, of his person in the Incarnation, and of his body in the Eucharist, which contains these three different mysteries. Let us contemplate these unities, mysteries, and communications for a time. Let us see that in the first of these mysteries there is oneness of essence and fertility of persons, in the second there is oneness of person and fertility of essence, and in the third there is oneness of body and fertility of spirit. For in the Trinity, we adore the oneness and fertility of the divine being, oneness in its essence and fertility in its persons divinely produced and producing. The Father produces his Son in wondrous oneness and fertility, and he even produces him as the one who receives from him a wondrous power and fertility to produce the Holy Spirit. This Spirit who is produced by the Father and the Son, not producing anything within the Trinity, produces beyond the Trinity the things of nature and of grace: those of nature, as though impressing on the world in its birth the productive power of all things;[5] and those of grace, as being sent by the Word to sanctify the whole Church at her birth.[6] Thus the first power and fertility, which is that of the Father, concludes in the production of the two divine persons; and the second, which is that of the Son, concludes in the production of one sole person, who is the Holy Spirit. And the Holy Spirit, not producing anything within himself, is himself alone binding the divine persons produced and producing, and he produces beyond himself the intimation, image, and resemblance of divine and uncreated being by producing this world. Then following this, he unites this world that is produced with its principle, which is God, in the mystery of the Incarnation. In this we see in passing one same order and progress in created and uncreated being, and an imitation and resemblance of the image to the model. For just as in uncreated being the persons are produced, and their production is brought to completion in their oneness by the Holy Spirit who is their eternal and ineffable bond, so also when created

---

5. Gn 1[:2] (original marginal note). Cf. Plotinus, *Ennead* 3.8, vol. 3, p. 395: "What is it [sc. the One], then? The productive power of all things."

6. Acts 2[:4] (original marginal note).

being is produced, this same Holy Spirit binds and unites it to its principle, by uniting it to the Word who produced all things as the Word of the Father and unites them all with his Father as the incarnate Word, by the power of his incarnation, the greatness of his offices, and the efficacy of his mysteries.[7] We see in this yet another point that is worthy of particular consideration, which is a very remarkable difference between the sources of the earth and those of heaven. For the sources of the earth and of time are less broad and deep at their origin than in their rivers, which increase and get larger the farther they get from their source. By contrast, we see clearly here that the living sources of heaven and eternity have a greater fullness and breadth in themselves than in what emanates and is produced from them, and that the divine fertility, although always producing in the Trinity things that are equal, continues as though to shrink the closer it gets to us and the farther from its source.[8] For the Father, who is the fontal source of the deity and the first source of the divine fertility, produces in himself two divine persons. The Son, who is the second person producing in the Godhead, brings his fertility to a close in the production of a single divine person. This third person, producing nothing eternal and uncreated, produces the Word as incarnate. And this incarnate Word, as the new principle of a new being and as father of the age to come, produces the order of grace and of glory that is completed and extends to making us gods, but gods by participation only and not by subsistence as in the Incarnation, nor by essence as in the Trinity. That is, it is completed in making us the temples of the Godhead that is communicated among the divine persons and the living images of this supreme, divine, and uncreated being. This is where the communication of God concludes within himself and beyond himself: within himself in the Holy Spirit and beyond himself in the spirit that is holy and sanctified by grace. As it has its original source highly and divinely in the communication of the Father to the Son, and of the Father and the Son to the Holy Spirit,

---

7. Jn 1[:3–4] (original marginal note).

8. Cf. Plotinus, *Ennead* 3.8, vol. 3, p. 395: "But what is above life is cause of life. [...] [It] itself flows out, so to speak, as if from a spring. For think of a spring which has no other origin, but gives the whole of itself to rivers, and is not used up by the rivers but remains itself at rest."

it is easy for us to believe and understand that just as in this first mystery of the Trinity there is oneness and fertility together (according to our earlier assumption), so also is there oneness and fertility in the second mystery, which is that of the Incarnation, in which we likewise adore oneness and fertility—oneness of person and fertility of essence. This is plain not only in the plurality of the essences that are in this mystery and are united in oneness of subsistence, but also because the divine and human essences are so joined together that they constitute a new existent and a new principle of life in the world, as the disciple of Life and Truth (that is, St. John) says in several places. This humanity, by the deity that is present, subsisting, and living in it, is a source of life; for in Jesus all is life and quickening, as will be said in the discourse on the life of God in this mystery. This humanity, bearing within it by union with the Word the deity and sonship that is distinct and natural to the only Son of God, is a living and powerful source of the adoptive sonship that begins on earth and continues in heaven. In the third mystery (that is, in the Eucharist) we adore the oneness of this body that is glorified and accompanied by a wondrous fertility of grace and spirit, for this deified body communicates Jesus' spirit, love, and grace to those who receive him as he ordains by his word. This mystery is a new power of the Son of God on earth. In this divine, august, and singular sacrament, he wanted to impress with his own body, substance, and holy humanity the Spirit of grace, love, and oneness within his Church.

Thus, in the first of these mysteries, the Father gives and communicates his essence to his Son. In the second, the Son gives and communicates his person to our humanity. And in the third, the Son gives and communicates his body and his humanity to men. And the Son of God, lowering himself thus by degrees so that he might honor his Father in the mystery of his self-humbling, and stooping even to us so that he might exalt us to him, should be contemplated by Christians and adored in his grandeurs and humilities. They should love him by the strength of his love that joins him with his Father in the oneness of the Holy Spirit and that joins him with our humanity in the oneness of his divine person. For as we contemplate these high mysteries, we see how the only Son of God, receiving from his Father his own essence, wants with his Father, with a necessary will, to communicate this essence to the Holy

Spirit. By this natural and mutual regard and love between them, he is brought to produce this divine person and be united again with his Father by the oneness of this Spirit that is produced, just as he is originally united with him, or rather, is one with him, by oneness of essence. He also wants, in the fullness of time and with a free will that is worthy of an infinite gratitude, to give his divine essence, his own essence, to a created nature and to unite himself with his creation by his own substance and subsistence. As he moves forward along the paths of his love and goodness and sees that he bears within himself the ineffable communication of the deity to our humanity, Jesus wants to bear this humanity that is united with his deity in our hearts and bodies, so that he might sanctify them in him and unite us with him. And Jesus, thus uniting himself to us, unites us to his humanity, and by his humanity unites us to his deity, and by himself unites us to his Father. This is the course and progress, this is the going-forth and the return, of the eternal Word's voyage as he comes forth from his Father's bosom and comes down from the highest heaven to humble himself on earth and unite himself with our humanity. This is the purpose and intention of this blessed voyage and ineffable going-forth: to cause us to return into God and to raise us up from earth to heaven. This is the state and end of the mystery of the Incarnation, a mystery so high and powerful that it reaches from earth to heaven and from heaven to earth and joins man to God and God to man. It is a mystery that is represented for us by this ladder of Jacob, for the Scriptures describe it to us as so high that its two ends join earth with heaven, God with man.[9] So also we see that the incarnate Word reaches down to earth and sanctifies it by his humanity, and that he reaches up to heaven and glorifies it by his deity. When he was residing visibly on earth by his humanity, he was also living gloriously in heaven by his deity. This is why the Son of God, speaking of himself on earth, spoke of himself as being in heaven and said to the Jews, *Filius hominis, qui est in caelo*.[10] For he was then both on earth with them and in heaven with his Father, since in this mystery, as in Jacob's ladder, heavenly things are joined with earthly, the highest with the lowest, and God with man. For on this ladder there are many rungs, like many degrees by which God

---

9. Gn 28:11–15; Jn 1:51.
10. Jn 3[:13] (original marginal note). "The Son of man, who is in heaven."

comes down and abases himself to man, and man mounts up to God. And it seems to me that I see the unities that are evident in God's fertility in the divine communications, by which God, as he communicates within himself, comes to communicate himself even to man and unite himself to man in honor of the wondrous unities that the human spirit conceives of and adores in his divine being. For a greater clarification of this discussion, we may distinguish two excellent orders of divine unities: the first comprehending the unities that are in God's being and the second containing those that are in God's works. The first that we adore in God is the oneness of essence, supreme and original oneness, unoriginate oneness, which gives rise to the origin of the others. It is the oneness that is the first perfection acknowledged and assumed within the divine being, a oneness that by the fullness of its perfection is the source of the divine fertility. And following the order that we can conceive among divine things, we can say that from this oneness of essence comes the second, which is the oneness of principle. In it, the persons of the Father and the Son produce the Holy Spirit, who is himself the third oneness—the oneness of spirit and personal love, binding and unifying the divine persons together with a oneness that is distinct from the unities of essence and of principle from which it proceeds.

These are three unities that are in God and remain always in God himself. In honor and imitation of them there are three other divine unities that are comprehended in the second order, which we have said are the unities indicated in God's works. For the mystery of the Incarnation, which is the first and highest of God's works and which has for its principle the oneness of essential and personal love that is in the Godhead, is a mystery of oneness, in which a divine person unites the two natures of God and of man. As this oneness of the Word subsists in these two different natures, it is followed in the Church by the miraculous oneness of Jesus' soul and body that are present in various places, in heaven and on earth, which is the second wondrous oneness in God's works, established by the divine mystery of the Eucharist. This remarkable twofold oneness in Jesus—the one in his person in the Incarnation and the other in his body in the Eucharist—is the wellspring of the oneness of grace and spirit, which is the third oneness, the principle of the new life that is communicated to souls on earth and in heaven.

Thus God, according to his power and word, *attingit a fine usque ad finem fortiter*.[11] Thus God, who is oneness, leads all things to oneness, and by distinct degrees of unities comes and descends to man, and man goes and mounts up to God. Man arrives finally unto the enjoyment of the supreme and original oneness of the divine essence, by the sight, the light, and the enjoyment of the glory in which this divine essence (which is one and oneness both) is impressed on our spirit, communicated to it, and makes it blessed. Thus, from the lowest point of earth and from the depth of our nothingness, we mount up from degree to degree to God, and God, from the highest heaven and the throne of his greatness, comes down and abases himself even to us. Thus, in the state of religion, we go from one mystery to another, from one oneness to another, from one communication to another, and from one marvel to another as we contemplate the secrets and truths that the faith teaches us. As we contemplate God therefore in himself, his state, and his works, that is, in his deity, his humanity, and his sacrament and sacrifice—or more clearly, in his three mysteries: the Trinity, the Incarnation, the Eucharist—we see that by a secret and profound counsel his supreme goodness and majesty reaches out to reduce all things to oneness and to encompass all things, that is, the Creator and the creation, in a wondrous circle of oneness. It even reaches out to unite them at the point and center of the divine oneness by the mystery of the Incarnation and by the oneness of a person who is both uncreated and incarnate. For the Word is as a wondrous center of oneness, set amid the divine persons, in that he proceeds as the one and produces as the other. He is also set amid created and uncreated being by the mystery of the Incarnation, as mediator of the one and of the other. And this center of oneness draws all things to God, to himself, to oneness, by a strong and sacred chain of mysteries and unities linked together, like many links attached and bound together. This indeed deserves a fuller discussion, but let us set that aside for another time. Let us take up for now the use of this thought, so that we might rise up to God, unite ourselves to his Word, join ourselves to our Mediator, give ourselves to the rule of his cross, deliver ourselves to his love, his Spirit, and his

---

11. Wis 8[:1] (original marginal note). "Reaches mightily from end to end."

grace, commit ourselves to his leading, abandon ourselves to his counsels and purposes for us, and humble and abase ourselves before him. For we have let our spirits wander among the variety of created things and let our hearts be divided by worthless and perishable objects, instead of uniting them with the supreme oneness of the Godhead and reaching out toward the oneness of grace and the mystical life, in which God impresses and communicates his holy oneness to the spirit that is prepared, purified, and lifted up, to make it one in spirit with God and cause it to experience eternally the wondrous effect of this sacred saying: *Qui adhaeret Domino, unus spiritus est.*[12] High and sublime oneness, worthy of God and his grace, worthy of his Spirit and love, worthy of his mysteries and unities, and worthy of the power that he deigns to use to call our souls, draw our hearts, and make us, by a heavenly and infused quality, ready and open to the wondrous oneness that he wants to impress and communicate to the soul by the efficacy of his mysteries, the power of his Spirit, and the dignity of his grace and love.

But let us return from ourselves to God and from our wretchedness to his grandeurs. Let us return to the point and center of our discussion and note that the oneness, fertility, and ineffable communion that is in the Holy Trinity is the object that this Trinity regards, honors, and imitates in its work of the Incarnation—a work and mystery of divine and wondrous oneness, fertility, and communication. For God is the cause and model of all that proceeds from him, and the more that works and things are sublime and excellent in themselves, the more they regard in God something very precious and particular to which they have their relation and from which they draw their source and origin. Consequently, this ineffable communication that God makes of himself beyond himself, in the fullness of time in the mystery of the Incarnation, and that is so high and singular that it is and always will be unparalleled among created things, assumes and looks upon as its model this internal and eternal communication that is in the Godhead and that is the highest and most incomprehensible point that faith adores in the Godhead. All human and angelic spirits are dazzled by the sight. In the one, a God is communicating his essence; in the other,

---

12. 1 Cor 6[:17] (original marginal note). "He who cleaves to the Lord is one spirit."

a God is communicating his subsistence. In the one, a Father is giving his deity to his Son and to his Holy Spirit, that is, to the two persons proceeding in the Godhead; in the other, a Son, father of the age to come, is giving his deity to the soul and body of man, that is, to the two parts constituting our humanity. In the one, God's essence that is communicated to the persons makes them divine and adorable; in the other, the person of the Son of God makes this flesh and this soul, to which he communicates himself, divine in its subsistence and adorable in its state. In the one, we have a natural and necessary communication among the divine persons; in the other, we have a substantial but free and voluntary communication of the person of God to the nature of man. And this second and temporal communication looks upon this great, supreme, and wondrous communication that is in the Godhead as its model and as its source and origin. I say that it looks upon it as its model, for it is so deeply represented and so perfectly imitated in this second communication that the Fathers acknowledged the one in the other and demonstrated the one by the other—that is, the oneness of the Son with the Father in the Most Holy Trinity by the oneness of the Son with us in the Incarnation and the Eucharist. This is evident in the learned and authoritative teachers St. Cyril and St. Hilary, two brilliant luminaries and precious ornaments, the former of the Greek Church and the latter of the Latin.[13] I say that it looks upon it as its source and origin, because God, producing within himself, wills to produce beyond himself; and God, communicating himself within himself, wills to communicate himself beyond himself. God is the fullness of life, love, and communication: the fullness of life in his Son, fullness of love in the Holy Spirit, and fullness of communication in these two persons who proceed. He is the fullness that pushes outward this mystery of the Incarnation, an ineffable mystery of life, love, and communication, just as water's fullness, at the source, constantly pushes and spurts new water out of the fountain and pours it into the channels and streams that come forth. This communication of God beyond himself in this mystery of the Incarnation looks upon, acknowledges, and honors this per-

---

13. Cyril, [*Commentary on*] *John* [4.2]. Hilary, *The Trinity* 8[.13–17] (original marginal note). Cyril of Alexandria, *Commentary on John*, trans. P. E. Pusey (London: Walter Smith, 1885), 236–39; Hilary, *The Trinity*, 284–88.

fect communication, this original communication, this supreme and eternal communication, this adorable communication that is adored by men and angels but also singularly and worthily adored by the ineffable communication that the eternal Word makes of his essence and divine person to our humanity in the mystery of the Incarnation. It is a mystery that in its substance, state, and circumstances adores and will continually adore eternally this original communication that is in eternity among the divine persons. For the eternal Word, just as he proceeds from the Father and receives his own essence from him, so also does he desire to honor this divine communication that he receives from his Father, in which his being, state, and greatness consist, as we have discussed elsewhere. He honors it by a new being, a new state, and a new mystery, which bears a singular communication of himself and his deity to our humanity. And as we will say in another discourse, the Son of God, being born in his deity, wanted to honor his eternal birth by a temporal birth and to be made man by being made Son of man, so that he might honor the birth that he has from his Father by the one that he has from his Mother. Thus the Son of God, receiving from his Father and communicating to the Holy Spirit his divine essence within eternity, wanted to honor this ineffable communication by the wondrous communication of himself to our humanity. In this we see that he is always God, always Son, and always relation to his Father; always God even in this humanity, and always Son loving, honoring, and regarding his Father even in this new and temporal communication and always dedicating to him his eternal person and his new essence.

Here is the origin and principle, here is the high and final end, here is the primary intention and the true model of this great work of the Incarnation that we must contemplate, proclaim, and adore. So, leaving aside for another time the secrets worthy of being considered and adored in the ineffable communication that is among the divine persons, let us set forth, step by step, the great and wondrous state of the communication that faith adores between the eternal Word and human nature, through the sacred mystery of the Incarnation. Let us note that the ternary that is divinely consecrated to God in his persons is also divinely consecrated to him in his divine communications.[14]

---

14. A ternary is a trinity or set of three.

For although in the Godhead there are three persons, there are only two communications, just as there are only two processions. But one of these divine persons is communicated doubly—namely, the eternal Word, for he gives and communicates his essence to the Holy Spirit in the Godhead, and in the humanity he gives and communicates his person to a created essence. In this way, we have three communications that are truly, rightly, and absolutely divine, just as we have and adore three divine persons.

For in this communication that is in the mystery of the Incarnation, the eternal Word communicates his august person, his own subsistence, his uncreated existence, eternal essence, divine efficacy, infinite majesty, greatness, holiness, sovereignty, life, love, glory, and, in a word, according to the apostle, the fullness of his deity.[15] This deserves as many discourses as there are points proposed. But we have not been given this leisure by those who in the past have dared (through an astonishing audacity and novelty) to call theology a vain thing and who without theology dare to judge and censure doctrines that they do not understand. For this reason, setting aside the rest for another time and a fuller discussion, let us adore the Son of God's wondrous presence in this humanity and contemplate God's majesty residing in himself, in his creatures, and in the humanity of his only Son, as in three quite different dwelling places. For he is in his creatures without giving them any dignity, holiness, or beatitude by this kind of presence. He is in them all, whatever quality and condition they may have—embodied, spiritual, heavenly, earthly, good, evil, eternally blessed, or eternally wretched—without drawing them to any higher degree or to any manner of being that differs from their state and kind. He is in them all equally, without placing in them any distinctions, and each one remains within the limits and boundaries of its own nature and condition. He is in them simply to give them being, life, and movement according to their kind, and to preserve them in it. In truth, this presence powerfully afflicts the hearts of those who love God. It makes the wound of this love always fresh and new, since the sole object of their love is always intimate and present. But it is to grace that we must attribute this holy

---

15. Col 2:9.

affliction. It is grace, not this presence, that produces this effect on this presence. It is grace that establishes a new manner of God's presence and gives this holy and divine impression, by which souls find that they are being and living in God, according to this word of his apostle: *In ipso vivimus, movemur et sumus.*[16] They live blessedly and contentedly in this sight, which assures them that nothing on earth or in heaven can separate them from their only love, not even hell. For sin alone has this unhappy power, which is the only hell of holy souls and the true hell of hell itself.

God is therefore in his creatures as the one who comprehends them, sustains them, and maintains them in their being. But God is within himself, comprehending himself, for he is comprehensible to himself and incomprehensible to any other. In himself he is without the world what he is also with the world. In himself he does and ordains by his providence before the world what he does also with the world. In himself he is sufficient to himself by the fullness of his being. In himself he lives with a life worthy of his essence and a life that is the source of the life of nature, of grace, and of glory that fills the earth and the heavens. In himself he knows and loves himself; this is his sole occupation in eternity, and by his example it will be our life for an eternity. In himself he is blessed within himself and delights in himself, which is his bliss and the sovereign origin and object of ours. In himself he ordains by an eternal counsel all things that are to be produced in their time, dedicating them to his glory, as the one who is the principle and end, the idea and model, of all created being. In himself he dwells in infinite and inaccessible light, truly inaccessible in himself, that is, in the outpouring and infinity of his splendor, but he makes himself accessible, that is, by the power of his love and the light of his glory. In himself he is alone and also in company: he is alone in the oneness and singularity of his essence, and he is in company, company worthy of him and equal to him, by the divine, perfect, and adorable communion of persons who subsist eternally in his deity. And these divine persons are not only bound together in communion but are intimately within one another by the oneness of their essence, the divinity of their origin, their mutual

---

16. Acts 17[:28] (original marginal note). "In him we live and move and are."

comprehension, and by their essence being one with their relationships. For the secret of faith and theology teaches us that the divine essence, perfectly one and perfectly communicable, is one same essence in each of the divine persons; that God produces, in himself and not beyond himself, what is equal to him; that the emanations are immanent; that the uncreated persons possess, contain, and comprehend one another; and that the divine relations cannot be conceived without conceiving the divine essence, which is formally the same as they, although by a wondrous secret the divine essence can be conceived without conceiving the relationships that complete it. These are the points on which the teachers establish the intimate, mutual, and reciprocal residence of the divine persons within one another.

Finally, God who is thus divinely and blessedly within himself willed to be blessedly and divinely in the humanity chosen and drawn from the Virgin's substance, and to be in it in a manner wholly fitting and particular to the greatness, holiness, and deity of this mystery. He is therefore in this humanity as in a sacred temple that he built for himself by his own hands, that he consecrated to himself as his most worthy and perfect work, and that he consecrated to himself by himself, that is, by the unction and application of his divine essence. For the holy Fathers understand this verse of David as referring to the unction of the deity subsisting in this humanity: *Unxit te Deus, Deus tuus, oleo laetitiae prae consortibus tuis.*[17] St. Jerome, St. Augustine,[18] and the best commentators of this age explain the verse thus: *Unxit te o Deus, Deus tuus, etc.*[19] These are great words that speak of Jesus Christ to Jesus Christ himself and that are addressed to him as God, *O Deus!*; as God's anointed one, *Unxit te Deus*; and as his God's anointed one, *Unxit te Deus tuus.*[20] This is how we must parse these holy words and

---

17. Ps 44 [45:7] (original marginal note). "God, your God, has anointed you with the oil of gladness above your companions." Cf. Heb 1:9.

18. Jerome, "Letter 65, To Principia, A Commentary on Psalm 45 [44]," in *Epistolae: Medieval Women's Latin Letters*, trans. Joan Ferrante et al., Columbia University Libraries, 2014, epistolae.ctl.columbia.edu/letter/425.html; Augustine, *Answer to Maximinus the Arian* 2.16.3, in *Arianism and Other Heresies*, trans. Roland J. Teske, WSA, pt. 1, vol. 18, p. 293.

19. "Your God has anointed you, O God, etc."

20. "God has anointed you"; "Your God has anointed you."

weigh them according to the sanctuary scale[21] in order to know their importance and excellence. So let us note how the prophet addresses his words to Jesus and says to him, *O Deus*; and speaks to him of his God, *Deus tuus*; and says that his God anoints him, *Unxit te Deus tuus*. Jesus therefore is God, for the prophet names him so in addressing his word to him: *O Deus!* Jesus is God of God, he is God the Son of God, and he has God for his God, according to this word, *Deus tuus*. He is God in his first nature; he is God, Son of God, in his person; he has God for his God in his new nature.

The first two propositions are evident in the faith; let us explain the last one. The mystery of the Incarnation assumes two natures in the Son of God: one divine and the other human. By this the eternal Father has two attributions with regard to his Son, for he is his God by reason of his humanity, which it pleased him to clothe him in for men's salvation, just as he is his Father by reason of the deity, which he received from him by eternal generation. And similarly, just as Jesus Christ our Lord has henceforth a twofold nature, so also he has a twofold regard toward God: toward God as his Father in his deity, and toward God as his God in his humanity, whose Father is God just as he is God of every creature. Furthermore, he is also the God of this humanity in a specific way, on which the truth and vigor of his sacred word, *Deus tuus*, is founded. This is why the resurrected Jesus Christ said to his apostles, *Ascendo ad Patrem meum et Patrem vestrum, Deum meum et Deum vestrum*,[22] where he speaks without distinguishing his different natures, which the prophet acknowledged by the spirit of prophecy and expressed in these words: *Unxit te o Deus, Deus tuus*. For Jesus is God, is God of God, and is God's anointed. He is God in his eternal essence, like the Father and the Holy Spirit. He is God of God and Son of God in his divine person, having God for his Father, which belongs to him alone among the divine persons. And he is the anointed of God in his temporal essence, which belongs singularly to God and is consecrated to him by a wholly specific unction. I say, to God the Father, for he is the one spoken of in this verse and of whom it is said to the

---

21. To weigh with strict accuracy, evaluate with sober judgement.
22. "I ascend to my Father and your Father, my God and your God." Jn 20:17.

Son, *Deus tuus*. He is the one to whom it belongs to be the God of his incarnate Son. He is the one to whom it belongs to send and give his Son. And it is he who, by an ineffable love, gives him to this humanity and by this means becomes the God of this humanity, in a manner so high and excellent that it corresponds to him only in regard to it and does not befit him in regard to other creatures. In giving his Son to this humanity, the eternal Father gives in this Son the same deity that he gave him when he begot him within eternity. Thus, he is singularly the God of this humanity, not only by his grace but by his very deity, by which he consecrates it by conferring on it the unction of the deity, which makes this man God and communicates to human nature the divine essence, subsistence, and sonship. This completes the meaning of these profound words: *Unxit te, o Deus, Deus tuus, oleo laetitiae prae consortibus tuis*. For we must always remember that in this mystery this sacred humanity does not receive only the unction of accidental grace. It receives and bears the unction of substantial grace, that is, the unction of the deity, which the Son of God received from his Father and communicates to this humanity, by virtue of which this man is God truly, perfectly, and substantially. This man, I say, who is called Jesus, alone among all the children of men, is God by uncreated grace, God by divine unction, God by communication of divine substance and subsistence, and God by deity itself. For this reason, the prophet speaks to Jesus these holy words: *O God, your God has anointed you with the oil of gladness above your companions.* From this we conclude two kinds of consecration of this humanity: one by the Father, who gives it his Son, and the other by the Son, who gives it himself. Both of these are worthy of a fuller discussion. Both are included in this verse, which expresses great mysteries to us in few words and the wondrous relations of the Father to the Son, as Father and as God; of the Son to the Father, as Son and as incarnate Son; and of this humanity to them both, since it belongs to the Father as the humanity of his Son, and it belongs to the Son as his own humanity. But let us leave the fuller and clearer explanation and exposition of this verse for another time, and let us go back to adoring God in this humanity. For he is in it as in the ark, not as in the ark of the Old Testament but as in a new ark, the ark of the new covenant, where he placed the propitiation of humankind, where the manna of the deity rests, where he gives his oracles, and where he receives the adorations of his people and his Israel. Not in a corner of Judea but in the universe, not on the earth only but in heaven, and not for a time but for an eternity. In short, he is in this humanity as in that which does not bear only the mark and presence of his deity in the manner of most holy, glorious, and exalted things, but that does so in a manner wholly distinct and singular to him and in so high and august a way that it seems to be close to, to imitate, and to adore the existence, dwelling place, and rest that God has in himself.

This is what caused St. Paul to say, speaking of Jesus Christ, "In him all the fullness of the Godhead dwells bodily" (*In ipso inhabitat omnis plenitudo Divinitatis corporaliter*).[23] This is a sacred, profound, and mysterious text, containing in these few words three parts and propositions that are great and important to the dignity of this mystery: the presence and indwelling of Jesus' deity, the fullness of the deity that dwells in him, and the singularity of this indwelling, which is defined by the condition appropriate to this mystery by this word *corporaliter*.[24] For it is the very deity and not a grace or ray of it. It is the very substance of this uncreated sun and this divine and personal light that dwells in Jesus: *In ipso inhabitat, etc.*[25] The deity does not dwell in him according to one of his perfections only, but all the fullness of the deity dwells there: *omnis plenitudo Divinitatis*.[26] And this fullness of the deity dwells in this humanity really and matchlessly, substantially and personally, according to the fullness and vigor of these sacred words: *In ipso inhabitat omnis plenitudo Divinitatis corporaliter*.

But, reserving the last two points for another discussion, let us now consider the first one, and let us note that God indeed dwells in all things, but it is not this sort of indwelling that St. Paul is speaking of. He means to say something greater and more excellent about so great a work and so excellent a subject. We must not reduce the greatness of the divine mysteries and oracles to the meanness of our understanding and thoughts when we contemplate and consider them. They must be

---

23. Col 2[:9] (original marginal note).
24. "Bodily."
25. "In him dwells, etc."
26. "All the fullness of the Godhead."

measured according to themselves and their own dignity, not according to us and our baseness. We must rise up and be proportionate to their greatness.

God therefore has two kinds of dwelling places: one in himself and the other in his creatures. The one corresponding to this mystery, which this apostle speaks of here and which he ascribes to Jesus, honors and looks upon as its model and origin the greatness and dignity of God's dwelling place within himself, not the one that he has in his creatures. It is not this second kind of dwelling place that this text of St. Paul expresses to us, for this great apostle has a greater, holier, and more exalted meaning. And just as this mystery is wholly singular and fitting to the deity, so also this presence and dwelling place of God in the humanity (which accords with this mystery and is expressed in these words, and which is fitting to Jesus and belongs only to him) is not this dwelling place of God that is common and ordinary to inanimate and insensible things—things that are good and evil, embodied and spiritual, of nature and of grace. This eagle of the apostles goes higher, he pierces the skies, goes beyond the orders of created things, and rises to the throne of the Godhead, and there he fixes and arrests his sight on God himself.[27] As there is in God a distinction of essence and person, a plurality of persons who are distinct from one another, and a kind of residence and indwelling that is fitting and specific to persons who reside in one another and in the deity that is common to them, this eagle of the apostles, as he contemplates this mystery, sets and arrests his sight on God and on this dwelling place that God has in himself. From there he swoops all the way down to us, in order to give us this word and encompass in it a high and exalted meaning that is worthy of this mystery's sublimity and also worthy of his flight and his rapture unto the third heaven.

This dwelling place, therefore, that is expressed in these sacred words is a dwelling place of God that draws to itself this created being in which he dwells, exalts it above all created being, and (preserving it in its human nature) gives it being in his being, joins, unites, and deifies it in himself. He does this in such a way that it has no being except in

---

27. Each Gospel writer has been traditionally identified with one of the "four living creatures" spoken of in Ezek 1:5–10 and Rv 4:6–7. John is identified with the eagle.

uncreated being, as though God desired to imitate and represent, in a subject and nature so base as human nature is, the state of the divine and uncreated persons who subsist and exist only in the Godhead. Being distinct from one another, they are yet one and the same with the divine essence. For in this way, this humanity, remaining in the distinction and difference of its own nature, without any alteration and confusion, has one same subsistence and existence with the deity, and God dwells in this precious, singular, and excellent way in Jesus. To be precise, this new and singular presence of God in this humanity is a divine imitation and a formal expression that the eternal Word wanted to make when he contemplated the manner of being and residence that the divine persons have in one another and in their one common essence. A great, precious, and exalted object! An object indeed worthy of being imitated! And of being imitated by so powerful and precious a worker as the eternal Word, who is the understanding, wisdom, and power of the Father, by whom all things were made! A precious object, which could not be imitated except by him, nor worthily expressed except in a singular mystery! For a thing so high and great could not be expressed sufficiently in the inferior order of nature nor even in that of ordinary grace. It was reserved for the order that surpasses both nature and grace and joins them by a new bond as it surpasses them. In this supreme and new order, God who is and dwells in all things, either by his nature or by his grace, is and dwells in this humanity by both grace and nature. By grace, but uncreated grace, substantial grace, personal grace, grace that surpasses and that is the foundation of all grace; and by nature, which meets here with grace and, what is much more, is the same grace: grace in its communication with regard to us, and nature in its condition with regard to God. For it is the nature and substance of God himself that is the grace personally communicated to this humanity and that sanctifies and deifies it in him. As God therefore wants to dwell in this humanity by this substantial, divine, and uncreated grace (which is his own nature) and by his nature (which is this supreme grace that he deigns to confer matchlessly on this created being), he wants to dwell in this humanity in a manner so high and sublime and worthy of himself that it is a deep and living representation and a perfect imitation of the way in which the Godhead dwells in itself and its persons in it. This thought is great and high, worthy of the conception of the apostle who speaks this oracle, and worthy indeed of the greatness of this mystery, which bears the most worthy, most efficacious, and the most holy presence that God can have in any created thing and is most similar to his dwelling place and rest within himself. But we cannot follow this eagle's flight and this apostle's rapture in the sight and understanding of this truth. Let us go on and follow step by step, leading our minds by degrees, trying to lift them up gradually from the lowest to the highest point of this presence.

Let us say then that God's presence in human nature by this mystery should not be conceived and considered as a bare and simple presence and a mere proximity of two things that have no relation or bond with one another. Nor should it be considered as a presence of God that is purely natural, simply resulting from the use of his power that creates and preserves the nature of things in which he dwells. Nor should it be conceived as a presence of God that results from and accompanies his love, closeness, and intimacy with the soul, as in grace, or even by his love when fully realized and we have perfect enjoyment of him, as in glory. It should be conceived as a presence wholly distinct and particular to the matchless and singular state of this new mystery; a presence that imitates the eternal dwelling, rest, and communication of God in himself; a presence working and actuating this humanity with a new being, a divine and uncreated being (without affecting or confusing either one); that is, a presence of God that applies to this humanity the deity of his essence, the infinitude of his power, the singularity of his love, the property of his subsistence, the actuality of his existence, and the intimacy, depth, and fullness of his divine, supreme, and uncreated being. In brief, presence of such a kind that this humanity receives from it a communication of God that is so deep, high, and perfect, so secret, intimate, and particular, that it is suffused by his essence, quickened by his Spirit, existing by his existence, sustained by his subsistence, and deified by his Word.

For just as God the Father dwells in himself and has his rest within himself, in such a way and manner that in this dwelling place and rest he continually communicates his essence to the divine persons, so also God the Son dwells in this humanity and rests in it, while continually communicating to it his own subsistence. And the Word, who dwells in his Father as in his Father, wants to dwell also in this humanity as in his own essence. For he makes it distinctively his own by this subsistence. Just as he has his dwelling place and rest in the deity as in his eternal essence, he also wants to take his rest and dwelling place in this humanity as in his new essence and wants to dwell there henceforth for eternity. Only in the deity alone and in this humanity is God present, dwelling, and residing like this and occupied in an ineffable and substantial communication of himself. For on earth he pours out his grace, and in heaven he gives his glory, but it is only in the Trinity and in the Incarnation that he has a fitting, direct, and substantial communication of the deity, either by essence as in the Trinity or by subsistence as in the Incarnation: two distinct mysteries and communications, both of them fitting, singular, and adorable in the Godhead. In the one, God communicates his essence, and in the other, he communicates his subsistence, which is one and the same with his essence. In the one, God is Father in giving his substance to his Son, and in the other, God is man, giving his subsistence to humanity. By a means so precious, by a communication so powerful and divine, God is man and man is God. God is man clothing himself in our humanity, and man is God subsisting and living in the Godhead. There is in the world a Mediator between God and men, who is man so that he might bear the death that men deserved and who is God so that he might triumph over the death that men could not vanquish and give them his life and eternity. It is the only Son of God who is this Mediator, who was made man for men's sake, and who by a wondrous love and power exalts us by humbling himself, glorifies us by suffering, makes us gods by making himself human, and makes us immortal by dying.

Thus the long-desired work of redemption is prepared. Thus is established and introduced into the world the most great mystery of the Incarnation that is to accomplish it, the mystery that St. Paul exalts and magnifies with these great words: *Manifeste magnum est pietatis sacramentum, quod manifestatum est in carne, iustificatum est in Spiritu, apparvit angelis, praedicatum est gentibus, creditum est in mundo, assumptum est in gloria!* ("Great without question is the mystery of piety, which is manifested in the flesh, justified in the Spirit, seen by angels, preached to the Gentiles, believed in the world, and taken up into glory!")[28] A great mystery that begins on earth and ends in heaven, where Jesus is at the right hand of the Father! A great mystery, which, in joining earth to heaven, joins God to man, joins him for an eternity! A great mystery, of a greatness and quality that is opposite to that of the mystery of the Trinity, for the one is great in sublimity and the other is great in humility, the one is natural and necessary and the other is free and voluntary! A great mystery, truly great in condescension, in love, in piety, worthy of bearing this beautiful name and praise that the apostle gives it: *Magnum pietatis sacramentum!* And following the nature of sacraments, this mystery and sacrament is composed of two natures, one outer and the other inner, one divine and the other human, one visible and the other invisible, for it is the basis, origin, and model of the other sacraments. They are all, following it, composed of two natures by relation to the Incarnate Word, who wanted to depict and represent his mystery of the Incarnation in his works and sacraments, in his Church. It is the Sacrament of sacraments, with a manner of grace that is more divine and august than the other individual sacraments. It is a sacrament and mystery full of God, full of grace, and full of light, which contains and manifests the invisible God in the visible flesh of man and which sanctifies humanity by the Spirit of the Godhead, according to these beautiful words: *Manifestatum est in carne, iustificatum est in Spiritu.* A powerful and universal mystery, which spreads its rays and effects everywhere, giving light to the angels and salvation to the world! *Apparvit angelis, praedicatum est gentibus, creditum est in mundo.* A mystery wholly divine and heavenly, that rises from earth to heaven, establishes there its permanent home, and draws and calls us all into glory: *Assumptum est in gloria.* A worthy end and crown of so great a mystery!

For this, may God be blessed forever in himself and in his only Son, Jesus Christ our Lord, whom the Father willed to give us in this mystery by a singular love and gift. He calls himself "the Gift of God" in these beautiful words that he spoke to the Samaritan woman: *Si scires donum Dei* ("If you knew, O woman, the gift of God").[29] So let us give ourselves to him, for he is the Father's gift and he gives himself to us. Let us be

---

28. 1 Tm 3:16 (original marginal note).
29. Jn 4:10 (original marginal note).

his, for he is ours, he is wholly ours—in his deity, *nobis datus*, and in his humanity, *nobis natus*.[30] This is what his prophet and his Church say. Let us go to him, for he comes to us, and he has the words of eternal life. Let us cleave to him, for in him our humanity cleaves to his deity. Let us love him, for he is our life, our glory, and our love! Let us adore him, for he is God, he is our God, God and man forever. And loving him, praising him, and blessing him in his grandeurs and marvels, let us yearn for him, let us long for his glory. Let us desire that he bless us and be accepted, served, and adored throughout the world. And let us close with this wish and these words of his prophet: *Benedicat nos Deus, Deus noster, benedicat nos Deus; et metuant eum omnes fines terrae* ("May God, our God, bless us, may God bless us; and may all the parts of the earth, even those most distant, revere and adore the greatness and power of his Majesty").[31]

---

30. "Given to us"; "Born to us."
31. Ps 67:6–7.

Discourse 8

On the Communication of God in This Mystery

An Ancient who was renowned in the study and knowledge of the things of nature made so much of seeing the sun that he said he had been born to behold and contemplate this great body of light, this beautiful star of the universe.[1] It communicates its splendor to the stars and planets, spreads its rays to the ends of the world, makes all things visible and apparent by its aspect, and by its motion it marks out our days, seasons, and years. So greatly did he prize the sight of this great heavenly body. But we are more blessed than this ancient philosopher. We have been raised up in a better school, instructed in a higher philosophy, enlightened by a much more luminous sun, and endowed with its infused light that is supernatural and divine. Let us say with truth that we are born on earth and born again in grace so that we might see the Sun of Righteousness, the uncreated and personal light, light from light, God from God, the only Son of God and only Son of Mary: Jesus Christ our sovereign Lord. Thus, he who created us by his power and redeemed us by his mercy gives us an eternity in which to behold this beautiful object, in the light of his glory, and while we await this blessed state, he offers it to us on earth as a primary object that should exercise our faith and piety in the knowledge and love of him. So let us think of him, let us speak of him, and as we continue our discourses

---

1. Presumably Eudoxus of Cnidus, mentioned in discourse 2.

let us pursue his light, fathom his grandeurs, set forth his marvels, and carry our thoughts further into the state, the secret, and the singularity of this precious mystery.

The sun, whose sight this ancient philosopher prized and loved so much and that we find so beautiful, is only an image of Jesus, who is a sun in the world of grace and of glory. He is the sun of as many suns as there are and will be saints in heaven, who all receive their splendor and luster from him as from a wellspring and inexhaustible fountain of light. For each is more brilliant and radiant than the sun, Scripture says,[2] and they have no other brightness than that which is given to them by Jesus, who is the great star not of the firmament but of the empyrean heaven and the principle of light not for time but for eternity. This sun that we see with our mortal and perishable eyes symbolizes and represents for us the excellences and perfections of that one, who is reserved for eyes endowed with glory and immortality. By this sun's similarities and differences from that one, it raises us to a more perfect and complete knowledge of him, for he is both its archetype and architect. It teaches us to value and recognize more deeply the nature of eternal things within the sensible view of temporal things.

For if the sun that is subject to corruption is so beautiful, grand, quick, graceful, and regular in its motions that we cannot marvel enough at this great work of the hand of the Most High; if, by the beauty of its nature, as a clear and shining eye it excels above all visible creatures; if it completes its periods and revolutions with so beautiful an order and measure that our minds are not adequate even to conceive such great speed with such great uniformity;[3] if by its influence and light it is so necessary to the universe that the universe immediately feels a disturbance in its being and feels its vigor eclipse when the sun goes into eclipse, although this occurs for such a short time and not in all places; in short, if this sun is such that one can never have one's fill in regarding it, how excellent must be, in beauty, in greatness, in brightness, in majesty, and in all kinds of perfections, the Sun of Righteousness, the Sun eternal, the Sun that creates the day of grace and divides it from the night of sin, the Sun that presides over time and

---

2. Phil 2:15.
3. Perhaps a reference to Johannes Kepler's *New Astronomy* (1609).

eternity, the Sun that separates the true light from true darkness, the Sun that enlightens both the earth and the empyrean heaven? How resplendent then will this true Sun be in his light? How prompt in his motions and in his appearing? How regular in his motion? How powerful in his influences? How efficacious in his attractions, and how necessary to the universe? If a blind person suffers great loss for never seeing this sun that appears to our eyes, what loss is it to the sinner to be deprived—deprived forever—of the sight of him who is his life and truth, who is and calls himself the true light of the world, and who is truly, wondrously, and divinely a sun, a sun very different from this one? For this sun is for the body only and is set forth only to the eyes of men and beasts; but Jesus is the Sun not of men only but also of angels. Jesus conveys a light that extends not only to eyes, to immortal eyes, but also to spirits, to spirits endowed with glory. Jesus is the Sun of both the visible world and the intelligible world, in his humanity. He is even a Sun, a Rising Sun, in the archetypal world, in his deity. This sun cannot be called the prince and father of light, for light was created and performed its office before the sun's creation, giving light to the universe and separating day from night. The sun was created afterward, to be a body supporting this most pure and genuine light and equipped to serve as a coach and chariot to bear this firstborn light. But Jesus is the true light, Jesus is one substance of light, Jesus is the wellspring of light, Jesus is the splendor of uncreated light and the father and prince of light, who extends and communicates it on earth and in heaven, in time and eternity, and the one without whom there is no true light in the world. This sun is not in fact the father of nature but just one part of this nature. For heaven and earth were made before it, and before it the earth was covered and heavy with its offspring; for the earth had carried in its womb and pushed forth abundantly a thousand kinds of flowers, grasses, and plants before the sun was created. So it cannot be considered the author of what is born from the earth. But Jesus is the author of nature, of grace, and of glory. Jesus is the one by whom all things were made and by whom they are made new and established in a new being. When God formed this sun of the corruptible world on the fourth day of Creation, he set it in the firmament, and there it is and will remain always, illuminating the earth from the heavens. But when

God formed the true Sun, the Sun of the eternal world, in the fullness of time, he set him on earth, and from the earth by his birth he enlightened the heavens. Even the angels came down to earth to seek his light. And now he is both on earth among his people in his Eucharist and in the empyrean heaven among his angels and saints, on the throne of his Majesty, illuminating the heavens and the earth and filling heaven and earth with his glory.

Now, this ancient philosopher, who so greatly prized the sight of his sun, was quite able to be content in seeing and regarding it often. But he could not depict this sun in itself; he could not transform himself into this sun. He could not become a sun regarding this sun. He still remained as himself, despite this regard and sight. He was still on earth and not in the heavens with his sun—still in his base and earthly nature and not clothed in this sun's brightness, splendor, and vivacity. But we have an additional advantage over this ancient philosopher, beyond those that we have described above in regard to the Sun who is truly ours and truly Sun, in whose sight we should be occupied. For we do not have only the power of contemplating and regarding a sun as this ancient philosopher did, but we have a much different Sun to contemplate, and we also have the power of depicting and forming him in us. He depicts himself in us by the rays of his grace, as with lively colors. He draws and raises us to him by his efficacy, he transforms us in his qualities by his power, and he makes us heavenly, resplendent, luminous, and eternal as he is. He even establishes his throne and tabernacle within us by a divine mystery, and we are conveying this Sun in the world.

The excellent art of painting is an imitation of nature, which represents to our eyes by its industry what God produced in the world beyond himself by his power. But this art appears weakest when it wants to depict the sun—the most noble of the bodies that God formed in the universe—for there is so much vigor, splendor, and brightness in this heavenly star, which cannot be expressed by the shadows and tints of the earth. The impotence of this art is nowhere so evident as in the depiction of this excellent object, for there is so much visible and sensible distance between the image and the exemplar. The profession of Christianity is in fact an art of painting, which teaches us to depict, but within ourselves, not on an external medium, and to depict there one single object. For we are not to depict the world within ourselves but to efface it—a world that is the sole object of men's sight and the painters' art. We are not to bear the image of the old man within us, but that of the new man. And, to speak more clearly, we are to depict within ourselves one single object, the most excellent object that is, and the one on which painting has least purchase; that is, we are all to depict within ourselves a sun, the Sun of the sun, the Sun of Righteousness, the Sun of the empyrean heaven and of eternity: Jesus Christ our Lord, who is the living image that the Father formed and expressed in himself. We are to spend our life in this beautiful and noble exercise, in which we express and form within ourselves the one whom the eternal Father expressed in himself and whom he expressed to the world and to the Virgin's womb by the new mystery of the Incarnation. In this noble and divine exercise, our soul is the worker, our heart is the board, our spirit is the brush, and our affections are the colors to be used in this divine art and excellent painting.

But how much distance there is between this imitation and image of Jesus Christ that we form in ourselves, following the apostle's counsel, and its original and exemplar? Certainly, nothing can artlessly represent the sun except the sun itself, which is the most excellent painter in the universe and the best painter of itself. For if we just expose to it a polished glass, it instantly creates the true and vivid image of itself in this glass, which no painter can imitate or even regard, for it is so brilliant and sparkling, so lively and vigorous, and the brightness, splendor, and beauty of its exemplar is expressed so artlessly and naturally. So also is Jesus the true painter of himself, and just as he has so many excellent relations with the sun, he also has the one of depicting himself and impressing his perfect image and likeness on the soul. For after we have tried to depict him imperfectly within us by our spiritual thoughts and affections, in the life on earth, he wants to represent himself much more perfectly in our hearts and spirits purified by his grace, which he does in the life of heaven. There, as we are exposed to his aspect and to the rays of his light, he represents himself in us as in a highly polished glass. Drawing us to him, lifting us up to him, he makes us like him and communicates his heavenly and glorious qualities to us. In these two kinds of paintings of one same object that are so different, the state and leading of the soul take place in two very different kinds of life: the one in which by its labor and industry accompanied by grace, it works and impresses on its ground the spirit and efficacy of Jesus; and the other in which Jesus himself, by the abundance and fullness of his light and luster, himself acts and works and impresses his spirit and likeness upon it.

But to lead us into the understanding of our mysteries by means of the same comparison with the sun that impresses its image on the mirror that is exposed to it, let us posit what does not belong to the earthly sun so that we might better understand what belongs to the Sun of the empyrean heaven. Regarding this sun's vivid and sparkling image in this mirror, let us imagine what would happen if this sun that impresses its image and representation on this glass were to come down from heaven, to apply, impress, and incorporate itself in this glass and become one single body and substance of light and brightness. How different that would be from the painter's dead image on a canvas and from the likeness impressed on the glass by the sun's rays! For there it is only an instance of the sun that its aspect impresses on this glass, but here it would be the sun itself in its own substance and light that would have suffused this glass, not by its rays but by its substance, and that would become one single body and principle of light. This is what the eternal Word, the true Sun in eternity, the Rising Sun in the Godhead, does in the sacred humanity of Jesus. He is not content to depict his image and likeness in it, as he does in us, but he comes forth from his Father's bosom, he comes down from the highest heaven to the lowest point of earth, he applies himself to this humanity, he unites himself with it, and he communicates to it his existence, subsistence, and person. And just as his Father who produces him eternally has impressed his own essence on him, he also, by a new production that he receives in human nature, impresses his subsistence and person on this humanity. He communicates to it his glory, splendor, and deity; he completes and accomplishes this created being with his uncreated being; he unites himself with this humanity, establishes himself in it, and incorporates himself in it. By an excellent mystery, according to the Holy Spirit's word, the Word is made flesh and dwells in us, full of life and glory, full of grace and truth,[4] full of light and majesty, as the one who is the only

---

4. Jn 1:14.

Son of the eternal Father and who is a new principle of life, glory, and deity communicated to the world.

It is the subject of the present discourse that this ineffable communication of the deity gives life and subsistence to our humanity. In order to understand this well, we must assume the earlier discourses: that the faith, in its light and piety, distinguishes, confesses, and adores two things in God, that is, his essence and his subsistence. It also distinguishes, confesses, and adores in these mysteries two kinds of divine communication, which set the foundation and establish the two principal mysteries that endure for all eternity, that the Church announces and proclaims to the world by God's authority, that the earth receives and adores in the humility of its faith, and that heaven will cause us to see in its light and glory. For the communication of essence establishes the mystery of the Trinity, and the communication of subsistence establishes the mystery of the Incarnation. And just as this essence that is divinely residing and communicated to the divine persons is their existence, greatness, deity, majesty, and their supreme, uncreated, and absolute perfection, so also the subsistence that is divinely communicated to human nature is this humanity's greatness and the cause, basis, and origin of all the excellences, perfections, and bliss that are and ever will be communicated by the Godhead to this humanity. This is why deep and particular consideration of this subsistence is most necessary for the perfect understanding of this mystery and is most worthy and high in itself.

So let us contemplate this mystery and raise ourselves up to acknowledge that when the eternal Word enters into this humanity that he wants to unite and join with himself for eternity, he does not communicate to it only his holy presence, as many uninstructed people might think. Nor does he communicate only some of his perfections that he shares with the other divine persons. In giving himself to this humanity, he gives and communicates to it something that is so great, so high, so divine that it is the same as the divine essence—the divine essence that is the ocean of all created and uncreated perfections and contains them all in oneness, in simplicity, in eminence. And this very thing that the eternal Word gives and communicates to this humanity (in addition to this wondrous sameness with the divine essence) is moreover so distinctive, particular, and intimate to his person that we have no words adequate to express it worthily, what we call in the Godhead by this august and singular name of "subsistence": subsistence whose particular feature it is to be incommunicable even within the divine being, to constitute the second person of the Trinity, and to distinguish him from the other divine persons.

Whence it comes that this mystery, which is primary in the Christian religion and the origin of Jesus' other mysteries, in his life, death, and glory, is in an order and state so particular and wondrous that it is both singularly divine and singularly distinctive to the divine Word. These are two points of very great consideration in this mystery, and from which many great results and consequences follow. Because this mystery is singularly divine, since it is founded and established in a being that is one and the same with the divine essence, that is, in subsistence, which is so perfectly one same reality with the divine essence that our minds cannot even conceive of it without this essence. For although they can divide things that are most joined together, and our thoughts separate essence from relations, they cannot separate relations from their common essence, by a wondrous secret within the Trinity and by a marvel in Marvel itself. For the same means that makes this mystery divine makes it also singularly distinctive to the Word, since it is founded in this subsistence that is so distinctive to the Word that it belongs only to him. For of the two things that we distinguish and adore in God, essence and subsistence, both are singular and remarkable in the oneness that corresponds to each one. But it is so fitting to the essence of the Word that, being one, it is yet equally and divinely communicable to the divine persons and corresponds to the Father and the Holy Spirit as much as and as well as to the Son. The subsistence of the Word, on the other hand, is perfectly one and perfectly incommunicable in the Godhead, and it is so distinctive to the Word that it corresponds to him only and constitutes his being distinctively. Whence we see clearly that this communication of the Word to humanity is made by what is so intimate to the Word as is subsistence, and so distinctive to him that it belongs only to him and not to the Father or to the Holy Spirit, with whom he shares even his essence. And yet, by the privilege of incomparable love that—O greatness! O marvel!—does in this mystery what is not found for a deep reason in the divine nature in the mystery of the Trinity, this subsistence that is incommunicable in the divine being is communicated, by an outpouring of love, into created being. And this subsistence is appropriated to human nature, to a new essence, an essence that is other, a created essence, and deigns to fill out in this essence the offices and uses of human and ordinary subsistence. This indeed demonstrates the excellence and singularity of this intimate, high, and sublime communication that takes place in the sacred mystery of the Incarnation. For faith adores two kinds of divine communications, which are very different from one another: one is the communication by nature in the Trinity, which communicates the essence and produces the person, but which produces it as incommunicable; and the other is the communication by love in the Incarnation, which communicates the person, and in the person the essence, and communicates this person that is incommunicable in the Godhead. O power! O privilege of love in regard to the Godhead itself, since it even communicates what is incommunicable in the Godhead! But this point deserves a separate discourse on the love of God in this mystery.

Let us continue our discussion, and let us say that this subsistence, communicated to this humanity in place of its human subsistence, makes and founds a singular and wondrous appropriation of the Word to this human nature, and of this human nature to the Word, and of us all in it and by it to this same eternal Word, and to the Most Holy Trinity as a whole. To understand this, we must note that this humanity does not belong to the Word only as the creature belongs to its Creator or as the vassal belongs to his Sovereign Lord—which is a right and quality that pertains equally to each of the divine persons—but it belongs to him in a sense in the same manner (who will dare speak it?) that the divine essence belongs to the Word. For the incarnate Word has two natures and essences, and this humanity is the second and new essence of this Word, just as the deity is his first and eternal essence. The Word wanted the subsistence of his deity to be the subsistence specific to this new essence (that is, to his humanity) as though by the strength and power of his love he had wished to share one same thing, a thing indivisible and incommunicable in itself, between two natures so unequal and different, by giving the same subsistence of his deity for the subsistence of this humanity. In this way we see that this humanity, subsisting to the same extent that the Godhead subsists, belongs to the Word by the title, right, and quality of essence, which is the same title that the divine essence holds and that corresponds to this uncreated being. But it is with this difference: that the human nature is the new essence of the Word, and the divine nature is his eternal essence; that the human nature is a willed essence, and the eternal essence is a necessary essence; that the human nature is an essence taken on and espoused by love, and the divine essence is given and received by nature.

Would I dare go further in fathoming this belonging that our humanity has to the eternal Word, and in giving thanks for the blessed and honorable right and the dear and precious quality that it bears, of being truly and properly one of his essences? For it is not yet enough to say that this human nature belongs to the Word by a kind of belonging that corresponds to no other created thing, and that it belongs to him in the same way that it does to the divine essence. We must go one degree further and say that it belongs to the Word in a sense that is so fitting to him that it does not even correspond to the divine essence, which is nonetheless the incarnate Word's first essence. For it has a singularity of belonging to the Word that is not found even in the divine nature. This singularity of belonging is so fitting to him that nothing belongs to the Word as this human nature does. Neither in created being nor in uncreated being is there anything that so specifically, solely, and singularly belongs to God—to God, I say, by an outpouring of love united with our humanity. For it has all the same rights and titles of belonging that correspond to all created things, and it enters blessedly into the right and ownership of the essence of the eternal Word, as the divine nature. And further, it has a singularity of belonging and appropriation to the Word that other created things do not have and that even uncreated essence does not have with regard to the persons of the Trinity. For this human nature corresponds only to the Word alone among the divine persons, whereas the divine nature corresponds equally to each of the uncreated persons, because the faith instructs us that the divine essence, although it is the essence of the Word, is shared with the Father and the Holy Spirit. But the human essence, in the order of created and uncreated things, corresponds only to the Word in this kind of oneness, intimacy, and property of person, for it is so much his essence that it is not the essence of the Father and the Holy Spirit. It is the beloved of the Father, but this is not its essence. It is the spouse of the Holy Spirit by the bond of grace, but this is not its nature as it is the nature of the Word subsisting and living newly in the world. For this humanity is the essence of the Word by the bond and right of his own subsistence, for which reason the Word is ours by nature and by grace and is called singularly "our God" by the divine oracles: *Deus noster*, as being singularly ours by the state of this mystery.[5] By this we also ought to be singularly his, as by a mutual and reciprocal right. It is a right that is blessed and advantageous for us, but an ownership and right that is onerous for him, for he will give it as the earnest for our sins, the deposit for our transgressions, the companion of our wretchedness, and, in the end, he will put it on a cross and in a grave.

But leaving these thoughts for another time and contemplating the honor that this humanity receives by this mystery, let us rise up and say, O dignity! O greatness! O bliss of human nature, to be chosen to belong to the Word in such a way! To be chosen to belong to him by a manner of belonging that does not correspond to any other created thing! To be chosen to belong to him by a singular right that the faith does not permit us to ascribe even to his eternal essence, which all the faithful acknowledge as the essence of the other divine persons! Rather, faith instructs us that this humanity has no other person to whom it belongs or in whom it rests except the person of the Word. And this kind of belonging, matchless and singular in the Word, is yet more marvelous, in that it is both natural and supernatural to him. For it belongs to the Word as to the one who is his very person, and the belonging of the nature with the person is a belonging so intimate, so intrinsic, and so natural that the order of created things contains nothing greater. In addition, the dignity of this person who deigns to be the own person of this human nature is so eminent above all created nature that his greatness and highness seem not to enter into these limits. He is so divine that we cannot regard him without adoring him. For he is the person of the Word, he is the second person of the Trinity, equal to the first, and

---

5. Ps 66 [67:6] (original marginal note).

he is a person in whom the divine essence subsists from all eternity, as in one of his persons. This belonging, therefore, of the humanity to the Word is not only so distinctive and intimate; it is also so abundantly high and divine that it may rightly be spoken of and esteemed with wonder as both natural and supernatural—indeed, as natural as though it were not supernatural and as supernatural as though it were not natural at all. That is, so natural that no condition could be more intrinsic and no bond more intimate between things that belong to one same nature—all other natural unions and belongings being lesser than that of person—and so supernatural and exalted above nature that neither men nor angels can even conceive of a greater exaltation and eminence than that which this humanity has, united with the person of the Word.

Now, in communicating himself to human nature thus, the eternal Word first communicates his subsistence. And because the divine essence is the essence of the Word and is the same, by being one, with the subsistence that he communicates to this humanity, it follows that the divine essence, as essence of the Word, is also joined and communicated to this human nature. I say, as essence of the Word, for it is also the essence of the Father and of the Holy Spirit, and as such it has conditions (to use theological language) that it does not have as essence of the Word. It is not joined to our humanity as the essence of the Father and of the Holy Spirit but as the essence of the Word. And as the essence of the eternal Word, no one can dispute that it is not united with this same nature that the Word is united with, since the person of the Word comprehends his essence and his subsistence. Therefore, if the person of the Word is united with this humanity, the Word's essence and subsistence is united with it. This humanity of Jesus Christ our Lord bears and receives in itself not only God's personal being but also his essential being. For the Word is God, God is man, and man is God, according to the most familiar and commonly held notions of the faith. The Word is God by this divine essence, God is man by this humanity, and man is God by the deity that the humanity receives in the subsistence of the eternal Word. It is not possible to understand how this personal being of God can be communicated without God's essential being, which it comprehends and encompasses in its formal conception. This is also the commonly held doctrine of theologians, although it does not seem to be well understood by the authors of defamatory pamphlets, who demonstrate by this that they are as unpracticed in Christian charity as they are uninstructed in the understanding of these mysteries and of the Council of Toledo that they cite without understanding it, as will be said elsewhere.

But let us reserve that for another time and not add heat to this discussion. Let us go on to say and assume that the humanity of Jesus Christ our Lord is united with the person of the eternal Word, that is, with his subsistence and with his essence; that it is united originally with his subsistence and subsequently with the essence; that it is united with the essence by means of the subsistence and not with the subsistence by means of the essence; that it is united with the essence of the eternal Word as being the Word's essence and not that of the Father or the Holy Spirit; that it is united with the essence that is shared by the Father and the Holy Spirit, not as it is shared and subsisting in their persons, but as it is subsisting in the specific person of the eternal Word; and that it is united by the Father, the Son, and the Holy Spirit with the subsistence of the Son, but that it is possessed only by the Son in this way that constitutes the mystery of the Incarnation. This is what the Council of Toledo wished to define, in this article that has been poorly cited, understood, and applied by some critics of this age.[6]

Now this eternal essence, as the essence of the Word, is divine, infinite, supreme, and sovereign over all created essence. In a word, it is an abyss of grandeurs, of perfections, of marvels. Therefore, all its grandeurs, excellences, and perfections, by means of this subsistence and because of and as a result of this subsistence, are communicated to this humanity. For these perfections subsist in the subsistence of the eternal Word; they subsist therefore in this humanity, since their subsistence is the same as that which accomplishes and completes this humanity. I said specifically, "by means of this subsistence," and I then intentionally added, "because of and as a result of this subsistence." From this it must be noted that this is not a simple variation of redundant words. These terms are different, and they convey different things. They mean great things that the tongue cannot express, nor the mind

---

6. Eleventh Council of Toledo (675 AD).

conceive. Faith adores these things on earth under its veil of darkness, and heaven reveals and manifests them in its light. What we can say and conceive of them in general, in the baseness and darkness of earth, is that the grandeurs and perfections of this divine essence, insofar as they are communicable to a created being that remains created, and in all the ways that they are communicable to it, without any conversion and confusion of one nature with the other, are in actuality abundantly and worthily communicated to this human nature, according to the divine economy and dispensation. They are communicated to it in order to enhance, actuate, perfect, dignify, and deify this humanity, in the way that inferior things may be actuated and perfected by supreme things, human by divine, and created things by uncreated being, and in a manner that is wholly fitting, wholly corresponding to the greatness, dignity, and sublimity of the mystery.

We must be content with these general and confused words, for lack of intelligence to fathom and explain the extent, sublimity, and depth of mysteries. For who could conceive and express what is either formally or effectively, firstly or subsequently, substantially or accidentally, or originally or secondarily encompassed in these words about the personal union of the divinity with the humanity? About the supreme and ineffable communication that is between God and man? About that which God gives to man and works in man, who is man and God together, that is, Man-God? And about that which this man, Son of God and Son of man together, works toward God and for God, in view of his appointed tasks and in the abundance of his powers, grandeurs, and excellences? O union! O communication of God in this ineffable mystery! O love! O life of God in this sacred mystery of life and love! O life! O love of man in God! O greatness! O holiness of God in this most high and holy mystery! Each one of these thoughts deserves its own discussion. Let us reserve them for another time and be content with saying here that if one degree of grace makes a soul worthy of God; confers an excellent deification upon it, as the holy Fathers say; and makes it "partakers of the divine nature" (*Divinae consortem naturae*), as the first and prince of the apostles says,[7] what excellent deification,

---

7. 2 Pt 1[:4] (original marginal note).

what divine communication, what sublime and intimate cleaving to the deity, what result, what extent of states, effects, and marvels will there be in this sacred humanity that receives into itself not one degree of grace but an abyss of grace? Not an abyss and an ocean of accidental grace, but of substantial grace, the origin and fundament of all grace? Not a created being communicated to men and angels, but uncreated being, the deity, which is right and fitting only to the divine persons and which by an ineffable power and love is communicated to this humanity, to this humanity alone among all created things, which is sublimely and intimately suffused, deified, and sanctified by the deity?

Let us follow the same example of grace so that we might learn where God yet desires to exalt this humanity, by giving it a new and subsequent communication of himself as a result and in honor of the earlier one that establishes and introduces the sacred mystery of the Incarnation into the world. For if for one degree of grace, which is only a quality of accident, God gives himself to man in the state of glory for all eternity, what will he do for his only Son Jesus Christ our Lord? And what will he give him? What new, abundant, and ineffable communication of himself will he make to his humanity, in which resides not one degree of grace but an abyss of grace? And not only an abyss of graces, but the ocean from which flow all the graces that are poured out in heaven and earth—that is, in which he sees residing the substantial grace, the uncreated grace, the being, person, and life of the deity, life subsisting, living, and working in this humanity for the glory of the eternal Father? Let us not reduce our mysteries to the meanness of our thoughts. Let us rise up to God and see that he is not content to give simply and specifically only his subsistence to this humanity, but that in this subsistence he gives himself; he gives his efficacy, power, and holiness; he gives his glory, existence, and majesty. In short, he gives it what he is, what he can give by an infinite love, and what it can receive from him by a power that is supreme.

God extends and communicates himself infinitely, and on the basis of his goodness alone he makes a great profusion and communication of himself to his creatures. What more will he then do by the new right and basis of the subsistence that he has given by love to this humanity, a subsistence that is one and the same with his own essence? God acts in his works according to his dignity, wisdom, and love; he communicates himself more or less, according to the dignity of his works and the proportion of the subjects that enter as though into interchange, communion, and communication with him. In this work therefore that is the chief and sovereign of God's works, and in this humanity that God himself desired to make worthy and capable of an infinite communication of himself, by the right that it has to be the humanity of the only Son of God, by the basis it has to subsist by his own and divine subsistence, and by the privilege it has of being sanctified by the deity itself, God will do in the world, by his goodness and wisdom, all that his power and love can do that is great, precious, singular, and marvelous. God will make a new communication of himself to this humanity that is worthy of his greatness, worthy of the sonship of his only Son given to this nature, worthy of his own and divine subsistence, worthy of a humanity filled with God and sanctified with the same deity, worthy of the state and greatness of this mystery, worthy of the infinite love by which he wrought it, and worthy of the wondrous things that he wants to do and work by it.

We therefore must believe and assume and, summing up what has been said, we must conclude and note, as the faith instructs us, that the divine essence is united with human nature by means of the divine subsistence. And therefore, the perfections of the divine essence are subsistent in the humanity, since their subsistence is the same as the humanity's subsistence. And passing further into the contemplation of this mystery, faith and piety, joined in this holy exercise, raise us up and bring us to recognize how, as a result and because of this subsistence and in its honor, God wants to communicate his being, glory, and greatness to this humanity in a new and singular manner—that is, in a manner that corresponds to this humanity alone, just as this humanity is the only one to which the subsistence of the deity is appropriated. That is, just as in the order of existing things we return to a subject so high, worthy, and exalted that it exists even in uncreated being by the communication of the divine subsistence and existence to our humanity—for there can be nothing in this order that exceeds in dignity an existent so noble and a subject so divine—so also in the order of the communications of God's graces and favors with his creatures. We must return to a sort of communication of grace and favor, of glory and splendor, of the divine being—a communication so high and sublime that it is infinite, if there be room for the infinite. It is such that there can be nothing greater in its type or kind, and such that it can properly be made (according to the laws of the divine wisdom that orders all things in number, weight, and measure) only to the one who bears and receives the divine subsistence. Just as there is only the human nature that receives it in the person of Jesus Christ, so also it alone is open to the greatness, sublimity, and fullness of this communication. It alone is to receive it, and it is right also that this nature receive it, as a result and in honor of this supreme state of hypostatic union to which it is exalted—alone exalted—by means of the divine subsistence. And this communication is as excellent, new, and singular in the world as this mystery is new, excellent, and singular.

This is what I think the Son of God was awaiting at the end of his labors. This is the state and sovereignty that he should receive after triumphing over the devil, sin, and death on his cross. This is what is contained in this beautiful prayer that he speaks upon completing his life and his mysteries, when he gives the kiss of peace and speaks the final farewell to the Synagogue and to his Church in the Jewish and Christian Passover that was completed at the same time at the private gathering in Jerusalem. This is what is suggested in many places in Scripture; this is what the Son asks of his Father with these words: *Clarifica me tu Pater apud temetipsum*.[8] This is what the Father says to his Son with these words, shortly before his death: *Clarificavi et iterum clarificabo*—words all the more worthy of consideration given that they are the Father's final words to the Son that are reported in the Gospel.[9] This is what the Church, raised up in the knowledge and love of her Savior, Head, and Spouse, confesses to be just and worthy that he receive, declaring it so by the mouth of one of the greatest apostles: *Dignus est Agnus, qui occisus est, accipere virtutem et divinitatem, etc.*[10] This is what is suggested to us in several other texts of Scripture that we will cite and explain elsewhere, for all his words, desires, and

---

8. "Glorify me, Father, with yourself." Jn 17:5.
9. "I have glorified and will glorify again." Jn 12:28.
10. "Worthy is the Lamb, which was slain, to receive power and divinity, etc." Rv 5:12.

prayers are given after the mystery accomplished in the Incarnation. These texts therefore speak of a glorification distinct from that which is specifically and necessarily encompassed in the state of the mystery, and they speak of a communication that assumes the same mystery of the Incarnation and that corresponds to its greatness and dignity. The first words that we quoted and that are reported in St. John 17 are the Son of God's own words, and the Son of God speaking not to men but to his Father. Words worthy of such a Son and such a Father, and of such a Son speaking to his Father about himself! Thus, the only Son of God is both author and subject of these divine words. These are words of the Son of God on his final day, a day on which, even among men, words are the most serious, important, dear, and remembered. And they have this additional advantage: that they are words of the Son of God not only on the last day but in the final hour of his free and public life among men and his apostles. For after these words, he leaves the cenacle in Jerusalem and goes to the cross and to death.

Let us listen then with humility, reverence, and love to the Son of God speaking, speaking to his Father, speaking to him of himself, and speaking to him as he is going toward death. We will see that he asks him for a new state, a state that he does not yet have: *Clarifica me tu Pater*. He asks him for a state of glory and splendor, for he uses this word: *Clarifica me*. He asks him for a state of glory with respect not to men but to the Father, dependent not on men but on the Father, for he speaks to the Father with these words: *Tu Pater*. These are words of particular love and efficacy, of the Son contemplating and loving his Father, of the Son speaking to his Father on the day of his final anguish and suffering. *Tu Pater* is what he says to him, as though saying that he is Son, and he is Father; that he is Son entering into the state of his griefs, humility, and cross; that he is Father in an eternal state of greatness and power; and that just as when he came into the world he received from him a state worthy of his love toward men and men's need, so also when he goes out of the world he awaits from him as from his Father a new state that is worthy of him, worthy of the Father, worthy of his cross and of an only Son's love toward his Father, and worthy of the love and power of a Father who is always the all-powerful Father and who is alone the principle and origin of this Son: *Tu Pater*. For, in the view and thought of the things that were close and imminent to him, and in the vigor of his words, we see that he does not speak to earth but to heaven; that in heaven he does not speak to the Holy Spirit, who is not his father or principle; and that he does not speak to God simply as God, for angels and men have that in common with him. We see that by a higher thought, by a particular elevation that is possible only to a spirit living and subsisting in the person of the only Son of God, and by a word that can be spoken only by the mouth of the eternal Word, he addresses God as Father. He addresses the Father as being his Father in a twofold way, according to these two natures. For he is his Father by generation in the Godhead, and he is also his Father as existing in this humanity, which receives and bears in its being the divine subsistence and sonship, by the communication of this person who is divinely begotten and lovingly communicated to this humanity. This is something of what is encompassed in the meaning of this word, *Tu Pater*—a word of singularity, a word of deity, for it regards the very deity and sonship of Jesus who is matchless and singular in the Godhead. For he is not God alone, since the Holy Spirit is also God as he is, but he is the only Son of God, and the Creed causes us to confess and adore him as the only Son of God. These are words therefore of both deity and singularity, words of particular love and efficacy of the Son to the Father in the humble and suffering state to which the love and honor of the Father reduces him, on his final day upon the earth.

In this state, therefore, so strange and pitiful, in the sublimity of these words and thoughts, and in the sight of the eternal Father who is and who has ever been only in a state of brightness, he asks him to communicate this enduring state and brightness. The Father has always been in this state of brightness, and he even produced his Son as the splendor and brightness emanating from him, by which he bears the name "Splendor of the Father." And if we contemplate his divine birth, he as much as his Father ought always to be in a state of brightness and splendor, not only by reason of his divine essence that is all light and brightness, following this word, *Deus lux est*,[11] but also by reason of the birth of his divine person who is produced as light and who in his

---

11. 1 Jn 5[:1, 5] (original marginal note). "God is light."

personal property is *the splendor of the Father's glory*.¹² But the love of his Father draws him from this state by abasing him to our wretchedness. And while the Father remained always in his state of brightness, the Son willed to come down from his greatness and splendor into the state of darkness to honor his Father, and into a condition of lowliness for love for men. He covered himself with the darkness of human life, common life, suffering life, and what is more—O abundance! O goodness!—he covered himself with the shadows of death that darkened the sun itself at full noon. And when he goes to enter into the extremities of this state, soon to being handed over by one of his disciples and forsaken by the others and even deserted by his Father, he asks that his humanity be established in this brightness and splendor that is fitting to his divine essence, his eternal birth, and his own person, and that is owed also to this humanity, since it is his humanity and this brightness has not yet been communicated to it. For the only Son of God united himself in such a way with our humanity that we see he is united with it as God in his divine essence, and as Son of God in his person, but not yet as splendor of the Father. This blessed and glorious state is reserved for after the economy and dispensation of the Son of God's painful and laborious life on earth.

This is the meaning, in my opinion, of these great words: *Glorify me, O Father, with yourself, with the glory that I had from you before the world was made*.¹³ He does not ask simply for a state of glory from men, that is, that men adore and confess him as Son of God, but for a state of glory from God his Father. He asks for a state of glory that depends specifically and singularly on the Father, and to obtain it he addresses the Father only. He asks for a state of glory that depends on his Father as Father and not simply as God, for he specifically asks for an effusion and communication of this brightness that he has from his Father and in his Father throughout eternity. For the glory that men render to the Son of God by believing in him depends on men, some announcing and others receiving the verities of the faith, and all manifesting by this belief the glory of Jesus—that is, the honor that he has in himself and that he deserves to receive from men as the only Son of God. The grace

---

12. Heb 1[:3] (original marginal note).
13. Jn 17[:5] (original marginal note).

by which they enter into this confession and render this honor to him is a grace that depends on God as God and not on God as Father of his only Son. For as Father he has relation only toward his Son, since he is not Father in the property of his person except in regard to this one and only Son. For it is clear that the only Son of God receives this brightness from him and from him alone in his eternal generation and before the world was made, to use these same words: *Clarifica me, tu Pater, apud temetipsum, claritate quam habui priusquam mundus fieret apud te.*[14] And he also looks upon his Father—his Father alone—as the sole principle of his being, life, and state, and as receiving from him the power to communicate to his human nature this brightness that he has received from him and that he holds from him. He looks upon him also in awaiting from him the hour and the moment to communicate it in its actuality, that is, as actuating, exalting, and perfecting by his splendor this humanity established in the glory of the eternal Father. So that just as the eternal Father, begetting his Son within himself, willed him also to be begotten in the world by the Incarnation, so also when he begets him within himself as light and splendor, he wills to produce him in the world and give him to this humanity in a state and quality of divine splendor, enduring for all eternity.

If one wished to reduce the majesty of these words to a lower understanding by relating this glory and brightness that Jesus Christ desired to the glory that men ought to render him by belief and confession of his greatness, I beseech that person to consider that it is uncreated and incarnate Wisdom who is speaking, who has a much higher meaning than ours and is in a state of glory so high and eminent that the belief and confession of men, adoring Jesus Christ as God, is only one ray of his glory and one emanation of his divine splendor. The glory, brightness, and splendor that he is speaking of in this text and that he awaits at the end of his anguish and labors is within him and not without, and is independent of the will of men. It is a glory and brightness that he has and bears within himself, not without. It is a glory that he receives from his Father, not from men. It is a glory and brightness that he possesses securely and unchangingly in the Godhead, not in

---

14. "Glorify me, Father, with yourself, with the glory that I had with you before the world was made."

the changeable belief and thought of human beings. It is the splendor of his deity communicated to his humanity as to a subject capable of bearing and receiving it forever, and of being fully and always actuated, suffused, and filled by it, without affecting this light's infinite being or this humanity's finite being; just as a translucent body is suffused by light without affecting either the body or the light that suffuses it, but with a radiance of light that is more brilliant, radiant, and ardent to our eyes than it was before. Thus, God's splendor united with human nature makes Jesus a principle of light to the world in a new manner and reveals a new meaning for this word of his: *Ego sum lux mundi.*[15]

Man therefore receives this light from Jesus and does not give it to Jesus. It is the glory and light of the world to believe in Jesus. If you wish, it is the outer light and glory of Jesus impressed on the world. But it is not the inner light and brightness of Jesus in himself, that is, the light that he received from his Father and that is impressed on his humanity. It is rather our glory and brightness to believe in him and to know him, and a glory, light, and brightness that emanates from his light, his splendor, and his glory. For his glory properly is neither increased by our faith nor reduced by our unfaithfulness. Jesus is God, and he enters by this means into the state, condition, and property of God's grandeurs. God does not receive any increase for creating the world or loss by losing the world. It is men who lose by losing the knowledge and grace of God and who are exalted by being raised up in the grace and love of God. So the world, by adoring Jesus' glory, receives glory and honor from Jesus, bears and manifests Jesus' glory, in itself. But it does not give glory to Jesus, for Jesus receives it only from his Father in his humanity, just as he receives it only from him in his divinity. This is why at this private gathering in Jerusalem, Jesus Christ, closed in with his apostles, rises up and addresses himself to God his Father. And then, speaking only to him alone in the privacy of his prayer, he opens his heart to him, he sets forth his desire, and he speaks these words—words that are worthy of being engraved by the hand of angels upon our hearts and minds: *Clarifica me, tu Pater, apud temetipsum, etc.*

---

15. Jn 8[:12] (original marginal note). "I am the light of the world."

So that we may understand these words more clearly, let us consider that the eternal Word, from all eternity, is in his Father, as his apostle teaches us at the beginning of his Gospel: *Et Verbum erat apud Deum*.[16] And he is in brightness and splendor in his Father, as these words of his prayer indicate: *Clarifica me, tu Pater, claritate quam habui*, which express to the eternal Father his desire to receive this splendor and brightness from him. *Quam habui*;[17] this is what he says. He therefore had this in his Father before the creation of the world, and he wants to have it in this humanity, since he resides in it by the mystery of the Incarnation just as he resides in his Father by the mystery of the Trinity. For when he came into the world to save the world and to die for our sins, he willed to unite himself with human nature in the subsistence of his deity but not in the splendor and brightness of his deity. He reserved to himself the right to receive this brightness after his pain and suffering, as something that was owed to the presence, subsistence, and life of the deity in this humanity.

He arises and speaks now to God his Father in this memorable prayer, asking that he be established in the use, exercise, and possession of the splendor and brightness that is due him and whose principle he has in himself, divinely and personally united with his humanity. It is as though the rational soul, existing before the body as the Platonists opine, were infused into the body of the small child who has the soul's life but not its light, with its intellectual light darkened as though buried in infancy and dispossessed for a time of the use of this light and understanding. If this soul were to enter into some glimmer and understanding of its state, it would surely rise up to its author who had infused it in this body and ask to be fully established in the use, exercise, and actuality of its understanding and of its own light owed to its essence. The effects and demonstration that the world had of it afterward would be only a result of this state, in which the soul would be in perfect use of reason, light, and understanding in this body. So also the Son of God has a being and state of divine light, brightness, and splendor during an eternity in his Father's bosom, before he resides in the Virgin's womb in this humanity. And this splendor and brightness

---

16. Jn 1[:1] (original marginal note). "And the Word was with God."
17. "That I had."

is covered and hidden in the humble and passible state of his human nature, which he united and joined with himself by the subsistence of his deity but without yet showing forth the brightness and splendor of his deity. For he asks that this splendor of his deity act and appear in fullness of power, vigor, activity, and actuality in this humanity, filling it with his glory and emptying it of its base and mortal conditions in order to clothe and adorn it with his glory, just as he emptied it of its subsistence in order to clothe it with the very subsistence of the deity.

The honor and glory that he awaits from men is something much lower and inferior, something extrinsic to his greatness, a result and dependency of his state of glory. It is but a ray emanating from this brightness, just as in the world the brightness of day is a light emanating from the sun but is not the light of the sun itself, in its globe and sphere. Of this light that it has in itself the sun loses nothing in the darkness of night or the ordinary eclipses that occur in its course and motion around the earth. It is the world that loses its day and light, but the sun does not lose its own, for it is always equally luminous in itself. Thus the world, receiving the light of Jesus, does not give light to Jesus, and in losing it does not take it away from Jesus. The brightness that he asks for with these words is not that which he can receive from the belief and piety of the world prepared to adore him, but that which his Father can give him in the power of his love and which was suspended, until then, for the love of men.

We must therefore sum up, from the preceding words, that there are two kinds of interchange and two ways in which God communicates to man in the mystery of the Incarnation. One precedes the mystery, and the other follows. The one is radical and original, and it contains in efficacy and seed the various states of the mystery. The other is extended, and it gathers in abundance all of the mystery's fruits. The one constitutes the mystery's essence; the other corresponds to its state and dignity. The one is the mystery's nub and essence, and the other is its fullness and enjoyment. The one gives the right to the grandeurs and excellences that are due to this humanity according to its new quality; the other gives the use, consummation, and possession of these grandeurs, excellences, and qualities. In the one, God is man and appears as man, and in the other, man is God and appears as God. In the one, God possesses man, but in the other, man possesses God. In the one, God enters into the being and state of man, and in the other, man enters gloriously into the being and state of God, is adored as God, and is seated at God's right hand. In the one, God is perceived by the senses as man (*habitu inventus ut homo*, as the apostle says),[18] for he is clothed with human conditions; in the other, man is God and appears as God, for he is clothed with God's features and grandeurs. In the one, man receives the title that makes him worth of glory and power; in the other, man receives this same glory and power that he is worthy of and says to his apostles, *Data est mihi omnis potestas in caelo et in terra* ("All glory and power is given me in heaven and on earth").[19]

These two points and states are very different, for the one causes God to be man and man to be God, and yet we see that the eternal Father does not treat this man as God. We see that he leaves him in infancy, in the common life, in the suffering life, as though God were not residing and living in this man. Nonetheless, God is in him according to this sacred word, *Deus erat in Christo mundum reconcilians sibi*,[20] which has deceived the sages of the world and even the demons in the craftiness of their understanding. The other state, assuming that this man is God by the mystery of the Incarnation, causes the Father to treat him as God, draws him from the baseness of human life, and causes him to enter into God's splendor and brightness, which was held back and now pours forth, spreads out, and is communicated to this humanity, suffuses it, actuates it, and fills it. Just as God, who is spirit, makes himself by this mystery able to be perceived, so also Jesus bears the majesty of God in a perceptible way, visibly impressed on his state. Heaven contemplates and beholds him in this glory, the earth believes in him and adores him, and hell feels and experiences him, where by the strength of Jesus' power the demons are constrained to bend the knee before him and render him homage as to their sovereign and their God.

These are the states of Jesus in this mystery. These are the two distinct communications that are encompassed in it: the communication

---

18. Phil 2[:7] (original marginal note). "Being found in appearance as a man."
19. Mt 28[:18] (original marginal note).
20. 2 Cor 5[:19] (original marginal note). "God was in Christ reconciling the world to himself."

of the deity, and the communication of the deity's splendor and brightness. It is this latter that Jesus awaits and that he requests in this prayer: *Clarifica me*. This is what the Father promised him with these words: *Et clarificavi et iterum clarificabo*.[21] If we had been at this private gathering in Jerusalem and present at this prayer of Jesus, we would have had to join our desires and prayers to his, and, as members of this head, spoken to the eternal Father through his mouth, having no desire but that of his glory. But sixteen hundred years have passed since his prayer was granted, his desire fulfilled, and the faith proclaimed to the world that Jesus is established in the glory of his Father. Let us enter therefore into the joy and pleasure of his grandeurs. Let us enter into this apostolic wish: *Omnis lingua confiteatur, quia Dominus Iesus-Christus in gloria est Dei Patris* ("May every tongue confess that Jesus Christ the Lord is in the glory of God the Father").[22] Great and precise words! Words that express to us two very important truths! One instructs and expresses that he is not only in the glory of men but fully and absolutely in the glory of the Father, glory as different and exalted above the glory that he receives from men as the Father is exalted above men themselves and uncreated being above created being; the other truth teaches us that he is now not only in the deity of the Father as he was formerly, but also in the glory of the Father resulting from his deity. In this deity he was established from the moment of the Incarnation and united with this essence that is the eternal Father's essence. But he was not yet fully established in the Father's glory. For despite this supreme and divine state, he remained in the swaddling clothes and in the manger, in infancy and in the helplessness of infancy, in flight and persecution, in sum: in the lowliness of human life, in the thorns of the cross, and in the darkness of death. Although in all these states he was truly God-Man, he was God-infant and helpless in a stable, he was God fleeing and hidden in Egypt, he was God living and unknown in a corner of Judea, he was God suffering and dying on a cross, and he was God dead and buried in a grave. In this humble state of lowliness, the deity of the Father was in him, the love of the Father was in him, and

---

21. Jn 12[:28] (original marginal note).
22. Phil 2:11.

the Father said of him, *In quo mihi bene complacui.*²³ But the glory of the Father was not yet established in him. He was in the Father's deity, he was in the Father's love, but he was not yet in the Father's glory. This glory was deferred by the Father's will toward his Son, by the Son's love toward his Father, and by the regard that the Father and the Son had for the needs and poverty of men. When the Father gave his deity to humanity by giving it the person of his Son, he suspended the giving of the entire and perfect state of his glory. For we see from the discussion of his life that he leaves it for a time in infancy and helplessness, in swaddling clothes and in the manger, in persecution and flight, in the known and unknown life, in the cross, in death, in the grave.

O strange division and wondrous separation, between even the deity and the glory of the deity! A division that takes place only in Jesus, and in him only so that he might represent, expiate, and remove the division that occurs between God and his creatures through sin! Is Jesus less adorable and lovable for having less glory in his life, since it is love and love alone that separates him from it, and since it is for us that he is separated from it? Since he is separated from it by love, let us love Jesus in his love, in his love that separates him from his glory. Let us adore Jesus in his deity, in his deity that abases him to our wretchedness. O love, O strong love, powerful love, love that exercises its power and severities upon the very person of a God in his new nature, which he unites with himself and makes live and subsist in him! O love that arrests the course of the divine emanations in the striving of the emanations of even his love, that is, in the infinite striving and effusion that he made of himself, in giving himself to man! Love brings him to give his deity to this humanity, and yet in the overflow of this emanation the glory is suspended and arrested for a time. He is worthy, infinitely worthy, to receive this glory, and in his time, he will possess it as that which is naturally due him. But he will be separated from it, and for so long a time, that is, all his life, by the power and fullness of his love—I say, by Jesus' love toward his Father. If the love is powerful, if it deprives, if it empties Jesus himself, empties him of something as great as his glory, will it not be powerful over our hearts? Will it not separate and empty

---

23. Mt 17[:5] (original marginal note). "In whom I am well pleased."

our minds of their perverse inclinations, their disordered pleasures, their illicit affections? If the love exercises its power and severities upon Jesus and puts him in the thorns, on the cross, in death, will it not put us in the thorns of penitence, in the cross of the Christian life, in the death of our earthly vices and affections? Ah! Since there is a love that crucifies, that crucifies a God, will it be less powerful over men? Will it not crucify us, in Jesus and with Jesus? And all the more because it is humiliation and opprobrium for Jesus to be crucified, crucified for sinners, but it is glory, it is greatness, it is bliss to be crucified for Jesus and with Jesus and to be able to say with his apostle, *Christo confixus sum cruci* ("I am crucified with Jesus Christ").[24] On this cross, crucified with Jesus, let us like him be lifted up and separated from the earth. For he himself describes his crucifixion to us as an elevation that separates from the earth. Let us therefore be raised and lifted up above earthly, worthless, and perishable things. Let us be crucified, in heart and mind, with Jesus and to Jesus, despising all for his love and glory. And let us say in spirit and in truth this apostolic word: *Existimo omnia detrimentum esse, propter eminentem scientiam Iesu-Christi Domini mei, etc.*[25]

An Ancient said that God, in creating the world, transformed himself into love, so rapt was he by the sight of this universe and so satisfied by its beauty.[26] But he had not seen this mystery, and he knew only this sensible world among the works of God. We therefore, raised up in a higher knowledge, on whom a better time has fallen (the fullness of time that bears the fullness of God and the fullness of God's love in this work of his, his masterwork) and rapt in the contemplation of this mystery, let us say that God, in making a new world, the World of worlds (that is, Jesus) transformed himself into love. For God is love and is only love in this work of his, in which his power, goodness, greatness, and majesty were converted and transformed into love. This mystery is love and nothing but love. For just as in it love joins God to man,

---

24. Gal 2[:19] (original marginal note).

25. Phil 3[:8] (original marginal note). "I consider everything as loss for the preeminent knowledge of Jesus Christ my Lord, etc."

26. Pherecydes, *Apud Proclum* (original marginal note). See Proclus, *Commentary on Plato's Timaeus* 3.1, trans. Dirk Baltzly (New York: Cambridge University Press, 2007), vol. 3, p. 107.

so also God's grandeurs and man's baseness are transformed there in love, by the power of the love that works this mystery and triumphs in this mystery in which God singularly placed his love and the triumph of his love together. Do we not see that in this mystery God's power is transformed into love? And that God, making himself powerless in it, no longer shows himself powerful only out of love? Do we not see that in this mystery God's greatness is transformed into love, and that God does not show himself to be great only out of love? Do we not see that even power and greatness are held captive by love in the helplessness and baseness of infancy? Do we not see that majesty is also transformed in love and changed into the softness and goodness of an infant? Thus, in this mystery God is love and nothing but love. Just as God's state and grandeurs are transformed there in love, so also man's state and baseness are transformed by the striving and power of love. God is man, but it is his love and not his nature that causes him to be man. For the divine nature is infinitely far from human nature and would always be so if the love as powerful and infinite as the nature did not so intimately unite the divine nature with human nature, uniting them in oneness of subsistence, existence, and person. God is an infant, but he is an infant by love and not by the neediness of his condition, as are the children of men. God is a child, the power and the deity being united powerfully, personally, and lovingly to infancy and helplessness. Thus, we should say with astonishment and wonder, *Suscepta est a maiestate humilitas, a virtute infirmitas, ab aeternitate mortalitas.*[27] For thus we see God suffering, God dying, and God dead on a cross and in a grave; but it is love and not his nature that reduces him to this state. His life, his cross, and his death are love, each of them nothing but love, life, and power. Jesus lives, loves, and rejoices in death and in suffering, and gives and merits for us life, love, and joy.

O love of God in this mystery! O love, triumphant over God and over God's love! O love, exercise your power over us and our love! Triumph over us, triumph over us in Jesus, according to the truth of this word: *Triumphat nos in Christo!*[28] Let us live in Jesus, let us love in

---

27. Leo, Letter 10 [sc. 28] to Flavian (original marginal note). "Majesty took on humility, strength weakness, eternity mortality." In *Letters and Sermons*, 40.

28. 2 Cor 2[:14] (original marginal note). "He triumphs over us in Christ."

Jesus, let us triumph in Jesus! May Jesus live in us, love in us, and triumph in us forever! Since love triumphs over God himself, may he triumph over us who are his subjects and creatures! Since God's love alone triumphs, may God's love alone be what holds us captive, and not our passions and agitations of mind. May God's love alone lead us in triumph as its captives! Since love wills to triumph over God and over God's love in this mystery, may the power of this triumphant love, and of this mystery in which it triumphs, be exercised upon us and our wills forever.

The consideration of the divine subsistence communicated to humanity in this mystery as the subsistence belonging to the Word and as one with the divine essence caused us to enter into this discussion and served as a basis and foundation for the points that we have set forth concerning the communication of God in this mystery. For God communicates his subsistence, and in his subsistence his essence, and in his essence the perfections of his essence as subsisting personally in this humanity. In its time, it makes a diffusion and communication of its glory, which is reserved, held back, and suspended at many points of its states and effects by an ongoing miracle, a special miracle, matchless and singular in the state of this mystery and specific to Jesus alone, just as the deity and the splendor of the deity are specific to him alone, excluding any other. This communication of the glory and splendor of the deity, made in its time to Jesus and established in its culmination and perfection in heaven, is a thing so great in itself and establishes a state so eminent and exalted that all that God has ever produced beyond himself in the order of nature, of grace, and of glory is not equal—it cannot even be compared—to this communication of glory, splendor, and brightness that is made to Jesus, in his soul and body, as a result of the communication that he received of the divine essence and subsistence. He is, he alone, a world, a great world. He is, he alone, a greater world than these three worlds together of nature, of grace, and of glory. He is a world of grandeurs, of glory, and of marvels, who holds in eminence, governs in power, quickens in influence, and surpasses in excellence these three created worlds and all those that can be created. For the order and state of the substantial and hypostatic union is a being transcending all the possibility of created being. The grace and glory that is owed to this state of hypostatic union, and that follows and accompanies it, is also a grace and a glory that exceeds all the states of grace and of glory. For he who is the sustainer of this humanity and the origin of this glorious state of his—that is, the eternal Word—is God, and he is God bearing in the deity the splendor of the eternal Father, to whom glory and splendor belong, not only in the deity of his essence but also in the property of his person. When therefore the Word makes a specific communication of himself to his human nature, he will make a special communication of his brightness, splendor, glory, power, and sovereignty, and everyone will have to confess it. Let us say then to the profane, in verses borrowed from a profane writer,

> *Terrarum Deus caelitumque Christus*
> *Cui par est nihil, et nihil secundum.*[29]

And let us say to the Jews in the voice of a prophet and king, their king and prophet, *Hic est Deus, Deus noster in aeternum, ipse reget nos in saecula* ("He is God, our God, for all eternity; he will govern us for the ages").[30] Let us say to Christians in the voice of the prince of the apostles, *Hic est omnium Dominus.*[31] And let us say to them again, in the voice of one who eminently merits the name of apostle by his labors and the efficacy of his spirit,

Deus, Domini nostri Iesu-Christi, Pater gloriae, constituit illum ad dextram suam in caelestibus supra omnem principatum et potestatem et virtutem et dominationem et omne nomen quod nominatur non solum in hoc saeculo sed etiam in futuro: et omnia subiecit sub pedibus eius, etc. Et donavit illi nomen quod est super omne nomen, ut in nomine Iesu omne genuflectatur caelestium, terrestrium et infernorum ("God, Father of our Lord Jesus Christ, the Father of glory, has established him at his right hand in the heavenly places above all principality and power, virtue and domination, and above all that has name, not only in this age but also in the age to come; and has put all things in submission under his feet and has given him a name that is above every name,

---

29. "Christ, God of the lands and heaven, who has no equal and no second." See Martial, Epigram 12.8. Martial's words are, *Terrarum dea gentiumque Roma, Cui par est nihil et nihil secundum* ("Rome, goddess of the lands and nations, who has no equal and no second"). In *Epigrams*, vol. 3, bks. 11–14, trans. D. R. Shackleton Bailey, LCL 480, p. 97.

30. Ps 47 [48:14] (original marginal note).

31. Acts 10[:36] (original marginal note). "He is the Lord of all."

so that at the name of Jesus every knee shall bow, of those in heaven, and on earth, and under the earth").³²

This is the end where Jesus' grandeurs and humilities are brought to completion. This is his secure and abiding state, abiding for eternity. This is his life, glory, and rest, his unchanging rest. This is the object of our eternity and the end where our lives, our crosses, and our discourses should be concluded. We should pass our life in thinking of him, speaking of him, and suffering for him, so that we might live in him as he lives in his Father, be united with him as he is united with his Father, and be in communion with him as he is in communion with the divine persons, that this apostolic wish of his beloved disciple might be accomplished: *Societas nostra sit cum Patre et Filio eius Iesu Christo* ("May our communion be with the Father and with his Son Jesus Christ").³³

For we must note again that this divine subsistence, which as we have explained in this discussion is communicated to the humanity, is the subsistence of the eternal Word, which has as its distinctive feature that it is the hypostatic form constituting the person of the Word. Thus, as it constitutes a person proceeding from the Father and producing the Holy Spirit, as such it is a bond most fitting to bind and join this humanity to the Most Holy Trinity. For this subsistence has a perfect relationship to the divine persons: to the Word as to the one whose own subsistence it is, to the Father as to its origin and principle, and to the Holy Spirit as to the endpoint produced by the principle, that is, by the person that it constitutes. This subsistence, therefore, that is communicated to this humanity is a most fitting bond, a sacred bond, a divine bond, a substantial bond, a personal bond, by which it enters into an incomparable state and greatness, into a very great and perfect communion, and into a most sublime and high communication with the three divine persons. Just as it is communicated, is communicated only, to this one humanity, so also this humanity enters, enters alone, into this greatness, communion, and ineffable communication. For just as this subsistence is only for it, so also this communion, to this degree, is only for it. And in order to express in a few words what was fully discussed,

---

32. Eph 1[:17–22]; Phil 2[:9–10] (original marginal note).
33. 1 Jn 1[:3] (original marginal note).

and to reduce it as to a brief sketch, let us say that when the eternal Word enters into this humanity and gives it something as great and intimate as his subsistence, this humanity enters into the matchless and singular order and into the supreme state of the hypostatic union and is superior to all that is created and can be created. This divine subsistence, being one and the same with the divine essence, wondrously deifies this human nature and makes it divinely human and humanly divine. For it is human in its own nature, and it is divine in its existence and subsistence, so divine that it has being only in uncreated being. This same subsistence—as it is constitutive of the person of the Son, and the particular subsistence that the eternal Father gives him in begetting him, and as it is necessary to the production of the Holy Spirit, in that it establishes a person who produces him—establishes in this humanity (which makes it thus blessedly and gloriously consubstantial with the deity) a belonging, an appropriation, and a substantial and divine relation, in regard to the Eternal Father, who is the origin of this subsistence; in regard to the Son, whom it constitutes; and in regard to the Holy Spirit, who is produced by the person that it accomplishes. And thus it returns, divinely but differently, this sacred humanity to the three divine persons, as a nature that is divinely and gloriously consubsisting with their deity in the hypostasis of the Word and that belongs to them in so high and sublime a manner and by a means so sacred and divine.

O what exaltation of this humanity in the Godhead, since it has being only within uncreated being! O what right and power of God over this humanity, which subsists only in his deity! O what appropriation of the Most Holy Trinity to this human nature! An appropriation that is founded not only in the shared perfections of its essence but in the origin and distinct property of its persons, that is, in the Father as Father, in the Son as Son, and in the Holy Spirit as Spirit proceeding from the Father and the Son. O what belonging and relationship of this humanity, both to this essence and to these divine persons, since it is the one created essence that belongs to them in so particular a way, and which in its being and its singular and exalted state imitates, adores, and regards the divine essence in its being, state, and oneness that subsists in the three uncreated persons! The latter is divine and the former is deified; the latter is uncreated and the former, for its existence, has uncreated existence; the latter is one in the Godhead of the persons, and the former is matchless in the excellent deification that it possesses. And just as the divine essence is communicated divinely and ineffably in the Trinity, so also in the Incarnation the divine subsistence is communicated to this humanity, which enters by this means into very great union and very close communion with the three divine persons. It has communion with the Father, having for its personal being the being begotten by the Father, and established by this means in the eternal sonship. It has communion with the Son, being his spouse, the only spouse of the only Son of God—a spouse not by accidental but by substantial grace, a spouse not in regard to the body only and the least part of oneself but in regard to the body and the spirit and its entire substance; totally, equally, and divinely joined and united with the Word, and united not in superficial oneness but in powerful and penetrating oneness down to the innermost part of every human being; not in temporal and transitory oneness but in enduring and eternal oneness, always matchless, always spouse, and always united really and personally with the eternal Word. It has communion with the Holy Spirit, being by these grandeurs and mysteries joined together by origin and derivation in a particular way with this third person of the Trinity. For this humanity receives in itself the divine and personal being of the very one who gives the Holy Spirit his being and subsistence.

In these high and sublime thoughts, we must note that just as in the being of God we consider and adore two things, one that is absolute and the other relative, one singular and the other plural, one communicable and the other incommunicable, one the essence and the other the subsistence, so also in the mysteries of our faith we adore two perfect, divine, and adorable communions. One is founded in the communication of the divine essence to the divine persons, and the other in the communication of the divine subsistence to human nature, which joins the eternal Word with our humanity and our humanity with the three divine persons. In each of these two distinct communications, we adore an ineffable fullness: in the one, the fullness of the divinity in the sacred Trinity, and in the other, the fullness of the divinity in Jesus Christ, our sovereign Lord, in whom, according to the apostle, dwells bodily all the fullness of the deity, as we will say in the following discourses. Two mysteries, two communications, two fullnesses, and two communions that we are to contemplate, serve, love, and adore, following the teachings of the Christian religion, and that are firmly and divinely founded and established in these two points that the faith distinguishes and adores in God—that is, in the essence, which founds the communication, the fullness, and the first, supreme, and adorable communion of the Most Holy Trinity, which is the end, cause, and model of all communions, divine, human, and angelic; and in the subsistence, which founds the second, divine, and adorable communion of the Word with humanity, and of humanity with the three divine persons. In these two communions are founded and established all the communions of heaven and earth, of God, angels, and men, of time and eternity. For they are all established to represent these two supreme and perfect communions as intimations and images and to adore them as servants and tributaries. All malign and illegitimate communions will be destroyed by the power of these two, and all those that will be lawfully established in the order of grace, of nature, and of glory owe tribute and homage of servitude and praise and are in a state of relationship, submission, and dependency toward these two divine communions of the Most Holy Trinity and of the Incarnation of the Word.

I give it to you, O eternal Word, and I adore you as Word proceeding from the Father and producing the Holy Spirit. I adore you as established in this first and supreme communion, by your divine emanation and ineffable production, in which you are the Son of the Father and the principle of the Holy Spirit. I adore you as setting the foundation and establishing in your person the second and divine communion of the two natures, the one divine, the other human, the one eternal, the other temporal, the one created, and the other uncreated.

In honor of these two supreme, divine, and adorable communions that regard and concern you, O eternal Word! O Man-God! O our Immanuel! I offer you this small society newly established in our day, which has the honor of bearing from its birth the mark and livery of its Lord and of having some kind of likeness to its head in tolerating opposition in its beginning.[34] I do not ask that these winds cease, but

---

34. Bérulle may be referring to the French Oratory, or to those who have taken the vow of servitude.

that as they agitate it, they might strengthen it in the one who is to be its upholder and support. I do not ask that these storms end, but that it might draw from them a lasting fruit, and that in these storms *Dominus dirigat corda nostra in charitate Dei et patientia Christi* ("the Lord direct our hearts in the love of God and patience of Jesus Christ").[35] This is the wish and word of a great apostle, agitated by similarly importunate and restless persons, as he himself calls them: *ab importunis et malis hominibus*.[36] In their midst he had recourse to and addressed the one who is the Lord absolutely and who has dominion over storms and winds, and over the spirits of winds and storms. He desires with these words and teaches us by his example to desire in similar encounters, that the Lord on these occasions might direct our hearts and affections *in charitate Dei et patientia Christi*. This apostolic person, according to the fullness and depth of his wisdom, marks out for us in two words the two points and two poles of the soul's firmament within these movements: *charitas Dei, et patientia Christi*. We who navigate through this life and aim for the port of heaven and salvation, and who must first pass through the torrid zone of afflictions, look upon both poles. Let us not lose sight of these two beautiful pole stars, and in the midst of the waves that surround us, let us contemplate and honor the love of God giving his Son to the world and to the cross, and the patience of Jesus accepting and bearing his cross for the salvation and example of the world.

Give us this grace, O Jesus! and cause this fledgling society that is still a bit frail to be more and more established, founded, and rooted in you. Cause it to draw life, influence, and leading from you; to have motion, concern, and power only for you; to render a particular homage to you and to your sacred humanity; to serve you on earth; to bear the mark, impression, and imprint of your servitude; to render to you its effects; to follow your leading; to devote itself to your interests; to carry out your desires; to be the slave of your greatness and power, of your love, your Spirit, and your cross; to be one of the instruments of your power; to honor your mysteries; to announce your counsels; and to solely and singularly depend on your sacred mystery of the Incarnation. And just as your state, your life, and your difference within

---

35. 2 Thes 3[:5] (original marginal note).
36. 2 Thes 3:2. "By importunate and evil men."

created and uncreated being lie in this mystery—for your person alone among the divine persons is united with your humanity, and your humanity alone among created things is united with your deity—so also I ask of you that our life, our state, and our difference on earth and in heaven be drawn from you and from your sacred humanity. And that in this special piety, devotion, and servitude to the mystery of your Incarnation, your deity made human, and your humanity made divine, might be our life and state, our spirit and particular difference, among the other holy and honorable societies that are in your Church. These seem to have wanted blessedly to share the robe that you left when you went up on the cross, in sharing among themselves the variety of your efficacies and perfections, by which they serve you on earth—some having chosen penitence, others seclusion, and still others obedience as the principal mark, object, and exercise of their institution. While honoring them all as we ought, we choose for our primary mark and difference this particular piety and devotion toward you and toward your sacred humanity, toward your life, your cross, and your Spirit, toward your glory, your grandeurs, and your states, and toward every one of your mysteries. For we desire and intend to renew our love, our belonging, our submission, and our servitude toward you. This is what the devil, the enemy of Jesus and of the servitude that we owe and that we vow to Jesus, regards, fears, and persecutes. This is what some people, to my mind ill-advised, blame and slander without understanding it. This is what we ought and want to preserve and increase in these storms and tempests. This is the end and subject of these discourses and our firm and abiding resolution. Thus, let us live and persevere, and thus, Jesus, be our life, subsistence, and love, unto the ages of ages.

Discourse 9

On the Love and Communication of God in This Mystery

One of the first and most important words of the Eternal Word on earth, which his beloved disciple recounts at the beginning of his Gospel, is a private word about the love of God, about the love of God giving his Son to the world: *Sic Deus dilexit mundum ut Filium suum unigenitum daret, etc.* ("God so loved the world that he gave his only Son, so that whoever believes in him may not perish but have eternal life").[1]

This is the Son of God's first catechesis and instruction to a prominent teacher of the law, and it is one of the private words of his sacred cabinet. For it is a word that Jesus gives intimately at home; he spoke it not out in the countryside but at home and in his house, and not to a multitude but to a great teacher of the law. It is a word that he spoke to one person, intimately and individually, and that he offered in a private conversation that he was having with a prince of the synagogue. Thus, it is recounted to us by one who is secretary of his state and cabinet: the favored beloved disciple and apostle St. John.

Let us hear, revere, and fathom this sacred word. For he who speaks is God, the one he is speaking of is God, and what he speaks of is the love of God, which in God is God himself. He speaks of a love of God that is so high, excellent, and divine in its effect that it gives and communicates a God to the world. For—O greatness! O marvel!—just as

---

1. Jn 3[:16] (original marginal note).

there is in God a love that produces a divine person (that is, the mutual love of the Father and the Son, which results in the production of the Holy Spirit), so also is there in God a love that imitates this supreme, inner, and productive work, which similarly results in a divine person as the object of this love, and which gives and communicates this person to human nature so that it might be completed and accomplished in its own subsistence. The one is natural and necessary love; the other is free and voluntary love. The one is love working in the Godhead, and the other is love working outside the Godhead. The one brings God's emanations to completion within God himself, and the other brings God's emanations to completion outside God himself. The one consummates the mystery of the Trinity, to use St. Hilary's term, and the other consummates the sacred mystery of the Incarnation.[2] These two loves differ in their endpoints and objects, but if their origin is considered, they are but one same being and one same substance of love in the Godhead.

It is this love that Jesus is speaking of in this sacred text, and he speaks of it with elevation, astonishment, and wonder. This is quite remarkable given who it is that is speaking and saying these words, *Sic Deus dilexit mundum, etc.* We must adore Jesus and listen to him willingly as he speaks, for he is the Word of the Father. We must adore and follow Jesus as he rises up in the sublimity of these lofty thoughts, for they are worthy of his grandeurs and understanding. And we have a particular stake in this divine subject that Jesus is contemplating, because in this thought and word Jesus rises up in astonishment and wonder concerning the love of his Father toward the world and the remarkable gift that the Father makes of his Son to the world through this love. This Jesus in whom all the treasures of divine knowledge and wisdom lie, this Jesus who is capable of God and is filled with God according to his infinite capacity, this Jesus who is by this fullness made incapable of ignorance and sin—this Jesus is astonished, and he marvels at the Father's love and the Father's gift. In wonder, he offers these great words: *Sic Deus dilexit mundum.*

Let us follow his example in this astonishment. For if this subject

---

2. Hilary, *The Trinity* 7.41, p. 271.

is worthy of lifting Jesus up in wonder, what should it not work in our minds, which, according to the common opinion of philosophers, are all the more suited to marveling since we have less intelligence and understanding? For this subject was well able to draw from the eternal Word these sacred words, words of astonishment and wonder, *Sic Deus dilexit mundum*—four words that are each worthy of deep consideration and that each justify this astonishment of Jesus. Can it be? Is God, infinite and eternal God, capable of loving outside himself? Is he capable of loving something as base as this base world? And is he capable of loving like this, and this abundantly? Yet Truth himself speaks those four words: "God so loved the world." But, can it be? Can God, who is fully, eternally, and divinely self-occupied within himself, in knowledge, love, and enjoyment of his eternal grandeurs and bliss, be occupied with something as mean as this base world, which is only a point in regard to heaven and a nothingness in regard to God? Can he think of so base and useless a creature as man, about whom his prophet says to him in his light, *What is man, Lord, that you deign to remember him, and the son of man that you deign to take account of him?*[3] Can it be? Can God, who is sufficient and fulfilled in himself, God who fills himself and all things by the fullness of his being, love something outside himself? For love seems to suggest a want and void in the one who loves, as though he were not yet satisfied and filled with the enjoyment and possession of what he loves. Does God, who is completely sufficient in himself, who is filled with the holy, pure, and divine love of his infinitely lovable essence, filled with this love from all eternity, still have room for a love that is other to dwell in him, and a love of something as base and contemptible as the world, and man, which is not an object for so worthy a love? In truth, this is a point worthy of astonishment in the contemplation of moral things, that God can love something outside himself. For God is so eminent, so far from, and so exalted above all created being. God is so blessedly filled and occupied in the love of his being and in a love that fills up, completes, and expends—or, to say it better, fills in the infinity of its act and object—all of God's power and actuality to love. And yet we believe, we see, we experience

---

3. Ps 8[:4] (original marginal note).

that God, while loving himself, also loves this world, and that he loves it with an extreme love. This is the subject that affects Jesus sensibly in this holy cabinet. This is the subject that lifts, delights, and holds him in astonishment and wonder. This is the subject that draws from the sacred mouth of the eternal Word these sacred words: *Sic Deus dilexit mundum, etc.*

It is clear that God in the greatness of his being must have perfect knowledge, not only of himself but of all things. For this knowledge is worthy of him, and he is not abased by it; rather, God remains on his throne, and the things that are known are raised there by the power of his intellect, giving them a kind of spiritual and divine being in the idea in which he knows them. For it is the distinctive feature of every kind of knowledge (sensitive, intellectual, and divine) to transform and raise the things that are known in the quality and dignity of the power that knows them. Thus, material things have a being that is in some way immaterial in this instance, making them visible and perceptible to the outer and inner senses, according to the eminence and quality of the sensitive faculty that receives and perceives them, and they have an intellectual being in the mind of the angel and man who contemplate them. This is one of the excellences that we observe in the understanding, above the will: the understanding transforms its object into itself, whereas the will is transformed into its object. This is also one of the points that makes knowledge different from love. Knowledge draws the object to itself and does not lower the knower to the objects that are known but raises and proportions the known things to the proportion and dignity of the one who knows them. Love, by contrast, brings the soul to the object that it loves, and by a gentle power it lowers and inclines the lover to the thing that is loved. This general difference between love and knowledge is highly significant, especially because it gives rise to a particular difference, even between the knowledge and the love of God that we can acquire on earth. Knowledge places the object in us and does not place us in the object. Love, on the other hand, places us in the object and transports us there so powerfully that, according to this sacred saying that is authorized by various philosophies, the soul is more where it loves than where it lives, and it has more life and presence, more occupation and concern, in the one than in the other. It follows that the soul on earth possesses God through knowledge not as he is in himself but as he is in the soul, and that the soul beginning on earth possesses God through love as he is in himself and not as he is in the soul. For love transports us from ourselves to him, and, what is more, makes us such as he is, by deifying and transforming us in God.[4]

What a blessed condition of the soul that is raised up in the school of the love of its God, if it knew how to understand and make use of it! And what a strange condition (if we may say so in passing) among Christians, even the most eminent and wise of Christians, who, not being able to know God as he is in himself, and being able to love him as he is in himself, still strive much more to know him than to love him! This is why there are so many schools and academies for raising souls up in this difficult, uncertain, and incomplete knowledge, and there are so few (and these so rarely frequented) for raising up and perfecting the soul in the love and the high and eminent possession of its God by the way of love. Yet in this mortal life we cannot know God as much as we want. We can love him as much as we want, rising up from degree to degree by his grace, in his love. And from the degree of this love on earth depend the state and degree of the knowledge that we will have of God eternally in heaven. For we will know God as much as we have loved him, not as much as we have known him, on earth.

But let us leave for another time this fundamental point of mystical theology. Let us dedicate this secret to the school of the love of God and to its disciples. Let us return to the previous point that we noted, for it serves as the basis and foundation of this discussion and of our mystery. Let us add further that just as from the general difference between

---

4. Cf. Ficino, *Platonic Theology* 14.10:

Human love of God is greater in this life than human knowledge of Him, because nobody truly knows God. [...] It is better to love Him than to know Him. [...] In knowing God, moreover, we take His vastness and contract it to match the concept of our own mind, but in loving Him we take our mind and expand it to match the immeasurable vastness of the divine goodness. In the former we pull God down to us, in the latter we lift ourselves up to God.

Trans. Michael J. B. Allen, I Tatti Renaissance Library (Cambridge, Mass: Harvard University Press, 2004), 317–21.

love and knowledge we have concluded a special difference between the love and knowledge of God, so also from this special difference we conclude that (justly and rightly in the school of Christians) the beatitude of the earth is principally attributed to the love and charity of God, and that of heaven is principally attributed to the knowledge and sight of God. For from the earth, love joins us to God as he is in himself, transporting us outside of ourselves to God. The knowledge that we have of God on earth unites us with God not as he is in himself but as he is in us—that is, as he is in our mind and in the understanding that we form of him, which we do not know except ambiguously and obscurely, *in aenigmate*, as says one who knew him in the third heaven.[5] The knowledge of God that we have in heaven, on the other hand, has this privilege and power above the knowledge and understanding of God that is given on earth: it unites and joins us with God as he is in himself. And this all the more, since in heaven his own essence is united with our spirit and actuates it by his light much more nobly than a translucent body is actuated by the ray that suffuses it. His essence raises our spirit up to know God as he is in himself, establishing us in a state of life corresponding to God himself; for the life of God, whose being and nature is intellectual, is to know and behold himself, that is, to behold the first, most noble, and most worthy object of all knowledge. Since the angel and man have only a shadow of being and light in comparison to the being and light of God, they are therefore naturally capable of receiving only an intimation and image of the knowledge that God has of himself. He does not raise them higher during the course of their meritorious way and life but is content to give them power, through his grace, to love him, and to love him as he is in himself, according to the nature and condition of love. This is why on earth love has preeminence over bliss, and it is why knowledge recovers this preeminence in heaven that it does not have on earth. For just as on earth love possesses God as he is in himself, so also in heaven the knowledge of God causes us to behold and possess him as he is in himself, as God in love impresses and unites himself with our essence and powers so that we see him as he is, according to the vigor

---

5. 1 Cor 13[:12] (original marginal note). "Darkly."

of this apostolic word and promise: *Videbimus eum sicuti est.*[6] For bliss consists in possessing God, possessing him as he is in himself, and this is accomplished on earth by love and in heaven by knowledge.

Just as here man's bliss has its root and origin in man's love toward God, so also this love has its origin in God's love toward man and in the abundance of this love of God, giving his Son and his love to the world. It is this love that astonishes the Son of God in this sacred text, when he says in wonder, *Sic Deus dilexit mundum.* This is a point most worthy of astonishment: that love, so great a love, of the world might be in the Godhead. This is a secret that philosophy has not fathomed; it has indeed spoken of God's greatness, as first cause, but little or not at all of his love toward the things that exist outside of his being and that are other to his essence. This is a point reserved to the light of faith, which, since it is more exalted, reveals about God what nature cannot teach us. And this is a point most worthy of being taught to us by the eternal Word, who is himself the subject of this love. For he is the one who is given to the world by this love. And we see in this word how he uses his first words and teachings to speak of this love, and how, despite the infinity of his understanding and wisdom, he finds cause to be astonished and bear witness to this astonishment by speaking and saying to us, *God so loved the world.* For it does not seem to correspond to God's greatness, nor to the world's baseness, nor to the quality and condition of love. By a blind and disordered power, love is detrimental to the lover and favorable to the thing loved, and it transports, transmutes, and transforms the one who loves into the state and condition of what he loves. Thus, great things are lowered and decline to the condition of the base objects of their affection, and, by contrast, mean things are raised up, ennobled, and increase if they are borne to the love of things greater and more exalted in condition. This is the common sense of philosophers, confirmed by the daily experience of those who love. It is also the teaching of the faith, which, since it reveals to us a love greater, higher, and more powerful than the one that is restricted within the limits of nature, it gives us a clearer knowledge and stronger experience of this truth. It makes us see in our mysteries the wondrous power of

---

6. 1 Jn 3[:2] (original marginal note). "We will see him as he is."

this love, which raises man up and abases God and causes the world to feel what is at stake for man in loving God and for God in loving man. For by this love, men are exalted and made gods, according to the word of God himself: *Ego dixi, dii estis*.⁷ And in loving man, God is humbled and made man, in such a way that we have, by this love's strange and wondrous power, a God-Man on the earth and men gods in heaven.

Returning therefore to the point of our discussion, let us say that the love of other things does not seem to be worthy of God, does not seem compatible with the majesty, eminence, and immutability of his nature, and that neither his greatness nor his goodness should tolerate and undergo it. For it seems that God must necessarily be abased and manifestly affected by the love of things that exist outside the greatness of his being, and that because he has in his essence an infinite goodness comprehending all goodness and equaling his power to love, he cannot extend his love outside himself. Is it not blessed enough for created things to be in God's hand and power and be led by him so that he might fully use them according to his will, since he is the Sovereign and Lord of all things? But to be the object of a God's love—this surpasses their condition and seems to touch the power, goodness, and greatness of the divine being. It seems to make equal, or bring very close together, the baseness of the creature and the greatness and highness of the Creator. And yet—O marvel! O abyss!—the God whom we adore is a God of love. He has so great a love for the world that the only Son of God himself—who fully knows the being, state, and condition of the one who loves and of what is loved, that is, who knows God as his Father and who knows the world as the work of his hands—is astonished and offers these words full of astonishment: *Sic Deus dilexit mundum*.

O love of God toward the world, worthy of the world's marveling and adoration! O love of God toward the world, worthy of confounding and condemning the world, which is without vigor and love toward this love! O great and extreme love, by which God gives and abandons his Son to the world, his only Son, his Son equal to himself, his Son who is another himself! Strange love, in which God seems to take no thought of his greatness and misjudge the meanness of his creation! For

---

7. Ps 81 [82:6] (original marginal note). "I have said, you are gods."

he humbles himself to earth, he treats of uniting himself with the earth, and by this treaty two such different and dissimilar parties (that is, God and man) enter into union, a union that endures forever; two parties so far apart, placed at the two ends of the ladder that Jacob went up, which is the representation and model of this accord and communication of God with man. For this mysterious ladder reached from earth to heaven, and God appeared at its top and man at its base. The distance between these two ends is therefore the distance between heaven and earth. This distance is very great, and it cannot be represented to our senses as any greater than the distance that is between the highest heaven and the lowest point of earth. But by using faith and our minds, we are able to see that the distance from man to God is greater still, and is so in many ways, if we consider these two objects each in his own nature and condition. For there is the distance of nature, the nature of the one being infinitely far from the other, since the one is Creator and the other is creature. There is the distance of quality: the one is holy, holy by essence, and the other is a sinner, a sinner by birth. There is the distance of will: God in himself abhors sin and iniquity, and man is willfully a sinner and the slave of sin. But by an infinite love God overcomes all of these infinite obstacles and distances. He desires to enter into union with a thing so base, to enter into relation and kinship with men, and he wants there to be among men a Man-God. Can it be? God, all-powerful and eternal God, wills to join himself to nothingness and unite himself to man and become flesh as man is, for this is how he himself speaks by the mouth of his beloved disciple. And in addition, he wills to take on the flesh descended from sinners and covered with the darkness of sin, and to bear it heavy-laden with grief, suffering, and the marks of sin; for the flesh of Jesus is truly flesh descended from sinners, and, according to the apostle, it is "the likeness of the flesh of sin" (*in similitudinem carnis peccati*).[8] Do not do it, O great God! It is enough, it is too much, to humble yourself to the nothingness of the creature. Unite yourself at least with the most excellent of them, the angel, and not with the most wretched that is man, who no longer bears this first image and likeness of your deity; for it was effaced by sin.

---

8. Rom 8[:3] (original marginal note).

But if, nonetheless, you want to make yourself man; if, by an adorable secret of your love, you prefer the lowest nature to the highest; do not choose this flesh drawn from the body of sin, derived from a wretched and sinful Adam, and do not come to the earth that is contaminated by sin. Create a man apart, not derived from men, and create a new world and paradise for this new Adam, since you deigned to create a world and paradise for the old Adam and for his descendants, who so little honored, loved, and preserved your grace, your love, and your paradise. Work, O great God! in keeping with your greatness and wisdom, and dedicate this great world to yourself, to you alone. And since in yourself you have no true relation except to yourself (that is, since in your essence there is no real relation except among the divine persons and there is no created nature or person with which you have a real relation), cause this supreme work of yours to resemble you. Cause this work that encompasses and contains you, and whose center and circumference you are, to have no relation except to you, no relation to the men and sinners who wished to be separate from you. They do not dedicate themselves to you; let this work therefore not be dedicated to them. Do not do something so great for a thing so base, wretched, and far from you. And therefore, in not doing this great work except for yourself, create also a new world, a new paradise and heaven for this new Adam, since you made one for that Adam who so quickly forsook your love and obedience. The reason, greatness, and dignity of this work wants it so.

But it occurs completely otherwise, for—O goodness! O love! O abundance!—this new man is made for the old man. And God himself—who would dare think it?—participates in this work only because and as a result of the participation that sinners have in it. In a very real sense, this work is performed only because of sin and in consideration of men, according to this oracle of the Creed: *Qui propter nos homines, et propter nostram salutem descendit de caelis, et incarnatus est de Spiritu sancto, ex Maria Virgine, et homo factus est, etc.* ("Who came down from heaven for us men and for our salvation, and took on human flesh by the working of the Holy Spirit, of the Virgin Mary, and was made man"). The Son of God, therefore, according to this teaching of the faith, comes down from heaven and is made man for the salvation of men, that is, he takes on human nature for men's sake, and in this nature he does not take on for men's sake only the quality of being passible. For it is not a simple circumstance and quality that is employed for men, but the mystery of the Incarnation's very nub and substance. It is not a simple condition of this humanity as passible and suffering, but it is humanity itself in its nature and circumstances that the Son of God takes on for the salvation of men, if we follow these words of life and truth that state explicitly and distinctly that he comes down from heaven and goes up on the cross for us. These words distinguish these two different movements, his coming down from heaven and his going up on the cross, and attribute them both to the same cause, that is, to men's sin. And thus this great work of the Incarnation is done for men, and if there were no sinners on earth there would be no Man-God in heaven and on earth. This is why God, who makes himself man for men's sake, also becomes Son of man and the descendent of men. And we see in St. Luke how Adam, a sinner and in his nature the source of sin, enters into the genealogy of the Son of God.[9]

But at least—O great God!—since you will and you deign to take on human flesh, flesh derived from Adam, honor this flesh, raise this humanity up in its state, condition, and qualities, in this life already! Let it not be passible! Let it not suffer! Let it not be subject to the weather's abuse! Let it not be exposed to the baseness of birth, the weakness of infancy, the woes of life, the horror of death, and let the first moment and use of its natural life be a life that is fully formed in the use of all its powers and grandeurs! For you are the author of this life and the maker of this work, and what comes forth straight from your hands is always perfect in all its conditions, as we see in the creation of the world and in the production of Adam. Let Jesus therefore come forth from your hands and from your power not as a child dwelling at his birth in a stable and manger, but as an Adam formed in an Eden and dwelling in a paradise, beginning the first step of his life in the full development of his being, with the perfect use of his life, and with the power, possession, and dominion that is due him and that he has on the earth! Let him appear not as an infant, but as a full-grown man! Not

---

9. Lk 3[:38] (original marginal note).

in swaddling clothes and in the manger, but in the grace and majesty of his state and in the splendor and glory of his person! For is it not a great enough humiliation for an only Son of God to be humbled in the nothingness of human nature, without being humbled further to the base and abject condition of infancy and suffering? Let Jesus therefore live on earth without this lowliness and wretchedness, for he is the King of glory and the Splendor of the Father! Let him not be subject to times and seasons, for he is the Son of the Eternal One, and with him he made the seasons and times! Let him not be weary and tired in his travels, for he is the way and the path and he is the strength of the Father! Let him not be consumed by the ardors of the sun, for the sun is the work of his hands and he is himself a sun, he is the Sun of the sun! This sun here below borrows its light from him, and it will serve and acknowledge him during his life by its brightness, just as it will acknowledge him in his death by its darkness when it ceases to shine in the eclipse (so to speak) of its Sun and ours, who is the true Sun of Righteousness and the principle of all light and splendor. In sum, let Jesus be blessedly and gloriously living from the first moment of his life and not subject to suffering and death! For he is life, the true life, and one moment of his life is more precious before God and honors him more than does an eternity of the life of men and angels in grace and in glory.

A state so exalted, a state so privileged and delivered from the baseness of human life, is indeed what Jesus' grandeurs and the dignity of his twofold birth, eternal and temporal, deserves. For the greatest of his prophets said of each, as of a marvel untellable, *Generationem eius quis enarrabit?*[10] And all created nature has this same wish and concurs in its own way in this same desire. If it could speak, its voice and clamor would reach the heavens, petitioning the eternal Father for its Liberator, for deliverance and release from this abject condition. For surely it groans and suffers greatly in the humble and suffering state of its Lord, since, according to the apostle, it groans and suffers in the servile, abject, and suffering state of his children: *Omnis creatura*, he says, *ingemiscit et parturit usque adhuc, etc., et expectatio creaturae revelationem filiorum Dei expectat* ("All creation groans and is as though in

---

10. Is 53[:8] (original marginal note). "Who will explain his generation?"

labor of childbirth until now, and the expectation of all creation awaits the revelation of the children of God").[11] That is, it awaits the blessed state of glory, owed and promised to them, to be accomplished and made manifest to the world. From this we can summarize two expectations and groanings of the universe, which are well worthy of deep and particular consideration: the expectation of the coming of its Liberator, which earth and heaven name and call on this occasion, *The Desired of All Nations*; and the expectation of the complete fulfilment of the deliverance that he is to make from the servitude that every creature bears because of sin.[12] This is the groaning of the universe, groaning and suffering in the humble and suffering state of its Savior—during which we see heaven and earth being affected and shaken, and the universe as though entering into convulsion and fainting during the eclipse of this Sun of Righteousness fainting upon the earth—and the groaning that we learn of from this precise text of the apostle, who says that all creation groans for the complete and perfect fulfilment of the deliverance that is due to the elect and children of God, who are afterward to be delivered from the servitude of corruption by the culmination of their glory and to be perfectly made new by their perfect renewal. This is the creation's state and expectation and groaning both with regard to itself, that is, to its deliverance, and with regard to its Liberator, that is, Jesus. But just as it has much more relation with its God and Liberator than with itself, so also the expectation and groaning that regards him and that it has toward him is much greater and is worthier of a much greater consideration than this one that regards it.

Leaving then for another time the elaboration and application of other points, let us note how all creation, according to the proportion of its being, is united and concurs in one same wish and sentiment for the glory of Jesus and to see him released from the humilities of the life into which he enters. But if all creation is thus in favor of his greatness and deliverance, the Creator has very different thoughts. The eternal Father has a counsel upon his Son that is farther from this wish of the universe than heaven is from the earth. For he wills that his Son be abased to our wretchedness. He wills that he bear our cross and sins.

---

11. Rom 8[:22] (original marginal note).
12. Hg 2[:8]; Gn 49:26 (original marginal note).

And he wills that we see the one who is life, our life, dead on a cross and in a grave, and that in his death we may regain life. And to this purpose, see how the eternal Word comes forth from the bosom of the Father,[13] opens heaven, and comes to earth. *Exivi a Patre, et veni in mundum*, as he himself says.[14] A coming that is blessed for man and precious for the earth! For the earth is to receive and contain henceforth the eternal Word in a state and in a manner of being in which he was not in heaven, since it is on earth and not in heaven that he carries out his work, that he is made a creature for his creatures, and that he unites himself with human nature so that he might suffer for men's sake in this humanity. Let us contemplate the state, order, and progress of this work, and, postponing for another time the consideration of the Son of God on his cross and in his sufferings, let us apply ourselves to beholding and adoring him in this divine mystery of the Incarnation. The subject is so worthy, and what is at stake for us is so great, that we ought to consider the time well spent and our mind well occupied in extending a bit further what was said as though in a word and set forth as though in embryo at the beginning of this discussion.

God, therefore, in the fullness of time that he ordained in his eternal wisdom, lowering the heavens (according to the voice of his prophet), comes down to the earth and chooses a province, a Nazareth, and a Virgin so that he might accomplish his mystery and perform a great work in her virginal womb—a work greater than that which he performs in the heavens themselves.[15] By the efficacy of his love and Spirit, he draws from her a pure and holy substance, with which he wills to unite himself in an ineffable and particular way. And he wills to communicate himself to this substance drawn and derived from the Most Holy Virgin's immaculate body, not by a simple effect of grace and power, nor by the sole state and gift of glory, nor by something proceeding from and inferior to him, nor even by something joined with him—as occurs in the union that he willed to have with us after this mystery through the Eucharist, in which he communicates himself by a

---

13. Is 64 (original marginal note).

14. Jn 10:28 [sc. 16:28] (original marginal note). "I came forth from the Father and have come into the world."

15. Ps 18:9, 144:5. Cf. Is 45:8, 64:1.

substance that is deified in him but different from him, joined with him but not the same as him. But in this mystery of the Incarnation, God wills to join himself to man's nature directly, himself, applying himself to this created being by what is so intimate and intrinsic to himself that it is the same as his divine essence and is constitutive of his own person. By this powerful application and this holy and divine union, the Word in entering into this humanity does not destroy it, does not negate it, does not convert it into his divine essence. Instead, by the same power and love that abases and applies him to this humanity, he preserves and maintains it in its created nature and in the condition that is universal, essential, and necessary to all created being. He preserves it in its nature and entity only so that he might make it capable of his grandeurs and deity. For he wants to make it wholly his own. He wants to make it capable of receiving him, that is, of receiving the second person of the Trinity into itself, as its own person. He wants to exalt it to a state and dignity that is new, singular, and untellable. He draws it to himself and causes it to enter into his divine and uncreated being. He receives it as his only and beloved one in the bosom of his deity. He receives it, I say, as his only, and so much his only, that it is his alone even in the Godhead. In this sense and in this way that is so intimate and particular, it does not belong even to the Holy Spirit or the eternal Father, as is said elsewhere. For, receiving it so loftily into his being, he receives and establishes it forever in his greatness, his deity, and his own person, as having no subsistence except in his own. In this way, the same God who made the world makes in an instant a new world, a world incomparably greater and more beautiful, ornate, divine, and lasting than the one he made in six days, for this one will pass away, as the very author of this world says in Scripture.[16] For Jesus is a world, and if the philosophers call man a little world, Christians have good reason to call Jesus a great world. He is a world that makes new and perfects this world. He is a world that binds and contains the three worlds together, which the Platonists constituted in their universal economy of the things existing in the universe. You are wondrous, therefore, O Jesus! You are Man-God, and in this state and quality you are a world, a very great world! You are

---

16. Mt 24:35.

a world, a world completely heavenly and supernatural, a world wholly excellent and divine! You are a visible and intelligible and archetypal world, and these three worlds are recapitulated in you by your different natures, by your various states, powers, and graces, and by the supreme oneness of your divine person that is uncreated and creates all things! For you are a visible world in this body that is precious and adorable in heaven and on earth and in the beauties that accompany it, which give luster and splendor even to the sun and the empyrean heaven, of which it is written that *the Lamb is the Light*, so radiant is it.[17] You are an intelligible world in your deified soul, which holds all blessed spirits in its power, circumference, eminence, and capacity, drawing, delighting, and filling them with your grandeurs and infinite perfections! You are an archetypal world in the Godhead, united personally with humanity!

These three worlds would well deserve a full discourse, but we must postpone it to another time and return to the preceding point. In order to explain more clearly, distinctly, and plainly a mystery that has so much light and so much darkness both (because the abundance and greatness of its light makes it truly inaccessible, but it bears the eternal light on earth and the splendor of the Father within our nature), let us raise our thoughts gently and gradually into the knowledge and contemplation of the perfect union that is between divine and human nature. For these two natures are joined together not by a simple communion and moral union of dignity or authority but by a real and physical bond, as the Council of Ephesus defines it on pain of anathema. As there are two kinds of real union in it, the one of substance and the other of accident, these two natures are joined together not only by a kind of real and physical union that is purely of accident, but by a union that is real, substantial, and divine.[18] I mean that the eternal Word does not limit himself to uniting and applying himself to our flesh and

---

17. Rv 21[:23] (original marginal note).

18. Part 3, anathema 3 (original marginal note). See Council of Ephesus, "Anathematisms of St. Cyril against Nestorius" 3: "If anyone shall after the [hypostatic] union divide the hypostases in the one Christ, joining them by that connexion alone, which happens according to worthiness, or even authority and power, and not rather by a coming together, which is made by natural union: let him be anathema." In Percival, *The Seven Ecumenical Councils of the Undivided Church*, 211.

humanity by a simple union of grace, and by the power of his presence and assistance, his residence and indwelling, in the way that attending forms are united to their matter, planetary intelligences to their orbits, the pilot to his vessel, the body to its clothing, or the host to his home. Instead, he applies himself to human nature in a much different, higher, and more particular manner, and he wills to unite himself with it by a kind of real, substantial, and hypostatic union, constitutive of one same underlying substance and one same person in these two natures that are so distinct and far apart.

This is why I said in the preceding discourse that this manner of God's presence and residence in humanity is an imitation of that which the divine persons have with each other. For they are in one another in such manner that there is one common substance that is the Father's, the Son's, and the Holy Spirit's and that unites them, or rather, makes them One, in oneness of essence. Just as there is one substance (if it were lawful to speak thus), that is, one common subsistence that is in the divine nature and in human nature and that unites these two natures in oneness of person. And just as the Father is in his Son by real communication of his own essence, so also the Son is in this humanity by the communication that he makes to it of his own subsistence. This bears a communication so high and great, so particular and divine, that God is made man and man becomes God, and two things so different, far apart, and unequal are united and joined together so intimately, perfectly, and divinely that man is God and God is man, in strict truth, in reality of substance, in oneness of subsistence, in property of person, and in eternity of duration.

And as there are within the divine being two kinds of distinct realities—the one absolute and the other relative, one common and communicated and the other specific and incommunicable, and both of them substantial, uncreated, and eternal—it seems that human nature participates, as it were, in the eternal and all-powerful God. For of these two kinds of being, the one is communicated to the divine persons and the other is communicated to human nature. And just as by the first communication the eternal Word is God, so also by the second the same eternal Word is man, and man is God, and the eternal Word is made man by the same principle that is constitutive and distinctive of his person in the deity, that is, by his own subsistence applied and communicated to human nature. The bond that unites two natures that are so far apart is so intimate to the deity that it is one, one and the same, with the divine essence. It is made so specific to our humanity that it enters and suffuses, it actuates and quickens, it sanctifies and deifies all of the human nature, the body, the soul, and all the parts and powers of this little world—or rather, of this great world that is Jesus—and does so to the very bottom and center and innermost part of his human essence. It takes in this nature the place of human subsistence, completely and perfectly, exalting this nature that has been divested of its natural subsistence unto the being and person of God, and causes it to enter by this right into his divine grandeurs and dignity. This bond and oneness of the human nature with the divine person is so firm and abiding, so secure and permanent, that it will last for eternity. For nothing can dissolve this powerful, strong, and perfect bond or break apart this divine and personal oneness.

May you be blessed, O great God, *God of gods*,[19] King of glory, for having willed like this to humble your grandeurs to the earth and join your deity so closely to our humanity! May you be blessed again, God eternal and incomprehensible in your goodness, wisdom, and love, for having done this for eternity! For as long as God is God, God will be man. May you be blessed forever for having performed this great work for us and for having made yourself man for man's sake! Since you deign in this way to give us so great a share in your grandeurs and in the secret of your love, in so great a work, let us take part in you; let us enter into your purposes, interests, and concerns; let us be yours completely, completely yours forever. May we belong to you in a manner that approaches, imitates, and adores the belonging that your humanity has in regard to God's Majesty, so that we may prove true in us this word of your apostle who expresses our state (that is, both our greatness and our duty) in these three words of great authority and substance that he says to us on your behalf and in the efficacy of your Spirit: *Omnia vestra sunt, vos autem Christi, Christus autem Dei.*[20] In response, we must, we

---

19. Ps 49 [50:1] (original marginal note).

20. 1 Cor 3[:22–23] (original marginal note). "For all are yours, and you are Christ's, and Christ is God's."

desire, we long to be yours perfectly and eternally, in honor and imitation of the perfect and wondrous belonging of your humanity to your deity forever. You desired, O great God, by love toward man, that all the works of your hands might be for man, and you have subjected this world to our use and utility. This is what the apostle says to us in these few words: *Omnia vestra sunt*. But by an abundance of incomparable love, you who are above all things, O Jesus, you also want to be ours, to be ours in your person, by a kind of possession that belongs to us alone. Taking no thought of your greatness and of our nothingness, you want to be ours in such a way that there may be nothing that is so fully, perfectly, and absolutely ours as you, O my Lord Jesus, who deign to be ours more than all things and above all things, just as you are above all things in the eminence of your being and singular state. It is as though you wanted to equal your belonging, in regard to men, with the infinity that corresponds to your greatness, and to be infinitely theirs just as you are infinite in yourself.

Since you are ours in this way, let us be yours, O Jesus my Lord; let us be yours, not only by the excellent right of your perfections, both divine and human, that subject us fully to your greatness, but also by this new and powerful right of love that brings you to want to be ours and compels us in return to be yours. Let us be yours, therefore, because you are ours. Let us be yours as you are ours. Let us be wholly yours as you are wholly ours. Let us prove true this word that your apostle says: *Vos autem Christi* ("You are Jesus Christ's"), to which he adds, *Christus autem Dei* ("Jesus Christ is God's"). O great Jesus, who could conceive the state of your belonging to God and to us? This subject deserves its own discussion, which we will treat another time if you deign to give me the grace to do so. I will content myself in saying here, in three words, that you belong to the eternal Father, as his Son, as his only Son, as the one who has his life and essence. In honor therefore of your belonging to the eternal Father, let us be yours, and let us belong to you as to our father. For we are born of you by grace, as you are born of the Father by nature. You are so much the Father's that you say to him solemnly on your last day, and you continue to say to him in eternity, *Tua mea sunt, et omnia mea tua sunt* ("What is yours is mine, and all that is mine is yours").²¹ O love! O communication of the Son toward the Father! In honor and imitation of this, let us use the same words toward you and say to you, *Tua mea sunt, o Domine Iesu! Et mea omnia tua sunt.*

Alas! I truly must say to you, *Tua mea sunt* ("What is yours is mine"). For it is only too true for the sake of your glory and your greatness. Your Spirit is mine, and you give it to me in baptism. Your body is mine, and you give it to me in the Eucharist. Your glory is mine, and you give it to me in your paradise. Your greatness is mine, and on earth it is abased to my wretchedness. Your life is mine, and on the cross I put it to death by the wretched power of my transgressions. May I say to you, then, with as much truth and as much homage and fidelity toward you as you show affection toward us in giving everything of yours to us, *Omnia mea tua sunt* ("All that is mine is yours"). My life, my being, my love is yours. All that I am, by your mercy, in the being of nature and of grace, is yours. My time and my eternity are yours. All that I hope for and await according to your promises, in your glory, is yours. Finally, my God and my Lord, all that I am is yours, all that I have is yours, and is incomparably more yours than mine. For it is mine only through you and for you. In honor, then, of all that you are in yourself and toward us, and of all that it pleased you to do and to suffer for us, I offer myself and dedicate all to you. I give and deliver myself into the power of your Spirit, your love, and your cross. And in homage to the wondrous gift that you design to make of yourself for us, I give myself and relinquish everything to you, from this moment on and forevermore.

21. Jn 17[:10] (original marginal note).

Discourse 10

On the Three Births of Jesus

Preface

We find in the book of life three wondrous births of Jesus, who is the life of God and men: his birth in his Father's bosom in the life eternal, his birth in the Virgin's womb in the life temporal, and his birth from the grave in the life immortal. These three births are accompanied by marvels worthy of Jesus and worthy of his source and origin in these three different lives. For in his birth in the divine and uncreated life, it is a twofold marvel that God begets and that God is begotten. In his birth in human and incarnate life, it is a twofold marvel that a virgin brings forth a child and that a God becomes incarnate. In his birth, or rather, rebirth, that sets him in the life celestial and glorious, it is a marvel that a grave is a source of life and that a place of death is a source of immortal life. But this is how God, who is wondrous in himself, in his works, and in his saints, is also wondrous in his only Son, who is another himself; in his masterwork, which is the Incarnation; and in the Holy of Holies, who is Jesus Christ our Lord, foretold and named this way by one of his prophets.[1]

These three births of Jesus, in which he lives by these three kinds of life that are holy, different, and adorable, are expressed in the word of life and in the express word of the eternal Father saying to himself and to his Son, *Ego hodie genui te*.[2] For these are the words that St. Paul

---

1. Dn 9[:24] (original marginal note).
2. Ps 2[:7] (original marginal note). "Today I have begotten you."

in Hebrews 1 applies to the eternal generation, proving by the strength and authority of this text that Jesus Christ belongs to God the Father by a kind of belonging and emanation from him that is different from the angels', because he begot him, according to this express word: *Ego hodie genui te*. This belongs only to the Son of God and not to the nature of the angels. For this proof would be proofless and implausible if this text that this great apostle quoted and produced did not mean truly and literally the eternal generation, which is divinely described to us in these terms, in which the present is joined with the past, *Hodie genui te*, by a wondrous skill, to explain the one who is always born and always being born and who has a kind of procession that is without end and without beginning. By an unfathomable secret, it is accomplished in such a way by the past term that it is always being accomplished by the present term.[3] The same St. Paul, led by the same Spirit of God and speaking to the same Hebrews in Acts 13, quotes this same text and applies it to the resurrection of the Son of God, which is a kind of new birth of Jesus into immortality. For resurrection is commonly called in the Church rebirth and regeneration. And the Son of God himself, who is its author, and who, as the eternal Word of the Father, has singular grace and property in his words, calls it this by his own mouth, speaking of the day of judgment in which the general resurrection will be accomplished: *in regeneratione cum sederit Filius hominis in sede maiestatis suae*.[4] Thirdly, the same Holy Spirit who dictated this word to the prophet David and who explained it by his instrument (that is, by one of the greatest apostles, St. Paul), concerning Jesus' eternal generation and resurrection, explains and applies it to Jesus' temporal birth in the world, by the voice of the Church in her offices of Christmas Day. God is prolific and fertile in his works and in his words, and he wanted this same memorable word to be applied in one same spirit to these three different meanings and these three states and mysteries of the eternal Word: to the mystery of his birth from his Father, the mystery of his birth from his Mother, and his birth from the grave, where like a phoenix he comes forth reborn into a new life.

3. The past term is *genui*, "I have begotten," and the present term is *hodie*, "today."
4. Mt 19[:28] (original marginal note). "In the resurrection, when the Son of man will sit in the seat of his majesty."

On the First Birth of Jesus

These three births are truly wondrous, and the first has neither time nor day, for it never begins and never ends. Rather, from it come the days, times, and ages that begin and end. Our eternity itself, in grace and in glory, originates here. For it is by his Son that the Father made the ages, as the apostle to the Hebrews says: *Per quem fecit et saecula.*[5] It is by his Son that the Father establishes us in his grace and in his glory, as all Scripture says. We must adore him as a Dayspring by his first and divine birth, to which all that is dawn owes tribute and homage. We must, I say, adore him as the Dayspring, but as an eternal Dayspring, a Dayspring that remains forever in its noonday by the fullness of its light. And it is forever in its dawn by the condition and perfection of his birth that always continues and never ends just as it never begins, in which he is born in such a way that he is forever being born in eternity. O marvel! O prodigy of this birth, in which Jesus is a Dayspring! An eternal Dayspring! Eternally Dayspring! The Dayspring to which our dawn and our birth owe homage, in nature and in grace, and our eternity owes homage in glory! For this reason, when the catechumens in former times entered the Church on their baptismal day in a solemn and notable ceremony, they would turn themselves toward the east as a sign of their homage and cleaving to the eternal Dayspring who is Jesus Christ our Lord.[6] Thus it is entirely clear that we are all regenerated in baptism in the name and remembrance of this divine birth and sonship, being baptized in the name of the Father as Father and in the name of the Son as Son. In this powerful and precious name, we can enter into the Church and into grace, so much so that our own condition in Christianity and our state in the faith mark out this truth for us and compel us to preserve the honor and remembrance that is owed to this divine and eternal birth of Jesus, the source of our rebirth in the Church. If the Church has assigned no day in the year for celebrating its feast day and remembrance, this is because of its greatness: it has no

---

5. Heb 1[:2] (original marginal note). "By whom also he made the ages."

6. See Cyril of Jerusalem, Lecture 19, "First Lecture on the Mysteries," in *Catechetical Lectures*, trans. Edwin Hamilton Gifford, *NPNF* 7, pp. 144–46.

day on earth because its feast and its day is the day of eternity, in which it is continually adored in the dwelling place and the state of glory.

But this blessed and divine birth that has no time and is before all times has a place and rest that is most worthy of it. It has an eternal place, that is, the bosom of the Father, where dwells the Son of God. For his beloved disciple, the eagle of his evangelists, who soared the highest and saw most clearly into his state and mysteries, who rested intimately on his breast and spoke to us clearly of his grandeurs and eternal birth, teaches us about this sacred resting place of the eternal Word in two places in his first chapter. In the one he says, *Verbum erat apud Deum*, and in the other, *Unigenitus qui est in sinu Patris*.[7] The Word therefore dwells in the Father's bosom as in the place of his birth, where the eternal Father conceives and forms him, begetting him within himself and not in another's womb, by an action that is wholly pure, holy, divine, and immanent, performing the office of both father and mother in regard to his Son and eternal Word.

Whence it arises that Scripture, by a wondrous secret and mysterious profundity, in one same verse ascribes jointly to the Father the two conditions of father and mother in the generation of their children. God says of himself to his Son, in this Psalm 109, *Ex utero*, or, in the manner of the Hebrew speech, *Ex vulva ante luciferum genui te*.[8] For it belongs to the father to beget and to the mother to conceive and bear in her womb the child that she has conceived by the father. Both of these are fitting to the eternal Father, who begets, begets in himself, and who carries in his bosom his only Son, bearing and begetting him there eternally. For this bosom (if we wish to speak using Tertullian's terms) is his matrix and his eternal dwelling place.[9] In keeping with this testimony of holy Scripture, the greatest and most ancient philosophers have had some glimmer of this truth, and one of them has spoken these words: *Intelligentia illa Deus, cum maris et foeminae vim haberet, genuit verbum*.[10]

---

7. "The Word was with God." Jn 1:1; "The Only Begotten who is in the bosom of the Father." Jn 1:18.

8. "From the womb." Ps 110:3; "From the womb before the light-bringing I begot you."

9. Tertullian, *Apology* 21, p. 34.

10. [Hermes] Trismegistus (original marginal note). "God, having both masculine and feminine power, begot the Word." See Hermes Trismegistus, *Poemandres*, in The

To express the same thing, the great Orpheus, according to what Clement of Alexandria has reported, uses these words, *expers matri-pater*, in speaking of God.[11] He creates a new word out of these two words, *pater* and *mater*, in order to ascribe to God in a single word these two offices and functions that are shared between the father and mother in human and natural generation and are united in God, who as Father begets and as mother conceives and carries within himself his only Son. By this means, the Son of God, who has in the fullness of time a Mother without a father, has in eternity a Father without a mother, but a Father who performs the functions of father and mother, begetting him within himself and carrying him in his bosom. Thus, the bosom of the Father is his matrix and dwelling place, his eternal dwelling place. It is one of the secrets and one of the grandeurs and marvels of the divine generation that the Father is, in regard to his Son, both father and mother; that the bosom of the Father is the Father's matrix, in which his only Son rests, rests for eternity; and that the Son is in the Father's bosom and dwells there matchlessly and eternally. To these ends, the greatest of the prophets and psalmists and the greatest of the disciples and evangelists agree in several ways of speaking: *Sinum patris appellat evangelista, quem psalmista uterum appellaverat*,[12] as the greatest teacher of the Church perceptively remarks.[13] I say not only that the Father's bosom

---

Theological and Philosophical Works of Hermes Trismegistus, Christian Platonist, trans. John D. Chambers (Edinburgh: T& T Clark, 1992), 4. Many theologians and philosophers, most notably Augustine, believed that Hermes Trismegistus was an ancient precursor of Plato and perhaps a contemporary of Moses. Jean Dagens writes, "When Bérulle sees in Trismegistus and Orpheus the greatest and oldest of the philosophers, this is an echo of the whole humanist age, and in particular of Marsilio Ficino. [...] The baroque era was surely that in which Trismegistus had greatest prestige." Dagens, *Bérulle et les origines de la restauration catholique (1575–1611)*, 21.

11. [Clement of Alexandria,] *Stromata* 5.7 (original marginal note). "Lacking a mother-father," or possibly "lacking a mother's father." See *The Stromata, or Miscellanies*, trans. A. C. Coxe, ANF 2, p. 473.

12. "The evangelist calls 'bosom of the Father' what the psalmist called 'womb.' "

13. *Qui est sinus, ipse est uterus*. Augustine, Discourse on Psalm 109 [110] (original marginal note). "That which is the bosom is the womb." See Augustine, *Exposition of Psalm 109*:

From the womb before the morning star I begot you. What can that mean? God has a Son, yes, but surely not a womb? If we think of the human, fleshly body, then no, he

is his dwelling place but also that it is his eternal dwelling place. For it is fitting to note that the Son of God is not like the children of men, who are born not fully developed and remain in their mother's womb for only a certain period of time. After this they come forth and enter into the world, and it is in the world that they come to completion in their being and birth and live on their own outside of their mother's person and substance. This birth is common and natural.

But there is still on earth, although not of the earth, another kind of birth that is loftier. It is a birth that is not common but particular and not bodily but spiritual. It is a birth that is not by nature but by grace, a birth not of the children of men but of the children of God, and a birth that takes its origin from this birth of the eternal Father and that perfectly corresponds to it as to its exemplar. For in this birth, the Church is the mother of the faithful, begetting her children in the honor and power of the fatherhood of the eternal Father, *a quo omnis paternitas in caelo et in terra nominatur*.[14] The Church as mother, by grace and not by nature, has this advantage over temporal mothers, that she begets and keeps her children in her womb always, without delivering them, and thus they always live and are always carried in the Church's bosom. They live in faith, as the Scripture says,[15] not by their own understanding but by that of the Church, just as children who are carried in their mother's womb live by her substance. And if some, as the heretics, come out of the Church's womb in order to live by their own understanding rather than by the Church's understanding and substance, they are no longer children but are as monsters[16] in spiritual generation, who tear

---

does not, any more than he has a bosom; and yet scripture says, *The only-begotten Son, who is in the bosom of the Father, has made him known* (Jn 1:1). *Bosom* and *womb* mean the same thing here; both are figurative expressions for what is hidden. What, then is implied by *from the womb*? From a hidden, secret place, from my very self, from my intimate substance.

In *Expositions of the Psalms*, 278.

14. Eph 3[:15] (original marginal note). "From whom all fatherhood in heaven and earth is named."

15. Rom 1:17; 2 Cor 5:17.

16. A *monster* is this context is a malformed fetus or infant, typically one that is stillborn or that dies soon after birth.

apart their mother's belly like vipers in order to come out and who violate the Church's integrity.[17]

This point is most worthy of consideration, and the relation is truly wondrous that spiritual birth has with the divine birth of him who is the first begotten of the Father and by whom we are all begotten in his Church. For, following this remarkable progress of the three births (temporal, spiritual, and divine), the children of grace and of the Church, as children of God, have a more perfect condition than do the children of men, and a dignity that is more like that of the only Son of God who is their model and exemplar. And, just as in this condition they remain always in the bosom of the Church that is their mother and always live by her own substance, so also the eternal Word dwells always in the bosom of his Father and lives always by the same essence and the very substance of his Father, who conceives in himself his only Son, begets him perfect, and begets him in his bosom as in his matrix. There he is always perfect, always blessed, and always living by his own substance, for he lives and subsists with his Father in the oneness of essence. In this way, therefore, the eternal Word dwells in the bosom of his Father as in the place of his birth, and he dwells there eternally. He dwells there matchlessly (which is another kind of excellence and greatness of his eternal birth), for he is the only and eternal Son. This term "bosom" is fitting and assigned to the generation that belongs only to the Son. As Son, he expends, or, to say it better, fills up and completes, all of the Father's power to beget, to such a degree that the Holy Spirit, who proceeds from the Father as he does, is not begotten as he is. The Holy Spirit is therefore in the Father's heart and love and not in the Father's bosom, to speak precisely according to the holy Scriptures and the sacred teachings of our religion.[18]

The place, then, of this first and eternal birth of Jesus is the bosom of the Father. But there is a second and temporal birth, which occurs in the Virgin's womb and in the stable at Bethlehem. Its time is the darkness of night and the severities of our winter, so that it might melt the ice and heat the coldness of our hearts and draw us out of our

---

17. It was believed that vipers were born by gnawing their way out of the mother's belly. See Herodotus, *History* 3.109, p. 258.

18. Jn 1:18.

darkness into his light. The first birth has for its day the day of eternity; the second has for its time a night, a night of winter and of December; and the third, which is his birth in his glory, has for its time a dawn, a dawn of spring, a dawn of March, the month that is blessedly assigned to the birth and rebirth of the world. In the first, he has received a life that never began and will never end. O greatness! O marvel of eternity! In the second, he begins a life in order to end it, being immortal yet born mortal in order to die. O outpouring! O marvel of love, mercy, and goodness! In the third, he begins a life, but he begins it in order never to end it. O greatness! O marvel of life, power, and glory! Let us say again: In the first birth, he is born immortal and impassible. In the second, he is born passible and mortal, born for death, destined to death as death's Host and Victim. In the third, he is born and comes forth from the power of death so that he might never die again and might enter into life immortal and glorious. In the first, he is born and is being born in the glorious bosom of his Father, without ever being able to withdraw. In the second, he is born and comes forth from his Most Holy Mother's blessed womb, yet remains divinely within her at the center of her heart. In the third, he comes forth reborn into the life beyond the grave and the tomb, never to return there again, although our hearts by the affections and exercises of piety should be, on earth, the monuments of his death and the living sepulchers and repositories of his body in the Holy Sacrament; of his body, I say, that is presented and expressed as dead mystically and sacramentally in the Eucharist. In his first birth, he is the firstborn of God, and Scripture calls him the *firstborn of all creation*, for "in him all things are created" (*in ipso condita sunt universa*).[19] In the second birth, he is the firstborn of the Virgin, and through him all the children of men are redeemed to God. And in the third, "He is the firstborn among the dead" (*primogenitus mortuorum* in St. John, *primitiae dormientium* in St. Paul), and by him all will be resurrected in glory.[20] Three births and three remarkable primogenitures of the Son of God, to whom we owe all that we are and all that we can be, in time and eternity. For we owe our natural being to his first birth, our new being in grace to his second birth, and our

19. Col 1[:15–16] (original marginal note).
20. Rv 1:5. Cf. Col 1:18; "The first fruits of those who sleep." 1 Cor 15:20.

glory and resurrection to his third birth. In the first he is born of God, God from God, Light from Light, eternal Son of his eternal Father. In the second he is born man, Son of man, but Man-God, from a Virgin Mother of God. In the third he is born man in the glory of God, man the father of men as children of God, and man seated at the right hand of his Father for eternity. How many marvels, how many grandeurs in his births! Who could contemplate them? Who would be able to describe them?

Let us lead our minds further in his grace, efficacy, and light. Let us fathom these secrets, and let us say that in his first birth we marvel and adore a God begetting and a God begotten, without difference of nature, without inequality of person, without dependency of origin, and without posteriority in the passage of time. O Father who is three times great and blessed! O Father who is wondrous and singular in his fatherhood! O Father whose fatherhood was unknown for four thousand years! It is so far beyond all capacity; it is so full of marvel. For it is a marvel in eternity and a marvel in the Marvel itself, that is, in the Godhead, in which all is itself marvelous! This is why the world, in its darkness and before the birth of the true light of the universe, adored the Godhead for so long without adoring the fatherhood in the Godhead, although this deserved so great a homage for being a marvel, the origin of all marvels created and uncreated. O Son, three times great and blessed! who is equally adorable and wondrous in his sonship, which is the second of the eternal marvels that we believe and adore in the Godhead! It is the marvel that all the marvels of heaven and earth, all the marvels of nature, of grace, and of glory, serve in their inferiority to this one, paying homage in their emanation to the first emanation that is in God himself. And to this emanation, in a wholly particular manner, honor and homage are rendered by the marvel of the work in which the deity, the subsistence, and the divine sonship are communicated to human nature by the sacred mystery of the Incarnation, in which the one who is the only Son of the Virgin is the only Son of God, coeternal and coessential with his Father.

O abyss! O outpouring! O marvel! For (in order to give still more light to this great thought, which encompasses many), it is not a marvel that we have a God, and that this God we have is infinite in his grandeurs and perfections. Nature itself clearly teaches this to us; the marvel is rather that some are so insensible and stupid to this voice of nature that announces the glory of its Creator. But the marvel of marvels is that there is a God begetting and a God begotten and that in the divine being who is perfectly one, perfectly pure, and perfectly simple, there is fatherhood and sonship. I say that this is the marvel of marvels, for the other marvelous things are in inferior, subordinate, and created being, but this is a marvel within the divine, supreme, and uncreated being. It is a marvel that dazzles all the light of nature, a marvel that needs the light of grace to be believed and the light of glory to be seen. It is a marvel that is comprehended only by the eternal Spirit and has no light that can render it comprehensible to created spirit, which will always marvel, adore, and become lost in the sight and contemplation of this marvel. It is served by all the other marvels of heaven and earth, of nature and grace. In a singular way, it is also served and paid homage by the marvel of the sacred mystery of the Incarnation, the supreme state of a Man-God, and the singular position of a Mother of God by whom this mystery is accomplished in the Most Holy Virgin, in perpetual homage to this divine fatherhood and this eternal sonship.

By this eternal and wondrous birth, and in the blessed state of this life, Jesus is God, Jesus is Son of God, Jesus is the Son of the living God, Jesus is the only Son of the Father, and Jesus is one principle with the Father of a divine person, that is, of the third person of the Most Holy Trinity. Each one of these points is distinct in itself and contains its own secrets and marvels, and each one deserves the creation's homage and elevation. But every creature does not consent to give us this leisure. While we await the God of peace to dispose them to it, let us say, in a few words, that Jesus is God. For although we behold him on earth as a man, in the manger as an infant, and as dead on the cross, we must adore him as God and say to him with his prophet, "In you is God, and there is no other God but you. Truly you are a hidden God, and the God of Israel, Savior" (*In te est Deus, et absque te non est Deus, vere tu es Deus absconditus, Deus Israel salvator*).[21] O God hidden in infancy, in humanity, in common and unknown life, in suffering life, in death!

---

21. Is 45[:14–15] (original marginal note).

O God! O life! O God in man! O life in death! O life supreme, life eternal, and life unchanging! Life supreme within lowliness! Life eternal within the measure of our days! Life unchanging within the inconstancy and mutability of our condition! O life divine! Life glorious, life adorable! Life divine in humanity! Life glorious in suffering! Life adorable on the cross and in death! Life quickening death itself! Life the source of all life, the life of nature, of grace, of glory! Life to which all life pays homage if it is created or has relation if it is uncreated. For it is the life of a God, the Son of God, by whom all creatures are made and to whom they owe their homage as to their Creator. Even the eternal Father, who is the first living one and the principle of life in the Godhead, has his relationship to him, as to his Son and as to the endpoint of his divine and ineffable generation. The Holy Spirit, who is the third person, after whom there is no other person living and uncreated in eternity, corresponds to him, as to the one who is the Son of the Father and is his principle with the Father. And we therefore, as Christians who have received from him the power to be children of God, according to his beloved disciple, owe both relation and homage to his person, his birth, and his divine life.[22] Homage for he is our God, and relation for he is our father and our life.

Jesus is God, Son of God. For these things are distinct: the Father is God and not Son of God, the Son is God and not Father, and the Holy Spirit is God and not Son of God. For Jesus is the only Son of God, as we will say in what follows. He is God in his essence, he is Son in his person, and this name of Son is a name equivalent in its position to the name of Father in eternity. This sonship says nothing less, for it says something that is equal to the fatherhood of his Father. O life proceeding, but life coeternal and coessential with his Father! Life emanated, but also life immanent in his Father! For he says to his Father, *I am and live in you, and you are and live in me!*[23] Life, fullness of life, for he says to him elsewhere, and even as his life is about to be taken from him, *Omnia tua, mea sunt* ("All that is yours is mine").[24] Life that is inseparable from him, for no one can take this deity from him, just as the Father

---

22. Jn 1[:12] (original marginal note).
23. Jn 17:21.
24. Jn 17[:10] (original marginal note).

himself is not able and does not will to give it to him, for he produces him by the blessed necessity and powerful fertility of his nature. All that he has, he holds from his Father, to whom also he speaks these words, *Omnia mea, tua sunt* ("All that is mine is yours").²⁵ And just as all that is his is his Father's, so also all that is his Father's is his. And he says elsewhere, *Omnia quaecumque habet Pater, mea sunt* ("All that my Father has is mine").²⁶ And just as he holds all from the Father, he dedicates all to the Father, and as his personal life is a kind of life wholly relative to the Father, he is in his eternity dedicating himself to the Father, and by what is his own he is himself the relation to his Father. In view of this, let us adore him, love him, imitate him, and dedicate all to him and through him to the Father. For the Son's relation is his life and subsistence, and thus the relation that we will have to him will be our life and our subsistence forever and will establish us blessedly in his eternity.

Jesus is the Son of the living God, according to this word that St. Peter learned from the eternal Father: *Tu es Christus filius Dei vivi.*²⁷ As the only Son of God the Father, he is distinct from the Father and from the Holy Spirit. As the Son of the living God, he is also distinct from us and from all children by adoption. This compels us to seek out a deep and hidden meaning in this word that calls Jesus Christ the Son of the living God, for it is not added baselessly and in vain. It is not said only to distinguish the true God from the false gods that were being adored on the earth, as some might think. This word is spoken not among the pagans but among the apostles, who had never adored false gods. It is spoken in the school and family of Jesus and in his holy presence: a great school and wholly instructed in great and particular things, a school worthy of its founder and worthy of the eternal Word. This word is so high and sublime that Jesus Christ himself dedicates it to the revelation of the eternal Father, and it bears the truth on which the Christian Church is founded and for which the Son of God delivers himself to death. For it is fitting to note that since the Son of God had to die, he desired to die for the confession of this truth, which regards his life and his divine and eternal sonship. When he had confessed it

---

25. *Ibid.* (original marginal note).
26. Jn 16[:15] (original marginal note).
27. Mt 16[:16] (original marginal note). "You are Christ, the Son of the living God."

to Caiaphas, who was questioning him on this point, he was judged deserving of death and handed over to the Gentiles to be executed, because he had declared himself to be the Son of the living God. For if Jesus, who is life, is to die, he is to die so that he might honor his divine life and sonship, give his life to his children, and make them all children of God.

What must we then expect from a word spoken by the prince of the apostles, learned from the eternal Father, and praised by Jesus Christ in the assembly of his own that he constitutes the teachers of light? And what are we to understand in these sacred words of St. Peter: *You are the Christ, the Son of the living God*? Certainly not a low and common meaning, but one much higher and more exalted. Not a life simply being contrasted with the state of false gods that have no life, but a life worthy of him who is the first living among all the living, the one who alone lives of himself, without principle and origin among all the living and even among the divine and uncreated persons. In truth, this word that Jesus Christ honored in this way and that he remunerated with the principality of his Church in the person of him who proffered it, this word that is fundamental in the faith and doctrine of salvation, will have a meaning worthier and more exalted and will ascribe to the Son of God a quality greater than the meaning that common and uninstructed people could understand by it. Since it is revealed from heaven by the eternal Word's express testimony, heaven itself must reveal its meaning and interpretation to us, and the Father who is in heaven must explain to us the greatness of his Son, the greatness of his Son's birth, and the greatness that is specific to the Father in the birth of his Son. These grandeurs are hidden and comprehended in these few words, for these are words from heaven—words taught by the one who is the Father of the eternal Word, if we may use this word in imitation of the most excellent authors of this age to refer to him who is the substantial Word, or, to repeat the same word, the substantial and personal word of God.[28]

---

28. Bérulle is using three different French words in this passage: *mot*, denoting "word" in the sense of lexical item, and *parole* and *verbe*, denoting "word" in the sense of language or speech.

These grandeurs are hidden and comprehended in these few words [*mots*], for these are words [*mots*] from heaven, words [*mots*] taught by the one who is the Father of the

Let us contemplate, then, this mystery and this word. Let us rise up above the earth and above ourselves, and—addressing ourselves to the Father of light and to the Son of the living God who is Light from Light and the light of the world—let us note and assume that he is named from heaven the Son of the living God with a venerable meaning that is worthy of the light of heaven and of his birth and greatness, and with singular honor to his Father, whom faith adores as the sole one among all the living who lives of himself, who lives with a life that has no principle and origin, and from whom all that is living, either in the Godhead or outside the Godhead, draws its life, origin, and principle. In this public and solemn profession of faith, therefore, made in the presence of Jesus Christ and at his request, in his name and in the name of the sacred company of the apostles, the prince of the apostles calls God living not to distinguish him from false gods that are dead and not truly living and that do not deserve to be compared to the greatness and majesty of the living God. Rather, he calls Jesus Christ the Son of the living God in contrast to another kind of children who are truly living and truly children of God and whom the eternal Word, the infallible and ineffable word of the Father, names and calls gods in a true and lofty sense. This makes them worthy of this high and sublime quality and denomination and of being named in this way by the very mouth of God. It makes them cleave to his deity and participate in it, as being truly gods by participation and truly children of God by adoption. But—and this is worthy of deep consideration—they are children begotten by a God dead and dying on a cross, whereas Jesus is begotten by a God living and immortal, a God alone living of himself in his eternity, a God living and giving life to his Son and through his Son to all things. He gives the very life of this Son, who emanated from him, to the sacred Humanity, in which, by suffering death on a cross and losing a high and divine life, the source of the life of grace, he gives life, the true life, to all his children. For we must carefully note that just as the greatness of our faith teaches us to adore a God begetting and a God begotten in eternity, so also does it teach us to adore in our

---

eternal Word [*Parole*], if we may use this word [*mot*] in imitation of the most excellent authors of this age to refer to him who is the substantial Word [*Verbe*], or, to repeat the same word [*mot*], the substantial and personal word [*parole*] of God.

mysteries a God living and a God dead. It teaches us that the living God has condemned us in his wrath, condemned us to death and hell, and that God dying and dead on a cross delivers us from death, gives us life, and makes us his children blessedly living and divinely begotten by the blood and death of Jesus Christ our Lord, only Son of God.

O living and powerful death, since it contains life, it gives life, and it begets—which belongs only to what lives! O strange and marvelous generation of Jesus, in his death and cross! A generation that stands counter to the entire state and power of nature, in which only the living beget and not the dead, and again, only the living when they have attained the state and highest point of their life and development! May I say that it is to this active and powerful generation of Jesus, dead and begetting his children divinely and painfully on the cross, that this passage from Isaiah refers: *Generationem eius quis enarrabit?* For this great saint, prince, prophet, and evangelist, all in one, speaks of this generation at the time and moment of his passion. In his rapture upon the state of Jesus on the cross and in death he speaks these divine words: *Oblatus est quia ipse voluit, etc. De angustia et de iudicio sublatus est. Generationem eius quis enarrabit? Quia abscissus est de terra viventium: propter scelus populi mei percussi eum.* ("He was offered because he willed it, etc. He was delivered from the anguish and condemnation. Who will explain his generation? For he was removed from the land of the living; I have struck him for the sin of my people.")[29] O true God living and dying! God living in eternity in the bosom of the Father! God dying in the bosom of the cross in the fullness of time! God lovable and God adorable as living and as dying! For, living and dying, you are always God, always powerful, and always wondrous. As God living, you are begotten in the bosom of the Father and you do not beget, for he whom you produce with the Father is your Spirit and not your son. You produce him in the Godhead without being his father, and he produces you in the humanity without being your father, for you are not his son. You are the Son only of the eternal Father and the Virgin Mary. O greatness of the Father! O singularity of Mary!

But this significant point is mentioned only in passing, and it

---

29. Is 53[:8] (original marginal note).

deserves its own discussion, in honor of the divine fatherhood and the venerable motherhood of her who is Mother of the one whose Father is God and who alone has a position in relation to Jesus that is not found even in the Holy Spirit. (This is not to the Holy Spirit's discredit, for in these divine and eternal persons, to produce and not to produce, to have and not to have, is equally perfect.) But in the person of the Virgin, to produce the Son of God and to have this great position is a precious and singular perfection that raises her above any other created person and brings her as near as is possible to the eternal Father. For she is Mother as he is Father; she is Mother-without-father as he is Father-without-mother. And this excellently corresponds to the excellence of the divine fatherhood: she alone is Mother and he alone is the Father of Jesus. Thus, O Jesus, are you begotten in the Godhead, and you do not beget. In the state of the cross and in the power of death, you have what you do not have in the life of the Godhead. For, dying and dead, you beget us, and you are truly father in your humanity. You are father, I say, of as many children as there are and will be righteous ones on earth and saints in heaven. Our life, the life of grace and of glory, owes homage to your cross and death for its birth, power, perseverance, and eternity.

We are all therefore, O Jesus, your true children, the children of God, of God dead. You are the Son of God living, and the only Son of the living God. The life of your deity proceeds only from God living, and the subsistence of your humanity, which gives God's being and life to this humanity, emanates only from God living. The very grace that rests in this humanity—grace that surpasses all the grace of angels and men and is the origin of all grace—this grace, I say, or rather, this abyss and ocean of grace, has no dead God on which it depends; it depends solely on the deity that is living, subsisting, and flowing in this humanity. It is due to the greatness of your divine and human births and precedes and accompanies your state on the cross and in death. From this state proceed the grace and glory of both men and angels and the very glory that you have received in your body in the resurrection. O living and dying God, let us be yours, let us live and die like you. Let us live in you; let us die through you and for you. By dying like this, let us live forever, and let us live with you in the life that you live with the Father.

For you are life, and in calling us to yourself you call us to life. In establishing us in you, you establish us in life, and you speak to us these holy words, words of life: *Ego vivo, et vos vivetis*. You speak them to us when you are going to death, death for you and life for us. That is, when you are going to the cross, you say to us in the person of your apostles, *Ego vivo et vos vivetis, quoniam in patre meo et vos in me, et ego in vobis*.[30] "I live, and you will live," for you are life, O my Lord, you are the source of life and the source of our life. But because you are the Son of the living God, you are life in such a way that the source of your life is in your Father: *Ego in patre meo*.[31] Because we are your children in you, the source of our life is in our father, and we have our life in you as you have it in your Father. By a blessed circle and return, you are in us and we are in you, we will live in you, we will live from you, we will live by you, we will live with you forever. Jesus therefore is the Son of the living God and gives life to his children, gives life to them by dying. And we are truly the children of God, that is, the children of God dead, just as Jesus is the Son of God, but the Son of God living.

But in order to sum up in a few words what we have discussed concerning Jesus' eternal birth and divine life, let us say that Jesus is God as the Father and Holy Spirit are; that Jesus is God, Son of God, which distinguishes him from the Father and Holy Spirit; and that Jesus is the Son of God living, which distinguishes him from us, who are the children of the God dying and dead on a cross. And just as among the divine persons he alone is the Son of God living, so also among men he alone, even in the state of grace and of glory, is the Son of God living. He is not the son of God dead as we are, not only because his sonship is not by adoption, since he has rightful and natural sonship, but also because, having infused and created grace like other men, and having it much more fully and abundantly, his grace alone among all the graces of men and even of his Mother has this privilege and singularity: that it comes from the life of God simply and does not come from the death of a God, as does ours.

It remains for us still to demonstrate how he is the only Son of

---

30. "I live, and you will live, because I am in my Father, and you in me, and I in you." Jn 14:19–20.

31. "I am in my father."

God and the principle of the Holy Spirit with the Father. These are two secrets and singularities, two powers and excellences of his divine life and eternal birth. For he does not alone proceed in the Godhead, but he alone is Son in the Godhead. He alone proceeds from the Father alone, which does not apply to the Holy Spirit, who proceeds from the Son as well as from the Father. He alone proceeds by generation, for the Holy Spirit proceeds in another manner. Thus, he alone proceeds from the Father as Father, for the Holy Spirit proceeds from the Father as principle and not as Father. It is one of the secrets and marvels of eternity that although there are two processions of two persons, both of them divine, both living, both proceeding from one principle of life, and both equally like unto their principle and origin, one of these persons is Son in the Godhead and the other is not. By the oracles of the faith, there is but one Son of God, just as there is but one God. I am well acquainted with the arguments that are put forth in the School concerning this difficulty, but I am also well acquainted with the capacities and temperance of those who argue them and who know as well as I do the objections that are made against these arguments and replies. Since they are not suitable to a discourse for the public, I do not wish to go into them. It is enough to instruct and abase our spirits in the sight of things so great and to be able to say, with truth, that the reason and principle of this distinction is a secret that God has reserved to himself and has not revealed to his Church.

The Fathers and teachers acknowledge and confess frankly the profundity that lies in this eternal birth, birth from light, but birth from light inaccessible to created light, which must adore and cannot fathom it in its darkness. The eagle of the teachers and the great teacher of St. Thomas, the prince of the School (I mean St. Augustine) says, *Quaeris a me: si de substantia Patris est Filius, de substantia Patris est etiam Spiritus sanctus, cur unus filius sit, et alius non sit filius? Ecce respondeo, sive capias, sive non capias. De Patre est Filius, de Patre est Spiritus sanctus, sed ille genitus, iste procedens.* ("You ask me why, if the Son is of the Father's substance and the Holy Spirit is of the Father's substance, the one is Son and the other is not Son. I reply to you, either you understand it or you do not. The Son is of the Father, the Holy Spirit is of the

Father, but the former is begotten, and the latter, proceeding.")[32] And further on,

Quid autem inter nasci et procedere intersit, de illa excellentissima natura loquens, explicare quis potest? etc. Distiguere inter illam generationem et hanc processionem nescio, non valeo, non sufficio. Ac per hoc quia et illa et ista est ineffabilis, sicut propheta de Filio loquens, ait: Generationem eius quis enarrabit, ita de Spiritu sancto verissime dicitur, processionem eius quis enarrabit? ("Now what difference is there between being born and proceeding? Who is he who, in speaking of this nature so excellent and sublime, will be able to explain it? etc. To distinguish between this generation and this procession, I confess that I do not have the knowledge, power, or ability to do this. And therefore, as the generation and the procession are ineffable, as the prophet says in speaking of the Son, 'Who is the one who will tell us his generation?' so also I will say to you in speaking of the Holy Spirit, 'Who is the one who will tell us his procession?'")[33]

Who will not admit defeat after this great and faithful servant of the God of hosts? Who will not keep silent after this great teacher and pastor of the Church, the oracle of his age and of the ages following? I prefer to say as he did in another place and on another subject but with the same spirit of understanding, wisdom, and temperance that accompanied him everywhere: *Cui haec responsio non satisfacit, quaerat doctiores, sed caveat ne inveniat praesumptiores.* ("He who will not be satisfied with this response, let him seek out more learned men. But let him beware lest he encounter more presumptuous ones.")[34] And if the reader appeals to St. Ambrose, St. Augustine's teacher in the faith, he will find in him the same humility and temperance, adoring and confessing the unfathomable secret of the divine and eternal generation: *Mihi impossibile est generationis istius nosse mysterium, vox silet, mens deficit, non mea tantum, sed et angelorum.* ("It is impossible for me to comprehend the mystery of this generation. Words fail me, my spirit becomes lost in it, and not only mine but also that of the angels.")[35] Let

---

32. [Augustine,] *Against Maximinus* 3.14 (original marginal note). In *Arianism*, 280.

33. See Augustine, *Answer to Maximinus the Arian* 2.14.1, in *Arianism*, 280.

34. Augustine, "On the Spirit and the Letter," trans. Peter Holmes and Robert Ernest Wallis, Nicene and Post-Nicene Fathers, First Series, ed. Philip Schaff, vol. 5 (1887; repr., Peabody, Mass.: Hendrickson Publishers, 1995), 111.

35. Ambrose, *On the Christian Faith* 1.10.64, trans. H. de Romestin, E. de Romestin, and H. T. F. Duckworth, *NPNF* 10, p. 212.

us be content with the teaching of these two great pastors, bright luminaries, precious ornaments, and firm foundations of the Church's state and doctrine. Let us learn therefore to adore and not to seek out feeble reasons concerning a subject that reason cannot attain and that God has not revealed. Let us give glory to God, and as we confess our impotence and the greatness of the eternal generation, let us adore in humility the Word's birth in his Father's bosom. Marveling at the greatness, depth, and sublimity of this eternal birth, let us honor Jesus' blessed and divine seclusion in this birth in which he alone is in the bosom of the Father as Son, just as he alone subsists as person in human nature and as he alone lives in the world as mediator of humankind, alone worthy, alone capable, and alone powerful to take our sins away by his blood and merit. In these three respects, the Son of God has no company, either on earth or in heaven, either in eternity or in the fullness of the ages. He alone is Son in the Trinity, alone subsisting in the Incarnation, alone filling the office of mediator in the redemption of human nature.

The last point proposed is that Jesus with the Father is one principle of the Holy Spirit, producing a divine person within eternity. For he is the Wisdom of his Father, he is fertile wisdom and not infertile, and he is wisdom producing not just anything but an eternal love. And just as the Son is produced in oneness by the sole person of the Father who is his principle, so also does he produce in oneness; so much does oneness have its place in divine things, and we give it so little place in the things of earth. For although the Father and the Son are two persons producing, they are not two principles, and, what is ineffable, they produce in oneness of principle and thus the endpoint of this wondrous production is oneness also. For the Holy Spirit is personally the oneness of the Father and the Son divinely united in oneness of love and spirit, and the eternal rest of these divine persons lies in this love and oneness. O Godhead! O fertility! O oneness! O power! O wisdom! O love! O oneness of essence! O oneness of principle! O oneness of love that encompasses, that comprehends, that completes the infinite and uncreated state in its nature, its persons, its emanations! What secrets and great things there are to say of these divine subjects, these persons either proceeding or producing, these internal and infinite emanations within a Being most simple and unchanging.

But it is better to marvel and adore them in profound silence, and it is more becoming to our meanness and to their greatness to remain in this humility and reserve than to try to say little about things so great. The principal fruit of these thoughts is to acknowledge and confess that the God of the Christians is great, *Deus magnus et vincens scientiam nostram*.[36] God great in his essence, great in his persons, great in his emanations. God Father, God Son, God Holy Spirit, always God, always great, always one. One as God, one as Father, one, or rather, only, as Son. One as principle producing, one as Spirit and as personal love produced, and one as sovereign Lord and Creator of heaven and earth. For we go from oneness to oneness in contemplating divine things, uncreated and eternal things, just as we go from oneness to diversity in contemplating human and temporal things: a lovely and noteworthy difference in the conduct and progress of our minds in these two different movements and contemplations! But we must reserve the elaboration for another time. It is time to end and conclude this discussion of Jesus' eternal birth, in which he is God, he is Son of God, he is Son of the living God, he is the only Son of the eternal Father, and he is the principle with him of one divine person.

These are the grandeurs of your first birth, O Jesus my Lord! May I adore them before I end and go on to the following discourse! May I engrave them in my thoughts all the more deeply since it seems that you want to take no thought of them, out of love for us, and to hide them from the world under the veil of our humanity and in the shadows of your mortality! I must break through these shadows and veils; I want to confess and adore God in man, life in death, and glory in the cross. For he is always God, always life, and always glory, indeed, the splendor of glory. And if he desires to take on a new state for our sake, we must not be ignorant of his earlier state. So before he is established in the Virgin's womb, I want to confess and adore him in the bosom of the Father. Before he enters into the state that his love gives him, I want to adore him in the state that his nature gives him. Before beholding him as temporal, I want to contemplate him as eternal. Before prostrating myself at his feet, as made man, I want to prostrate myself before

---

36. "God is great and goes beyond our knowledge." Jb 36:26.

his majesty, as being the majesty of a God. For it is for this reason that his beloved disciple teaches us of his eternal essence and dwelling place before he teaches us of his incarnation.[37] He tells us, in a few words, that he was God and that he was with God, before telling us that he became incarnate.

Let us rise up therefore with thoughts worthy of a subject so high and so divine. Let us seek after the Word in God, for he is God and he is in God, he is God from God, he is God in God, and the bosom of the eternal Father is his center, rest, and dwelling place, his unchanging center, unvarying rest, and eternal dwelling place. There he lives with the same life as his Father. There he possesses the same essence and enjoys the same glory as his Father. There he is as old and as powerful as his Father. There he is the splendor of the glory and the divine imprint of his Father. There he is God as his Father is. There he works as his Father does and produces with his Father the Holy Spirit, a divine person, an eternal and personal love. There he both proceeds and produces, always proceeding and always producing, always proceeding from a divine person and always producing another divine person. In this emanation and production lie his life, his state, and his greatness. There he is life and light. There he is the source of life and light. There he is the source of life and of light in himself and beyond himself: in himself as principle of the Holy Spirit, and beyond himself as principle of grace and glory. O life! O splendor! O state of the divine Word in this divine dwelling place of his in the Father's bosom! O dwelling place! O bosom of the Father! There, O eternal Word, I want to adore you in your grandeurs, and elsewhere in your humilities. There I must adore you in your deity, and elsewhere in your humanity. There I want to adore you in your eternal emanation, and elsewhere in your temporal emanation. So before you enter into a womb that is other to your divine essence, I adore you in the bosom of the Father, as in the source of your life, the center of your rest, the throne of your glory, the culmination of your grandeurs, the dwelling place of your bliss, the paradise of your delight. There you live, there you reign, there you work eternally. There you are and you appear always God, always Son, and always principle

---

37. Jn 1:1–2.

of the Holy Spirit. There by a wondrous secret and power you have a being always proceeding and always producing. There you are always great, always blessed, and always unchanging in your being, your life, and your eternal bliss.

On the Second Birth of Jesus

From the throne of these grandeurs where the Son of God lives by his first and eternal birth, and from this blessed and glorious state where he lives and reigns from all eternity, he comes down and humbles himself to earth and to the Virgin's womb in order to take there a second birth. We contemplate him laid out on the hay and straw, in the stable and the manger. Not in the midst of angels but of shepherds, not among the divine persons but among the cow and ass. Our senses perceive him not most high but most lowly, not most powerful but most powerless, not producing but produced, not creating but receiving a created being, not eternal but beginning to live, and being born in order to die. The Son of God's humilities in this birth are marked and evident and ordinarily treated, but because we are discussing Jesus' grandeurs we will speak of the grandeurs of this birth, confessing God in man and greatness in humility, by the light of faith and the spirit of truth. For God is always God and always great, God in humanity, great in humility. And just as he exalts humanity by deifying it, so also does he lift humility up by magnifying it and by impressing a new and incomparable greatness on the lowliness that he humbles himself to, to the honor of his Father and for the salvation of men.

This birth of Jesus on earth has many kinds of grandeurs, for he is born in the Virgin without affecting her chastity, following this word of the Angel: *Quod in ea natum est, de Spiritu sancto est.*[38] He is born of the Virgin without affecting her integrity. In these two words, *Qui conceptus est de Spiritu sancto, natus ex Maria Virgine,*[39] the faith tells us these two most high and important truths to the honor of Jesus, his Most Holy Mother, and the humble birth that he desired to have of her.

---

38. Mt 1[:20] (original marginal note). "What is born in her is of the Holy Spirit."
39. "Who was conceived by the Holy Spirit, born of the Virgin Mary."

A twofold birth: one inner, *in ea*, and the other outer, *ex ea*.[40] Both are worthy of Jesus and Mary; both have their privileges and advantages, which we will set forth another time. And just as in the one, the divine Word is made flesh in the Virgin and by the Virgin; the Virgin conceived, conceived divinely, the only Son of God without affecting her virginal purity, and she blessedly received this seed from heaven without earthly voluptuousness; so also in the other, after nine months, the Virgin gives birth to him without pain and without affecting her integrity, remaining virgin and mother both. This divine child comes forth from his mother as the ray comes forth from a polished crystal, suffusing it without breaking it apart, and as light comes forth from the sun, leaving it as whole as though it had not come forth. For we can borrow heavenly qualities from heaven in order to honor the one who comes from heaven and of whom St. John says, *Qui de sursum venit, super omnes est. Qui de caelo venit, super omnes est*.[41] But if from heaven we lower ourselves to earth, since Jesus is born on earth, the earth will also render honor and testimony to its Lord and will give us some example to clarify and illustrate this miraculous integrity. Let us say then that he comes forth from the Virgin as the flower comes forth from its stem. For he is also the flower of Israel, the flower that embellishes the world. The flower comes forth from its stem without rending it, without affecting it; on the contrary, the flower is the ornament and embellishment of the plant or tree that bears it.

But these grandeurs, which on earth correspond only to Jesus' birth, are not so distinctive and specific to it that they cannot belong to the birth of a man who is purely man, if God would like to honor him by a similar favor and cause him to be born of a virgin mother by a similar power. Let us rise higher, then, and contemplate the grandeurs that are distinctive and particular to Jesus' birth—grandeurs so high and excellent that they can belong only to a God being born into the world. For the more the Son of God hides and humbles himself in this mystery, the more the Father reveals and manifests him, and the more men must confess him and speak openly of him. Since the eternal Fa-

---

40. "In her"; "Of her."

41. Jn 3[:31] (original marginal note). "He who comes from above is above all. He who comes from heaven is above all."

ther produces new lights on earth so that he might honor and manifest his Son,[42] and he inspires hearts with new movements of his Spirit so that they might know and speak of him,[43] let us follow these lights and impulses. And by such holy and blessed leading, let us devote ourselves to seeking, discovering, and making known the remarkable grandeurs in his abasement and in his humble, new, and human birth.

His birth takes place on earth, but its origin is in heaven. It occurs in a little town of Judea, but its emanation is of the eternal Father. Something as lowly in appearance as the birth of the infant Jesus in the stable of Bethlehem, on the hay and straw, among the cow and ass, has a source so high and wondrous as the bosom of the eternal Father, who is the highness, the greatness, and the marvel of eternity. For the Word, as Son, is encompassed in the bosom of the Father, and he does not come down to earth and to our humanity except by his Father's sending. The Father does not send him to become incarnate except by the same power with which he begets him in himself. In this way, the principle of his eternal generation is the principle of his sending, his birth, and his incarnation in the world. Let us follow this thought, and for a greater clarification of this truth let us say that just as this birth of the Son of God into the world assumes the sending of the same Son of God to the world, so also this sending assumes his eternal procession and comprehends and brings with it the ineffable generation of this eternal Word. This humble birth is blessedly bound and joined with the Word by means of this sending, as by a common bond. The eternal emanation is its origin, and the temporal emanation is its effect. In one same person begotten by power within eternity and sent by love within time, that is, in one same incarnate Son of God, it binds and joins together his divine and eternal birth and his human and temporal birth.

For as we contemplate this most humble and high mystery, we see by the eyes of faith that he who is born in the Virgin's womb and is made man is the very one who is in the bosom of the Father and is God by his divine and eternal birth, just as he is man by his human and temporal birth. We see that the one who comes down to earth to draw the earth to himself and become by new right the Sovereign of the uni-

---

42. Mt 2:2 (original marginal note).
43. Lk 2:27 (original marginal note).

verse, is the very one who formed the earth with the Father, and by the very power that he received from the Father. He does not come down to earth except by the Father's sending and so that by his self-humbling he might establish his Father's greatness, power, and glory. We see that the one who seems as though he comes forth from the bosom of the Father to enter the Virgin's womb does not, however, forsake the Father's bosom. He is divinely in the bosom of the Father and also humbly in the Virgin's womb. He has this twofold residence, of which the one is as wondrous by the abundance of his love as the other is adorable by the abundance of his greatness. Let us conclude, then, that this incarnation and birth on earth regards the bosom of the Father as its source and origin, from which it is blessedly derived on earth. But I pass beyond, and I say (and this is worthy of careful consideration) that it is distinctive and singular of this new birth of the eternal Word (and it is his preeminence and privilege) that among all the things that proceed from God and that are brought to completion outside of God, it alone is encompassed and comprehended in the Father's personal property as Father and in the generation of his Word, who is the first emanation of God. In his honor and power and efficacy the mystery of the Incarnation and the birth of the Son of God is accomplished in our humanity.

In order to better understand this truth, let us take up the discussion at a higher level and note that God, by his essence, is the center and circumference of all things. All things are in God: in their eminent being by his greatness, in their principle by his power, and in their perfect idea by his wisdom. By virtue of these three distinct points, God contains and comprehends all that is created. But the eternal Father, as Father and in the property of his person, is the center and circumference of his Son. The Son regards him as his center, the center in which he is, lives, rests, and has his eternal dwelling place. For the Son is in his Father as in the one who comprehends him, as an infinity equals and comprehends another infinity and as the divine persons, by a secret adorable to our finite and limited minds, mutually comprehend one another. In the eternal Father as Father, there is only his Son and what regards the person of his Son, who is sole in the Godhead and who willed to be sole in our humanity also. Even the Holy Spirit, who proceeds from the Father, is indeed in the Father as in his principle, but he is not in him as in his Father. For he does not proceed from the Father as Father, and he is not the Son of the Father. This position corresponds only to the one who is named the only Son and whom the Father has given us in calling him by the name of his beloved Son in whom he is well pleased.[44] The Son is in eternity the first emanation of the Father, alone proceeds from him by true and natural generation, and has his residence and dwelling place in the Father's bosom, for "bosom" is fittingly a term rightly assigned and appropriate to generation. The Son therefore is in the Father's bosom, for he is Son. The Son alone is in the Father's bosom, for he alone is Son. And the Father alone sends his Son to become incarnate, for he alone is the Father of this Son. For the sendings in the Godhead correspond only to the principle of their procession, according to the common voice of all sacred theology. Let us then say boldly and openly that the Father alone sends his Son to become incarnate, and (what is worthy of deep consideration and establishes the principal point of this discourse) that he sends him as Father. Consequently, he sends him by the same power by which he begets him (a power that belongs only to the Father) and not by the power by which he creates the world, which is a power common to the three persons of the Holy Trinity. It is clear therefore that this sending and communication of the Son of God to the world originates in the Father and in the Father alone.

From this we learn a beautiful difference between this sending and new production of the Son of God and the production of the creatures. For whereas the creatures proceed from God as God and not from God as Father, this temporal sending of the Son of God to earth has as its distinctive and singular feature that it proceeds from God as Father, in addition to the eternal emanation of the same Son. This sending also has as its distinctive and particular feature that in addition to the eternal emanation it is encompassed and hidden, alone encompassed and hidden, in the bosom of the Father, from whom alone it originates. This is why in my opinion the apostle in several places calls the mystery that is accomplished by this sending, *The mystery hidden from all eternity in God*.[45] For we must note this beautiful principle, which

---

44. Mt 17:5 (original marginal note).
45. Eph 3:9.

ought to serve as the foundation of our thoughts and the guide of our conduct, that all that proceeds from God remains in God himself in a certain manner, as in its principle. Whence it comes that the created things, as coming forth from the divine essence, remain in this essence; and thus this sending and incarnation that proceed from the bosom of the Father have a kind of residence in the same bosom of the Father, as in their principle. And just as it alone among all other things has this prerogative of proceeding from the bosom of the Father alone as from the one who, alone begetting his Son, alone sends him to become incarnate, so also it has this prerogative of alone being encompassed, residing, and hidden in the bosom of the Father as in his glory, rest, and principle. In this we must marvel at the excellence of this work of the Incarnation among all the works of God, and we must confess and adore the profundity and singularity of this mystery among all the other mysteries of earth and heaven, of grace and of glory. It is a mystery in which the principle of the eternal generation is the principle, the sole principle, of the temporal sending of the one who comes to be born among us. Before this, he is in the Father's bosom as in his eternal rest, in the wellspring of his being, and in the origin of his sending, birth, and incarnation on earth.

From a source so high, deep, and powerful, and from an origin so great, profound, and divine, what should we expect if not something most great and surpassing the stature of men and of angels? Since Jesus' birth on earth proceeds from this source and comes from this principle, will it not be like its principle? That is, will it not be great and wondrous like him, divine and ineffable like him? Was not the greatest of the prophets, rapt in the contemplation of this mystery, correct to say to us, *Generationem eius quis enarrabit?*[46] For it does not have as its distinctive and singular feature only that it is encompassed and comprehended in the person of the Father as in its principle; it also has another kind of relation to him and to the eternal generation, since it corresponds to it not only as to its origin but also as to its model. For

---

46. "Who will explain his generation?" Is 53:8; Acts 8:33. Cf. Leo, Sermon 23: "We believe that the saying, 'Who will recount his generation?' pertains not only to that mystery by which the Son of God is co-eternal with the Father, but also to this beginning by which 'The Word was made flesh.'" In *Sermons*, 87, 121.

the Son of God does not desire only to be made man. He desires to be made man by birth, as he is God by birth. And he desires to be Son of man as he is Son of God.

This deserves to be set forth further. Let us say, then—and we must take pleasure in thinking and saying it many times, for this point is delightful and also concerns the delight of the Son of God, who takes pleasure in being Son of man among the children of men. Let us say, then, that as the eternal Word contemplated himself and saw that he was God in his divine essence, he willed to take on a new essence and be made Man-God for the salvation of men. And seeing that he was in the Godhead by birth and origin from his eternal Father, he wanted to be in this humanity by birth and origin from his holy Mother. Thus, he wanted to be in a state corresponding to his state in the Godhead and to be Son of man on earth as he is Son of God in heaven. He wanted to have his humanity by human sonship as he has the deity by divine sonship, and to bear the same name of Son in each nature, that is, in his eternal nature and in his temporal nature. So much does he take pleasure in his divine and eternal birth! So much does he desire to express and imitate it in a second birth! So much does he want to honor and make it known by a new state! And so agreeable is he to this name and state of sonship that constitutes him Son of God in the Father's bosom and Son of man in his Mother's womb! It is for this reason that in Psalm 71, which the rabbis themselves apply entirely to the Messiah, in verse 18 where we have *Sit nomen eius benedictum in saecula; ante solem permanet nomen eius*,[47] the Hebrew wording reveals to us a secret worthy of this mystery, as remarks the learned Génébrard, the luminary of this age and very accomplished ornament of this celebrated faculty of Paris. For this great teacher, explicating this verse and not finding in Latin any name vigorous enough to express the strength of these Hebrew words, creates a new word out of them that cannot be translated into French. This obliges me to use it in this treatise and give it currency under the authority and safe conduct of this excellent author, although it will seem a bit strange to those who seek more elegance in words than vigor. I will say then, following him, that where we have *Sit nomen*

---

47. "May his name be blessed forever; before the sun his name endures." Ps 72:17.

eius benedictum in saecula: ante solem permanet nomen eius, the Hebrew says, in speaking of the Messiah, "*Filiabitur proprie, seu filius erit: Filius appellabitur nomen eius, etc.*,"[48] and that the ancient Hebrews observed that this word "son" placed in this text is a name belonging to the Messiah—the most beautiful name he has and the one in which he most takes delight. It is a name that marks his deity, in which he is Son of God; a name that marks his humanity, in which he is Son of man; a name that marks his origin, his twofold origin, that is most dear and precious to him. For he does not subsist among the divine persons except by the relation that he has as Son to his Father, whom he loves and regards with an eternal love, and he does not live and subsist among men except by the birth that establishes the relation and relationship that he has as son to his Most Holy Mother, whom he cherishes and loves above all others on earth as his single source and origin. In addition, in this verse this name marks out for us the birth of the Word in eternity, *Ante solem filiabitur nomen eius, etc.*,[49] that is, before the sun was created he has the name, being, and position of Son. And it marks out for us the time of his birth on earth, at midnight, before the dawning light, *Ante solem filiabitur nomen eius*, that is, before the sun had risen. For the original text can bear both meanings and can be applied to the Messiah's divine sonship and to his human sonship. It instructs us that it is his distinctive feature to be Son; that this name does not correspond to him merely by being given to him, as many names that are given to persons on earth, but that it is a name that he takes from his birth and his origin; and that it is a name that is born with him and that he is born with before the sun's birth, *Ante solem filiabitur nomen eius*, a name that will endure as long as and longer than the sun. Thus, it is the august and sacred name by which it pleased the eternal Father

---

48. "Strictly speaking, his name 'will be sonned,' or, he will be son: his name will be called son, etc." Gilbert Génébrard, *Psalmi Davidis* (Paris, 1588), 200, https://numelyo.bm-lyon.fr/f_view/BML:BML_00GOO0100137001102338642. Génébrard (1535–97) was a noted scholar of biblical Hebrew. At issue here is the interpretation of the Hebrew word *yinnon* that occurs in the Bible only at this verse and is translated in the Latin as *permanet* ("endures"). Génébrard expresses what he believes to be its meaning with a nonce word, *filiabitur*, created from the noun *filius* (son) plus the verbal endings *-bi* (future-tense marker) and *-tur* (passive-voice marker).

49. "Before the sun his name will be sonned, etc."

to give and present him to us on earth, in saying to us, *Hic est filius meus dilectus*.⁵⁰ For these are the words that the Father himself uses to announce and manifest him to St. John in the desert and to the apostles in the glory of the Transfiguration. He makes known this name in the universe, and it is worthy of being taught to men by the eternal Father and foretold by his prophet in this memorable text that tells us, in the Hebrew: *Ante solem filiabitur nomen eius*, and in our version: *Ante solem permanet nomen eius*. By these two different terms, this name's origin and eternal duration are expressed to us, for it will endure as long as the sun—that is, for eternity, in which Jesus will be forever both Son of God and Son of man.

From this sacred word and this name of Son that is particular to the Messiah, according to the truth of this sacred text, we sum up a new greatness of this human and temporal birth. For just as God's first emanation and communication within himself is by eternal birth and generation, so also God's first and supreme emanation and communication beyond himself is by this temporal birth, in which the Son of God is the Son of man and the Son of man is Son of God in the sacred mystery of the Incarnation. It is a most remarkable greatness in this birth, to produce in the universe and bear to the creation the highest communication of God that can be made beyond himself. God—great and wondrous in his thoughts and counsels upon the children of men, and much more in his thoughts and counsels upon his only Son—in wanting to make the greatest and most ineffable communication of the divine being that created being can receive, does not choose another way to give him to the world than this humble birth that we adore on earth: a birth that abases God so that we might be exalted, and that raises up a human substance even to the subsistence of the Word. One same manner of emanation causes the Son of God to come to the earth in the fullness of time and establishes the Son of God within eternity and gives him being in the Godhead. So that the same one who is Son of God might be Son of man, and that the whole state of sonship that is right and natural, but truly divine and supernatural, might be revered, consecrated, and adored in one same person, who receives his

---

50. "This is my beloved son." Mt 3:17.

two different natures in the same manner, who possesses these two essences (the one eternal, the other new) on the same basis (that is, by birth), and who is established by birth in the Godhead and by birth in the sacred Humanity. For all this, may he be blessed on earth and in heaven forever.

From these grandeurs others follow, and we go from one greatness to another as we contemplate Jesus' birth. For this human birth is a mystery of life, since the one who lives by the Father, who is produced as living by the property of his emanation, who is the true life and who gives himself the name of Life in an absolute way, and who is life and the source of life in himself and beyond himself, desires to take on life in this mystery so that he might be our life forever. It is a mystery of light, for the one who is Light from Light, who is emanated from the Father of lights, who is emanated from him as light and who, in the property of his person, is the Splendor of the Father, being light in his essence and in his person, by this mystery comes into the world so that he might be the light of the world, as he himself says: *Ego lux veni in mundum, etc.*[51] *Ego sum lux mundi.*[52] And so he is born with light at midnight and enters upon the earth with a heavenly light that lights up the darkness of night and gives a twofold light to the shepherds. And just as at his death the world's light was overshadowed and turned into darkness, so also at his birth a new light, a light extraordinary to the world, appeared that gave light to kings, the East, and Judea, the heavens thus marking and honoring Jesus' birth as the birth of a new light in the world.

This birth is a mystery of holiness, according to these angelic words: *Quod nascetur ex te sanctum*, a premier mystery of holiness even among Jesus' other mysteries.[53] For it bears and works in the universe the greatest holiness and most eminent sanctification that is and can be and in which all the other remarkable holinesses and sanctifications on earth and in heaven are founded. This is the birth of the Holy of Holies. This is the birth of a God-Man and of a Man-God. This is the birth of the order and state of the hypostatic union, which carries outside of

---

51. "I am the light that has come into the world, etc." Jn 12:46.
52. "I am the light of the world." Jn 8:12.
53. "The one that will be born of you is holy." Lk 1:35.

God the highest and most eminent holiness possible and is the closest to the superessential holiness of God himself, which this supreme order and state encompasses and comprehends in itself, as its form and principle. For this new holiness on earth and in heaven, and this wondrous grace of the hypostatic union, has its birth in Jesus' birth and takes its origin in this mystery. From here it comes and spreads to all Jesus' other mysteries, states, and works. For, to be precise, the other mysteries of the Son of God are mysteries of either holy actions or sufferings, but this mystery is a mystery of substance, and a mystery producing in the world the very substance of holiness, from which his holy actions and sufferings proceed, in which they rest, and in which subsist all the other various and divine states that he has, either on earth or in heaven. Let us acknowledge this mystery, then, as a mystery of life, a mystery of light, a mystery of holiness, a mystery of substance and not only of action or accident; a mystery of substantial holiness, primordial holiness, original and foundational holiness; of all of Jesus' mysteries, all his works, and all his states. Let us receive from this mystery a grace, a holiness, a light, a life, a life of light, and a light of life in Jesus, as effects that are fitting and proceeding from the state and condition of this mystery, in which the Son of God gives and manifests himself to the world. Concerning this, we see that here, more than at any other time, any other state, or any other mystery of his life, he gives life and knowledge of himself. For it is in this birth that the angels announce him, the shepherds testify to him, the star reveals him to the magi, the magi make him known in Judea, the Holy Spirit reveals him in the temple, and St. Simeon and St. Anne prophesy of him to all who await the redemption of Israel. And the holy souls who desire to share in Jesus' holiness, life, and light should have recourse to the efficacy of this mystery as to a mystery of holiness, of life, and of substantial or, rather, supersubstantial light, and as to a source of holiness of life and light in the world.

This birth of Jesus has another quality and property that is most worthy of Jesus and of the previous ones. For it is a mystery of honor and homage, a mystery of praise and adoration to the Godhead by the humanity subsisting in this mystery. To understand it well, let us note that each mystery of the Son of God has something distinctive and particular of its own, not only in its effect but also in its state. And that just as his cross is properly a mystery of suffering and expiation, so also his birth is properly a mystery of offering and adoration. It is a mystery in which we see that the eternal Father acquires both a new adorer and a new host. For Jesus, the perfect, supreme, divine Adorer, is born in this mystery, and he is born as Host, as host of praise, and as host that receives his fulfilment in this same mystery and performs in it his function and office, rendering praise and adoration to the eternal Father.

These points are clear to the one who penetrates even a little into the state of this most high and humble mystery. To proceed in step: First, it is in this mystery of Jesus' human birth in Mary and of Mary that the true and matchless host of the eternal Father is prepared by the incarnation of the Word (which occurs in this birth), in that this humanity, which is capable by its nature, is rendered worthy by subsistence of being a host of perfect praise and adoration to the supreme Majesty. Second, it is in this mystery that this host, chosen and set apart like this from the common run of men by the hand of God, who singularly applies himself in forming and producing it, in the same instant that it is produced is consecrated by the unction of the Deity and by the ineffable and hypostatic union that is made in this same birth. And in the third place, it is in this mystery that the host, chosen and consecrated in this way, is offered and presented to God by the oblation that Jesus makes of himself as he comes into the world, according to St. Paul's memorable text.[54] One same moment and one same mystery, that is, the mystery of Jesus' human birth, accomplishes and comprehends these three points that are necessary to the perfect state of hosts as such. This divine host accomplishes his office at the same moment that he is formed, completed, and dedicated. The first moment of his life and divine subsistence is the first moment of his elevation and oblation to the eternal Father. Jesus adores, by a new adoration, an original adoration, a divine adoration, an adoration adorable and adored by the angels who behold him—Jesus, I say, adores the Deity through the humanity at the same moment that he is formed in the Most Holy Virgin's womb and enters into the world.

54. Heb 10[:5–9] (original marginal note).

Now, as this mystery of the Son of God's human birth is a mystery of absolute and universal homage to the Deity by the humanity deified in this same mystery, it is also a mystery that is consecrated to the distinctive and particular homage of the eternal birth by the temporal birth, and of the divine sonship by the human sonship. This state of birth and human sonship is a state that truly imitates, adores, and regards the eternal birth and sonship, to which it has a perfect and divine relation as to its origin and model. For Jesus is born in the Virgin's womb because he is born in the bosom of the Father; Jesus is Son of man because he is Son of God. This humble birth and human sonship is derived from a source so high and powerful as the bosom of the Father, and on earth it properly regards the Father as Father and as begetting his only Son. By the property of its state and condition, on earth it imitates and adores a thing as great as the eternal generation, which is a marvel and source of marvel in eternity. As the Son of God is Son of man in such a way that he will always be Son of man, he therefore has in himself a permanent state and everlasting quality that continually regards the divine sonship as its model and origin. I beg the reader to be careful, for I do not say only that the Son of God adores this sonship by his own thoughts. I say that by this mystery he is in a state and has a quality that in itself adores the eternal Father as Father and that adores the divine birth of his only Son and his eternal sonship.

This point is great and deserves to be well understood. It is founded in a great and universal proposition that must serve as the foundation of our discussion and the rule of our conduct: that all that proceeds from God regards God and renders honor to God. This is a proposition so true that it occurs even in the divine persons, who mutually honor and regard one another, and the subsistence and life of the Most Holy Trinity lies in these relations and regards of honor and love. And if from this high state of the divine and immanent processions we descend to the things that have come forth from God and exist outside of himself, it is easy to note the truth of this proposition in them all and recognize that what proceeds like this—not from God in God himself but from God outside of God—regards and renders homage and adoration to God, adoring in its created condition the grandeurs of uncreated being. The order of seraphim adores by its seraphic state, which is a state of love, the uncreated love from which it emanates. The order of cherubim adores by its state, which is a state of light, the uncreated light from which it comes forth. The order of thrones adores by its rest and stability, the rest and stability of God in himself and in his own perfections. The being and life of existing and living things adore the being and life of God, who is their cause and principle. The intellectual natures adore intellectually the supreme intelligence, who is God, to whom it belongs by essence to behold and know himself and all things in himself.

But just as all created things proceed from God as God, and not from God as Father or as Son, etc., so also they regard only God's essential being, and manifest only his essence, not his persons, and by their condition they pay homage only to the essential and common perfections of the divine persons. Thus, the Son of God's eternal birth had nothing outside of God and in the creation properly appointed to praise and adore it. The angels adored it by intellect and knowledge, but not by state and condition. Men were ignorant of it in the darkness of their faith. A thing so great and primary in God as the divine fatherhood and divine sonship was without this proper and singular kind of homage and recognition like that which created things rendered to the perfections of the divine essence by the state and condition of their being. But it pleased God to establish on earth this divine mystery of Jesus' birth. By this means, there is on earth what is not in heaven, and there is among men what is not among the angels, that is, there is a new birth and wondrous sonship that has as its distinctive and singular feature that it regards not only God's essential being but also his personal being. This birth alone among all created things regards it, and regards it in a singular and eminent quality that belongs to it only. Thus, it pays homage, divine homage, to the personal being of the Father begetting his Son, to the personal being of the Son begotten of his Father, and to the divine generation that by this internal emanation binds the Father to the Son and the Son to the Father with a most intimate residence and most adorable oneness. Instead of created things' regarding God's perfections only as traces, intimations, and images of such divine things, this mystery of Jesus being born of his Most Holy Mother, and this birth and human sonship, regard and adore a thing so great, distinctive, and divine as are the personal properties, and regards them in a great manner. For it regards and adores the Father as the one who is its origin and principle (according to the previous argument), it regards the Son as the one who is its endpoint and subsistence, and it regards the divine birth that the Son has from the Father as its cause and model.

Jesus therefore bears within himself a state that regards and adores his eternal state. Before his birth, there was nothing on earth or in heaven that properly regarded, perfectly expressed, and divinely honored the Father as Father and his Son as Son in the state of his divine birth and eternal sonship. By his state, Jesus alone adores the divine persons and emanations that the angels adored in heaven by the acts of their understanding and will but not by this kind of adoration that we are speaking of, which is very different. For we are speaking of an adoration that is by state and not by act. It is an adoration that does not emanate only from the faculties of the mind and depend on its thoughts, but one that is secure, permanent, and independent of powers and actions and that is deeply impressed on the depths of the created being and in the condition of its state. Thus, we are saying that before this new birth there was nothing that, in itself and its condition, either naturally or personally, adored and rendered homage to these divine objects, nothing that bore in its origin, being, and state the relation, mark, and impression of a thing so great and high.

If the greatness of this proposition prompts someone to penetrate and understand it further, I beg him to consider the sound foundation that we have laid and to note this truth again: that all that is created proceeds from God as God and not from God as Father or from God as Son. And that therefore all that is created regards and honors God's essential being but not his personal being. For the personal being, as personal, works and impresses nothing of itself outside the Godhead, and thus nothing in created nature belongs to the distinction, property, and singularity of the persons. Things so great and marvelous in the Godhead as to be Father of a God Son and to be the only and eternal Son of God have nothing on earth or in heaven, in time or eternity, that regards them specifically and pays homage, by the property of its state, to the property of these two divine persons, one of whom is Father and the other is Son. That belongs only to this one birth derived from the Virgin and to the blessed and wondrous state of motherhood from which it proceeds. For this birth, sonship, and motherhood regard God's personal being and properties by regarding the eternal Father who, as Father, gives his Son to this humanity, and by regarding this same Son who, as Son of God, is made Son of man and is born in this human nature. Just as only this human birth and sonship of Jesus regards God's personal being, so also this personal being properly regards outside of itself only this birth, in which the Word divinely impresses his own person on our humanity and forms a living, express, and glorious image of his eternal birth, by a temporal birth. This new birth and sonship is the one subject that the Son of God, as Son, looks upon outside of himself and that he looks upon as his living image and imprint, which bears the resemblance and impression of his substance and his eternal emanation. Following his example, we must likewise contemplate and regard this birth and new sonship as an excellent and precious font and as a divine subject on which he impresses his being and represents his personal greatness. Just as the eternal Father in his eternity produces his Son and, in producing him, looks upon him as his living image and as the one to whom he communicates his essence, so also the Son of God, working on earth this mystery of the Incarnation, produces himself by a new production, by making himself Son of man as he is Son of God, and as he contemplates himself in this mystery he sees himself to be in a new state, which honors his eternal state and pays homage to his divine birth by his human birth. A birth in which God truly humbles himself to become Son of man, but in humbling himself he exalts, honors, and deifies this humble birth and makes it worthy to sublimely, perfectly, and divinely adore his eternal birth.

This is the state of this humble birth in the eyes of the Father of lights. This is his condition in the sight of heaven and the angels, a state and condition very different from that which appear to the eyes of men, who see only base things in so great a thing. But such is earth's wretchedness, which has darkness, blindness, and shadows for its portion, and such is heaven's blessedness, which has the wellsprings of all light within itself. Since we receive from heaven and not from earth this very light that is to enlighten our eyes, it is from heaven that we must receive the true light that is to enlighten our minds. It is in the light of heaven that we must contemplate the one who comes down from heaven and who covers his grandeurs with our baseness, his lights with our darkness, so that he might be, might live, and might treat with us.

In view of this object, let us let our senses go. Let us rise up above ourselves. Let us behold the state and conduct of heaven and the angels upon the one who is born on the earth. They stoop down to earth, delighted by this new object's greatness and drawn by its power. They leave heaven so that they might behold and adore on earth a greatness that is not in heaven. They make themselves the followers and servants on earth of a Majesty hidden and unknown on earth, and they behold in this birth many more grandeurs than our senses perceive humilities. Let us imitate the angels. Let us approach like them this divine child. Let us see this light being born, but in his light, and like them we will see that this humble birth of Jesus originates in the bosom of the Father. We will see that it is an imitation on earth of the eternal birth and a state belonging and consecrated to the homage of the divine birth. We will see that causes so high and great can conclude and result only in great things. This birth, therefore, so high in its origin, so exalted in its object, so sublime and holy in its ends, this birth, I say, that has for its principle the bosom of the Father, for its model the eternal birth, and for its end to be a state adoring the Father in the generation of his Son and the Son in his emanation from the Father, will be as great in its state and effects as it is in its causes, ends, and origin. We see therefore that this birth concludes in the production of a Man-God, of a Man-God not by grace but by nature, not by the working of the deity but by its communication, not by indwelling but by subsistence, and not in union but in oneness of person.

The light and power of nature knows no greater miracle than man. And thus, when God created the world, he ceased in man's production as in the final and supreme of his works in the order of nature. But the light and power of grace is much more exalted than that of nature. And God himself, author of nature and of grace, God, I say, in the breadth of his knowledge, light, and power, knows no greater miracle than the Man-God, since God himself is encompassed and comprehended in the circle and circumference of this miracle. The Ancients brought all their eloquence to bear upon celebrating man's grandeurs and perfections, and rightly, for man is truly a great miracle. In his substance we see two such different natures that are united in a wondrous way. One is wholly spiritual: it stirs up a thousand things without moving, ascends to heaven and descends to the depths without changing place, files away the entire world in the cabinet of its memory without holding it any place therein, joins together all past times in one without sequence, is wholly in this body and in each part of this body as in its universe, and is an image of God and of God's sovereignty and work on earth. The other is embodied: animal and sensible, by which he lives, senses, imagines, and is an epitome of this universe in his structure and composition. From these two natures united together an excellent composition results, having existence like the elements, life like the plants, sensation like the animals, and intellect like the angels.[55]

This is the most perfect and wondrous mixture in nature, in which it seems that God desired to epitomize his works and reduce to miniature the greatness of his universe, or, rather, produce a new universe and little world. It is a little world that encompasses with more marvels all the perfections of this great universe, a little world that in the midst of the universe carries as it were an epitome of God in man's mind and an epitome of the world in his body's wondrous composition and structure. This so perfect mixture is without confusion of natures, for each remains distinct in its essence and powers and works, but they are wondrously united in subsistence and in the oneness of one same person, composed of two such different natures.

It seems to me in these thoughts that man, who is the image of God

---

55. Cf. Hermes Trismegistus, *Ascelpius*, in *Hermetica*, 69–70. Cf. Bérulle, *Œuvres de piété*:

For man is composed of very different parts. He is a miracle on the one hand, and a nothing on the other. He is heavenly on the one hand, and earthly on the other. He is spiritual on the one hand, and bodily on the other. He is an angel, he is an animal; he is a nothing, he is a miracle; he is a center, he is a world, he is a god. He is a nothing surrounded by God, wanting of God, capable of God, and filled by God, if he wills.

In *OC*, 4:10. This view of humankind as the whole in miniature, or as occupying a middle, sharing in what is higher and what is lower, is commonplace in Neoplatonic thought. But whereas the Neoplatonic philosophers taught that man can ascend to the higher and ultimately to the One by his own efforts, Bérulle speaks of grace and of virtue—that is, human effort assisted by divine grace.

by whom he is made, is also the image of the Man-God by whom he is made new, and that in making man, God makes as it were a prelude to the mystery of the Incarnation. This is why he attends to man's production in a different way than he does in creating heaven or earth or any part of this universe. He enters into his council and deliberates about it within himself. He takes in his hands a piece of earth, from which he wants to form him. He forms and molds it by himself, not by his angels. He breathes into it the breath of life and marks and impresses on it his most perfect image. He makes it sovereign among his works. And as the only eternal, invisible, and universal God, he sets it down among his works as a temporal, visible, and particular god. Contemplating this procedure of God in man's creation, who will not marvel at the particular care that he takes in this one work? And who will not be astonished by this self-humbling of the greatness of God, who from that moment involves himself in mud and mire so that he might create man, and who applies himself to the loam of the earth? Yet he will go on to a greater outpouring and will involve himself even further in the earth's mire. He will apply, he will involve, he will deepen himself therein without bottom or shore, and one day he will speak this word by his prophet: *Infixus sum in limo profundi, et non est substantia.*[56] For he will unite himself so closely with the loam of the earth and with the mire of our nature that he will cause himself to become earth and mire. He will become flesh, and flesh is earth in its outcome, substance, and origin. God said to man, *Terra es, etc.*,[57] and calls man "earth" three times by his prophet.[58] Flesh therefore is earth by the voice of him who made both earth and flesh and who drew flesh from the earth. For the Word is made flesh, and thus the Word is made earth; and for this reason, from the Creation he loves to take earth into his hands and form the earth that he wants to unite and incorporate with himself one day.

Thus it seems to me that God, who sees things future in things present, saw in this work of Creation that of the Incarnation, and he delighted to think of the second Adam as he formed the first, and to form this piece of earth in his hands, because in it was this part and portion of

---

56. "I stick fast in deep mire, and there is no foothold." Ps 69:2.
57. "You are earth, etc."
58. Gn 3:19.

earth and substance that he wanted one day to quicken by the spirit of his deity and unite to himself, by communicating and impressing on it not his likeness but his essence, his subsistence, and his deity. There is therefore a great relation between the work of man's creation and that of the incarnation of the Word, as between two excellent works: the one supreme in the order of nature and the other supreme in the order of grace. For just as in man's creation there is a mixture, so also is there a mixture in the Incarnation. And the great theologian exclaims, *O mixturam novam, O temperamentum admirandum!* ("O wondrous temperament, O new mixture!")[59] A mixture without mixture—that is, without the imperfection of mixture. As this first mixture is of two natures, the one spiritual and the other bodily, this second mixture is of two natures, and much more different: the one divine and the other human, the one created and the other uncreated. Just as the soul and body make up a composition, which is man, so also from the deity and humanity joined together results a divine composition, who is Jesus. And just as to the man are appropriated the conditions and actions of his two different natures, so also to the Man-God, to our Immanuel, are appropriated the perfections, qualities, and actions of his two natures, although so different. For God is man, is measured by time, is passible, is mortal, and suffers and dies on a cross. And man is God, is eternal, is impassible, is immortal, and causes this humanity and all those on earth who pay him homage to be forever triumphant, glorious, and immortal. Just as God made in man an epitome of the world and himself, so also did he want to make in the Man-God (in a much more excellent manner) a divine composition of created and uncreated being, an epitome of himself and the world, or, to say it better, a new world, a much more excellent one, an incomparable world, the sustenance, salvation, support, and end of the world. In this new, incomparable, and divine world, he does not reduce but extends and diffuses his divine grandeurs and perfections, in which the profusion and fullness of the deity shine out singularly and are made equally lovable and adorable.

Would that it pleased God for us to have as much good fortune, eloquence, and intelligence in the state of Christendom to celebrate the

---

59. Gregory Nazianzen, Oration 45, "Second Oration on Easter," in *Select Orations and Letters*, 426.

grandeurs and perfections of the Man-God as the Ancients had in the state of paganism to treat of the excellences of man. But we must leave this subject to the spirits in heaven, who by the eminence of their glory and light are worthy of fathoming the singularities of this masterwork of grace and of nature. Our task in the baseness of earth is to honor in silence the depth of our mysteries. Ours is to accompany with the affections and effects of piety a faith that is stronger, more powerful, and more eloquent in works than in words and that was first made known to the world by works, miracles, and suffering rather than by discourses, presumption, and choice words. Our task as we confess Jesus' greatness and our meanness is to content ourselves with saying, in the humility and simplicity of faith, that man is God, that is, that man is at the highest and most exalted point that God's power, wisdom, and goodness can set him. The Man-God is the center of all God's workings outside of himself. The Man-God is the masterwork of the Almighty. The Man-God is a divine composition in which God uses, applies, and expresses the grandeurs and perfections of his deity, majesty, and power. A composition in which the two natures are not mingled or confused, and yet they are as perfectly joined as though they were mingled and as individually stable in their natural properties as though they were separate. A composition that has union but not oneness of natures, and that has oneness but not union of persons, but oneness of person in his different natures that are perfectly and divinely united.

Whence comes the manner of speaking common among the Fathers, approved in the schools, and set forth in sermons: that the divine nature is incarnate, that the human nature is deified, and that its actions are humanly divine and divinely human—human in the nature by which they are produced and divine in the person who produces them by this nature. Whence comes also the attribution so famous in antiquity, and the mutual communication of such different effects, qualities, and properties in one same subject, who is, lives, and acts in two such different natures, and who is mutable in the one and immutable in the other, passible in the one and impassible in the other, mortal in the one and immortal in the other. Whence it comes, in short, that Jesus' state and life always has its humilities exalted by the marks and ensigns of the deity, so that the greatness of God might be made known in man's lowliness, and that the world might see that just as these two natures (the one divine and the other human) are perfectly united in Jesus, so also in Jesus humility is joined with greatness throughout the course of his life and in all its many states.

I prefer to revere so lofty a subject by a sacred silence than to profane it by my base conceptions and feeble words. Holding them back, therefore, in reverence, and in profound humility toward things so great, let us permit the authoritative and great theologian of antiquity to speak, and let us listen, for he treats of them worthily and describes them with the authority of his learning and the flowers and ornaments of his eloquence.[60]

The Son of God was born, but he was begotten from all eternity. He was born of a woman, but of a virgin woman; the former is human, the latter is divine. In the one he is without father; in the other he is without mother. Both are divine. He was carried in his mother's womb, but he was confessed by a prophet who was likewise in the womb of his own mother, leaping before the eternal Word, for whom he was created. He was truly swaddled, but at his resurrection he stripped off his burial shroud. He was put in the manger, but he was honored by angels, indicated by the star, and adored by the magi. Why do you take offence at what can be seen, not considering what is spiritual in it? He was a fugitive in Egypt, but he put to flight the errors and idolatries of the Egyptians. The Jews found in him no grace or beauty, but David calls him the most beautiful of the sons of men. And on the mountain he is as brilliant as a lightning flash and more shining than the sun, causing to appear there a sample of his glory to come.

In truth, he was baptized as a man, but he broke the bonds of sin as God, and he commands us to have confidence in him as in the one who has overcome the world. He endured hunger, but he fed thousands of men, he is this bread of life, he is this bread come down from heaven. He was thirsty, but he said in a loud voice, *If anyone is thirsty, let him come to me and drink.* And he promised those who believe that he will cause fountains of running water to come from them. He was tired from work, but he is the rest of those who are weary and heavy laden. He was heavy with sleep, but he is light on the waters, he commands the winds, he lifts St. Peter up as he sinks into the waters. He pays the tribute, but by a fish, he is the prince of those who demand tribute. He is called a Samaritan, he is considered demon-possessed, but he restores

---

60. Gregory Nazianzen, Oration 33, 1, On the Son, and 3, On Theology (original marginal note). See Gregory Nazianzen, Oration 29, *Third Theological Oration, On the Son*, in *Select Orations and Letters*, 308–9.

health to the one who went down from Jerusalem and fell among thieves, the devils acknowledge and confess him, he chases them out and causes legions of spirits to plunge into the sea, and he sees the Prince of Demons fall from heaven like lightning. He is stoned, but he is not hit or injured. He prays, but he also grants the prayers of others. He sheds tears, but he wipes our tears away. He asks where Lazarus has been laid (for he was man), but he raises Lazarus from death to life, for he was God. Truly he was sold at too cheap a price, for thirty pieces of silver, and yet he redeems the world by an inestimable price, that is, by his own blood. He is led like a poor sheep to the slaughter, but he nourishes and feeds Israel and does so each day still, and to everyone. He was silent as a lamb, but he is himself the Word, announced by the voice of one who was crying in the desert. He has borne our griefs and was covered with stripes, but he heals every stripe and takes away every grief. He is raised up upon the wood and crucified there, but he redeems us by the wood of life, he saved the thief hanging with him on the cross, he covers with darkness all that is visible. He is given vinegar to drink and fed with gall, and who is he? The very one who changed water into wine and sweetened the bitter waters, the one who is sweetness itself and the object of all our desires. He gives his life, but he has the power to take it up again, the veil of the temple is torn (for secrets then were made plain), the rocks are split apart, the dead are raised. He dies, but he gives life, and by his death he stifles death. He is put in the grave, but he comes back to life. He descends into hell, but he brings the souls out and goes back up to heaven. And he is to come to judge the living and the dead, accompanied by his angels and seated on the throne of his Majesty.

This is the man whom the eternal Father has given us in the abundance of his love and the extremity of our wretchedness. This is the second Adam, so different from the first. This truly is the Adam we need, to heal our wretchedness, to pay our debts, to fill up what we lack, to take away our iniquities, to carry out what we ought. Truly, the first Adam was holy, but he hardly persevered in his holiness; this Adam is holy, is forever holy, and is the Holy of Holies. The first might never have sinned, but the second cannot sin and is sinless by so high a principle and so high a means as is the hypostatic union, which, in the person of the Word, gives to his human nature the same right that makes God sinless. The first, in his grace, could not deliver any of his children from the state of sin, even from one single sin, the least sin. The second delivers his fathers and children; he delivers even the first Adam, who is the source of sin. He delivers us all from sin, from as many sins as there could be in the eternal duration of a world, so much is this source of life, grace, and holiness the deep, powerful, and efficacious source. The first Adam did not have the gift of stability in grace, for himself or for any of his own, but the second Adam gives the gift of stability and perseverance to his elect, and he will establish them one day forever in a lasting holiness and will make them all, for a whole eternity, sinless like him. In brief, the first Adam by his transgression was the cause of all his children's ruin and of his own ruin; and the second Adam is the cause of life, glory, and immortality of all who will confess and claim him as father. We who are filthy are all made clean in him, the dead are raised in him, the guilty are justified in him, the lost are saved in him, he who is our salvation, our life, our righteousness.

May you be blessed, O great God, for giving him to us! May you be blessed also for giving him to us by means of birth, so that by birth the world might possess in itself its Savior, your only Son, just as you possess him in yourself by birth. May you be blessed in this twofold birth of your only Son, born in you and born outside you, born of you by knowledge in your fatherly bosom and born by you and by love in the Virgin's maternal womb. May you be blessed in the grandeurs and humilities of this second birth. May you be blessed in the adorable power of this humble birth, a power that is humbly, secretly, and divinely hidden in infancy and helplessness, in the infancy of the one who *factus est tam parvus ut ederetur a foemina, sed est tam magnus ut non separetur a patre.*[61] A power that in this powerlessness produces a greater effect than it does in all the visible effects of its grandeurs and power. A power that in this powerlessness makes the greatest striving over nature, forms the greatest state in grace, and accomplishes the greatest and most eminent order possible in the world. A power that in this powerlessness produces the greatest effect of nature and of grace, that is, of the nature of God himself and of essential and uncreated grace. For the being, power, and nature of God do not and never will do any work greater and more miraculous than that which is done by this birth. And essential grace, which is God himself, will never com-

---

61. D. Aug. Sermon 52, *On Various Things* (original marginal note). "He became so small that he was born of a woman, but remained so great that he was not separated from his Father." See Augustine, Sermon 371, *On the Lord's Birth*, in *Sermons 341–400 on Various Subjects*, 312. Sermon 371 contains many themes that are present in Bérulle's text.

municate a greater grace than the personal grace of the eternal Word subsisting in our humanity. O wondrous power! O power blessedly and divinely joined with powerlessness! O most powerful and adorable powerlessness of Jesus' birth and infancy, in which we have a Man-God, a Child-God, a Virgin-Mother of God, and a fulfilling of the fatherhood of the Father in regard to his only Son, giving him forever the power and authority over him that he did not have in his eternity. We adore a Trinity of persons in the Godhead, but we must adore a trinity of effects and grandeurs in this mystery; for the birth of Jesus magnifies man by making him God, it magnifies the Virgin by making her Mother of God, and (if one can use this word in a certain sense) it magnifies the eternal Father, in his sovereignty, in his state, and in the extent of his power, giving him power not over a world but over the Lord and Savior of the world, his only Son, Man and God together.

This trinity of grandeurs is remarkable in this work of the Holy Trinity, which likes to impress its trace, mark, and impression on its works in proportion to their dignity, and which, as it performs this work as its masterwork, puts its particular mark upon it by impressing this trinity of grandeurs on this humble birth of Jesus. Of these three points, we have set forth the first. It remains to demonstrate how this mystery that abases the Son of God and magnifies man magnifies the Virgin and the state of the eternal Father and is truly a mystery of grandeurs hidden in the humility of Jesus' birth and infancy.

To clarify the second point, then, and to honor with our thoughts a state so worthy of honor as that of the Most Holy Virgin's motherhood (a state that God honors, by himself, by the birth and submission of his Son, and by the greatest effects of his grace and power), we must consider that there are three divine fertilities that can be noted in the secrets and mysteries of our faith: the fertility of the eternal Father begetting his Son within himself, his Son who is equal to him, eternal as he is, and God as he is; the fertility of the Father and the Son producing the Holy Spirit and concluding the divine emanations in the Godhead; and the fertility of the Most Holy Virgin newly begetting the same only Son of God and producing a Man-God in the world. These three fertilities are the origins of three processions that are truly and substantially divine and wondrous: that of the Son, by the knowledge of the Father;

that of the Holy Spirit, by the love of the Father and the Son; and that of the Son again, outside the bosom of the Father in our humanity, by the sacred mystery of the Incarnation that is fulfilled in the Most Holy Virgin's womb. A procession new but divine, a procession of the Son begotten in his Mother and coming forth from his Mother, a procession that is done by love, by the personal love of the Most Holy Trinity, who is the Holy Spirit. For it is by love that the Father sends his Son into the world to become incarnate; it is by love that this same Son gives and delivers himself to the world by this birth; and it is the Spirit, the person of love produced by the Father and the Son, whom the Father and the Son send and employ to make the Most Holy Virgin fertile and powerful to produce a Man-God in the world, so that the love that brings the fertility of God to completion within God himself also brings to completion the highest, most sublime, and most divine fertility there may be outside the internal emanations of the Godhead. And just as from the love of the Father and the Son proceeds this person of love, after whom there is no person nor procession in the Trinity, so also from the love of the same Father sending and from the same Son giving himself to the world, proceeds this mystery of love, which cannot be followed by any work or mystery surpassing it in the state of the Godhead's works. It is so high, so great, and so divine that there is no work that equals it, there can be none that exceed it, and there will never be any that approach it except from a truly infinite distance.

I said specifically that there were three processions, as there were three fertilities. For although there are only two persons who proceed, one of them proceeds and is born in two ways. Thus, there are three processions, since the second person proceeds in two ways, that is, by knowledge in the Godhead and by love in the humanity. Thus, this second procession of the eternal Word on earth follows and imitates the second eternal procession, which is a procession of love, a procession of the Holy Spirit. This most high mystery that we are discussing regards, imitates, and honors, in two different senses, the two immanent and eternal processions that are in the Godhead: that of the Word, as is amply said elsewhere, and that of the Holy Spirit, as is evident here. The only Son of God, being born a second time, is born by love in the Most Holy Virgin and from the Virgin's substance, as he is born by knowledge in the Father's bosom and from the Father's substance. The Virgin receives from the eternal Father this wondrous power of giving birth to God in human nature, of giving a new being to the Eternal and Unchanging One, of giving existence within the course of time to the one who exists in eternity, and of giving life on earth to the Son who lives and was living in heaven by the Father. The Most Holy Virgin receives this power from the eternal Father, who fills her with a divine, heavenly, and wondrous fertility so that she might produce on earth the one who is in heaven, conceive in her womb the one who is in the bosom of the Father, and be Mother of the one who has God himself for his Father.

This fertility of the Most Holy Virgin is rightly associated and compared to the divine fertility, for it is a perfect imitation of the fertility that we adore in the divine being. It is evident that both fertilities are brought to completion in God, and one same divine person is the endpoint who proceeds, the endpoint who accomplishes these two different kinds of emanations and generations, by which the very Word and very God who is begotten of the Father before the ages is begotten of the Virgin Mary in the fullness of time. Whence it comes that this fertility of the Most Holy Virgin has two singular prerogatives and excellences: for in Jesus it concludes in the greatest state that can correspond to created nature, that is, the state of hypostatic union; and in the Virgin it forms and constitutes the greatest position and dignity that can correspond to a created person, that is, the position and dignity of Mother of God, since it makes her mother of Jesus, who is God. In this way, both the created nature and the created person, that is, all that is notable in the order of created substances and that takes part in its being, is, by the humility of this birth, together exalted, although in different ways, to the highest point at which a created being can be placed—that is, the human nature in divine subsistence, and the human person in divine motherhood. This twofold greatness of the human nature and the human person that is accomplished in this mystery is a twofold effect of this humble birth of Jesus on earth. For in being born, Jesus is Son of man and has a virgin for his mother, and since he is Son of God, this virgin is Mother of God. Mother, I say, not only of a man who might later become God, but of this man who is Man-God at the same instant that he is conceived. Thus the sacred womb of the

Virgin is the holy place, the sacred temple, and the heavenly paradise in which the fullness of the Godhead dwells bodily, in which the Word takes on human birth and nature, in which God is made man and man becomes God, and in which is accomplished the most high mystery of the Incarnation and the ineffable secret of the oneness of one divine person in two such different natures. By this oneness, man is God, the Son of man is Son of God, and the Virgin (as mother of this Son of man who is Son of God and is God as is his Father) is Mother of God, which is the greatest position to which a created person can be exalted.

This point deserves its own discourse, an entire discourse that might fully treat this divine motherhood's state and grandeurs, its result and effects. While awaiting a greater leisure to permit me, let us say in a few words that this motherhood of the Most Holy Virgin takes its origin, luster, and authority from the divine fatherhood of him *a quo omnis paternitas in caelo et in terra nominatur*.[62] For he is Father of the one of whom the Virgin is Mother. Just as this position of Father is divinely reported to us in the Scriptures under this title and adorable name of fatherhood, so also this position of Mother that adores, imitates, and represents the eternal Father is properly expressed by this honorable title of divine motherhood. Just as all the marvels of the Son of God's divine birth are encompassed in the divine fatherhood as in their center and origin, so also the marvels of this same Son of God's human birth are comprehended in the divine motherhood as in the point and origin from which they are born and to which they correspond. Let us say to sum up, that this motherhood is a position so high and eminent that it regards only God above itself and all else as much inferior. It is a position so holy that it assumes a grace completely singular, a culmination of grace, a grace completely full of privileges. It is a position so precious that it is matchless on earth and in heaven. For earth bears many children of God by adoption, and heaven is full of saints and angels that are children of God, but heaven and earth bear just one Mother of God. She is matchless and singular in this position, just as there is but one only Son of God in the world. And just as there

---

62. Eph 3[:15] (original marginal note). "From whom all fatherhood in heaven and earth is named."

is among the divine persons only one uncreated person who holds the position of Father, so also among all created persons established in the order of nature, of grace, and of glory, on earth and in heaven, there is only one created person, there is only Mary, who has the position of Mother in regard to God and who is Mother of the one of whom God is Father. A position so high, so precious, and so holy that we cannot marvel at it enough. A position so divine that she approaches God so closely, approaches him in the position of Mother so much, that she conceives him, contains him, bears him, and begets him in herself and outside herself, in giving him to the world. And she gives him to the world together with the eternal Father, as Mother (if, in the oneness of person, the use of this term is permitted), Mother undividedly of the one of whom he is eternally Father.

What will I say of you, O holy Virgin? God makes you Mother of the one of whom he is Father! God exalts you, and on earth he makes you the Mother-without-father of the one of whom in heaven he is the Father-without-mother! God permits you to share with him in the greatest of his works, in the second emanation and generation of his Son, in the Incarnation of his Word, in the birth of Jesus. He permits you to share with him in a communion so noble and great that, before heaven and earth, as by an incomparable respect and honor, he causes the greatest of his works and highest of his mysteries (that is, the Incarnation) to depend on your consent. He asks, he awaits, and he receives this consent by his angel's report. He accomplishes his will, his highest and greatest will that he will ever have, only after he has received the testimony of your will cleaving to his own. He awaits this humble word, *Ecce ancilla Domini*, and this powerful *Fiat* from your mouth, a *Fiat* much more powerful in its outcome and effect than the one that God pronounced in the Creation of the universe.[63] For if that one then made the world, this one now makes the author of the world. What will I say of you, O holy Virgin? You enter into your nothingness, when God exalts you to his grandeurs! You declare yourself the servant of the one of whom he desires that you be Mother! And in this abasement you give into the hands of the angel your consent to the eternal Father's will,

---

63. "Behold the handmaid of the Lord." Lk 1:38; "May it be."

and you conceive the Most High in the very great act of your humility! When this consent is given, reported, and accepted by the eternal Father, by the power of the Most High you are the Mother of Jesus, you are the paradise of the second Adam, you are the temple filled with God incarnate! You are the ample dwelling place of the one who cannot be comprehended! What great qualities, wondrous powers, precious and singular effects! And yet things so great and divine are the results and effects of something as low as the humble birth of Jesus on earth and in the manger. For if God were not an infant and born of the Virgin, this great state and this precious position of Mother of God would not exist in the world. And thus, the absolutely greatest state that is possible in the jurisdiction of the incarnate Son of God's sovereignty and power, that is, the state and position of Mother of God, is and subsists only by this humble birth. For if he is not son, she is not mother, and he is son only by this humble birth and infancy that makes him Son of man, Son of the Virgin, just as he is Son of God, Son of the Father eternal. For if the Word had not become incarnate, or if the divine mystery of the Incarnation had been accomplished by means of greatness and power and not by birth and infancy, either Jesus would not be in the world, or Jesus, Son of God, would not be Son of man, and the Virgin would not be the Mother of Jesus, Son of God, and God in his person. Thus, this position of Mother of God has existence only in the mystery of the Incarnation and is dependent on the Word incarnate, the Word that is incarnate by birth. This humble birth, therefore, that takes place on earth, in Nazareth, in the manger, establishes this great and eminent position of Mother of God and is the source and origin of the grace and portion given to this position. And in this way, the greatest emanation of grace that proceeds from Jesus, coming forth from his love, merited by his cross, communicated by his power, which is the grace given and reserved to the position of Mother of God, would not exist at all in the treasures of Jesus' power and in the order accomplished by his grace and his glory. And the incarnate Word would be separated from the highest point of his state, the most beautiful jewel of his crown, and the most eminent dignity that arises from his power.

Let us recognize therefore that a thing so great, high, and intimate to Jesus as the position of Mother of God depends on his humble birth and cleaves to it. This makes me marvel at Jesus' power in the mystery of his birth more than his power in the mystery of his cross. For in suffering and dying he makes children by adoption, but in being born he makes a Mother of God, who in the eminence of her position and in the abundance of her graces bears a dignity greater, higher, and more joined with God than that which is comprehended in the whole state and extent of the sonship by adoption. O wondrous power of the humble infancy and birth of Jesus! O wondrous power of this powerlessness of the infant Jesus, who, in making himself small and a child, produces the greatest effect and greatest state there is in the order of nature, of grace, and of glory; for he forms and establishes the order and state of Mother of God, and as a result he establishes this kind of excellent grace and glory that is worthily fitting and distinctive to her whom God himself makes worthy of being the Mother of God! A distinct order, set apart from all the orders that are among the angels and saints! An order that she fills alone and in which she is matchless, just as the Son of God is matchless in the order and state of the hypostatic union! An order that contains a greater grace and glory than that which is comprehended in all the orders of heaven and all the states of the blessed spirits! The most excellent order there can be after the supreme order and dignity of the hypostatic union that is reserved for the only Son of God! An order that closely follows this divine and personal union, that is founded in it, and that is joined with it forever! But just as it is by his power alone and not by powerlessness that God becomes small, that he becomes humble, causes himself to be born and become an infant, suffers, trembles, and is wrapped in swaddling clothes, so also in his humilities and powerlessness there is a secret and wondrous power. And if I may compare what is incomparable, it seems to me that I find and adore a greater power in his birth than in his suffering, in the manger than on the cross, in Nazareth than at Calvary. For the power of Calvary and of the cross makes children of God by adoption, but the work and power of Nazareth and of the stable of Bethlehem makes a Mother of God in the world. And if the Son of God had wanted to be and to suffer in the world without being born of a woman, there would be children of God but there would be no Mother of God on earth or in heaven. Let us not separate in our thoughts what God has joined in their effects. Let us bless the one who wanted both to be born and to suffer and who wanted to join together in his own person these two divine powers, secretly hidden in the powerlessness and humility of his death and birth. And let us serve, love, and adore God dead and God being born into the world out of love for us.

In these thoughts, O blessed Virgin, O holy Virgin, we recognize three singular abodes and dwelling places of the divine Word: the one in the Father's bosom from all eternity, the other in the Mother's womb in the fullness of time, and the third in our humanity for all eternity. And reserving for another time the other dwelling places of the divine Word, let us adore him in your womb, in your womb by this mystery. Let us contemplate the secrets that take place in you and in your immaculate body, O holy Virgin. For God wants to be and to dwell in you in an eminent and singular way, distinct from that by which he dwells on earth and in heaven, in grace and in glory. He wants to dwell in you by the sacred mystery of the Incarnation, and he wants to be with you according to this word of the angel, *Dominus tecum*, and to be with us through you.[64] For in you he unites himself with our humanity, and by you he is made man and dwells among men.

Let us go into this more deeply and see that there are three mysteries in one (so fertile is it) and that in Jesus' birth there are three noteworthy and important unions of the eternal Word. The first is that of the divine nature with human nature, in which he is made man. The second is that of the divine person of the eternal Word with the human person of the Most Holy Virgin, in which he makes her his mother by making himself her son and thus becomes the Son of man. The third is that which he wants to have with us and with all humankind, in which he becomes the Redeemer of men by taking on a flesh derived from us, a flesh like ours, a flesh like the flesh of sin, a passible and mortal flesh, in which he is the Victim of men. By the first union, God is man, and man is God. By the second, the Son of God is Son of man, and the Son of man is Son of God. By the third, the Son of God and of man is the Victim of men and the Lamb of God who takes away the sins of the world. These three points, three states, and three unions are distinct

---

64. "The Lord is with you." Lk 1:28.

and different from each other. For God could have not become man. God could have been man without being Son of man. And God could have been born and become Son of man without suffering and dying for men. But his love carried him to this overflow, that he wanted to make himself man, Son of man, and the Victim of men. And in you, O holy Virgin, he wanted to enter into all of these unions. For it is in you that he takes up his humanity and becomes man, it is in you and from you that he becomes Son of man, it is in you and from you that he takes on this flesh in which he wills to suffer and die for men, it is in you that he receives the eternal Father's ordinance to suffer and die for men, and it is in you and in your womb that he accepted this will and ordinance from the Father and that he made the first offering and oblation of himself on the cross and in death. An oblation that began in you and in your womb, as in a sacred temple, made sacred by Jesus himself living in you and from you. An oblation not once interrupted until it had been carried out and consummated on Calvary. An oblation that is accomplished as you were present and attending at the cross, so that Jesus' first and last oblation might be honored by your presence and attendance and so that it might be concluded close to you, just as it began in you. For thus it is consummated and accomplished in this precious body that comes from you and was part of your substance, that is much dearer and more precious to you in Jesus than it was in yourself and than is this holy and venerable body in which you live and from which he was drawn by the omnipotence of the Godhead. O body forever holy, forever venerable! O body formerly part of Mary's body, and now the body sustained by the spirit of Jesus! O body holy in you, but in Jesus the source of holiness! O substance pure and immaculate in you, but in Jesus the origin of purity! O body sanctified in you, but deified in Jesus! O body venerable in you, but adorable in Jesus! O body beloved of you and truly lovable, as he was part of you and had life by the holiest soul that was in the world, but beloved by you so differently when it has life by Jesus and is quickened by the spirit of his deity! This body is always holy, always pure, always yours, but much holier, much purer, much more yours when it is the body of the divine Word than when it is part of your body. In this body thus yours and thus divine, Jesus makes and consummates his oblation on the cross, and you concur in a spirit of love and suffering in this oblation, suffering by spirit, love, and piety what he suffers by iron, spear, and the cross.

But leaving the cross and Calvary for another time and returning to Nazareth and to the manger, what will I say of you, O holy Virgin, and of the secrets that went on within you? What will I say of you and of the blessed state, lasting for all eternity, that you enter into by this humble birth of Jesus—of Jesus, I say, born in you and born of you? You bear in yourself the one who bears all things, you contain the one who contains all, and you have encompassed in yourself that which cannot be comprehended! He who is all dwells in you and is part of yourself, for the infant carried in the mother's womb is part of the mother, lives from the mother's substance, and thus—O marvel! O abyss!—he who resides in the eternal Father resides in you. He who lives in his Father from the Father's substance lives in you and from your substance. He who is in his Father without being part of the Father is in you and is part of you. And you, as sharing with the eternal Father, have undividedly with him that very one for your Son who has God for his Father. O supreme greatness! O infinite dignity! O incomparable love! O most lovable communion! O ineffable closeness! That you might approach the Godhead, O holy Virgin, and approach so closely! That you might approach him so honorably and intimately, so lovingly and divinely! For what is more intimate and more joined together with the son than the mother, and with the Son of God than the Mother of God, who conceives him within herself, who bears him in her womb, who carries and comprehends him as part of herself, as so noble a part, indeed, as the noblest part? For the state of mother has this privilege, in nature, of having and bearing two spirits, two hearts, and two lives in one single body. And the state of Mother of God gives this privilege to the Virgin by nature and by grace, of having Jesus within her, of having him as the noble part of her, and of having the spirit, heart, and life of Jesus so intimate and so joined together with her spirit, heart, and life that he is the spirit of her spirit, the heart of her heart, and the life of her life. O greatness! O abundance! O abyss! O abundance of grandeurs! O abyss of marvels! You give life to Jesus, for he is your son; you receive life from Jesus, for he is your God; and in this way you both give and receive life. And just as the divine Word both receives and gives being, life, and glory in eternity, receiving it from the Father and giving it to the Holy Spirit, so also you, O holy Virgin, who have the honor of being the Mother of the incarnate Word, you, I say, following and imitating his example, both receive and give life. You give life to Jesus and receive life from Jesus. You give life to Jesus, sustaining with your heart and spirit the heart and spirit of Jesus. And you receive, from the heart and body of Jesus living and residing in you, life in your heart, in your body, and in your spirit together.

But I find a much greater secret and profounder point, stranger and more wondrous. Dare I think it? Dare I proffer it? *Eloquar an sileam?*[65] Will the persons who take offence at the piety and devotion that is being proposed toward the Mother of God be able to bear it? Or, rather, must I, for souls weak in strength and understanding, omit high and great truths and withhold them from souls that are strong and capable of adoring God in his secrets, grandeurs, and marvels? Let us say, then, that in this wondrous ebb and flow of life and love between Jesus and Mary—between these two persons so noble and joined together, the noblest and most joined together after the divine and eternal persons and divinely joined in the state of Jesus' humble and secret birth in the Virgin—the Virgin as Mother gives life to Jesus, and in begetting and conceiving him, she gives him a life received and founded in uncreated existence and subsistence. A life incomparably higher and more divine than the one she receives from Jesus himself. For she plays a part in the union of the Godhead with humanity; she gives humanly divine life to Jesus; she gives new life to God; she causes God to be man and man to be God; she begets a living being, divinely living and divinely subsisting, who is God; she produces into the world the life of a Man-God; and from her substance she conceives, nourishes, and gives birth to God in herself and in the universe. And thus, her work is brought to completion in a Man-God, since she is Mother of God. Whereas Jesus, living and working in Mary, gives her a most high and sublime life indeed, but a life of grace, which is a quality and not a substance, and the life of a holy, most holy, person, but of a human person, not divine and

---

65. "Should I speak, or remain silent?" Virgil, *Aeneid* 3.30. See *Aeneid*, trans. A. Mandelbaum (New York: Bantam, 1961), 56.

uncreated as is her only Son. And this presence and working of Jesus in the Virgin is brought to completion within her in forming the state of Mother of God, which is a state much inferior and subordinate to that of the Man-God, which the Virgin, exalted by the Holy Spirit's working, establishes and forms by this birth. Jesus thus gives to the Virgin a life that is lesser in grace and in glory, one that is not this great and wondrous life that the Virgin produced when she conceived, incarnated, and gave birth to the Son of God in the world.

Let us sum up these grandeurs and delights that are hidden in the Virgin and in these two states joined together, of divine birth and motherhood. Let us say that this motherhood of the Virgin involves and contains two births of Jesus, each one having its distinctive grandeurs, privileges, and sweetness: the birth within the Virgin and the birth outside the Virgin. Both make up one complete and perfect birth, in these two different points and moments, and compose the blessed and divine state of the motherhood that the Virgin holds in regard to God. The birth within the Virgin is internal, and Scripture expresses it in these words: *Quod in ea natum est*.[66] The birth outside the Virgin is outer, and the Creed expresses it in this way: *Qui natus est ex Maria Virgine*.[67] The birth within the Virgin is carried out in Nazareth, after the angel's visitation; the birth outside the Virgin is carried out in Bethlehem, nine months after she conceived the Son of God in her womb. In the inner birth, the Virgin receives the eternal Word from the bosom of the Father in her virginal womb, so that he might become incarnate. In the outer birth, she produces outside her womb and gives the incarnate Word to the world. In the first, the Father gives her his Son; in the second, she gives the Father's Son to the world. In the first, her spirit is exalted, attentive, and cleaving to the Father, to the Word, and to the Holy Spirit: to the Father who gives her his Son, to the Son who gives himself to her, and to the Holy Spirit who comes upon her, prepares her, overshadows her, and exalts her to so high a power and working. And just as the Word is in her in a distinctive and singular manner, fitting to the condition of this mystery, so also does she cleave

---

66. Mt 1:20 (original marginal note). "That which is born in her."
67. "Who was born of the Virgin Mary."

singularly to the Word, for he desires to be hers and take from her a new substance to become incarnate within her and be henceforth flesh of her flesh and bone of her bone. In the second, she cleaves to the eternal Father and to the Father's will to give his Son to the world, she cleaves to the Son and to his desire to be born into the world, and by the sole striving of this love and will of the Father and the Son, without striving in nature, without affecting the Son and the Mother, and as a great author elegantly says, *sine contumelia naturae*.[68] Thus Jesus is born into the world in a manner worthy of the Mother and the Son, in a manner worthy of his eternal birth, and in a manner worthy also of his inner birth, carried out by the working of the Holy Spirit in the sacred womb of the Most Holy Virgin.

Thus Jesus being born into our humanity has a twofold birth from the Virgin: a birth from the Virgin within her in Nazareth, and a birth from the Virgin outside her in Bethlehem—both wholly divine, full of marvel, full of grace and delight, and full of grandeurs by the greatness hidden in the abasement of him who makes himself so small in order to make us great, who makes himself an infant in order to make us gods. The outer birth in Bethlehem occurs noisily and radiantly: the angel makes it known to the shepherds, the star to the kings, the kings to Judea, and the capital of Judea is convulsed with it. The inner birth occurs in the world discreetly, softly, between the Holy Spirit, the angel, and the Virgin, in the innermost part of her heart, in the secret of her bosom, and in the cabinet of Nazareth, while the rest of the earth knows nothing of this mystery. Even Joseph knows nothing, although he is an angel on earth, chosen on earth to be the sole participant at this great council, the son's tutor, the mother's spouse, the head of the family and of the eternal Father's house on earth, and about him the prophet tells us, *Constituit eum dominum domus suae, et principem omnis possessionis suae*,[69] for God establishes him in power and principality and as his lieutenant over the noblest part of his state and kingdom.

---

68. Cyprian (original marginal note). "Without affront to nature." The editors of the Cerf edition of Bérulle's works provide this reference as Pseudo-Cyprian, *On the Nativity*. This work is not available in English translation.

69. "He established him master over his house and ruler of all his possessions." Ps 105:21.

For the eternal Father's noblest kingdom is Jesus and Mary, and Joseph has power over each of them by the Father's will. And yet this angel, this prince, this spouse, this tutor of the Son and of the Mother of God is not admitted to the secret of this inner birth of Jesus, a secret that adores the secret of the eternal birth, just as the Son's intimate dwelling place in the Mother by this inner birth adores the Son's intimate dwelling place in the Father by the divine birth.

And henceforth the Virgin bears within herself a greater work, a greater state, a greater order, a greater glory, and a higher and more divine life than that which God established in heaven. She is a more glorious heaven, a more sacred temple, a more delightful paradise, and a more august dwelling than heaven itself. For Jesus is in her and not in heaven. God incarnate is in her and not in heaven. The life of Jesus, who is and calls himself Life, is in her and not in heaven. The glory of Jesus is in her and not in heaven. A glory henceforth greater than the glory of the angels, who were in heaven, and greater than the glory of both men and angels for eternity. Henceforth the Virgin possesses in herself the one whom the eternal Father possesses in himself. Henceforth, O Virgin, in sharing with the eternal Father you have undividedly the same one for son who has God for his Father. I say undividedly, for the Holy Spirit, who is God as is the Son and God as is the Father, does not have the position of father in regard to the one who holds and honors you as his mother, O holy Virgin, O sacred Mother, O Spouse of the Father, O Daughter, O Handmaiden, O Mother of God all together! In this humble and secret state of Jesus being born of you in you by his first and inner birth, you possess Jesus, and you are possessed by Jesus. I say more: you alone on earth are possessed by Jesus, and you alone possess Jesus. You alone possess the love of the Father, the treasure of the Holy Spirit, the secret of heaven, the delight of paradise, the rejoicing of the angels, the prize of men, the desire of nations, the salvation of the world, and the glory of the universe. O holy Virgin, divine and blessed, Jesus is in you, the Lord is with you, God is in you, and in you is hidden the God of Israel and the Savior of the world. O adorable secret! O favorable presence! O honorable communion! O precious communication! O delightful intimacy! O blessed possession! O, what secrets! O, what effects! O, what marvels between the son and the mother, bound to each other only, living in each other only, conversing with each other only! O, how blessed is this nine months' dwelling, how sacred and filled with mutual graces and effects, for there is not one single moment during all this time that lacks a singular working, delightful application, or precious influence! O mystery of secrecy, of silence, and of seclusion! For this is how it is fulfilled and how we must contemplate it. O mystery of love and delight, heavenly delight! For both the Son and the Mother are in this mutual and reciprocal state by heaven's design, by heaven's power, and by heaven's working. O mystery of honor and homage to the grandeurs of eternity! For the divine fatherhood is adored by this motherhood, the secret of the eternal birth by the secret of this temporal birth, the dwelling of the Son in the Father by the dwelling of the Son in the Mother. O mystery of incomparable greatness and dignity! O Mother of Jesus! At this moment you enter into the blessed and exalted state of being his Mother, you beget the one whom the eternal Father begets from all eternity, you beget him in you just as he begets him in him, you beget him from you and from your substance just as he begets and produces him from his own substance. You do not for one single moment lack the right of motherly power over him, and for an eternity the eternal Father lacked power and authority over his Son, for he is equal to him; and it is you who, in giving him a new birth, gives a beginning to the Father's power over the Son. By begetting this Son and giving him a new nature, you set him in a state in which the Father can exercise his power over him. Before this birth, the Father does not have power over him, for in eternity he begets him as Son but he begets him as God, equal to him and independent as he is. Such that if he is for an eternity the Son of the Father before being the son of the Mother, he is not the Son subject to the Father before being the son subject to Mary, for one same point and one same instant give cause and beginning to Mary's authority and to the eternal Father's authority over his Son newly born. O greatness of this humble birth! O honorable communion of the Virgin and the eternal Father, at the point of their authority over Jesus! Will we not respect two powers so joined together? Will we not serve, although differently, both the Father's majesty and that of the Mother, two majesties that are so holy, so similar? Will we not submit willingly to two powers so exalted, having one same object and one same moment and mystery as the origin of their power?

May you be blessed, O holy Virgin, in your grandeurs and in the blessed state that you enter into on this day and in this moment that is precious to earth and heaven, the moment in which you are Mother. O greatness of Mary! You are Mother of the one of whom even the Holy Spirit (yet without fault) is not Father. You are Mother of the one of whom the Father alone among the divine persons is Father. And the eternal Father who precedes you by an eternity in the production of his Son does not precede you by one single moment in the exercise of his authority over him. In you and in your womb begins the first power over so worthy a subject, and the highest, most worthy, and most desirable power that the eternal Father will ever have, which is the power over his incarnate Son.

This is the third point concerning the greatness of this birth, which we noted above and must now explain and by which we want to end and conclude this discourse on the grandeurs of Jesus' human birth. Let us note that the first person of the Most Holy Trinity has two qualities noted in Scripture: that of Father and that of God; that of Father in regard to his only Son, that of God in regard to his creatures. And just as these two objects and ends are indeed different, so also these two qualities are indeed distinct and separate. And (according to St. Cyril) we should marvel, adore, and love this divine person much more in his position as Father than in his position as God.[70] For in his position as Father he has a divine and infinite endpoint, and he corresponds to a person equal to himself. In his position as God, he relates himself to creatures infinitely distinct, separate, and far from him, according to all their possible kinds of being. As Father, he has power to beget his Son and does not have power over his begotten Son, but his power to beget him (that is, to beget a God) is so high and divine that it equals any other kind of

---

70. Cyril [of Alexandria], *Thesaurus. Magnum quid afferri Deo haeretici putant, quum non semper Patrem, sed semper Deum fuisse asserunt. Nec videtur ad contumeliam id potius pertinere. Nam ut Deus ad servientia et ad creatam naturam habitudinem habes, sic Pater ad Filium. Ita re maiore Deum privantes nunc sentiunt, etc.* (original marginal note). "The heretics think they are ascribing a great attribute to God by affirming that he has not always been Father but has always been God. Nor do they see that it pertains to an affront. For as God has a relation to what is servile and to created nature, it is the same of the Father toward the Son. Now, in thinking this way, they deprive God of a greater thing, etc." This work is not available in English translation.

power that could be ascribed to him. By contrast, as God he has power to create and has absolute and everlasting power over all that is created. It is the power by which *vocat ea quae non sunt, tanquam ea quae sunt* and by which all is living and all is nothing in regard to the Creator.[71]

These two qualities of Father and of God, which are distinct in the Godhead and separated in their objects, are wondrously joined together by this birth, by which he is Father of the one of whom he is God, and he is God of the one of whom he is Father. He is Father of this newborn child, for he is his Son, his only Son, to whom he says, solely and to the exclusion of any other, *Ego hodie genui te*.[72] He is God of this newborn child, for he is his Son in such a way that he is also his servant (his matchless servant), and he enters into this state of servanthood by this single birth, for which reason he says to him by his prophet, *Servus meus es tu, o Israel, in te gloriabor*.[73] And in chapter 42, *Ecce puer meus*, according to the evangelist;[74] and according to the prophet, *Ecce servus meus*.[75] And elsewhere, *Formans me ex utero servum sibi*.[76] The divine apostle also joins the two qualities together, with these holy words: *Deus et Pater Domini nostri Iesu Christi*.[77] Words worthy of being engraved on earth and in heaven and on the hearts of men by the hand of angels. Words that comprehend in few words the two greatest mysteries of the Godhead, the Trinity and the Incarnation; the two states of the divine Word, his eternal emanation and his temporal emanation; and the two qualities of the supreme and uncreated Being, his position as Father and his position as God. They mark the excellence of our religion, in which we adore a God who is Father and a Father who is God, both God and Father of our Lord Jesus, God and Father together in regard to the same object. For the one who is our God and

---

71. "He calls into existence the things that do not exist." Rom 4:17.

72. "Today I have begotten you." Ps 2:7. Cf. Acts 13:33; Heb 1:5, 5:5.

73. Is 49[:3] (original marginal note). "You are my servant, O Israel, in you will I glory."

74. Mt 12[:18] (original marginal note). "Behold my servant."

75. "Behold my servant." Is 42:1.

76. Is 49[:5] (original marginal note). "Forming me from the womb to be his servant."

77. "God and Father of our Lord Jesus Christ." Cf. Rom 15:6; 2 Cor 1:3; Eph 1:3, 17; 1 Pt 1:3.

our Sovereign—that is, Jesus, who is called *Deus noster*[78]—has a Father, for he is God from God, and he has a Sovereign, for he is Man-God. But just as these two natures (divine and human) are brought together in him, and just as by the ineffable union of these two natures he is both God and man, and just as by this mystery he is God in such a way that he is man and man in such a way that he is God, so also the very one who is his God is his Father, the very one who is his Father is his God, and these two qualities are joined together in one same person, that is, in the person of the Father, just as the two natures are joined together in one same person, that is, in the person of the Word, the only Son of the living God.

It is by this new mystery that these two natures are united. Before this, God, who is from all eternity, is also from all eternity the Father, Father always begetting his Son and always exercising the position of Father in regard to his Son. Before this mystery, God was for eternity without being the God of his Son, just as his Son during this eternity did not have the state of being his creature. God did not then exercise in regard to his Son the power that he has in this position of God and that he exercises now. For he did not enter into the use of this power and authority except by this divine mystery. It is a mystery in which God, who cannot become greater in himself, becomes greater in his work and in his mystery, which makes him God—God forever—of the one of whom he is Father from all eternity. It is a mystery that in this way reveals, honors, and increases the state and sovereignty of the eternal Father, and increases them by an infinite quality and dignity. For it is as nothing to God to have dominion over the creatures; they that are nothing are not worthy of being and of obeying him. But to have dominion over a Subject so worthy that he is infinite in his dignity, God in his nature, only Son of God in his person, this is a thing worthy of God himself. His power and dominion cannot rise higher, and his realm is filled with all the greatness and dignity that can belong to him.

O greatness! O abyss of this profound mystery that magnifies the eternal Father like this in his power and authority, magnifies him forever! O greatness! O power of Jesus' abasement, which forever exalts and

---

78. "Our God." Ps 67:6.

increases the eternal Father's greatness and power! O goodness of the Father, who does not desire to reserve to himself alone this new power that is given to him through the mystery of the Incarnation! For he communicates it to the holy Virgin and sets her in maternal power and authority over him, the one over whom he takes fatherly power and authority. And weak persons, little understanding the mysteries of God, do not want to enter into servitude in regard to the one with whom the eternal Father seems to share his position, power, and authority over his Son. I say, to share without division, without decrease, but by communication, by extension, for this is how heavenly, spiritual, and divine things are shared, and this is how the eternal Father honors and shares this power over his Son with the Virgin, to whom the one who is the Son of God, God himself, is set in submission, for our example and out of love for us.

But let us leave these persons to their base thoughts. Let us offer ourselves to the Father and the Son, and to the Mother. Let us adore the grandeurs of this mystery, this second birth of Jesus, which honors, exalts, and unites with a new bond these three persons together: the Father in the power that he has over his Son, the Son in the honor and homage that he renders to the Father, and the Mother in the position, power, and authority that she has in regard to the very one who is the Son of the Father. O fatherhood! O sonship! O motherhood! But it is better to end and to adore in sacred silence what the tongue and thought of angels cannot worthily announce either to men or to angels. Let us end, then, and sum up in a few words the grandeurs proposed in this discourse concerning Jesus' birth on earth.

The source of this humble birth is the bosom of the Father. Its model is the eternal generation. Its end is the greatness of God, and of God himself in the position of Father. Its distinctive feature is to give new birth to God, to give a new being to the Eternal and Unchanging One, to give a new essence to the only Son of God. Its outcome is the salvation of the universe. Its state of being is a mystery of honor, homage, and adoration of the most ineffable and incomprehensible things in eternity. Its own endpoint and effect are to make God man, to make a Virgin the Mother of God, to make sinners holy and children of God forever, and, by this means, to lay down on earth the foundations of the kingdom of heaven, the kingdom of God, the eternal kingdom, and, to say all in a word—O marvel! O greatness!—to produce on earth, for the earth and for heaven, a life so high, so powerful, and so divine as the life of the Man-God, a life uncreated and a life incarnate! Life divine and life human! Life glorious and life suffering! Life, source of life, for all eternity! Life destroying the power of death and the rule of sin! Life reconciling God to men! Life satisfying in strict justice a God of wrath, a God offended! Life redeeming, by its fullness, the emptiness and needs of human nature! Life meriting all that can be merited of God living, dwelling, and working in this sacred humanity!

On the Third Birth of Jesus

Contemplating these grandeurs, we have only to lose ourselves in this abyss and grieve with all created nature that this life so high, divine, and great lies under the rule of mortality and that this second birth gives to Jesus a passible, mortal, and perishable life. For Jesus is born in order to die, and yet his greatness should be immortal. But the eternal Father provides for a third birth, delivering him from the cross, from death, and from the grave and causing him to be reborn like a phoenix in this holocaust of his, to give him life in his bosom and in his glory and to make his state henceforth blessed, glorious, and eternal. This is the Father's will upon his Son; this is Son's power upon himself, his state, and his own life. This is what his greatness deserves and requires. Immortality is natural to it, for it is by a miracle that Jesus is mortal, just as we by a miracle are immortal. This is the wish of every creature that desires to live and to be reborn in its Creator. This is the particular need of men, who must be born again by his powerful resurrection. And this is in the end what so many humilities and sufferings deserve.

After six days of Creation, God ceased to work, and he entered into his sabbath and his rest. After so many days, months, and years, after the re-creation and redemption of the world, it is time, O Jesus, for you to cease not to work but to suffer and for you to enter into the eternal sabbath and rest. Enter therefore into your glory after so many sufferings. After so many labors, enter into your rest. You left this rest out of love for us, and you willed to exchange the dwelling place of life and glory, where you dwelt from all eternity, with the dwelling place of the cross and of death. Abandon now the bosom of the cross, the state of death, the abode of the grave, not to return into a mortal life but to return to the bosom of the Father and the dwelling place of heaven. It is enough, O Jesus, to have been on this earth of those who die, in this country of exile and banishment, in this vale of tears, in this place of woe, on the cross, in death, in the grave. It is enough, O Jesus, to have been mortal and passible for thirty-four years. It is enough to have been among us as one of us. It is enough to have been a pilgrim in Egypt and Judea. It is enough to have been in Bethlehem and at Calvary, in the manger and on the cross, in the grave and in limbo. These places are ones of death and suffering, and you are life and glory. This earth is one of exile and banishment, and you cannot be separated from the Father. These abodes of death and woe are fitting to us but not to you, and if they befit you it is only through us and for our sake. You are eternal, and these places are temporal. You were for eternity in rest and in glory, and this present state is one that is other to you, a state and abode so different from the one that belongs to you and that you possess from all eternity. For there you are in rest without anguish, in life without death, in glory without wretchedness. It is time to return to this state; it is time to be blessed, glorious, and immortal in the one as well as in the other of your two natures. For both are your natures, both are yours: one is yours by essence and the other by subsistence, one by eternal birth and the other by temporal birth, one by nature and the other by love. Be henceforth in both of these your natures as is fitting to your greatness. Be for eternity at rest, in life, and in glory.

Abandon this grave, therefore, O Jesus my Lord, and ascend into your rest. *Exurge in requiem tuam, tu et arca sanctificationis tuae* ("Ascend into your rest, you and the ark of your sanctification"), that is, you and your holy humanity.[79] For it is an ark like the other; it is an ark of covenant more than the other is; it is an ark much more yours than the other. It is an ark holier and more sanctifying than the other; it is an ark much more adorable than the other. And it is also the object of adoration of earth and heaven, of angels and men, for time and eternity.

---

79. Ps 131 [132:8] (original marginal note). Cf. 2 Chr 6:41.

An ark that bears the presence of your deity, and bears it in a manner so high, august, and powerful! It is thus your ark, the ark of your sanctification. Give us leave therefore to speak to you these words of your prophet: *Ascend into your rest, you and your Ark*, that is, your person and your humanity. This ark and this humanity is precious. It is formed by the Holy Spirit. It is drawn from the immaculate body of the Most Holy Virgin. It is united at the same instant with the deity, united inseparably. It is filled with infinite grace and dignity. Should a thing so great be mortal? For if the abundance of your love brings you to undergo our mortality, it is time to deliver this sacred and deified body from the cross and the grave and establish it in glory and immortality. It is the eternal Father's counsel upon his Son; it is his good pleasure to deliver him from death and the grave; it is his wish to say to him for a third time, *Ego hodie genui te*,[80] by a third birth, in which he desires to give Jesus a new life—a life more powerful and glorious than the one you robbed him of, O Jew. You put him on the cross; you confined him to the grave. But you are mistaken, O faithless people; this cross is the pyre from which this new phoenix, this bird of heaven, will be reborn into a better life. You are mistaken, O Jew; this grave will be a place of life and not of death, and of life more powerful and glorious than the one you robbed him of. This cross and this grave, which in your eyes is a grave of death, is in the Father's eyes a precious nest, from which his Son will be reborn and rise again and about which he tells us by his faithful servant: *In nidulo meo moriar, et sicut phoenix multiplicabo dies meos.*[81]

These are prophetic and wondrous words, a text woven with a great secret of seeming contradictions. For what likeness is there between life and death? And yet Jesus says in this text, *Moriar et multiplicabo dies meos.*[82] What relation is there between death and a nest, since a nest is

---

80. Acts 13[:33] (original marginal note). "Today I have begotten you."

81. Jb 29[:18]. In Pagnino's translation (original marginal note). "I will die in my nest, and like the phoenix I will multiply my days." Bérulle refers to the Latin Bible, first published in 1527, of Santes Pagnino (1470–1541), who translates the Greek *phoinix* as *phoenix* in Latin. Both the Greek and the Latin words can mean "phoenix" (the bird) or "date-palm." Much earlier, Tertullian had also interpreted *phoenix* at Ps 92:12 as the bird rather than the tree. See Tertullian, *On the Resurrection of the Flesh* 13, ANF 3, p. 554.

82. "I will die and will multiply my days."

a place of life, of birth, and not of death? And yet Jesus says, *In nidulo meo moriar*. For if Jesus, who is life, is to die, then his death is life for us, and the place of his death is the nest of the life that we receive in the death and by the death of the one who is Life, by whom all is life, and by whom death is life, even life that gives life. But there is much more, for his cross is a nest not only for us but also for him; it is the nest of his life and his rebirth into immortality. And therefore, he says in this prophetic word, *In nidulo meo moriar*. Let us then say that this cross of Jesus is the bed of his love and the nest of his fertility, where, lifted up between heaven and earth like a bird of heaven, he hatches his little ones. Let us say also that this cross is the bed and nest in which this new phoenix himself is born anew. For just as among all the birds of the air and animals on the earth the phoenix alone has the place of his death for the nest of his life, so also Jesus alone among mortals has the place of his death for the nest of his life and rebirth, drawing from his cross and his death the power and right to enter into a new and immortal life. O cross! O nest! O death! O birth! O dying life! O immortality! O immortality, source of immortality! I adore you, O Jesus, on the cross, as in the bed of your love and the nest of your immortality. At the foot of your cross, at the entrance to your grave, I prostrate myself before you, O Jesus, my Lord, whom I behold in the state and shadow of death, and I contemplate your griefs and my wretchedness and the purposes of the eternal Father upon you, and upon us through you. There I adore you as dying and begetting your children into immortality. There I adore you as dying and being reborn into a new life. There I adore you as dying and pouring out the seed of immortality, both for you and for us. There I adore you as being reborn into a heavenly life, acquiring a new right of glory, and entering into a new power over immortality. And I adore you in this blessed moment in which you pass from the cross to glory, from death to life, from earth to heaven, from the dying and pilgrim life to the heavenly and immortal life. O blessed, lovable, and adorable moment! You end the labors and the cross of Jesus! You give beginning to his immortality! You establish in his immortality our own! You give us cause to rejoice and say with the apostle, *Jesus Christ died once and will never die again; death will no longer have dominion over him!*[83] You triumph over death, just as death triumphed over Jesus! You render to Jesus what is owed him and what his love had suspended and arrested for so long! How precious this moment should be to us, the first moment of his realized glory, his heavenly life, his immortality! Blessed moment! The moment in eternity that gives principle to an eternity, to the eternity of such a life and such glory, the source and resource of eternal life, of men and of angels! Blessed moment in eternity!

But here I find a new striving and new surprise of your love, which wants to indicate its power and effects at the beginning of your new and immortal life just as it did throughout your pilgrim and mortal life. For in abandoning your body to its glory, it also suspends the place of this glory, and Jesus lives between heaven and earth, keeping company on earth for a period of forty days. O love! Always love and always triumphant! And triumphant over what is so high and divine as Jesus' life and glory! O triumphant love, triumphant over Jesus, even in the triumph over his glory! For just as you are born on earth into mortal life, in the birth from the Virgin, and earth is the place that is to receive you in this humble birth, so also are you born in heaven into immortal life, in this birth from the grave, and heaven is the place that should rightly receive you, in this blessed birth, into the state of glory. But love for your apostles, your disciples, and your Church arrests for a time this last birth's final effect, and your entry into heaven is deferred and suspended by a miracle, a miracle of love that you exercise upon yourself, suspending not the state of glory, as elsewhere, but the proper place of glory.

For the love that has the power to draw you from heaven to earth and from the bosom of the Father to the Virgin's womb arrests and suspends you between earth and heaven, in such a way that although you are reborn into the state of glory, you are not yet in the place of glory. You divide a mystery in two so that you might unite us with yourself. You set a space of forty days between the Resurrection and the Ascension so that we might be with you for this whole time. By your love, you divide that which the nature of things, supreme things, should join together, that is, the state of glory and the place of glory. O love in Jesus, strange in its nature and effects! For the property of

---

83. Rom 6[:9] (original marginal note).

love in itself is to unite, and the property of divine love is to lift up to heaven, yet the property of Jesus' love is to separate and draw Jesus to the earth. Love, O Jesus, draws you from the bosom of the Father and causes you to go forth, as you yourself say, in order to be in an earth and nature that is other. For you speak in this way: *Exivi a Patre, et veni in mundum.*[84] Love separates your human nature from the human person in order to deliver it to another person, to a person infinitely far from its own nature and condition. In your pilgrim life, love separates glory from the state of glory, and the glory of the soul and that of the body. By a strange striving, love separates this deified soul from this deified body, and yet they were joined together not only by the relation of their nature, as in us, but much more powerfully by their deity, in which they remain united in the state of their separation. And now that God reunites this deified body and soul by the mystery of the Resurrection, and renders to the body the glory that is due it, love separates the essence and state of glory from the place of glory, etc.

O love that separates and no longer unites! How many separations you make, and in regard to subjects so worthy and powerful! In a certain and excellent manner, you separate the Son from the Father, by the condition of a nature that is other, and yet their own nature joins them together in oneness of essence! You separate human nature from human subsistence, and yet it is, of itself and in all other respects, this nature's rightful endpoint and substantial fulfilment! You separate glory from the state of glory, and the state of glory from the place of glory, and yet these things are supreme, divine, supernatural, and divinely joined, and in all other respects outside of you alone they are inseparably joined together! This is a noteworthy difference between the love in God and the love in Jesus. For the love in God unites, and the love in Jesus separates. The love in God unites even to the oneness of essence, and the love in Jesus separates even to the division of essence, dividing the essence of man from the person of man, the essence of glory from the state of glory, and the deified soul from the deified body, which are two essences joined together by nature, by grace, and by glory. May

84. Jn 16[:28] (original marginal note). "I came forth from the Father and have come into the world."

this love, O Jesus, that is in you be in us. May this love that works in you work in us. May this love that triumphs over you triumph over us. May this love that divides and separates in you divide and separate in us; may it separate us from sin, from the earth, and from ourselves, so that we might live for you. And may this love occupy us with you, draw us to you, fill us with you. I see that this separating love founds, establishes, and accompanies three kinds of lives within you. May I contemplate and adore you in these three lives and at the three moments of your entry into them—three lives to which the whole life of men and angels should be dedicated, three precious moments to which all the moments of our mortality and eternity should be consecrated. The first is the moment of the Incarnation, in which Jesus begins to be Jesus and to live by an uncreated life, and the Word begins to have a new and incarnate life, a life divine and human, divinely human and humanly divine. The moment of the pilgrim and meriting life, in which the soul of Jesus is united with both a passible body and the life of glory, and Jesus by this means has a new kind of life. A life that is his alone! A life that is the origin of our eternal life! A life in glory and in suffering! A life that unites and joins together two such different states in one same soul, by a miracle wrought within Jesus Christ by Jesus Christ himself, wrought within him alone and continued for a period of thirty-four years on the earth! The moment of his heavenly and fully glorious life, in which Jesus is triumphant in life, in glory, in immortality. A life without suffering and mortality! A life that is nothing but life and nothing but glory! A life that will endure forever! These three moments give origin to three lives. These three lives have three different dwelling places, in which we must adore this sacred humanity of Jesus. O moments! O dwelling places! O adorable lives! This must be the object of our thoughts, this must be the subject of our occupations, this will be the purpose of our eternity. May I regard you, therefore, O Jesus, in these three moments! May I adore you in these three lives! May I contemplate you in these three dwelling places! For God is your dwelling place and shelter in these three lives, and God receives you in his bosom, his love, and his glory. You are in the bosom of the Father by your eternal birth, and in the fullness of time your divine person draws and exalts our humanity there. There the mystery of the Incarnation is treated, is resolved, is established. There God is man, and man is God. There this soul and humanity of Jesus consubsists with the deity. There the only Son of God, who rests upon the bosom of the Father, rests in this humanity. There this humanity has being only in uncreated being and has its life, subsistence, and state in a person produced in the Father's bosom, residing in the Father's bosom, and inseparable from the Father's bosom. There this man who is called Jesus is at the right hand of God by his power, in the bosom of the Father by his subsistence, and has his life and rest forever in the Godhead.

In truth, the Word was without this humanity for an eternity, but he will also be with it for an eternity. And in his divine essence, the Word has only ever regarded this human nature as in a perfect mirror, regarded it as a nature that would be his for an eternity. He has never been without this regard toward it, for his regard and love for our humanity is an eternal regard and love. From all eternity he looks upon it as his own essence, as that which is to be, one day and forever, one of his essences, and as the being that he wants to accomplish and complete from his own subsistence. O divine regard! O eternal regard! O regard full of love and honor! O regard that must draw our regard, our love, and our homage toward this humanity that God looks upon eternally and continually as his own, and that we must regard as our own, as our own by the Father's gift and the Holy Spirit's working, by the subsistence of the Son who is given to it so that he might work our salvation, and, in a word, by the power of the cross and of the death that he consummated in sacrifice and holocaust for us.

Just as you are, O Jesus, my Lord, in the Father's bosom by your first birth, so also you are in the Father's love by your second birth. For the Father who begets you by knowledge in the Godhead produces you by love in our humanity. Thus, he employs his spirit and love in this humble birth, according to the angel's word, and it is by love toward us that the Father gives the Son not only a humanity, but our humanity—that is, the humanity drawn from us, the humanity like our own, the humanity able to suffer and die for us. You who are in the Father, that is, in his bosom and love by your previous births, are now in the Father's glory by a third birth. For on the cross, in infancy, and in the pilgrim life, you are indeed in the Father but not in the glory of the Father, for it was not fully communicated to this humanity except by this third birth. But God wills now to end this state of abasement and humiliation. God wills to raise and exalt you above all that is created. God wills to set you at his right hand, in his rest, in his glory. God wills every tongue to confess you in this state, and as the apostle says, *Omnis lingua confiteatur quia Iesus-Christus in gloria est Dei Patris.*[85]

This is the life that you enter into by this third birth: a life of glory and greatness, a life that the apostles confessed and made known. The beloved disciple, nourished by the secrets of heaven in the school and bosom of Jesus, tells us concerning this life that he beheld your glory and that it is the glory of the only Son, the only Son of the Father.[86] The great apostle, caught up into the third heaven, tells us concerning it that it is the very glory of the Father, and that every tongue must acknowledge and confess it so. These are great and profound words, worthy of these two great apostles, the most instructed and exalted in the understanding and knowledge of Jesus. Let us listen to these words, meditate on these words, and invoke the leading and light of the Spirit who revealed and inspired these words to them. It is enough to tell us, O disciple of Truth, O beloved disciple, that you have beheld this glory and that it is the glory of the only Son, as of the only Son of the Father. If reason cannot attain so high, may piety lead us there by elevation and wonder. Let us say then: O glory of the only Son of God, as the only Son of the Father! O glory worthy of the Father, who is the source of all deity![87] O glory worthy of the Son, who is equal to the Father and is the splendor of the Father's glory! O glory worthy of his cross, his humilities, his self-emptying! O glory worthy of the honor and service rendered to the Father, honor and service that is infinite in dignity, in merits, in effects! O glory worthy of being the object of the glory communicated to angels and men! O glory worthy of being named preeminently the glory of the Father! For this is how the herald of Jesus' grandeurs and humilities

---

85. Phil 2[:11] (original marginal note). "Every tongue confess that Jesus Christ is in the glory of God the Father."

86. Jn 1[:14] (original marginal note).

87. Dionysius, *Divine Names* [2.7] (original marginal note). "We learn from the sacred scriptures that the Father is the originating source of the Godhead." In *Complete Works*, 64.

names it when he tells us that every tongue must confess *quia Dominus Iesus-Christus in gloria est Dei Patris.* Speaking to us of Jesus humiliated, of Jesus exalted, and distinguishing these two such different states, he tells us in conclusion that Jesus exalted is in the glory of the Father. He wants to comprehend and encompass in the sublimity of these few words that which is infinite and ineffable, and to mark out for us the way by which we are to enter into some understanding of this immense glory. For we must know the Father, we must know the Son, and we must know the mutual love of the Father and the Son, in order to know and measure the state and greatness of this glory that is the glory of the Father, of the Son, and of the Son by the Father and in his Father.

Scripture describes for us two voyages of the Son of God: the one in which he comes forth from the Father and into the world by the mystery of the Incarnation, *A Deo exivit*,[88] and the other in which he goes out of the world and to the Father, *Ad Deum vadit*.[89] The one is accomplished by Jesus' incarnation and human birth, and the other is accomplished by Jesus' glorification and glorious birth. The Son of God, therefore, having come forth from the Father, returns to the Father, goes back to the Father, and enters into the Father's glory, never to go out again. He lives forever in glory, power, greatness, and majesty worthy of the Son, worthy of the Father, worthy of such a Son and such a Father. Jesus is in the Father's deity, and the Father's deity is the Father's glory. Jesus therefore is in the Father's glory. And although this deity is communicated to Jesus from the moment of the Incarnation, it is now communicated to him not only in his subsistence and personal dignity but in his life and glory. O subsistence! O dignity! O life! O glory of Jesus! This glory of Jesus is not a glory like ours, just as Jesus' grace is not a grace like ours. Our grace and holiness are an accident and quality spread in the soul, and our glory is this same grace consummated and more fully realized, but proportioned to our grace in its being, quality, and degree. Jesus' glory is like his grace, and just as Jesus' grace is so different from ours, so also is Jesus' glory different from ours. Jesus' grace and holiness are of substance, and his glory is of substance; his grace is uncreated, and his glory is uncreated! The infused

---

88. Jn 13[:3] (original marginal note). "He came forth from God."
89. "He goes to God."

grace that flows in the soul and to the powers and faculties of Jesus' soul is a grace that emanates from this original and principal grace, from this grace belonging to Jesus, this grace constitutive of Jesus, and is an accident that depends on this eternal substance! So also the glory corresponding to this infused grace is a glory that emanates from this essential glory, which is communicated to Jesus in the communication of the Godhead, given to this humanity as essential and superessential life and glory.[90]

Let us rise up above ourselves and the glory of men and angels, and let us lose ourselves in beholding and contemplating this glory. For this glory is so high and divine that we can indeed say that this glory of Jesus is the splendor of the deity's glory, just as the person of Jesus is the splendor of the Father's glory. Thus, the same apostle, the worthy herald of Jesus' grandeurs, contemplating him in one of his epistles, tells us concerning him, *In ipso inhabitat omnis plenitudo Divinitatis corporaliter* ("In Jesus dwells all the fullness of the deity bodily").[91] This word is vigorous, worthy of this mystery's depth and the apostolic meaning. It comprehends two terms that are the crux of the discussion and the key to this great apostle's sublime and exalted message: the term *fullness* and the term *bodily*. He employs this word *fullness* in speaking of the Godhead in order to mark out for us the emptiness of the creature and make us consider all created being as a void that is filled with the fullness of God. For there are two beings in Jesus: created being and uncreated being. The uncreated being dwells in its created being as in its void, which he fills with his fullness—his entire fullness—not desiring to hold back any of what can be communicated to a created nature that remains created. He communicates his being to its nothingness, his greatness to its baseness, his dignity to its meanness, his power to its weakness, his glory to its mortality, his light to its darkness, his fullness to its capacity, his deity to its humanity, and his subsistence to the substance of the human nature in which he dwells as in his own nature. God dwelt formerly in this humanity, but he suspended the effects, states, and splendor of his presence. He dwelt in it

---

90. Jn 17[:5]. Hilary, [commentary] on Psalm 2:6–7 (original marginal note). This work is not available in English translation.

91. Col 2[:9] (original marginal note).

as in a nature that is other, for Jesus desired to be a stranger, pilgrim, and mortal upon the earth, because we ourselves were estranged from God. He wanted to be like us and to remove this perverse state in us by the humble and other state of his greatness that he bears upon the earth. But he dwells now in this humanity as in his own nature, and the eternal Father wants his Son to be and to appear in the state of his greatness, drawing him out of the nonage in which he willed to live for so long a time, in Nazareth, Egypt, and Judea. And just as the deity is the fullness of the humanity subsisting in the Word, so also in this blessed and glorious state is the fullness, fulfilment, and consummation of the mystery of the Incarnation. This is why he uses this term *fullness* and adds to it the term *bodily*, to tell us that the deity, the fullness of the deity, all the fullness of the deity dwells in Jesus, and dwells in Jesus bodily, that is, as in his own body. This is a great and lofty truth, which in two words says what is ineffable, marks out an infinity of grandeurs and marvels, and contains a deep abyss of meaning and light! All the fullness of the deity dwells in Jesus as in his own body.

To enter into the understanding of these great words, we must consider that God in his divine nature has no body. For he is all spirit, a spirit infinitely far from all bodies and even from all created spirits, by the eminence of his uncreated being. But his love gives him what his nature does not, since by the mystery of the Incarnation the Word is made flesh, and this flesh and this body are the flesh and body of God. This body is deified, as the Fathers say, and it is the ordinary language of the early Church.[92] That is, this body is made the body of God, and God dwells in it as in his body. And what God does not have by his essence he has by his goodness, condescension, and love. For the secret of the faith instructs us that the eternal Word is made man, takes a soul and a body to himself, and gives them existence and subsistence in his uncreated being, and this body has consubsistence with his deity, just as his divine person is consubstantial with his Father. For just as the person of the Father and the person of the Son have one same deity, so also this body and the deity have one same subsistence. An incomparable

---

92. Cf. Gregory Nazianzen, Letter 51, To Cledonius the Priest against Apollinarius, in *Select Orations and Letters*, 439–40, cited in Aquinas, *Summa Theologica* 3a.16, p. 4:2112.

dignity and a marvelous appropriation of this body to God, occurring by the power of the love that equals the power of nature, and that in God is God himself!

This wondrous power unites this body with God so intimately, closely, substantially, and personally that this body is adorable, adored by all created spirits, and also humbly adored, because it is the body of God by love and subsistence, just as though it were his body by his essence and nature. For pagans and Christians find themselves agreeing in one same thought, although pagans are led by the spirit of lie and Christians by the Spirit of truth. The pagans in their opinions give God a body by nature; Christians in their belief give God a body by love. But if this false and impossible supposition of the profane heathens were correct, this body would be the body of a god on another basis than that of love. It would be God's more naturally and necessarily, but it would not be God's more actually, and it would not be the body of a person worthier of supreme adoration. And this natural condition that heathenism would ascribe to God would diminish God's essence and dignity, making him embodied, and abasing him by nature to a thing so base as a body. But when God abases himself to it, and abases himself to it by love and condescension, as he does in this mystery that Christians adore, he remains always in his own greatness and in the dignity of his high, separate, and immaterial essence, and he enhances this body that he unites himself to with the greatness of his deity. He exalts it in its dignity without his deity's essence being abased. Instead of this body's being his by his essence, it is his by subsistence, which is one and the same as his essence. For if this body and soul were fitting to God by nature as they are by subsistence, what life, what glory, what greatness would befit this body that would be the body of a God, and this soul that would be the soul of a God? For this body and this soul and this humanity, thus joined with God by means of the hypostatic union, are truly and efficaciously, blessedly and divinely, the body of God, the soul of God, and the humanity of God by subsistence, just as they would be the body of God by subsistence if God had a body by his nature. The life, therefore, the glory, and the greatness that would necessarily befit this body by nature do rightly befit this body deified by love and subsistence and are conferred on it by God's goodness and love and power, for he regards this body as his body and as such he fills it with divine glory, splendor, and majesty.

The ancient philosophers were right to say that if God had a body, it would be that of the sun, for they saw nothing in the world worthier of being God's body, since it is a body that excels in its splendor, influences, and activity. But by this third birth, God wills to give his Son a body much more excellent than this, a body whose light overshadows the sun's light, a body that is the sun not of the earth but of the empyrean heaven, a heaven that contains in its immense extent both earth and sun, all the stars and the full breadth of the heavens themselves, a body that governs all the heavenly bodies and spirits, a body that has consubsistence with the deity. And this body is adorable and adored by every creature that pays homage to this body as to the body of its God and to this soul as to the soul of its God. Every creature delights in bearing the deeply impressed marks of Jesus' servitude and in feeling the effects of his divine and wondrous power. For God, who has no body by his nature and willed to have a body by his power, love, and subsistence, dwells henceforth in this body in a manner much more intimate and powerful than that by which the soul dwells in its body. For the soul, in the course of nature, is joined with the body only for a time. It must be separated from it, and once separated it can never return. If by an external power and very great miracle it is restored to the body, even then it can be preserved in it for only a few years. Without an ongoing miracle, it must be separated from it forever. But when the deity unites himself with this body and soul, it will never to be separated from it, and nothing will be able to alter even a little this perfect union. It will endure for an eternity. For as long as God is God, God will be man, and this body will be forever the body of a God.

We see then that the soul, greatly inferior to the deity in its power and activity, communicates its life and state to the body by uniting itself with the body (if it is vegetable, the body is vegetable; if it is animal, the body is animal; if it is human, the body is human and has a human life). All the more, the deity that dwells in this body in a more intimate, powerful, and august manner, that fills and actuates this soul and body with his own subsistence and communicates to this soul his life and being, communicates to it, as a result, a divine being and makes it divine in its state and subsistence. For if a holy soul makes a body holy, and a glorious soul makes a body glorious, what will this deity do, who is glory and holiness in himself and dwells in this soul as the soul of this soul, in this body as in his own body, and in this human nature as in his own nature? For we must note well that the eternal Word has two essences: one by nature and the other by love, one by eternal birth and the other by temporal birth, one by which he is God and the other by which he is man, but Man-God forever. And in this same essence and nature that his love gives him, he also has two births, one in mortality and the other in immortality, which are two very different states of this same humanity and two births that are just as different, in one same subject and one same person. The first birth is completed on the cross, and Jesus looks upon it from the first moment of this humble birth. The second birth is completed in heaven, and heaven awaits you and looks upon you, O Jesus, as that which is its own from the first moment of this rebirth. In the one, you are born, O Jesus; in the other, you are born again. You are born in Bethlehem as man; you are reborn from the grave as man, but as man immortal and making men immortal. The one birth regards the cross, and the other regards heaven: two very different endpoints, dwelling places, and thrones. In the former you die, and in the latter you live. In the former you suffer, and in the latter you reign. In the former you enter into our wretchedness, and in the latter you enter into the Father's glory. In the former you sit on the throne of your humility, and in the latter you sit on the throne of your majesty. In the former you are in the manger and on the cross, and in the latter you are in heaven and on the throne of glory. O life divine! O heavenly life! O glorious life! O life in which the fullness of the deity and the splendor of the glory appear, formerly veiled and hidden from our eyes by the thorns of the cross and the state of his mortality! Life that says fullness of glory, fullness of power, fullness of majesty! Life without humilities, without suffering, and without mortality! O true life! Life, fullness of life, and fullness of deity! Life that is only life, only power, only glory, only majesty! For just as God is life so much that everything in God is life, so also in this blessed state Jesus is life and everything in Jesus is life, and life triumphs in Jesus and through Jesus. It triumphs over the universe and triumphs blessedly for the universe: *Triumphat* *nos Christo.*⁹³ Let us humbly follow this triumphal chariot of Jesus, for we are his slaves and captives, slaves of his greatness and captives of his triumphs, and we share in his spoils, his trophies, and the precious ornaments of his victory.

As we contemplate these three births and three lives of Jesus—his divine birth by which he is God, his human birth by which he is man among men, and his birth in glory by which he is King of glory among men and angels—we must note how in these three births he is born sovereign, and every creature owes him the homage of its servitude and submission. In the first birth, he is sovereign for he is God. In the second, he is sovereign for he is King, and born King, as the Gospel says.⁹⁴ In the third, he is sovereign for he is established at the right hand in the glory and power of his Father, and he himself declares his sovereignty to us by these words: *All power is given to me in heaven and on earth.*⁹⁵ Words of great vigor and very great authority! Of these three births, his authority is less marked and more hidden in the second one, in the humility of his infancy and the state of his mortality. And yet in this humble and second birth, just as Jesus is both living and dying, so also both living and dying he expresses, maintains, and exercises his sovereignty. Those who want to rob him of his life in his infancy, and do rob him of it on the cross, cannot rob him of his kingship that he maintains and preserves when he does not preserve his life. Thus, we see that in his infancy, kings proclaim Jesus as King, a king fears him, and kings adore him. From his birth, he desires to cause a radiance of his greatness to appear and cause the Great to feel the secret power hidden in his manger, that is one day to appear before the face of the universe, to their astonishment. *Si tantum terruit cuna vagientis, quid faciet tribunal iudicantis?*⁹⁶ During his mortal life, when he pays the tribute for the sake of example, he shows that he has no duty to

---

93. 2 Cor 2[:14] (original marginal note). "He triumphs over us in Christ."
94. Mt 2:2.
95. Mt 2:28 [sc. 8:18] (original marginal note).
96. Augustine (original marginal note). "If the cradle of a wailing baby was so terrifying, what will a judge's court do?" The actual text of Augustine: *Quid erit tribunal iudicantis quando superbos reges cunae terrebant infantis?* See Augustine, Sermon 200, in *Sermons on the Liturgical Seasons*, trans. Mary Sarah Muldowney, FC 38, p. 64.

pay it as the Son of the King of kings. Therefore, he pays it by power and miracle, his apparent submission being enhanced with an effect of extraordinary power, marvel, and authority over the earth and sea, in such a way that the mark of his submission bears the mark of his power. When he dies, he causes himself to be proclaimed, in death itself, the King of the Jews, and he makes the same judge who condemns him to be the herald of his kingship. After death in the grave, he takes voice and employs his follower's tongue to be named Sovereign in the state and shadows of death and the grave. This is a follower well instructed in the school of Jesus, the school of love, the school of the Holy Spirit, and she calls Jesus Sovereign[97] by the impulse of the one who possesses her heart, guides her tongue, draws forth her tears, and attaches her to the cross and Jesus' grave, more alive in his death than in herself. What do you say, O lover, but divine lover? Jesus is dead, and you live in him. Jesus is dead, and you call him Sovereign, Sovereign without limit. Jesus is dead, and his body alone is in the grave. Believing in him, seeking him, loving him in this state, you call him Lord, speaking to the apostles, that is, to the teachers of the world and the disciples of Life and Truth. But the Holy Spirit guides your heart and thought and directs your tongue and words, for when Jesus is born, when Jesus dies, when Jesus is dead, he is still sovereign and does not lose his sovereignty any more than his deity, to which it is solely and inseparably joined. In this state of the cross and death, Jesus is sovereign. He does not produce any effects of his power over his sensible and rational creation, because he willed to suffer by it and for it, but he produces the effects of his power over his insensible and inanimate creation. For although he suffers and does not act, suffers and does not work, dies and does not live, he shakes the earth, he breaks the stones apart, he rends the temple veil, he covers the heavens with darkness, he robs the sun of its light, and he marks his sovereignty on earth and in heaven when he is robbed of life, he who is the light and marvel of heaven and earth.

Jesus, then, even in this state of humility, suffering, and death, is King and Sovereign. How much more should we acknowledge and confess him so in the state of his glory and immortality. As he enters into

---

97. Jn 20[:11–16] (original marginal note).

this state and in the midst of his triumph, ascending from the earth to enter into glory, he turns toward us, and as he addresses us with his words, he tells us clearly and authoritatively, *Data est mihi omnis potestas in caelo et in terra.*⁹⁸ He ends his sojourn on earth with these great words and this final message, to leave his power and authority more deeply impressed on our minds, our hearts, and our life, and to teach us that the end of his life, his cross, his death, and his rebirth into immortality is to reign and to establish the effects of this his power on earth and in heaven. Let us heed these holy words, spoken in this triumph. Let us cleave to Jesus who speaks and proclaims them to us. Let us deliver ourselves into the power of the one who triumphs over death and sin and who wants to triumph over us also as over that which is his, both by his greatness and by his victories. For he is Sovereign and we are his subjects; he is Redeemer and we are his captives. He is Sovereign and Redeemer by birth and by nature; and by birth and rebirth we are the subjects of his rule and the slaves of his power. He is always Sovereign and we are always his subjects, his vassals, his slaves, and this on many bases: slaves of his love, his greatness, his humilities, his cross, his spirit, his glory. To him we must render homage and the effects of our servitude, finding our life in obedience, our freedom in servitude, and our glory in the submission that we must render and want to render to Jesus, the only Son of God, the love and power of the Father, the King of glory, the Sovereign Lord of men and of angels.

---

98. Mt 28[:18] (original marginal note). "All power is given to me in heaven and on earth."

BIBLIOGRAPHY

Source Text

Bérulle, Pierre de. *Discours de l'estat et des grandeurs de Iesus.* 2nd ed. Paris, 1629. https://gallica.bnf.fr/ark:/12148/bpt6k319075m.

Other Works

Alter, Robert. *The Art of Bible Translation.* Princeton: Princeton University Press, 2019.

———. *The Hebrew Bible: A Translation with Commentary.* New York: Norton, 2019.

Ambrose. *On the Christian Faith.* Translated by H. de Romestin, E. de Romestin, and H. T. F. Duckworth. Nicene and Post-Nicene Fathers, Second Series, edited by Philip Schaff and Henry Wace, vol. 10. Peabody, Mass.: Hendrickson, 1896.

Aristotle. *Parts of Animals.* Translated by A. L. Peck and E. S. Forster. Loeb Classical Library 323. Cambridge, Mass.: Harvard University Press, 1937.

Athanasius. *On the Incarnation.* Translated by P. Lawson. Crestwood, N.Y.: St. Vladimir's Seminary Press, 1993.

Augustine of Hippo. *Sermons on the Liturgical Seasons.* Translated by Mary Sarah Muldowney. Fathers of the Church, edited by Thomas P. Halton, Ludwig Schopp, Roy J. Deferrari, Bernard M. Peebles, and Hermigild Dressler, vol. 38. Washington, D.C.: The Catholic University of America Press, 1959.

———. *Confessions.* Translated by R. S. Pine-Coffin. Harmondsworth: Penguin, 1961.

———. *Tractates on the Gospel of John, 11–27.* Translated by John W. Rettig. Fathers of the Church 79. Washington, D.C.: The Catholic University of America Press, 1988.

———. *The Trinity.* Translated by Edmund Hill. Works of Saint Augustine, edited by John E. Rotelle, Boniface Ramsay, David G. Hunter, and Allan Fitzgerald, pt. 1, vol. 5. Brooklyn, N.Y.: New City, 1991.

———. *On the Predestination of the Saints.* In *Four Anti-Pelagian Writings,* translated by John A. Mourant and William J. Collinge. Fathers of the Church 86. Washington, D.C.: The Catholic University of America Press, 1992.

———. *Sermons 148–183.* Translated by Edmund Hill. Works of Saint Augustine, pt. 3, vol. 5. New Rochelle, N.Y.: New City, 1992.

———. *Tractates on the Gospel of John, 28–54*. Translated by John W. Rettig. Fathers of the Church 88. Washington, D.C.: The Catholic University of America Press, 1993.

———. *Tractates on the Gospel of John, 55–111*. Translated by John W. Rettig. Fathers of the Church 90. Washington, D.C.: The Catholic University of America Press, 1994.

———. *Answer to Maximinus the Arian*. In *Arianism and Other Heresies*, translated by Roland J. Teske. Works of Saint Augustine, pt. 1, vol. 18. Hyde Park, N.Y.: New City, 1995.

———. *Arianism and Other Heresies*. Translated by Roland J. Teske. Works of Saint Augustine, pt. 1, vol. 18. Hyde Park, N.Y.: New City, 1995.

———. *On the Lord's Birth*. In *Sermons 341–400 on Various Subjects*, translated by Edmund Hill. Works of Saint Augustine, pt. 3, vol. 10. Hyde Park, N.Y.: New City, 1995.

———. "On the Spirit and the Letter." Translated by Peter Holmes and Robert Ernest Wallis. Nicene and Post-Nicene Fathers, First Series, edited by Philip Schaff, vol. 5. 1887. Reprint, Peabody, Mass.: Hendrickson Publishers, 1995.

———. *Commentary on Psalm 122*. In *Expositions of the Psalms* (*Enarrationes in Psalmos*) *121–150*, translated by Maria Boulding. Works of Saint Augustine, pt. 3, vol. 2. Hyde Park, N.Y.: New City, 2004.

———. *Exposition of Psalm 109*. In *Expositions of the Psalms* (*Enarrationes in Psalmos*) *121–150*, translated by Maria Boulding. Works of Saint Augustine, pt. 3, vol. 2. Hyde Park, N.Y.: New City, 2004.

Baillet, Adrien. *La vie de monsieur Descartes*. 2 vols. Paris, 1691. https://gallica.bnf.fr/ark:/12148/bpt6k75559n.

Belin, Christian. "Le 'discours en forme d'élévation' selon Bérulle." *Littératures classiques* 39 (2000): 253–64.

———. *La conversation intérieure: La méditation en France au XVIIe siècle*. Paris: Honoré Champion, 2002.

Bernard of Clairvaux. *Works of Bernard of Clairvaux*. Translated by Kilian Walsh. Kalamazoo, Mich.: Cistercian Publications, 1981.

Bérulle, Pierre de. *Discours de l'estat et des grandeurs de Iesus*. 1st ed. Paris, 1623. https://gallica.bnf.fr/ark:/12148/bpt6k65626015.

———. *Œuvres de piété*. Edited by Michel Dupuy. Vols. 3–4 of *Œuvres complètes de Pierre de Bérulle*, edited by Michel Dupuy. Paris: Cerf, 1995–96.

———. *Discours de l'état et des grandeurs de Jésus*. Edited by Joseph Beaude, Blandine Delahaye, Michel Join-Lambert, and Rémi Lescot. Vols. 7–8 of *Œuvres complètes de Pierre de Bérulle*, edited by Michel Dupuy. Paris: Cerf, 1996.

———. "Narré." Edited by Joseph Beaude, Blandine Delahaye, Michel Join-Lambert, and Rémi Lescot. Vol. 8 of *Œuvres complètes de Pierre de Bérulle*, edited by Michel Dupuy. Paris: Cerf, 1996.

Blümner, Hugo. *Home Life of the Ancient Greeks*. Translated by Alice Zimmern. New York: Funk & Wagnalls, 192–?.

Bonaventure. *The Journey of the Mind to God*. Translated by José de Vinck. In *Works of Bonaventure*, vol 1. Patterson, N.J.: St. Anthony's Guild, 1960.

---. *The Mystical Vine: Treatise on the Passion of the Lord.* Translated by José de Vinck. In *Works of Bonaventure*, vol. 1. Patterson, N.J.: St. Anthony's Guild, 1960.

Bourgoing, François. "Préface aux prêtres de la Congrégation de l'Oratoire de Jésus-Christ, notre Seigneur." In *Œuvres de l'éminentissime et reverendissime Pierre Cardinal de Bérulle*, edited by François Bourgoing. Paris, 1644. https://gallica.bnf.fr/ark:/12148/bpt6k6568438c.

Bradley, Henry. *The Making of English*. New York: Macmillan, 1924.

Bremond, Henri. *Histoire littéraire du sentiment religieux en France depuis la fin des guerres de religion jusqu'à nos jours*. 11 vols. Paris: Bloud et Gay, 1916–36.

Canfeld, Benoît de. *La règle de perfection / The Rule of Perfection*. Edited by J. Orcibal. Paris: Presses Universitaires de France, 1982.

---. *Renaissance Dialectic and Renaissance Piety: Benet of Canfield's Rule of Perfection. A Translation and Study*. Translated by Kent Emery. Binghamton, N.Y.: Medieval & Renaissance Texts & Studies, 1987.

Catechism of the Council of Trent Published by Command of Pope Pius the Fifth. Translated by Jeremiah Donovan. Baltimore: Lucas, [1829?].

Clement of Alexandria. *Exhortation to the Greeks*. Translated by G. W. Butterworth. Loeb Classical Library 92. Cambridge, Mass.: Harvard University Press, 1919.

---. *The Stromata, or Miscellanies*. Translated by A. Cleveland Coxe. Ante-Nicene Fathers, edited by A. Cleveland Coxe, Alexander Roberts, and James Donaldson, vol. 2. Peabody, Mass.: Hendrickson, 2004. First published 1885 by Christian Literature Publishing Company (Buffalo, N.Y.).

Clement of Rome. *Epistle to the Corinthians*. In *Epistles of St. Clement of Rome and St. Ignatius of Antioch*, translated by James A. Kleist. New York: Newman, 1946.

Cochois, Paul. "Bérulle et le pseudo-Denys." *Revue de l'histoire des religions* 159, no. 2 (1961): 173–204.

---. *Bérulle et l'École française*. Paris: Seuil, 1963.

Cognet, Louis. *De la dévotion moderne à la spiritualité française*. Paris: Fayard, 1958.

Copernicus, Nicholas. *De revolutionibus orbium cœlestium* [On the Revolutions of the Heavenly Spheres]. Translated by Edward Rosen. Warsaw: Polish Scientific, 1978.

Cyril of Alexandria. *Commentary on John*. Translated by P. E. Pusey. London: Walter Smith, 1885.

---. *Commentary on John*. Vol. 1. Translated by David R. Maxwell. Ancient Christian Texts. Downers Grove, Ill.: Intervarsity, 2013.

Cyril of Jerusalem. "First Lecture on the Mysteries." In *Catechetical Lectures*, translated by Edwin Hamilton Gifford. Nicene and Post-Nicene Fathers 7. Peabody, Mass.: Hendrickson, 2004.

Dagens, Jean. *Bérulle et les origines de la restauration catholique (1575–1611)*. Bruges: Desclée de Brouwer, 1952.

Dictionnaire de l'Académie françoise. 1st ed. Paris, 1694. https://www.dictionnaire-academie.fr/.

Dupuy, Michel. "Bérulle et la grâce." *XVIIe siècle* 170 (January–March 1991): 39–50.

Elowsky, Joel C., ed. *John 1–10*. In *Ancient Christian Commentary on Scripture*. New Testament 4a. Downers Grove, Ill.: Intervarsity, 2006.

———, ed. *John 11–21*. In *Ancient Christian Commentary on Scripture*. New Testament 4b. Downers Grove, Ill.: Intervarsity, 2007.

Euripides. *Fragments*. Translated by Christopher Collard and Martin Cropp. Loeb Classical Library 504. Cambridge, Mass.: Harvard University Press, 2009.

Eusebius of Caesarea. *Church History*. Translated by Arthur Cushman McGiffert. Nicene and Post-Nicene Fathers 1. Buffalo, N.Y.: Christian Literature Publishing, 1890.

The Evangelical Pearl. In *Late Medieval Mysticism of the Low Countries*, translated and edited by Rik van Nieuwenhove, Robert Faesen, and Helen Rolfson. Classics of Western Spirituality. New York: Paulist, 2008.

Ferrari, Anne. *Figures de la contemplation: La "rhétorique divine" de Pierre de Bérulle*. Paris: Cerf, 1997.

Ficino, Marsilio. *Platonic Theology*. Translated by Michael J. B. Allen. I Tatti Renaissance Library. Cambridge, Mass.: Harvard University Press, 2004.

Fox, Margalit. "Gregory Rabassa, a Premier Translator of Spanish and Portuguese Fiction, Dies at 94." *New York Times*, June 15, 2016.

Génébrard, Gilbert. *Psalmi Davidis*. 3rd ed. Paris, 1588. https://numelyo.bm-lyon.fr/f_view/BML:BML_00GOO0100137001102338642.

Gregory Nazianzen. "Second Oration on Easter." In *Select Orations and Letters*, translated by C. G. Browne and J. E. Swallow. Nicene and Post-Nicene Fathers 7. Peabody, Mass.: Hendrickson, 2004.

———. "Third Theological Oration, On the Son." In *Select Orations and Letters*, translated by C. G. Browne and J. E. Swallow. Nicene and Post-Nicene Fathers 7. Peabody, Mass.: Hendrickson, 2004.

Gregory of Nyssa. *Against Eunomius*. Translated by H. C. Ogle and H. A. Wilson. Nicene and Post-Nicene Fathers 5. Peabody, Mass.: Hendrickson, 1994.

Hermes Trismegistus. *Poemandres*. In *The Theological and Philosophical Works of Hermes Trismegistus, Christian Platonist*, translated by John D. Chambers. Edinburgh: T&T Clark, 1882.

———. *Asclepius*. In *Hermetica*, translated by Brian P. Copenhaver. New York: Cambridge University Press, 1992.

Herodotus. *The History*. Translated by David Grene. Chicago: University of Chicago Press, 1987.

Herp, Hendrik. *The Mirror of Perfection*. In *Late Medieval Mysticism of the Low Countries*, translated and edited by Rik Van Nieuwenhove, Robert Faesen, and Helen Rolfson. Classics of Western Spirituality. New York: Paulist, 2008.

Hesiod. *Precepts of Chiron*. In *Hesiod, the Homeric Hymns, and Homerica*. Translated by H. G. Evelyn-White. London: William Heinemann, 1914.

Hilary of Poitiers. *The Trinity*. Translated by S. Mckenna. Fathers of the Church 25. Washington, D.C.: The Catholic University of America Press, 1954.

Holloway, Paul A. *Philippians: A Commentary*. Minneapolis: Fortress, 2017.

Irenaeus of Lyons. *Against the Heresies*. 3 vols. Translated by Dominic Unger. Ancient Christian Writers. New York: The Newman Press, 2012.

Jerome. *Against Jovinianus*. Translated by W. H. Fremantle, G. Lewis, and W. G. Martley. Nicene and Post-Nicene Fathers 6. Buffalo, N.Y.: Christian Literature Publishing, 1893.

———. *Commentary on Matthew*. Translated by Thomas P. Scheck. Fathers of the Church 117. Washington, D.C.: The Catholic University of America Press, 2008.

———. "Letter 65, to Principia, A Commentary on Psalm 45 [44]." In *Epistolae: Medieval Women's Latin Letters*, translated by Joan Ferrante et al. Columbia University Libraries, 2014. epistolae.ctl.columbia.edu/letter/425.html.

John of Damascus. *Exposition of the Orthodox Faith*. In *Writings*, translated by Frederic H. Chase. Fathers of the Church 37. Washington, D.C.: The Catholic University of America Press, 1958.

———. "Homily on the Transfiguration of Our Lord Jesus Christ." Translated by Harold L. Weatherby. *Greek Orthodox Theological Review* 32, no. 1 (1987): 1–29.

———. *Exposition of the Orthodox Faith*. Translated by S. D. F. Salmond. Nicene and Post-Nicene Fathers 9. Peabody, Mass.: Hendrickson, 2004. First published 1885 by Christian Literature Publishing Company (Buffalo, N.Y.).

Justinian. *Digest of Justinian*. Translated by Alan Watson. Philadelphia: University of Pennsylvania Press, 1985.

Krumenacker, Yves. *L'École française de spiritualité: Des mystiques, des fondateurs, des courants et leurs interprètes*. Paris: Cerf, 1998.

———. "Entre histoire et mémoire: L'École française de spiritualité." *Théophilyon* 4, no. 1 (1999): 41–64.

———. "L'École française de spiritualité." In Alain Tallon et al., *Histoire du christianisme en France*, 263–76. Paris: Armand Colin, 2014.

Leo the Great. *Sermons*. Translated by Jane Patricia Freeland and Agnes Josephine Conway. Fathers of the Church 93. Washington, D.C.: The Catholic University of America Press, 1996.

———. *Letters and Sermons*. Translated by Charles Lett Feltoe. Nicene and Post-Nicene Fathers 12. Peabody, Mass.: Hendrickson, 2004. First published 1895 by Christian Literature Publishing (Buffalo, N.Y.).

Lescot, Rémi. "Introduction historique et théologique." In Pierre de Bérulle, *Discours de l'état et des grandeurs de Jésus*, edited by Joseph Beaude, Blandine Delahaye, Michel Join-Lambert, and Rémi Lescot, xiii–lxxi. Vol. 7 of *Œuvres complètes de Pierre de Bérulle*, edited by Michel Dupuy. Paris: Cerf, 1996.

Littré, Émile, ed. *Dictionnaire de la langue française*. Paris: Hachette, 1872.

McGrath-Merkle, Clare. *Bérulle's Spiritual Theology of Priesthood: A Study in Speculative Mysticism and Applied Metaphysics*. Munster: Aschendorff, 2018.

Martial. *Epigrams*. Translated by D. R. Shackleton Bailey. Loeb Classical Library 94–95, 480. Cambridge, Mass.: Harvard University Press, 1993.

Morgain, Stéphane-Marie. *Pierre de Bérulle et les Carmélites de France: La querelle du gouvernement 1583–1629*. Paris: Cerf, 1995.

———. "La prêtrise selon Pierre de Bérulle." *Revue d'histoire de l'Église de France* 83 (2007): 139–52.

Nicholas of Cusa. *On Learned Ignorance*. Translated by Jasper Hopkins. Minneapolis: Banning, 1981.

Nicot, Jean, ed. *Thresor de la langue francoyse*. Paris, 1606. https://gallica.bnf.fr/ark:/12148/btv1b8622102w.

O'Brien, Peter T. *The Epistle to the Philippians: A Commentary on the Greek Text*. Grand Rapids, Mich.: Eerdmans, 1991.

O'Day, Gail R. *John*. In *New Interpreter's Bible Commentary*, vol. 8. Nashville: Abingdon, 2015.

Olier, Jean-Jacques. *Traité des saints ordres*. Paris, 1676. https://numelyo.bm-lyon.fr/f_view/BML:BML_00GOO0100137001101213879.

Origen. *Contra Celsum*. Translated by Henry Chadwick. Cambridge: Cambridge University Press, 1953.

Oxford English Dictionary. Oxford: Oxford University Press. https://www.oed.com.

Pelikan, Jaroslav. *The Christian Tradition: A History of the Development of Doctrine*. Vol. 1, *The Emergence of the Catholic Tradition, 100–600*. Chicago: University of Chicago Press, 1971.

Percival, Henry R., ed. *The Seven Ecumenical Councils of the Undivided Church*. Nicene and Post-Nicene Fathers 14. Peabody, Mass.: Hendrickson, 2004.

Plato. *Philebus*. Translated by Harold M. Fowler. Loeb Classical Library 164. Cambridge, Mass.: Harvard University Press, 1925.

———. *Statesman*. Translated by Harold M. Fowler. Loeb Classical Library 164. Cambridge, Mass.: Harvard University Press, 1925.

———. *Timaeus*. Translated by R. G. Bury. Loeb Classical Library 234. Cambridge, Mass.: Harvard University Press, 1929.

———. *Republic*. Translated by Paul Shorey. Loeb Classical Library 276. Cambridge, Mass.: Harvard University Press, 1946.

Pliny. *Natural History*. Translated by H. Rackham, W. H. S. Jones, A. C. Andrews, and D. E. Eichholz. Loeb Classical Library. 10 vols. Cambridge, Mass.: Harvard University Press, 1938–62.

Plotinus. *Ennead*. Translated by A. H. Armstrong. Loeb Classical Library 440–445, 468. Cambridge, Mass.: Harvard University Press, 1969–88.

Plutarch. *Moralia*. Translated by Frank Cole Babbitt, W. C. Helmbold, Phillip H. De Lacy, Benedict Einarson, P. A. Clement, H. B. Hoffleit, Edwin L. Minar, et al. Loeb Classical Library. 15 vols. Cambridge, Mass.: Harvard University Press, 1927–69.

Proclus. *Commentary on Plato's Timaeus*. Translated by Dirk Baltzly. New York: Cambridge University Press, 2007.

Pseudo-Dionysius. *Celestial Hierarchy*. In *Complete Works*, translated by Colm Luibheid. Classics of Western Spirituality. New York: Paulist, 1987.

———. *Divine Names*. In *Complete Works*, translated by Colm Luibheid. Classics of Western Spirituality. New York: Paulist, 1987.

Ruusbroec, John. *The Spiritual Espousals and Other Works*. Translated by James A. Wiseman. Classics of Western Spirituality. New York: Paulist, 1985.

Seneca. *Moral Essays*. Translated by John W. Basore. Loeb Classical Library 254, vol. 2. Cambridge, Mass.: Harvard University Press, 1932.

Sidonius. *Letters*. Translated by William B. Anderson. Loeb Classical Library 296, 420. Cambridge, Mass.: Harvard University Press, 1965.

Teresa of Ávila. *The Book of Her Life*. In *Collected Works of Saint Teresa of Avila*, translated by Kieran Kavanaugh and Otilio Rodriguez, vol. 1. Washington, D.C.: Institute of Carmelite Studies, 1980.

———. *The Interior Castle*. In *Collected Works of Saint Teresa of Avila*, translated by Kieran Kavanaugh and Otilio Rodriguez, vol. 2. Washington, D.C.: Institute of Carmelite Studies, 1980.

———. *The Way of Perfection*. In *Collected Works of Saint Teresa of Avila*, translated by Kieran Kavanaugh and Otilio Rodriguez, vol. 2. Washington, D.C.: Institute of Carmelite Studies, 1980.

Tertullian. *Against Praxeas*. Translated by Peter Holmes. Ante-Nicene Fathers 3. Peabody, Mass.: Hendrickson, 2004. First published 1885, Christian Literature Publishing Company (New York).

———. *Apology*. Translated by Sydney Thelwall. In Ante-Nicene Fathers 3. Peabody, Mass.: Hendrickson, 2004. First published 1885, Christian Literature Publishing Company (New York).

———. *On the Resurrection of the Flesh*. Translated by Peter Holmes. Ante-Nicene Fathers 3. Peabody, Mass.: Hendrickson, 2004. First published 1885, Christian Literature Publishing Company (New York).

Thomas Aquinas. *Summa Theologica*. Translated by Fathers of the English Dominican Province. 5 vols. Westminster, Md.: Christian Classics, 1981.

Thompson-Uberuaga, William, ed. *Bérulle and the French School: Selected Writings*. Translated by Lowell M. Glendon. Classics of Western Spirituality. New York: Paulist, 1989.

Varden, Erik. *Redeeming Freedom: The Principle of Servitude in Bérulle*. Rome: Sankt Ottilien, 2011.

Vasey, Vincent R. "Mary in the Doctrine of Bérulle on the Mysteries of Christ." *Marian Studies* 36 (1986), article 11.

Vetö, Miklos. *Pierre de Bérulle: Les thèmes majeurs de sa pensée*. Paris: L'Harmattan, 2016.

Virgil. *Aeneid*. Translated by A. Mandelbaum. New York: Bantam, 1961.

INDEX

Abstract school of spirituality, 9, 11–12, 21–23, "state" in, 14n27
Acarie, Barbe, 2
Accident. *See* Substance
Adam, 16–17, 20, 71, 255–56, 306, 310–11; Jesus as the second or new, 20, 69, 71, 129, 157, 184, 255–56, 306, 310–11, 317
Adoption, sonship by: 19–23, 38, 84, 104; contrasted with sonship by nature, 62, 92, 134, 277–82; contrasted with motherhood of Mary, 315, 318; sonship by nature as source of sonship by adoption, 153, 190. *See also* Isaiah 9:6
Adoration: as elevation, 26–29; as latria, 106; as state, 302; by Creation, 27, 90, 300; Jesus begins and ends his life in, 106–9; Jesus' birth as a mystery of, 298–99, 330; of Golden Calf, 99–100; the Incarnation as a new and perfect, 46–48, 87–88, 299, 302
Alan of Lille, 169n12
Ambrose, 284
Ancient of Days, 45
Angel of Great Counsel, 55
Angels: as translation of Greek *angelos*, 39n5; as intellectual beings, 45, 71–74, 90, 102, 112, 122, 130–34, 174, 184, 186, 194, 206, 249, 251, 261, 308; as worshipers of God, 46, 48, 66, 121, 304, 343; at Jesus' birth, 109, 324; hierarchy or ranks of, 54–55, 131–32, 239, 300–301; John the Baptist as, 37; Joseph as, 324–25; man as, 20, 305n55; relation to deity, 46, 55, 102, 121, 131; state of, 300–301. *See also* Gabriel
Anne, 298

Annunciation, 37–41, 115, 159, 288, 297, 316–19, 323–24, 338
Apelles, 143. *See also* Painting
Apollinaris, Sidonius, 129
Aristarchus of Samos, 59n6
Aristotle, 47n7, 141n1
Ark, 67, 201, 332–33
Ascension, 28, 91, 200, 332–35, 348
Aspect, 57n2
Astronomy, 57–59, 209–12. *See also* Aspect; Influence
Augustine of Hippo, 85, 138n34; *Against Maximinus*, 283–84; as eagle, 283; *Confessions*, 23, 28, 49, 182–83; *Expositions of the Psalms*, 168, 270; *On the Predestination of the Saints*, 134–35; *On the Spirit and the Letter*, 284; *On the Trinity*, 50–51; *Sermons*, 159n26, 311, 346; *Tractates on the Gospel of John*, 17, 125n10, 135n28, 160; transmission of Neoplatonism, 9, 10n18, 269n10

Baillet, Adrien, 5
Baptism: of Jesus, 296, 309; relation to deity, 162, 265, 268; relation to the Church, 177, 268; relation to vow of servitude, 4–5, 177
Basil of Caesarea, 9
Beaucousin, Richard, 2, 11–12
Being: contrasted with state, 136; created being contrasted with uncreated, 341; essential being contrasted with personal, 301–3, 328; God as source and sustainer of, 68–69, 150, 169–72, 197–98, 291; God's communication of his, 184–89;

Being (*cont.*)
God's self-sufficiency and delight in his, 132–33, 168, 198, 248; Incarnation as entering into created being, 136–37, 203–6, 214–25; Incarnation as honoring uncreated being, 144, 155–57; Incarnation as new, 314, 330; Incarnation as union of created and uncreated, 18, 47, 62, 67, 77, 112, 115, 119, 167, 262, 307; Jesus as always beholding, 108; Jesus as transcending uncreated, 238–42; oneness as prior and superior to, 98; orders of, 184–85; relation to state, cabinet, and council, 136; relation of the divine persons to God's pure and simple being, 147, 275, 285; the spiritual nature, fineness, and immensity of God's, 169

Bernard of Clairvaux, 184

Bérulle, Pierre de: "Copernican revolution" of, 29, 59; influence of Abstract school on, 9, 12; influence of Teresa of Avila on, 9, 12; heresy imputed to, 4, 54; life and influence, 1–7; opponents of, 48–50, 82, 89–90, 177

Birth: Jesus' first, in the Father's bosom, 266–88; the first's primacy, 147–54; the first as completing the mystery of the Godhead, 147; Jesus' second, in Mary 288–331; Jesus' third, in the Resurrection, 331–48; the three together, 266–67, 272–74; relation of the first to the second, 144, 196, 227–28. *See also* Bosom; Isaiah 53:8

Body: God has a body by love and subsistence but not by essence and nature, 342–45; mystical, 42, 69, 104, 124; relation between Mary's and Jesus', 320–22; the soul as suffused throughout the, 169, 305; the soul as preexisting the, 231; Jesus' death separates and his resurrection reunites his soul and, 336; Jesus' death did not separate the deity from his soul and, 70, 125–26, 160, 336. *See also* Colossians 2:9; Crucifixion; Eucharist; Temple; Transfiguration; Victim

Bonaventure, 69n21, 184n4

Bond: as translation of *liaison* and *lien*, 22; Holy Spirit as, 62, 107–8, 119–20, 142–45, 188; Incarnation as, 330; of grace, 68–69; of hypostatic union, 20, 68–69, 112, 122–24, 141–42, 204, 219, 240, 261–63; of nature, 68–69; of the Trinity, Incarnation, and Eucharist, 164; of servitude, 68

Bosom: as translation of *sein*, 38n3; compared with matrix and womb, 269–72; Holy Spirit's dwelling place, 62, 186, 272; Mary opens the Father's, 38; of death and hell, 125; of the Church, 271–72; of the cross, 280, 332; of Jesus, 339; of Mary, 324; place of Jesus' first birth, 266–88, 290–94, 300, 304, 311, 313–14, 319, 323, 330, 335–38; place of Jesus' third birth, 331–32, 337–38; the Son does not withdraw but goes forth from, 155; the Son's dwelling place, 61, 89–90, 102, 161, 173, 180, 186–87, 191, 214, 231, 259, 292–94; the Word receives Humanity into, 260; where the Father produces the Son and Holy Spirit, 45, 133, 136, 145, 149. *See also* Matrix; Womb

Bourgoing, François, 1, 5–7; meaning of "state," 14–15, 22–23

Bremond, Henri, 7

Burning bush, 22, 62

Cabinet: contrasted with council, 41n15, 136; of man's mind, 305; of Jesus, 246, 249; of Mary, 39, 106, 324

Caiaphas, 181, 278

Camus, Jean-Pierre, 4

Canaanite woman, 44

Canfeld, Benoît de, 2, 12

Capacity: as translation of *capacité*, 52n17; in Augustine, 23; of Christians, 1, 22–23, 76, 85 ("naked capacity and pure void"), 161–62, 305n55; of God, 168, 247–48; of Jesus, 161, 224, 230, 247, 260, 285, 299, 341; of Mary, 23, 159, 317, 321. *See also* Comprehension; Nothing(ness); Poverty

Carmelites, 2–6, 177n20

Cave, 56

Chain, 156, 165–66, 193

Christians: as sons of God dead, 279–82; capacity of, 1, 22–23, 76, 85; compared with philosophers or pagans, 58–59, 81,

182, 260, 343; Jesus as stumbling block to, 49; strive more to know God than to love him, 250. *See also* Image

Church: as mother, 271–72; birth at Pentecost, 188; eastern orientation, 148n9; Index of Prohibited Books, 59n6; Jesus in, 121–23, 132; liturgy of, 96, 110, 149, 268; relation to Peter, 278; relation to vow of servitude, 4, 177; the Trinity and Incarnation as the two principal mysteries of, 176, 215. *See also* Council

Circle: God as, 59, 63, 61, 67, 111, 137, 139, 142, 147, 157, 169, 185, 193, 255, 261, 291, 304; God's bosom as, 287; hypostatic union as, 308; in Nicholas of Cusa, 63n14; Jesus as, 63, 67, 282, 291, 315; man as, 305n55; the Incarnation as, 47, 77, 109, 113, 121, 129, 131, 158, 193, 255

Clement of Alexandria, 143n3, 150n15, 159n26, 270

Clement of Rome, 146n5

Clement VIII, pope, 2–3

Colossians 2:9 ("In him all the fullness of the Godhead dwells bodily"), 64, 72, 197, 202, 242–43, 307, 315, 341–45

Composition: as translation of *composé*, 69n22; Jesus as, 69, 108, 128, 174, 307–8; man as, 305, 307. *See also* Hypostatic union; Temperament

Comprehension, 23, 45, 47, 52, 55, 127–28, 185–87, 198–99, 290–93, 304, 315–18, 321. *See also* Capacity; Poverty

Concomitance, 164. *See also* Eucharist

Condren, Charles, 6

"Copernican revolution," 29, 59

Copernicus, Nicholas, 59, 156n21

Coton, Pierre, 2, 150n15

Council: as translation of *conseil*, 41n15; contrasted with cabinet, 136; in God, 83, 101, 132–36, 158, 306; Joseph in God's, 324; Mary in God's, 41; of Chalcedon, 127; of Ephesus, 261; of the Church, 123, 145; of Toledo, 221; of Trent, 2, 4, 11, 137n32, 177

Covenant: of human persons, 123; the Incarnation as, 62, 67, 139, 164, 201, 332. *See also* Law

Creation: as dependent, 20–23, 41n15, 111, 152, 170–74; as emanation, 74; as image of God and his oneness, 51–53, 70–71, 94–95; from God as God, 292, 301–2; God's presence in, 223–24; groaning and shaken, 182, 257–58, 347; its homage and submission to Jesus, 67; multiplicity in, 51–54, 75, 117; of the world, 18–26, 37, 40, 46–47, 51–53, 58–59, 62, 65–66, 71, 84, 100–101, 106, 113, 117–18, 122, 128, 130, 132, 137–39, 168, 169n11, 171, 173, 180, 184, 191, 193, 211, 231, 253, 256–58, 273, 296, 301, 306–7, 316, 331, 347. *See also* Being; Order(s)

Creed: Athanasian, 78n33; Nicene, 152, 179, 227, 255, 323

Crocodile, 47

Crucifixion: as beginning in Mary's womb, 320–21; as deicide, 160; as humiliation and elevation, 28, 86–87, 90, 96, 104, 134, 181, 234–39; relation to salvation, 15–16, 19, 106, 219, 225, 244, 256–59, 265, 279–82, 299, 310, 317; relation to the Eucharist, 28, 144, 273. *See also* Body

Cyril of Alexandria, 17, 23, 195, 261n18, 327

David, 47, 134–35, 199, 267, 309

Dayspring: as translation of *orient*, 148n9; Jesus as, 16, 99, 148–50, 211, 214, 268

Death. *See* Body; Crucifixion; Victim

Deity: as translation of *divinité*, 42n16. *See also* God(head)

Demons: as deceived, 233; as opposing God, 98, 100, 170–71; as subject to God, 73, 90, 98, 171, 310; Jesus considered possessed by, 309; Satan as prince of, 310. *See also* Devil

Denis of Paris, 163n1

Denys de la Mère de Dieu, 3–4, 177n20

Dependence: as translation of *dépendance*, 41n15; of Creation, 20–23, 41n15, 111, 152, 170–74; of Jesus, 174–81, 226. *See also* Independence; Submission; Vow

Descartes, René, 5

Devil (Satan), 5, 129, 160, 225, 245; accuser, 89; prince of darkness, 89; prince of demons, 310; prince of the world, 106. See also Demons

Discourses: as a work, 7–8, 41–44; as genre, 26–29; circumstances of writing, 4–5, 49–50; message of, 13–24; sources and influences, 8–13; translation of, 24–26

Divinity: as translation of *divinité*, 42n16. See also God(head)

Duns Scotus, 19

Dust. See Earth

Duval, André, 2–3

Duvergier de Hauranne, Jean (Abbé de Saint-Cyran), 4

Eagle: Augustine as, 283; John as 203–5, 269

Earth: as dust, loam, mud, or mire, 71, 80, 103, 128–29, 133; as world or planet, 19, 59, 182, 211–12, 232, 236, 253, 259, 289–91, 301–4; handled by God, 306–7; Jesus becomes, 212, 306; joined to heaven, 62, 77, 97, 207, 254; reversal with heaven, 46, 130–31; shaken at the Crucifixion, 182, 258, 347

Eckhart von Hochheim (Meister Eckhart), 11

Egypt, flight into, 90, 109, 125, 234–35, 309, 332, 342

Egyptians, 47, 57–58, 309

Elevation: as genre, 26; as prayer and adoration, 26–29; in the Eucharist, 27; of Jesus to God, 76, 106, 227, 247, 299; on the cross, 28, 236

Emanation: beyond the Godhead, 51, 97, 113, 229; in Neoplatonism, 10; in the Godhead, 51, 60, 95, 110–11, 139, 186–87, 199, 235, 243, 267, 274, 285–87, 290–92, 296–97, 301–4, 313–14, 328; in the Incarnation, 63, 247; of the Holy Spirit, 61–62, 100, 110, 116–19, 142, 312; of the Son, 107, 139, 144, 153, 177; of the sun's light and heat, 74; to humanity, 66–67, 235, 287, 290, 296, 316–17, 328

Empty: as translation of *anéantir* and *dépouiller*, 61n11. See also Nothing(ness); Poverty; Self-emptying

Endpoint: as translation of *terme*, 40n11; Holy Spirit as, 62, 110, 116–19, 142, 240, 285; Jesus as, 118, 138, 276, 302, 314, 327

Epitome: as translation of *abrégé*, 39n9; Incarnation as, 39; Jesus as, 47, 141, 261, 307; man as, 138, 305–7

Erasmus, 9

Essence: God's existence is his, 94. See also Substance; Underlying substance

Eucharist, 44; as miracle of oneness, 103–6, 164, 192, 195; as principal mystery of the faith, 162–65, 187–88, 193; as a second, transitory, union with humanity, 18, 123–24, 125n11, 165–66, 212, 259, 265; relation to Crucifixion, 28, 144, 273; relation to priesthood, 11; relation to the Incarnation, 187

Eudes, Jean, 6, 7

Eudoxus of Cnidus, 58–59, 209–12

Euripides, 49

Eusebius, 15

Exemplarism. See Image; Model

Fall, 19, 98, 255, 310–11

Fatherhood: See God the Father; Isaiah 9:6

Fertility: in the Godhead, 133, 147, 150, 187–89, 194, 277, 312–13; of Jesus, 285, 334; of Mary, 38, 314; of the Holy Spirit, 18, 116–18; relation to love, 116, 313; relation to oneness, 95–98, 110–11, 187–92. See also Infertility

Feudalism, 43n18, 63n13, 170n15

Fiat. See Luke 1:38

Ficino, Marsilio, 9, 250n4, 269n10

Filiabitur. See Psalm 72:17

Firstborn, 19, 147–49, 273

First fruit, 19, 149–50, 153, 273

First mover, 130

Flower, 149–50, 289

French school of spirituality, 1, 7

"From what is his own," 175

Gabriel, 37–42, 115, 159, 288, 297, 316–19, 323–24, 338

Galileo Galilei, 59n6

Gallemant, Jacques, 2–3

Génébrard, Gilbert, 294–95
Genesis 3:5 ("You will be as gods"), 98
Glory: communication of, 224–39; Jesus' state of, 71–76, 225–35; deferred, 335–41. *See also* John 17:5; Order(s); State; Transfiguration
God the Father: as Father, 291–92, 301–3, 327–29; as father and mother, 269–73; as father-without-mother, 281; as font of deity, 61, 144, 153, 163, 339; as gardener, 77; as God living, 277–83; his fatherhood unknown before the Incarnation, 274. See also God(head); Trinity
God(head): as adored and adoring, 46; as hidden, 275; as one or oneness, 53, 94–100; as source, 10, 20–23, 150, 198, 293; as translation of *divinité*, 42n16; capacity of, 168, 247–48; communication to Creation, 184–85; communication in the Incarnation, 185–96; council of, 83, 101, 132–36, 158, 306; essence is existence, 94; fertility in, 133, 147, 150, 187–89, 194, 277, 312–13; his love, 246–55; in the Incarnation, 199–204; motto, "He who is," 170; presence in Creation, 197–98, 202–3; self-sufficiency of, 132, 168, 198, 248, 255. *See also* Being; Circle; Creation; Emanation; Holy Spirit; Jesus; Knowledge; Model; Sun; Trinity
God-Man. *See* Hypostatic union
God(s): false, 98–99, 165, 277–79; man as, 19, 159–60, 166, 189, 206, 253, 279, 324. *See also* Genesis 3:5; Psalm 82:6
Grace: bond of, 68–69; experienced by Creation, 197–98; Jesus as or source of, 38, 64–66, 74–75, 81, 117, 134, 154, 201–4, 223, 242, 281, 304, 311–12, 340–41; of Mary 315–18. *See also* Order(s); State
Grafting. *See* Incarnation
Gregory Nazianzen, 9, 17, 128, 142n2, 307, 309–10, 342n92
Gregory of Nyssa, 9, 125n10
Grignion de Montfort, Louis-Marie, 6

Heathens. *See* Pagans
Hell, 125, 171, 182, 198, 233, 280, 310; as limbo, 125, 332

Heretics, 16, 54, 67n19, 98, 105, 123, 327n70; as monsters and vipers, 271–72
Hermes Trismegistus, 81n36, 156n21, 169n12, 269, 305n55
Herod, 181
Herodotus, 47n7, 146n5, 272n17
Herp, Hendrik (Harphius), 11, 22
Hesiod, 146n5
Hierarchy: in Neoplatonism, 10; in Pseudo-Dionysius, 10–11; of angels, 54–55, 131–32, 239, 300–301; reversal of, 19, 46, 130–31. *See also* Order(s)
Hilary of Poitiers, 17, 125n10, 125n11, 138n34, 147, 152, 153n19, 173n17, 195, 247, 341n90
Holy Spirit: as bond, 62, 107–8, 119–20, 142–45, 188; as endpoint, 62, 110, 116–19, 142, 240, 285; as love and oneness, 62, 115–20, 142, 159; fertility and infertility of, 18, 116–18. *See also* Bosom; Emanation
Homage: as translation of *hommage*, 43n18. *See also* Feudalism
Host. *See* Victim
Humanism, 9, 150n15, 269n10
Humanity: as instrument, 64–65, 102. See *also* Hypostatic union
Humility. *See* Self-emptying
Hypostasis: in Christian doctrine, 42n16, 79, 81, 150, 167, 186, 240–41, 261n18; in Neoplatonism, 10, 169n11. *See also* Subsistence
Hypostatic union: as circle, 308; as eternal, 18, 126, 161; as lawful, 78–84; as perfect adoration, 46; as composition, 69, 108, 128, 174, 307–8; as temperament, 128, 307; as transplantation, 81; compared to marriage, 123; "humanly divine, divinely human," 70, 86, 106, 176, 241, 308, 322, 337; relation to vow of servitude, 17. *See also* Bond; Incarnation; Order(s); State

Image: communions as, 243; Creation as, 71, 95, 122, 184, 188, 301; man or Christians as, 1, 16–17, 128, 153, 164, 189, 212–13, 251, 254, 305–6; Jesus as, 58, 60, 97, 118–19, 143–44, 147–48, 153, 213–14, 303; sun as, 58, 170, 210, 212–14. *See also* Model

Imprint: 68–69, 89, 99, 124, 153, 180, 198, 244, 287, 302–3, 312

Incarnation: as bond, 330; as comprehending God, 45–47; as comprehending the world, 45–47; as covenant, 62, 67, 139, 164, 201, 332; as divesting and reclothing, 77, 233; as eternal, 124, 263; as grafting, 17, 77–78; as investiture, 17, 84; as model of the other sacraments, 207; as mystery, 45–48, 162–66; as new and perfect adoration, 46–48, 87–88, 299, 302; as oneness, 17–18, 52–53, 96–97, 120, 192; as reprise of Creation, 19; as self-emptying, 15–24; as sun becoming one with a mirror, 214; as triumph, 52; compared with Creation, 58; motive of, 19, 255–56; relation to the Eucharist, 187; relation to salvation, 15–19; relation to vow of servitude, 14; relation to the Trinity, 147, 187, 204–7, 262, 294–96, 304. *See also* Circle; Hypostatic union

Independence: of Jesus, 172–81, 229, 326; of uncreated Being: 151, 172–77, 326. *See also* Dependence

Infertility: of the Holy Spirit, 18, 116–18. *See also* Fertility

Influence, 38n4

Interchange, 17, 21, 84, 127–28, 224, 232; as translation of *commerce*, 84n40

Investiture, 17, 84. *See also* Feudalism

Irenaeus, 16–17, 52n18, 129n20, 159n26

Isaiah 9:6 ("Father of the age to come"), 19, 152–54, 164, 189, 195. *See also* Adoption

Isaiah 53:8 ("Who will explain his generation?"), 148, 257, 280, 284, 293; in Leo, 293n46

Jacob: house of, 41; ladder, 191–93, 254

Jansen, Cornelius (Jansenius), 4

Jerome, 39n7, 47, 67, 199

Jesuits, 2, 5

Jesus: as adorer, 19, 46, 87–88, 121, 299; action "from what is his own," 175; as ark, 67, 201, 332–33; as composition, 69, 108, 128, 174, 307–8; as dependent, 174–81, 226; as earth, 212, 306; as father of the age to come (Isaiah 9:6), 19, 152–54, 164, 189, 195; as first fruit, 19, 149–50, 153, 273; as firstborn, 19, 147–49, 273; as flower, 149–50, 289; as gift of God (John 4:10), 168, 207; as God dead, 279–82; as independent, 172–81, 229, 326; as lamb, 42n17, 225n10, 261, 310, 319; as mediator, 101, 193, 206, 285; as oneness, 192–93; as shoot, 149–50, 155; as source, 65, 134, 142; as sovereign, 346–48; as stumbling block, 49; as the second or new Adam, 20, 69, 71, 129, 157, 184, 255–56, 306, 310–11, 317; baptism of, 296, 309; begins and ends his life in adoration, 106–9; capacity of, 161, 224, 230, 247, 260, 285, 299, 341; fertility of, 285, 334; generation unexplainable (Isaiah 53:8), 148, 257, 280, 284, 293; living and working in Mary, 322; servitude of, 106–7, 157, 328; viewed as a sinner, 72. *See also* Ascension; Being; Birth; Bosom; Dayspring; Emanation; Endpoint; Epitome; Glory; Grace; Hypostatic union; Image; Lives; Model; Self-emptying; State; Sun; Transfiguration; Trinity; Victim; Will; World

Jews, 47, 99, 100–12, 268, 294–95, 333

John 3:16 ("God so loved the world"), 246–53

John 4:10 ("Gift of God"), 168, 207

John 17:5 ("Glorify me, Father, with yourself"), 225–35, 341n90

John 17:21 ("That they may be one, as we are one"), 69–70, 109, 114, 165, 195–96, 276

John: as beloved disciple, 246; as disciple of Life and Truth, 190; as eagle, 203–5, 269; as secretary of state, 246; Bérulle likened to, 1; Epistle of, 108; Gospel of, 15–17, 21n35, 28, 48, 109, 113, 164–65, 226, 289; Revelation of, 89, 149, 273

John of Damascus (John Damascene), 26n49, 73, 125n10

John the Baptist, 37, 296, 309–10

Jonathan ben Uzziel, 138n34

Joseph, 324–25

Justinian. *See* Law

Kenosis. See Self-emptying
Kepler, Johannes, 59n6, 210n3
Knowledge: draws the object to itself, 249; in God, 61, 133, 139, 145, 204, 247–51, 311–13, 338; limitation of man's, 12, 51, 90, 182, 251, 283–86; relation to reverence and love, 56–57, 90, 116, 248–52

La Salle, Jean-Baptiste de, 6
Law: as way of Jesus or God, 39, 166, 181, 243, 262; biblical, 58, 99, 112, 156, 170, 246; as right or positive law, 41n15, 48, 78–84, 80 (Justinian), 99, 126, 148, 176; of nature, 99, 120, 225. *See also* Covenant
Lazarists, 7
Lazarus, 103, 310
Leo the Great, 55n21, 60n7, 121n6, 237n27, 293n46
Letourneau, Georges, 7
Light. *See* Sun
Limbo. *See* Hell
Lives: in Creation, vegetable, animal, human, 71; of Jesus, divine, pilgrim, glorious, 71–72, 76, 266, 337, 346
Love: as motive of the hypostatic union, 18; free and voluntary in the Incarnation, 18–19, 247; God's, 246–55; in Jesus separates, in God unites, 336; natural and necessary in the Trinity, 18, 247; relation to fertility, 116, 313; relation to knowledge, 56–57, 90, 116, 248–52; relation to oneness, 116; that crucifies a God, 236. *See also* Holy Spirit; John 3:16
Luke 1:38 ("May it be"), 316
Luke, apostle, 113, 117, 256

Man: as Adam: 16–17, 20, 71, 255–56, 306, 310–11; as angel, 20, 305n55; as composition, 305–7; as sinner, 39, 65, 236, 254; his creation as prelude to the Incarnation, 306; immortality of, 182–83; mortality of, 129, 182–83; partition between nothingness and, 129. *See also* Adoption; Capacity; Epitome; Fall; God(s); Humanity; Image; Knowledge; Poverty; World
Man-God. *See* Hypostatic union

Manicheans, 152, 186
Marriage, 5, 29, 50, 69, 123
Martial, 239
Mary: as comprehending or capable of God, 23, 159, 316–17, 321; as mother of the Son of Man, 52n18; as mother-without-father, 280–81, 316; Bérulle's other writings on, 6; chastity and integrity of, 288–89; fertility of, 38, 314; grace of, 315–18; her *Fiat* (Luke 1:38), 316; Jesus living and working in, 322; Jesus' second birth, in 288–331; motherhood of, 18, 40, 312–27; opens the Father's bosom, 38; order or state of Mother of God, 303, 312–27; servitude of, 316–17; will of, 93, 316–17, 324. *See also* Annunciation, Womb
Mary Magdalene, 6, 347
Mass. *See* Eucharist
Matrix, 269–72. *See also* Bosom; Womb
Matthew 28:18 ("All power is given to me in heaven and on earth"), 91, 233, 346–48
"Me," 84–85. *See also* Self-emptying
Microcosm or macrocosm. *See* World
Mingle, 125, 308
Mirror, 11, 17, 22, 94, 148, 214, 338
Mixture, 128, 174, 305, 307
Model: Godhead as, 97, 119, 187, 195–96, 203, 243, 293, 300–304, 330; Incarnation as model of the other sacraments, 207; Jesus or deity as, 15, 21, 23, 26, 66, 84, 109–10, 120, 154, 181, 186, 188, 194, 198, 271–72; in angelic ranks, 131; in painting, 212–13; *See also* Image
Mohammed. *See* Muslims
Monophysitism, 3
Moses, 22, 62, 95, 109, 117, 150n15, 170, 269n10
Motherhood: in God, 269–73; in Jesus, 334; in the Holy Spirit, 117. *See also* Mary
Mountain, 56, 109, 309
Muslims, 99

Nature: bond of, 68–69; law of, 99, 120, 225. *See also* Adoption; Order(s); State
Navigation, 244

Neoplatonism, 9–10, 38n2, 305n55. *See also* Plato; Platonism
Neri, Philip, 3
Nicholas of Cusa, 63n14
Nicodemus, 246
Nothing(ness): Creation out of, 71, 129–30, 133, 248; in Abstract school, 22; in Mary, 316; of the creature, 20–23, 68, 76, 86, 108, 128, 160, 169, 171–72, 193, 254, 305n55, 328–29, 341; of man's effort apart from grace, 20, 86; of self-emptying, 20–24, 61, 85, 133, 168, 254, 257, 264; partition between man and, 129. *See also* Capacity; Poverty; Self-emptying

Olier, Jean-Jacques, 6, 11
One: as translation of *unique*, 46n5; in Neoplatonism, 10, 188n5
Oneness: as prior and superior to being, 98; as translation of *unité*, 43n20; contrasted with *union*, 119, 304; in philosophy, 98; in the Eucharist, 103–6, 164, 192, 195; in the hypostatic union, 54–55, 126; in the Incarnation, 17–18, 52–53, 96–97, 120, 192; of Creation, 51–53, 70–71, 94–95; of essence in the Godhead, of love in the Trinity, of subsistence in the Incarnation, 107–14; of God, 51–54, 98, 186, 192–93; of Jesus, 100–103; recognized by pagans and Jews, 98–100; relation to fertility, 95–98, 110–11, 187–92; relation to love, 116; the Holy Spirit as divine worker of, 115–16. *See also* John 17:21
Oratorians, 3, 5–7, 11, 243–45
Order(s): hierarchy of, 130; in Creation, 130, 184–85; multiplicity in, 54–55, 65, 97; new, 129–30; of the hypostatic union, 54–55, 121, 129–30; of Mother of God, 318; of nature, of grace, and of glory, 54–55, 64–65, 72, 85–86, 92, 97, 117, 129–31, 154, 174, 188, 198, 203–4, 211, 238, 243, 265, 274
Orpheus, 269n10, 270
Outpouring: as translation of *excès*, 61n12. *See also* Emanation; Neoplatonism

Pagans, 98–99, 139, 182, 277, 308, 343
Pagnino, Santes, 333n81
Painting, 118, 143, 154, 212–13; Christianity as art of, 242–43; Jesus as painter, 213
Pascal, Blaise, 60n8
Passover, 69–70, 105–6, 109, 113–14, 165, 225–35
Paul, 9, 107, 170, 198, 267, 239; 1 Corinthians, 59, 104, 112, 263–4, 273; 1 Timothy, 206–7; 2 Thessalonians, 244; Colossians, 54, 64, 112, 197, 202–3, 242, 341; Ephesians, 45–46, 54, 112, 131–32, 240, 271, 292, 315, 328; Galatians, 85, 158, 236; Hebrews (taken as written by Paul), 81, 114, 266, 299; Philippians, 20, 78, 90, 233, 339; Romans, 78, 135, 147, 161, 254, 257–58, 334–35
Pearl of the Gospel, 11, 14n27, 23
Pentecost, 39, 188
Person. *See* Hypostasis; Subsistence; Trinity
Peter, 222, 277–78, 309
Pherecydes, 236
Philippians, 2, 58, 78, 90, 210, 233–34, 240, 339
Philosophers, 10, 49, 59, 80–81, 95, 98, 129, 141, 209–12, 248, 269, 304–5, 344
Philosophy, 139, 350; compared with Christianity, 182–83, 236, 252, 260
Phoenix, 146, 267, 331–34
Pilate, 181
Plato, 9, 10n18, 56n1, 80, 81n36, 150n15, 169n11, 236n26, 269n10. *See also* Neoplatonism; Platonism; Philosophy
Platonism, 56n1, 98, 149–50, 231, 260. *See also* Neoplatonism; Philosophy; Plato
Plotinus, 9, 137n33, 169n11, 188n5, 189n8
Plutarch, 47n7
Poverty, 20–23, 68, 128, 170–73, 235, 248; as translation of *indigence*, 60n8. *See also* Capacity; Comprehension; Nothing(ness)
Predestination, 132–36
Priesthood, Bérulle's renewal of, 3; views on, 6, 11; of Jesus, 11, 42. *See also* Victim
Principle: as translation of *principe*, 38n2
Procession and return, 113, 130, 136–39, 157, 191–93. *See also* Circle

Prodigal Son, 93
Providence, 130–33, 136, 139, 198
Psalm 2:7 ("Today I have begotten you"), 180, 266–67, 328, 333
Psalm 45:7 ("God, your God, has anointed you"), 199–201
Psalm 72:17 ("He will be sonned"), 295–96
Psalm 82:6 ("I have said, you are gods"), 19, 24, 66, 159n26, 160n29, 253
Pseudo-Dionysius: *Celestial Hierarchies*, 55n20, 184n4; *Divine Names*, 45n1, 113, 115, 137n33, 144, 149, 153, 163, 166, 184n4, 339n87; orders and hierarchies, 19; person and influence, 9–10
Pythagoras, 59n6

Recapitulation. *See* Epitome
Relation(ship): as translation of *relation* and *rapport*, 22, 40n10; adjectival form *relatif*, 111n17; between Jesus and the Father, 21, 137, 154, 196, 277; in the Trinity, 255. *See also* Vow
Rest: within the Trinity, 61, 96, 101, 116–18, 137–42, 189n8, 202, 205–6, 269, 285–87, 293, 301, 331–33, 338–39; in Jesus, 118, 126, 138, 181, 206, 240, 298
Resurrection: of Jesus, 26, 71, 126, 160–63, 200, 267, 281, 309, 331–48; of Lazarus, 103; of the dead, 135, 273–74. *See also* Phoenix
Richelieu, cardinal, 4
Rising Sun. *See* Dayspring
Rome, 3, 4, 96n3, 158n24, 239n29
Root: of Jesse, 41; of Jesus, 41, 64, 113, 232, 244; of Mary, 41; of tree, 80, 81n36
Ruusbroec, Jan van (Ruysbroeck), 11, 14n27, 23, 56n1, 81n36

Sacrament, 64, 104, 123–24, 131–32, 144, 147, 190, 193, 206–7, 273
Saint-Cyran. *See* Duvergier de Hauranne
Seal. *See* Imprint
Self-emptying: as state, 15–24; as translation of *anéantissement*, 61n11; of Jesus, 20, 46, 61, 70, 73, 79, 83–87, 232, 235–38, 256–59, 306, 339. *See also* Capacity; Nothing(ness); State

Seneca, 182
Septuagint, 37n1, 46n3, 55n20, 117, 150n15
Servitude: in human societies, 79–80; of human nature, 82; of Mary, 316–17. *See also* State; Vow
Shoot, 149–50, 155
Silence: at the Incarnation, 39, 326; fitting to God and religion, 47–51, 78, 286, 308–9, 330; of Jesus, 310
Simeon, 298
Sin: and nothing(ness), 20; as hell or separation from God, 198, 235; image of God effaced by, 153, 254; in Gospel of John, 15–16; Jesus incapable of 91, 247, 310; Jesus' likeness to the flesh of, 72, 77–78, 254, 319; of Adam, 310; of man, 254–56; relation to salvation, 129, 139, 160–62, 210, 225, 255–56, 280, 330
Sinner: Adam as, 256; condition of, 72–73, 171, 211; Jesus viewed as, 72; man as 39, 65, 236, 254
Son of God: as independent, 21, 60, 83–84, 137, 172–78; as proceeding from the Father, 60–61; as principle of the Holy Spirit, 42, 61, 64; as image of the Father, 143; as middle in the Trinity, 142; his will, 143. *See also* Hypostatic union; Incarnation; Jesus; Self-emptying; Trinity
Son of Man, 18, 28, 38, 52, 54, 61, 108, 125–26, 134, 144, 157, 161, 174, 191n10, 196, 222, 248, 256, 267n4, 274, 294–96, 300, 303, 314–20, 336; in interpretive tradition, 52n18, 108
Sonship: by adoption, 153, 282, 318; by nature, 62–63, 84, 87, 92–93, 103, 107, 134, 137, 144, 153, 156–57, 174, 180, 190, 201, 224, 227, 242, 268, 274–78, 282, 294–96, 300–303, 330. *See also* Adoption; Psalm 72:17
Soul. *See* Body
Source: Adam as, 256, 310; as translation of *source*, 38n2; God as, 10, 20–23, 150, 198, 293; Jesus as, 65, 134, 142; of grace, 58, 81, 134, 279; of life, 61–62, 70, 276, 282, 287, 297, 331; water as, 189, 195

State: as translation of *état*, 13; contrasted with actions, 155, 302; contrasted with being, 136; contrasted with person, 80; in Abstract school, 14, 23; meaning of, 13–15; of communication and suspension of grace, 72–73; of angels, 300–301; of death, 332–34, 345–47; of firstborn, 147; of hypostatic union, 20–22, 54, 62–63, 69, 72, 103–8, 113, 118–20, 126, 129–34, 144, 157–60, 173–81, 225, 233, 238–39, 241, 260, 275, 297–98, 314, 318; of glory, 54, 76, 91–92, 209, 223, 226–32, 235, 258, 269, 335–40, 347–48; of grace, 15, 20, 26, 41, 45, 64–65, 180; of human life, 128; of Jesus, 14–15, 71–72, 74, 125, 154, 187, 196, 233–34, 257, 286, 300–302; of Mother of God, 303, 312–27; of nature, 20, 41, 78–79, 82–84, 180, 280; of relation, 137, 150, 154, 243; of self-emptying, 20–23, 70, 258, 281; of servitude, 14–15, 29, 68–70, 82, 86–88, 133, 155–57, 234, 328; of sin, 310; of sonship, 62, 84, 92, 156, 294–96, 300–304, 318

Striving: as translation of *effort*, 71n24; of God, 18, 71–72, 121, 125–26, 155, 235–37, 311, 324, 335–36

Suárez, Francisco, 176n19

Submission, 27, 87, 154, 243, 245, 312, 330, 348; as translation of *dépendance*, 41n15; of Creation, 67, 239, 346; of Jesus, 181, 347; of Mary, 41. *See also* Dependence

Subsistence, 17–18, 63–64, 75–85, 90–92, 107–13, 124–28, 137, 141, 160, 189, 205–6, 215–25, 238–42, 262–63, 338–43; as translation of *subsistance*, 42n16, 79n34. *See also* Hypostasis

Substance: of Mary, 100, 159, 185, 199, 259, 271–72, 313, 320–26; contrasted with accident, 64–65, 80, 122, 172, 223, 261, 298, 340–41. *See also* Essence; Underlying substance

Sulpicians, 6–7

Sun: as created, 58, 136, 149, 209–14, 232, 257, 261, 289, 294–96, 309, 344; as image, 10, 20, 56–60, 74, 170, 210, 212–14; as visible god, 156; eclipse of, 76, 160, 228, 257, 347; Egyptians' worship of, 57–58; God as, 20, 56–60, 148–49, 170, 344; Jesus as, 16–17, 56–60, 64, 74–76, 99–100, 121, 148–49, 156–58, 182, 202, 209–15, 232, 257–58, 344

Sun of Righteousness, 57, 59, 76, 121, 209–10, 213, 257–58

Temperament, 128, 307. *See also* Hypostatic union

Temple: as place of worship, 149, 298; of Jesus 67, 92, 199; of man, 164, 189; of Mary, 106, 315–17, 320, 325; veil of, 310, 347

Teresa of Avila, 2–3, 9, 28; *Constitutions*, 2–3; contrasted with Abstract school, 12–13

Tertullian, 138n34, 146n5, 155, 168, 269n9, 333n81

Thomas, apostle, 68

Thomas Aquinas, 64n16, 94n1, 138n34, 141n1, 283, 342n92

Transfiguration, 73, 296, 309

Tree: as translation of *phoinix*, 333n81; grafted, 77; flower of, 149, 289; man as upturned, 80–81; transplanted, 80–81

Tremblay, Joseph (the Gray Eminence), 4

Trinity: as principal mystery of the faith, 162–66; communication in, 185–96; fertility in, 133, 147, 150, 187–89, 194, 277, 312–13; relation of persons in, 66, 115–19, 142–47, 150–58, 185–99, 275–77, 283–85, 290–91; relation to the Incarnation, 147, 187, 204–7, 262, 294–96, 304. *See also* Bond; Bosom; Emanation; God the Father; God(head); Jesus; Oneness; Rest; Son of God

Triumph, 52, 94–97, 121, 126, 206, 225, 237–38, 335–37, 345–48

Underlying substance, 78–79, 83, 174–75, 262; as translation of *suppôt*, 79n34. *See also* Essence; Substance

Union: as completion of circle, 23; as participation in Jesus' self-emptying, 20–21, 29; as translation of *union*, 43n20; contrasted with oneness, 119, 304; in Abstract school, 12; man's first, with God

in likeness; man's second, with God in nature, 17, 128. *See also* Burning bush; Eucharist; Hypostatic union
Unity: as translation of *unité*, 43n20. *See also* Oneness
Urban VIII, pope, 5

Vapor, 128
Victim: animal as, 50; Christians as, 42; Jesus as, 11, 27–28, 106–7, 124, 144–46, 158, 163, 187, 193, 273, 299, 319–21, 331, 338
Vine, 69, 155
Vipers, 272
Virgil, 322n65
Virgin: as Hebrew *almah*, 39n7. *See also* Mary
Vow of servitude, 3–5, 14–17, 22, 28, 48, 68–70, 85–93, 155, 177, 243–45, 330; relation to elevation, 28

Want. *See* Poverty.
Will: in Abstract school, 12, 21; relation to adoration, 27–29; of angels, 302; of demons, 171; of God, 22, 107, 147, 173–75, 235, 253–54, 277, 316, 331; of Jesus 83–84, 143, 147, 173–75, 190–91, 320; of man, 5, 20–23, 91–93, 172, 183, 229, 254; of Mary, 93, 316–17, 324; relation to knowledge, 249; relation to submission, 41n15
Womb: as translation of *sein*, 38n3; of God, 60, 269–72; of Mary, 38, 60–62, 106, 109, 118, 180, 213, 231, 259, 266, 269–73, 286–91, 294, 299–300, 309–27, 328n76, 335; of the earth, 149, 211. *See also* Birth; Bosom; Matrix
Word. *See* Son of God
"Works of God outside of his self," 120, 137
World: in Neoplatonism, 10; Jesus as (great, new), 19, 47, 53, 74, 117–18, 182, 236, 255, 260–63, 305; man as (little), 9, 53, 138, 260, 304–5. *See also* Creation; Epitome
World Soul, 169
Worship. *See* Adoration

Zamet, Sébastien, 4

Also in the Early Modern Catholic Sources series

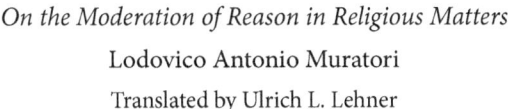

On the Moderation of Reason in Religious Matters
Lodovico Antonio Muratori
Translated by Ulrich L. Lehner

Jansenism: An International Anthology
Edited by Shaun Blanchard and Richard T. Yoder

*A Defense of the Catholic Religion: The Necessity,
Existence, and Limits of an Infallible Church*
Beda Mayr, OSB
Translated by Ulrich L. Lehner

*On Slavery and the Slave Trade: De Iustitia et Iure,
Book 1, Treatise 2, Disputations 32–40*
Luis de Molina, SJ
Translated by Daniel Schwartz and
Jörg Alejandro Tellkamp

*Metaphysical Disputations III and IV:
On Being's Passions in General and Its Principles
and On Transcendental Unity in General*
Francisco Suárez
Translated and annotated, with corrected Latin text,
by Shane Duarte

Metaphysical Disputation II:
On the Essential Concept or the Concept of Being
Francisco Suárez
Translated and annotated, with corrected Latin text,
by Shane Duarte

The Predestination of Humans and Angels:
Augustinus, *Tome III, Book IX*
Cornelius Jansen
Translated by Guido Stucco

The Catholic Enlightenment: A Global Anthology
Edited by Ulrich L. Lehner and
Shaun Blanchard

Metaphysical Disputation I: On the Nature of
First Philosophy or Metaphysics
Francisco Suárez
Translated and annotated, with corrected
Latin text, by Shane Duarte

On the Motive of the Incarnation
The Salmanticenses (Discalced Carmelites of Salamanca)
Translated by Dylan Schrader

www.ingramcontent.com/pod-product-compliance
Lightning Source LLC
Chambersburg PA
CBHW071952290426
44109CB00018B/2001